LEADING *the* WEST

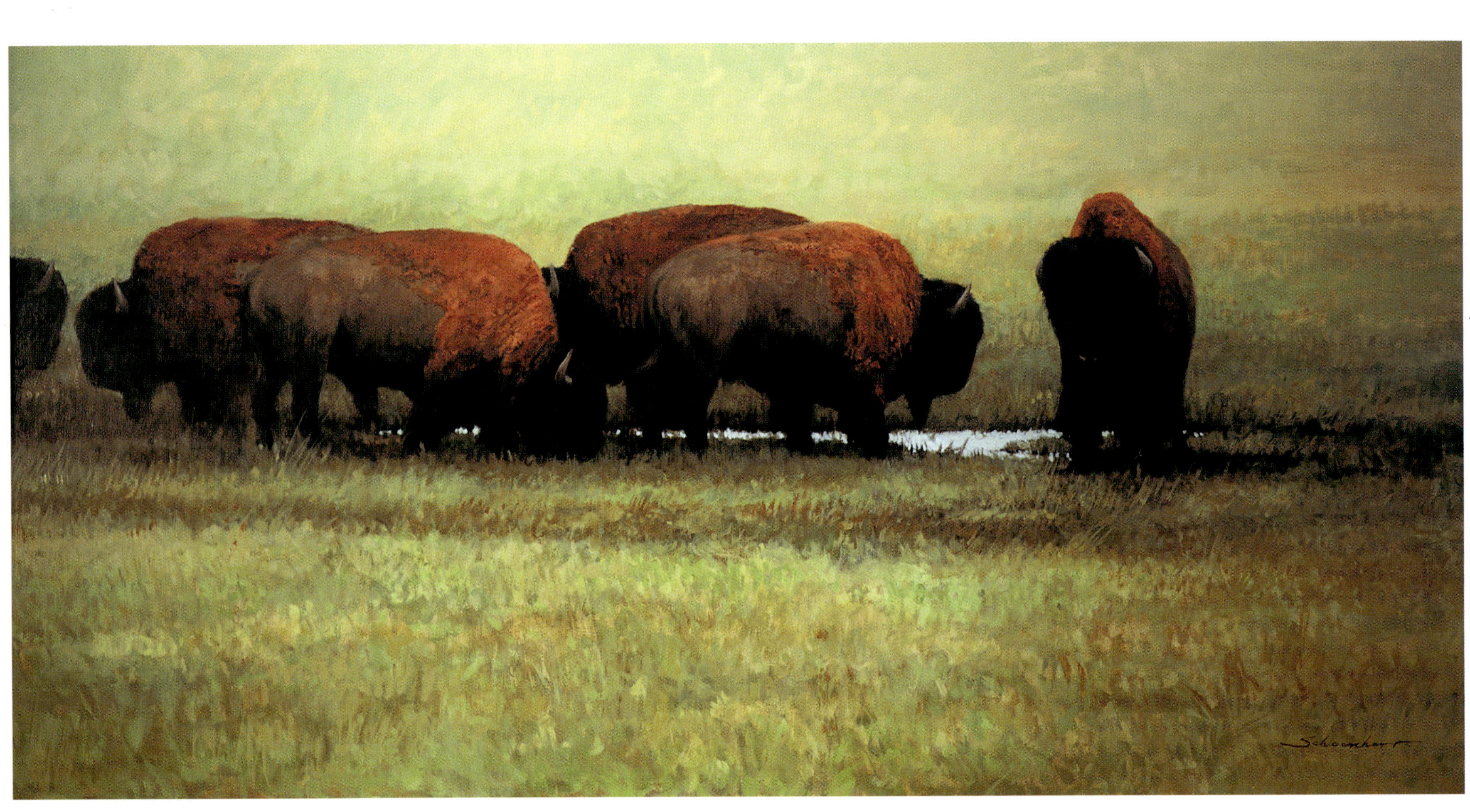

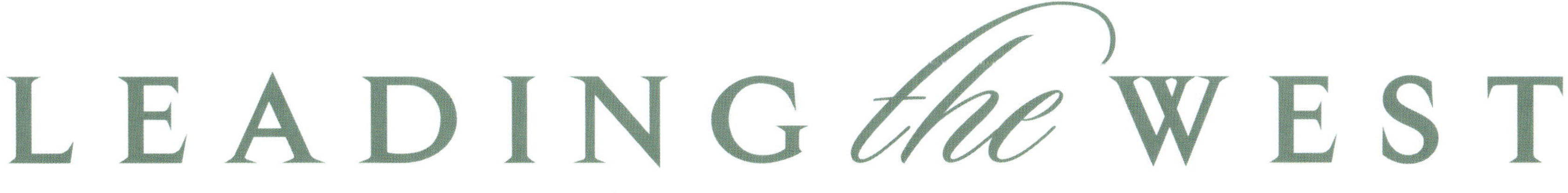

ONE HUNDRED CONTEMPORARY PAINTERS AND SCULPTORS

by DONALD J. HAGERTY

in cooperation with Southwest Art

foreword by Susan Hallsten McGarry

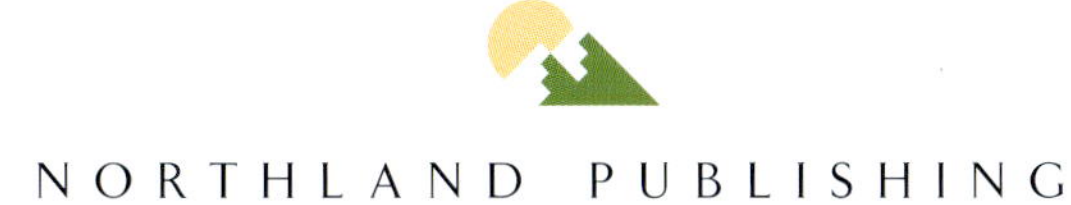

NORTHLAND PUBLISHING

Frontispiece: *John Schoenherr,* WATERHOLE, *oil on canvas, 36 by 72 inches, 1987. Private collection.*
Opposite: *Jeri Nichols Quinn,* LAVENDER SOFT SLOPES, *oil on canvas, 36 by 48 inches, 1989. Private collection.*

The text type was set in Janson
The display type was set in Arrow and Sloop
Composed in the United States of America
Designed by Nancy Rice
Art Direction by David Jenney
Edited by Erin Murphy
Production Supervised by Lisa Brownfield

Manufactured in Hong Kong by South Sea International Press Ltd.

Every attempt has been made to include appropriate ownership credits for the art pictured in this book. If you have any information that has been omitted or listed incorrectly, or that has changed since the date of the first printing, please contact the publisher at P.O. Box 1389, Flagstaff, Arizona 86002-1389.

FIRST IMPRESSION 1997
ISBN 0-87358-600-x (cloth)
ISBN 0-87358-691-3 (limited edition)

Library of Congress Catalog Card Number 97-9540
Cataloging-in-Publication Data
Hagerty, Donald J.
Leading the West : one hundred contemporary painters and sculptors/ by Donald J. Hagerty in cooperation with Southwest Art ; foreword by Susan Hallsten McGarry.
p. cm.
Includes bibliographical references and index.
ISBN 0-87358-600-X (cloth). — ISBN 0-87358-691-3 (lim. ed.). —
ISBN 0-87358-693-X (spec. coll. ed.)
1. Art, American—West (U.S.)—In art. 2. Art, Modern—20th century—West (U.S.) 3. West (U.S.)—In art. 4. Artists—United States—Biography. I. Southwest Art (Firm) II. Title.
N6525.H34 1997
709'.78'09045—dc21 97-9540

0634/10M/9-97
0671/500 ltd./9-97

TO REBECKA

TO THE MEMORY AND
LEGACY OF TOM LOVELL
(FEBRUARY 5, 1909—JULY 1, 1997)

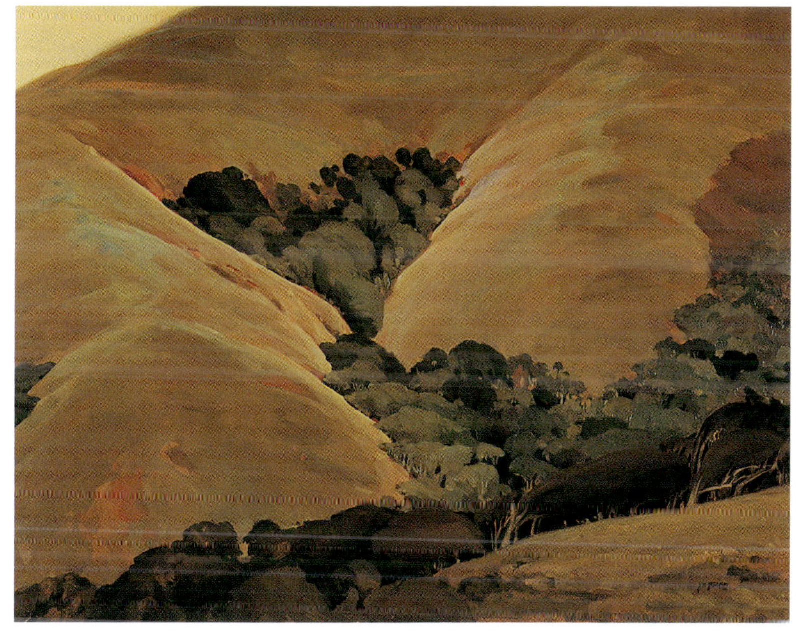

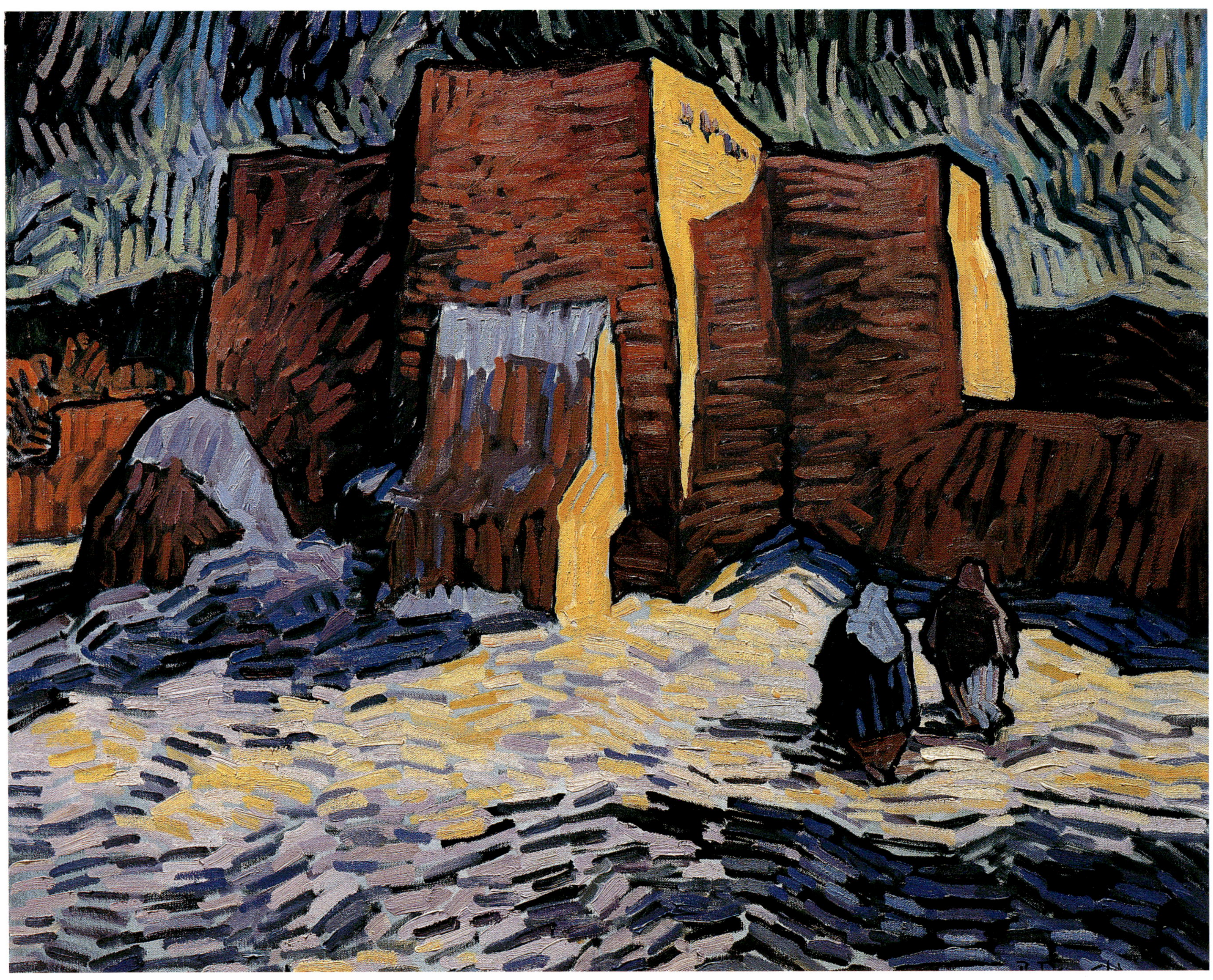

Robert Daughters, RANCHOS WINTER, *oil on canvas, 24 by 30 inches. Private collection.*

CONTENTS

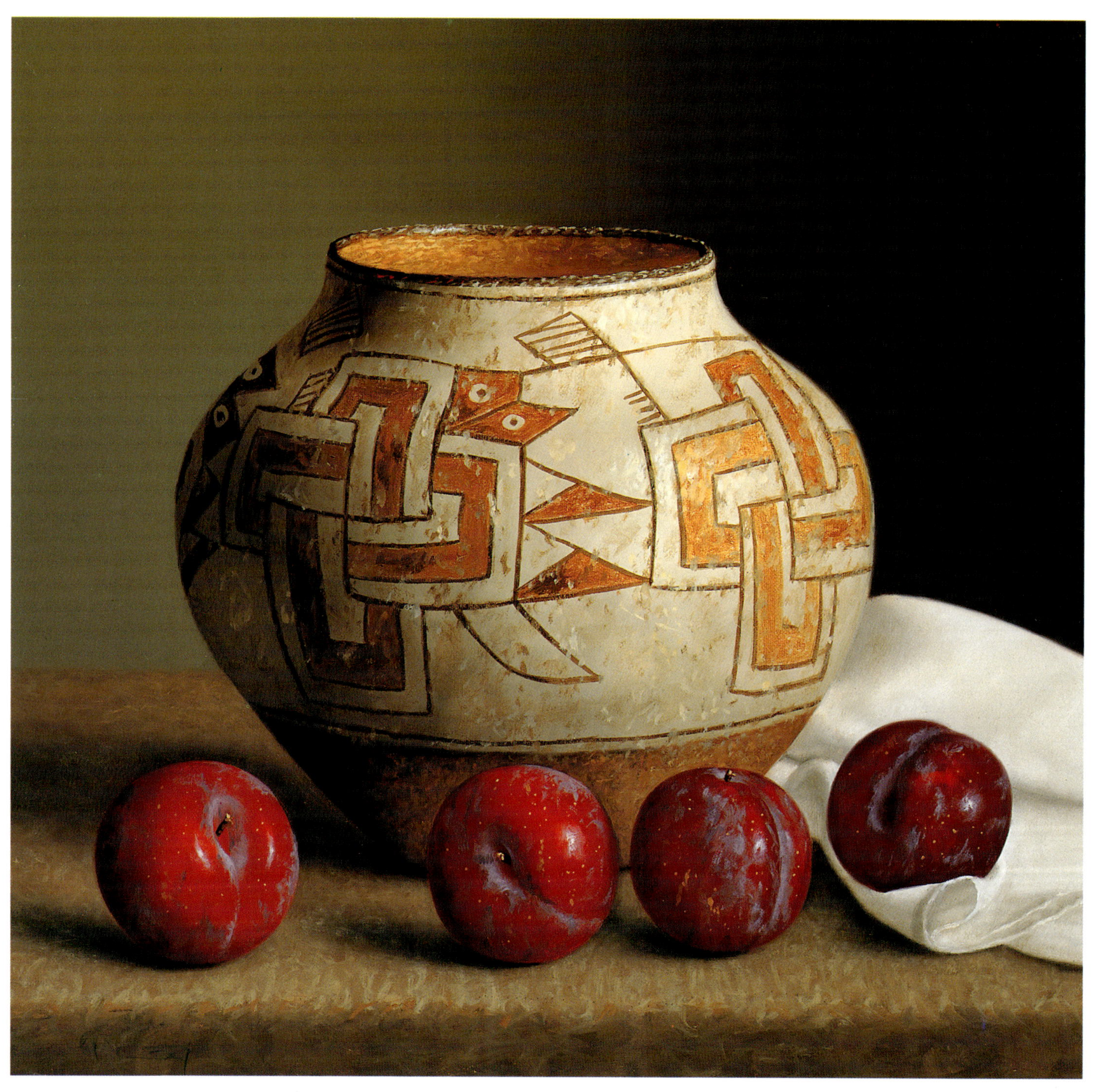

ACKNOWLEDGMENTS

THIS BOOK WOULD NOT BE POSSIBLE WITHOUT THE COOPERATION OF THE PAINTERS AND SCULPTORS represented here. Their willingness to submit examples of their work, reply to questions, and direct me to additional resources added immeasurably to my knowledge about contemporary art in the American West. They are all partners in the process of this book's creation. In particular, I want to acknowledge the valuable assistance of Tom Palmore, Thomas Quinn, and Chuck Forsman, who offered valuable suggestions about prospective artists. To them, and all the others, I extend my gratitude.

Credit must go to the publisher of Northland Publishing, David Jenney, and to Editor-in-Chief Erin Murphy, for the initial concept of the book. Susan Hallsten McGarry, editor-in-chief of *Southwest Art* magazine, enthusiastically supported the idea, and has written the insightful foreword to the book. Additional thanks are due all of the fine staff at Northland Publishing for their support and dedication to this project.

As usual, many individuals from galleries and museums stood ready to assist. My thanks go to Maria Hajic, National Museum of Wildlife Art; M. J. Van Deventer, National Cowboy Hall of Fame; Janet Hevey, Wheelwright Museum; Linda Corderman and William Lykins, Suzanne Brown Gallery; Mark Sublette and Amy Steeby, Medicine Man Gallery; Trudy Hays, Overland Gallery; Tom Nygard, Thomas Nygard Gallery; Abe Hays, Arizona West Gallery; Arlene LewAllen, Cline LewAllen Contemporary; John Cacciola and Theresa Reeves, J. Cacciola Galleries; Dirk Meyer and Kent Whipple, Meyer Gallery; Tina Goodwin, William Matthews Gallery; Lee Brotherton and Chris Moran, Trailside Americana Fine Art Galleries; Khimba Lee, Peyton-Wright; Nat Owings, Owings-Dewey Fine Art; Joanne Isaac, Steinbaum Krauss Gallery; Joy Tash, Joy Tash Gallery; Francis Namingha, Niman Fine Art; Brita Ericcson, Horwitch Newman Gallery; Ellen Popejoy, Corpus Christi Art Connection; Connie Farley, Concetta D. Gallery; Delia Tallman, Settlers West Galleries; Joyce Peters, Munson Gallery; Nancy Parker, Legacy Galleries; and Caryn Benard, Greenwich Workshop.

Other individuals assisted in many ways, including Eileen Bailey, Lui Andersen, Pam Carlson, Mary Bunn, Julie Shufelt, Mary Owen, Grace Gilson, Rosalyn Hurley, Nancy Pletka, Betsy Hook, Andy Ambrose, and Jean Smith.

Finally, I want to thank my wonderful family, Rebecka, Kristina, and James, for their interest and warm support throughout the creation of this book.

William Acheff,
SANTA ROSA PLUMS,
oil on linen,
10 by 10 inches, 1996.
Private collection.

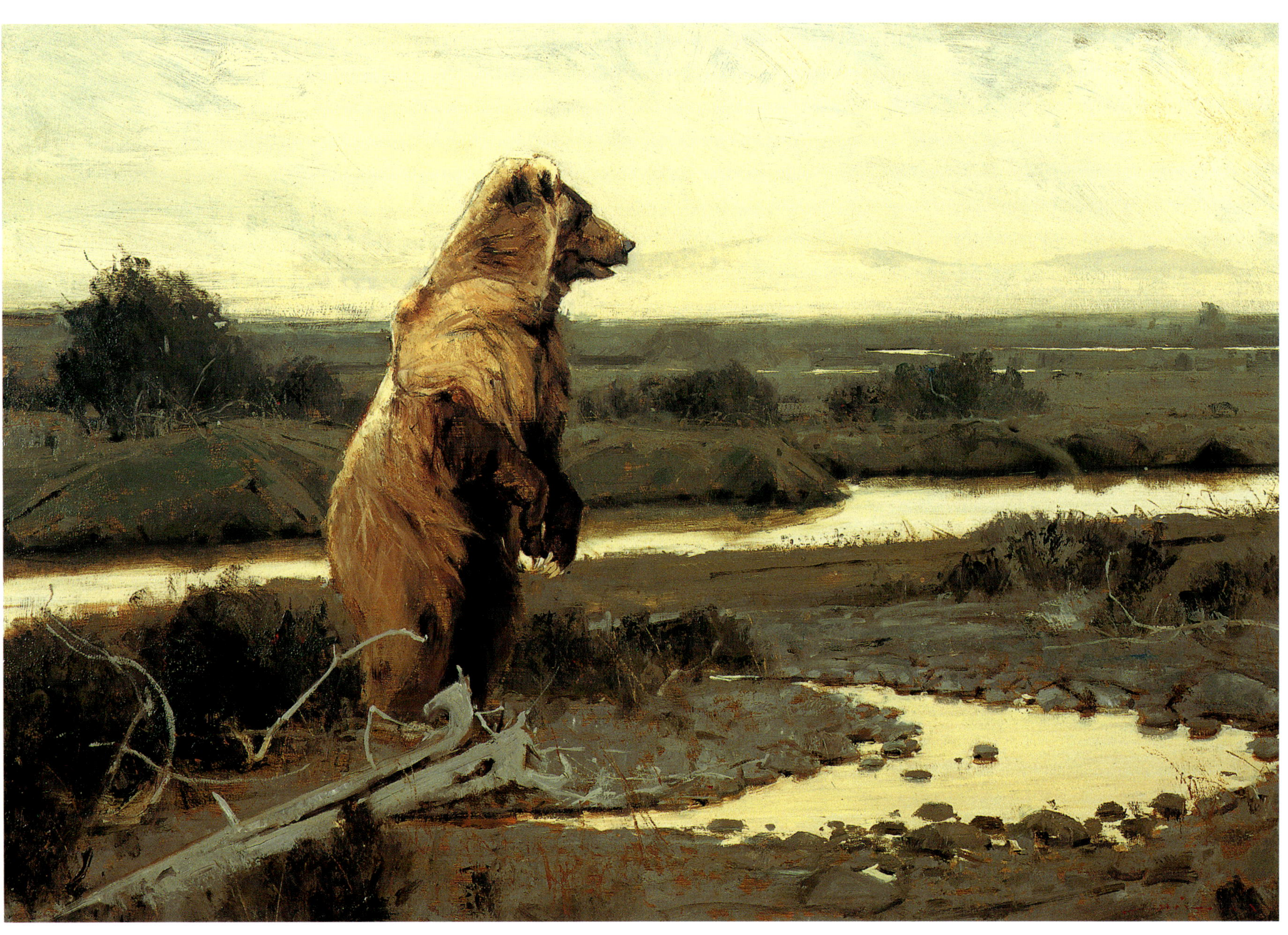

FOREWORD
Western Mythos

In selecting the artists for this book, Don Hagerty was faced with possibilities as vast as the Western American landscape. As *Southwest Art's* annual January collector's guide documents, thousands of artists work in and are represented by galleries in the West. Winnowing down the number to one hundred individuals required identifying and applying common criteria, then looking for the widest variety within that criteria.

What is the common denominator within the group represented here? First and foremost, Don was looking for artists inspired by the West, particularly the non-urban West—*pastoral, rural,* and *romantic* are adjectives that describe most of the artwork, he says. From the countless purveyors of such material, Don selected artists who display technical excellence and original visions, or as he puts it, those who possess "the touch." Once he compiled a group that met these criteria, he switched gears and focused on variety, hoping to make the one hundred artists a representative sampling of the subjects, styles, media, genders, and ethnic backgrounds of the larger body of artists working in the West.

Luke Frazier,
THE INTRUSION,
oil on canvas,
22 by 30 inches, 1992.
Private collection.

"I wanted this to be more inclusive than a traditional Western art book," he says. "I also admit that my personal bias played into the selections."

An Intriguing Mix

Two generations of artists are seen here, separated by a span of sixty years between the oldest, Tom Lovell (b. 1909), and the youngest, Luke Frazier (b. 1970). The majority are in their mid to late careers, and nearly two-thirds were born before 1945. Nineteen are women, eight are Native American, and three are Hispanic. Sixteen are sculptors and three work in both two- and three-dimensional formats.

Roughly 20 percent of the group came to their craft in nontraditional ways, including trial and error (e.g., Wilson Hurley, Bill Owen), mentorship or the inspiration of relatives (Lanford Monroe, Russell Chatham), or apprenticeships with masters (William Acheff, Peter Adams). Another 20 percent studied in California schools, and notably, eleven artists attended the Art Center College of Design in Pasadena, California (formerly in Los Angeles). Schools in Chicago and New York City each claim about 10 percent of the artists. The remainder were educated in Kansas, Utah, New Mexico, Arizona, Colorado, and a smattering of other states.

Many of the older artists began their careers as illustrators for magazines and books in New York or Chicago. Among them are Tom Lovell, Ken Riley, Bob Kuhn, Gordon Snidow, Don Crowley, Frank C. McCarthy, Paul Calle, Roy Andersen, Howard Terpning, Oleg Stavrowsky, and Joe Beeler. Others started out in professions such as the film industry (James Reynolds, Gary Niblett), architecture (Morris Rippel, Nelson Boren), or commercial art (Ed Mell, Don Coen).

All of the artists, however, were ultimately seduced by the heroes, themes, symbols, and legends that comprise the Western mythos, and all have chosen to make this complex of attitudes and beliefs the focus of their life's work.

Heroes of the Western Mythos

Hagerty's organization of such varied material is admirable. Based primarily on the images themselves, he offers a thematic exploration of the historic and contemporary West, focusing on the heroes at the heart of the Western mythos.

Among these heroes are real people. Ray Swanson's *Man of the Dineh*, Harley Brown's *Dog Rib Chief*, and Bill Owen's *Born to This Land* are portraits of contemporaries whom the artists have met or are lucky enough to call friends.

Other heroes of the Western mythos have evolved into archetypes, enriched by legend and modeled around cultural ideals. Indeed, the West is synonymous with our national image of freedom and rugged individualism, and those qualities have long been associated with the Western American cowboy. You see him in his finest moments in Grant Speed's *Ridin' a Rank One* and Ed Fraughton's *The Cowboy*. Bill Schenck's *Leaping into the Twilight of His Career* places the archetype in an equally archetypal landscape, commenting further on the cowboy's larger-than-life status with a shadow that thoroughly dominates the sky.

The romance of the cowboy archetype, however, has been somewhat eroded by the scrutiny of revisionist historians and artists who remind us of the hardships that go hand in hand with attempting to make a life off the land. Bill Owen will be remembered for documenting the ever-dwindling number of family-owned ranch operations. Many of Herb Mignery's images give a face to oft-forgotten Western characters like the black cowboy in *The Hungry Loop*. Tom Ryan's *Six Pack Saturday Night* comments on a more anti-heroic archetype. John Farnsworth's *Whiteface* places us eye-to-eye with the unsung beef-on-the-hoof that contributed substantially to the cowboy lifestyle, and in Gary Ernest Smith's *Solitary Man of the Field* we confront the hardscrabble farmer whose life is summed up by the haunting cow skull in Smith's *Eastern Oregon Gateway.*

Conflict and the Changing Archetype

Much of the West's archetypal imagery revolves around the theme of conflict, whether between man and animal, individual and society, or civilization and wilderness. Paul Calle's *In the Beginning . . . Friends* speaks to the earliest days of this conflict by positioning a mountain man and a Native American as star-crossed cohorts exploiting the land. As the flow of civilization inexorably eliminated wilderness, direct conflict with Native Americans became inevitable. Star Liana York's *War Magic* and Frank C. McCarthy's *After the Council* address the battles that ended in reservation life for tribes across the United States.

As the cowboy archetype has changed over the years, so too has the archetype of the Native American. Countless sociopolitical factors play into the trend, not the least of which are the Civil Rights movement, the space program, the conservationist movement, and the Vietnam War. Like all Americans, artists today are questioning values and seeking alternative ways of connecting to forces larger than the individual. This paradigm shift has many parallels in popular arts, not the least of which are seen in films such as *Little Big Man* (1970) and *Dances with Wolves* (1994), which pose the questions, Who was right and who was wrong? and, Who won and who lost in the conflict between wilderness and civilization?

Those same questions have influenced Western American imagery since the early nineteenth century, when Native Americans were pictured as anthropological phenomena and as savages in need of "civilizing." In the early twentieth century the picture changed to Native Americans symbolizing noble savages whose simple lifeways offered a panacea for the perils of industrialization. While these views still play a part in today's visions, the 1980s and '90s are dominated by images of pre-reservation Indians as individuals separate from society, living in spiritual harmony with animals and the land. George Carlson's *Boy and Eagle II* and Ken Riley's *As One* are outstanding examples of how this theme of spirituality melding animal strength and human intellect, instinctual and analytical powers, can be pictured with integrity and without the saccharin sentimentality that trivializes so much of the genre.

Guilt over Native American genocide and wanton destruction of the buffalo are undercurrents in much imagery, including Howard Terpning's poignant *Hope Springs Eternal—The Ghost Dance* and Tom Palmore's ironically titled *Gunsmoke,* in which a buffalo dominates the landscape, casting a wary eye at anyone who dares trespass on land it calls home. Much of this imagery is more complex, dwelling on parallel themes of suppression and spiritualism, as seen in Paul Pletka's tortured images of Penitentes and Plains Indians. Just as provocative are Bob Haozous's cookie-cutter symbols, juxtaposed to comment on the subservience of civilization to the larger forces of nature.

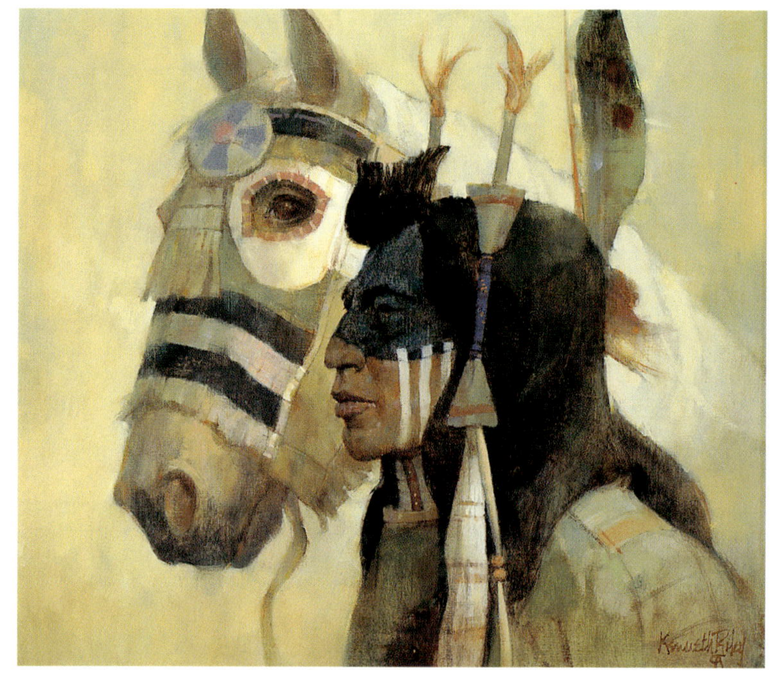

Kenneth Riley,
AS ONE,
oil on canvas,
13½ by 15 inches, 1996.
Private collection.

Women—not only as subjects of art but as artists—have been slower to gain recognition in the changing Western mythos. Undoubtedly the women's movement of the 1970s has been partly responsible for the growing numbers of women who are expressing their views of how the West was won. In Veryl Goodnight's *No Turning Back,* we see a historical reminder of our pioneer courage. In *Waterbearers,* Glenna Goodacre uses the classical theme of nurturing, clothed in Native American robes. In *Earth, Air, Fire, and Water,* Donna Howell-Sickles draws a parallel between the cowgirl and our global panoply of mythological goddesses. While these artists reach outward in their work, Native American painter Jaune Quick-to-See Smith looks inward, transforming symbols of popular culture into personalized glyphs and dream states that pulse with the mysteries of the unknown.

The continuing elimination of wilderness habitats where we may experience the unknown weighs heavily on today's image-makers. That consciousness has combined with a need to go beyond scientific vignettes and taxidermy mounts, resulting in some of the best wildlife art to have ever been created.

Today's wildlife painters and sculptors don't settle for what is better captured with the click of the camera lens. They qualify as *artists* by bringing equal doses of accuracy and aesthetics to their work, creating formally beautiful images that happen to have animal subjects. Examples are

Bob Kuhn's focus on design, color, value, and pattern in *Return of the Caribou;* the impressionistic surfaces of Sherry Salari Sander's *Goats at Rest;* and the stylized, curvilinear shapes of Gerald Balciar's *Riverside.*

Unlike earlier sporting art, in which animals were depicted as dead or about to become dinner, today's wildlife artists present the animal kingdom as precisely that: a domain where animal rights are inherent. The awe filtered into Thomas Quinn's *Blue Cougar,* Jim Morgan's *Backwater Sanctuary,* and Kent Ullberg's *Herdmaster* implies an admiration for and celebration of the creatures with whom we share the planet.

The Landscape of Mythos

Don begins his discussion of contemporary Western American art by focusing on the land, so it is fitting to conclude this discussion with the stage upon which the Western mythos was and still is conceived.

The ever-shifting Western frontier has been the subject of the Western American mythos since the eighteenth century, when artists were invited to join intrepid explorers on travels into uncharted wilderness. Although they entered the landscape as recorders, these artists undoubtedly saw themselves as adventurers no different from the men who set sail to find a New World known only through speculation and hearsay. Leaving the world they knew, artists such as Thomas Moran ventured into primordial places as deep as the Grand Canyon, as imposing as the mountains of Wyoming, and as mysterious as the land around the Yellowstone River.

That feeling of adventure is little changed for today's landscape painters. Crevasses such as P. A. Nisbet's *Taos Gorge,* Lindsay Holt II's *Light Place/Dark Place,* Curt Walters's *Palisades of the Desert,* and Barbara Zaring's *Canyon de Chelly* still inspire discovery, as do heights captured by Peter Holbrook in *Spider Woman* and Gregory Kondos in *Mt. Pedernal—A View from Ghost Ranch.*

The land, whether carved by the forces of nature in Merrill Mahaffey's *Canyon Morning* or by ancient peoples in Morris Rippel's *Echoes of the Anasazi,* is the common ground we share with adventurers from all eras. Like explorers Lewis and Clark, who opened the West to further exploration in 1804–06, Russell Chatham still meditates on the Missouri River in *The Seasons: The Headwaters of the Missouri River in April;* and, like the countless pioneers who settled the prairies,

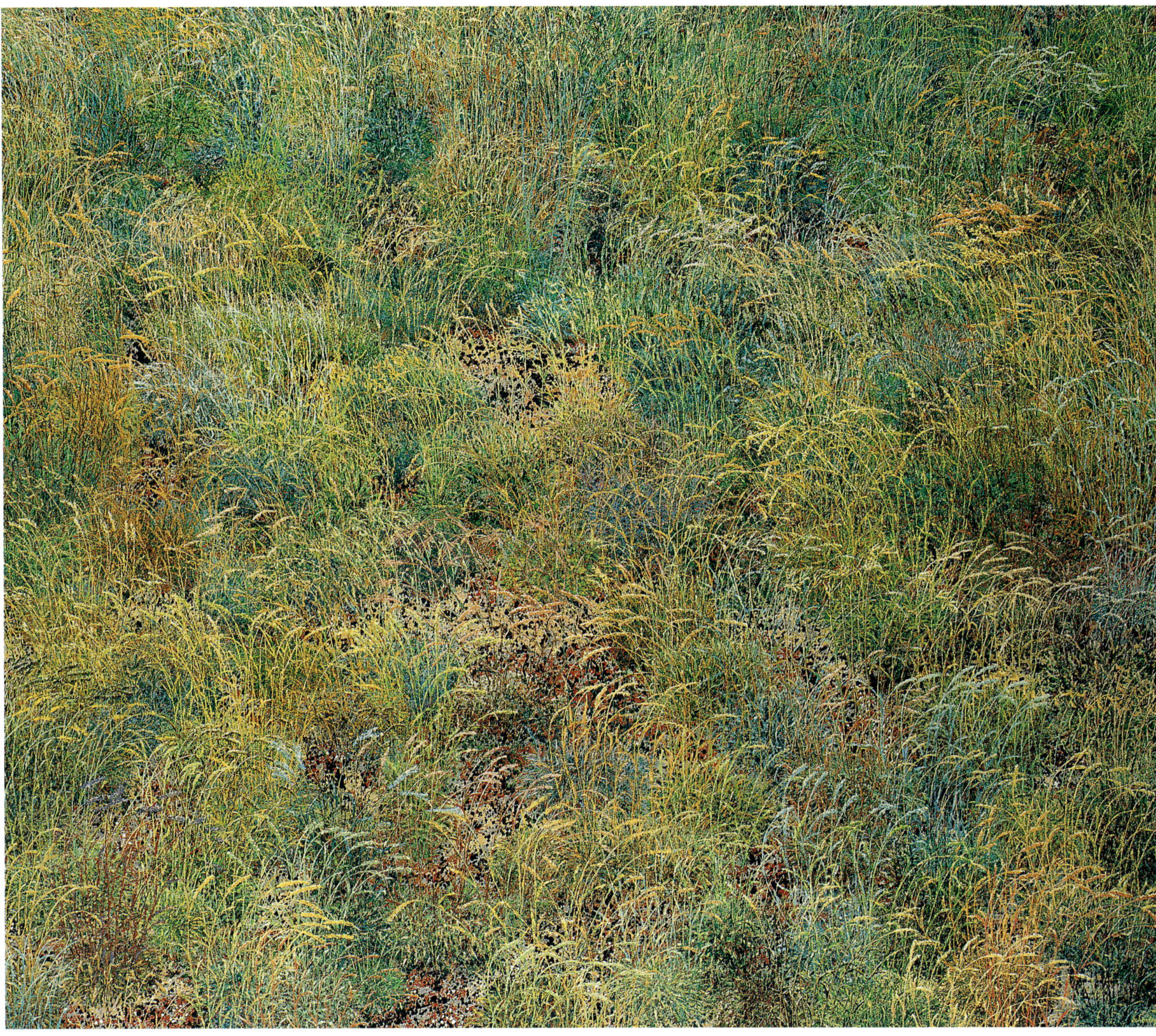

Elmer Schooley, FERGUSON'S PASTURE, *oil on canvas, 80 by 90 inches, 1992. Private collection; photograph courtesy of Munson Gallery.*

Elmer Schooley continues to be mesmerized by grasslands, as in *Ferguson's Pasture.* Response ranges from sensing the sublime, in Charles Fritz's *Towering Skies at Dusk,* to finding security in a comfortable mix of human-made structures and hillsides, as in Joellyn Duesberry's *Above Taos Valley* or Donna Clair's *Last Light on Truchas.*

For the adventurer who seeks illumination, the Western American landscape continues to offer opportunities for discovery. Roads guide us to unknown places over the horizon, as in Woody Gwyn's *Chimayo* and Chuck Forsman's *Crow Country,* and rivers continue to follow their own course, as in Wayne Wolfe's *Oxbow Bend.* For many of us, these pathways lead to enhanced self-awareness, waiting, for instance, in the primordial pool of Emmi Whitehorse's *Solar Pond* or at the climax of Page Allen's *Blue Highway.*

Allen described the landscape of adventure in the 1991 catalog for the Eiteljorg Museum's exhibit *New Art of the West: The Artist's Response to Nature.* It is a fitting summary of the heart of the Western mythos:

> I have always felt the tug of open space, the prayer of distant heights and the wonder of animals that inhabit the land. Landscape, like anything else, can be a metaphor for certain conditions of the human soul. I believe in the truth of this: that there is a correspondence between ourselves and our land, that nature does indeed shape us through beauty, mystery, change, and power. I look for images that manifest the fertile intersection of imagination and reality. The road to the horizon is one such image; there is longing, excitement, and mystery implicit in, as my daughter calls it, the "forever road."

—SUSAN HALLSTEN MCGARRY
Southwest Art
MARCH 1997

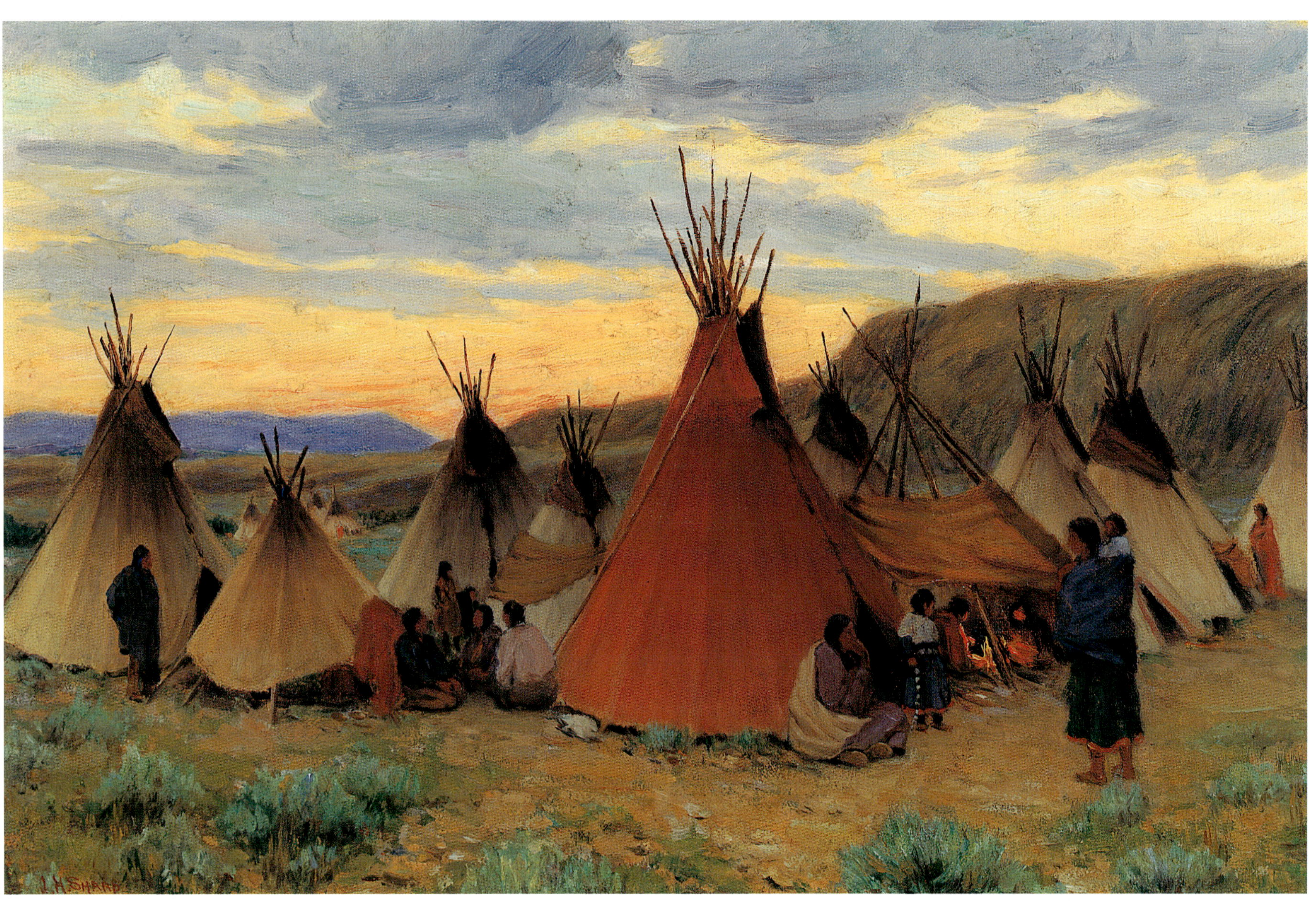

INTRODUCTION
The Visualized West

Joseph Henry Sharp,
EVENING, CROW RESERVATION,
oil on canvas,
12 by 18 inches, circa 1905.
Photograph courtesy of Thomas Nygard Gallery.

THE WEST. THE AMERICAN WEST. THE TRANSMISSISSIPPI WEST. THE OLD WEST. THE FRONTIER West. These are just a few of the many descriptive names that reflect the American experience with those lands and cultures beyond the Mississippi River. The West can start with geography, the border traced more or less along the 100th meridian. Westward lies an amazingly diverse topography—arid deserts, sagebrush plains, the canyonlands and mesas of the Southwest, the towering Sierra Nevada and Rocky Mountains—all different from the human-scaled landscapes of the East. Of course, there are other Wests: the Native American West, the Hispanic West, the Cowboy West, and nowadays, the Urban West or New West. These are realities, up to a point. Historian William Goetzmann calls the West "The West of the Imagination," a region that exists in our minds through stories, myths, legends, and sagas, a concept larger than the geographic reality. As such, whatever we want the West to be, it is.

The West is not always due west. As young artist Maynard Dixon made preparations in early 1900 to venture forth from San Francisco for his first extended journey through Arizona and New Mexico, he exclaimed, "I'm going East to see the West." Even then, despite the rich history of California in the development of the region, the West meant something different than California—it was a mythic region that lay somewhere between the Sierra Nevada Mountains and the rolling prairies of the Great Plains. Now, as then, the West is a cornucopia. It is Mary Austin's *Land of Little Rain.* It is Wallace Stegner's "The West is America, only more so." It is Clint Eastwood's *Unforgiven,* Alan Ladd's *Shane,* Mark Twain's *Roughing It,* and Larry McMurtry's *Lonesome Dove.* It is the great playa that fills Nevada's Railroad Valley, the red sandstone walls of Arizona's Canyon de Chelly, and the ramparts of Wyoming's Grand Tetons.

Artists ventured to this region in the early nineteenth century to create and document the awesome landscapes and their human and animal inhabitants. George Catlin and Karl Bodmer pushed up the Missouri River in the 1830s to record with grace the vibrant lives of Plains Indians. Alfred Jacob Miller became the only painter to reveal the wild, free life of the mountain men and fur trappers in the heart of the Rocky Mountains. Later arrivals included landscape painters Albert Bierstadt and Thomas Moran, whose heroically sized work drew inspiration from the lofty peaks of the Rocky Mountains, the wonders of Yellowstone, and the sublime grandeur of the Grand Canyon.

By the late 1880s, and into the early twentieth century, other artists turned not to the symphonic imprint of the landscape, but to romantic melodrama and nostalgia. Two artists, Frederic Remington and Charles M. Russell, define an era that saw the concept of the "Old West" emerge, specifically the "vanishing Old West." Through the paintings and sculpture of Remington and Russell, and a host of artist-illustrators active in what is called the "Golden Age of Illustration," stories of the West were told as exciting narratives: sagas on canvas or embedded in bronze. Russell in particular used his art to comment eloquently on what he did not like about his own time, lamenting "the West that has passed," as he called it.

Sometime in the early twentieth century, this art, and the art and artists before Remington and Russell, began to be referred to as "Western art." Western art, which can trace its beginnings back to the restless, nationalistic energy of an expanding nation driven by Manifest Destiny, often centers on the rupture between the past and the present, and is about transient time and loss. A complex and problematic domain, Western art did not begin as a regional art, but certainly has evolved as one.

To some degree, this book reveals the many facets of Western art, a distinctive, representational art of paintings, drawings, and sculpture that portrays animals and men, and rarely women, in natural, often pristine settings—the West of trappers, plainsmen, soldiers, old-time cowboys, and Indians, but also contemporary cowboys and ranch life. Cowboys and Native Americans, past and present, usually dominate Western art because they express so well the intense nostalgia for a way of life that has disappeared, or is perceived as about to disappear. The subjects of cowboys and Indians dominate traditional Western art, and much is left out to include these two elements. But the continued promise of Western art is the inclusion of a much wider array of subjects, styles, and techniques. Animals and wildlife, humor, irony, satire, and spirituality are bona fide elements. The selection of artists for this book was driven in part by that premise.

From the early 1900s to after World War II, a large number of artists continued to exploit the rich pictorial roots of the West and keep the historical threads alive. A dozen artists serve as examples of the generation that bridges Remington and Russell and today's artists. These individuals approached their art with styles that ranged from modernist candor to quiet, elegiac tones.

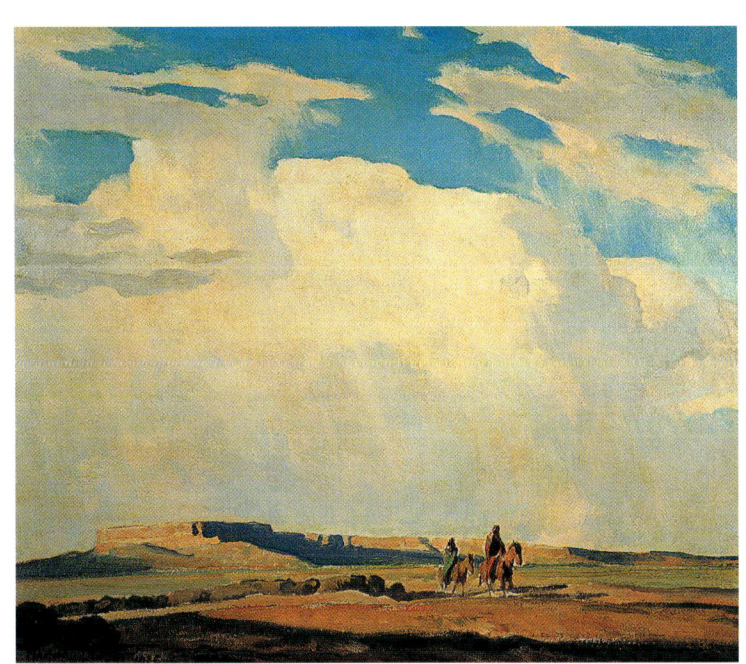

Maynard Dixon, NAVAJO LAND, *oil on canvas, 26 by 30 inches, 1925. Private collection; photograph courtesy of William Karges Fine Art.*

Among the dozen is Joseph Henry Sharp (1859–1953), a founding member of the Taos Society of Artists. Around 1892, Sharp met the painter Henry Farny in Cincinnati, prompting him to renew his interest in Native Americans. A year later, Sharp visited New Mexico. While in Europe during 1895, he encountered Ernest Blumenschein and Bert Geer Phillips, then students in Paris, and told them about his travels in New Mexico and a remote village named Taos. A quiet, isolated hamlet then, Taos eventually became an internationally known art colony.

In 1902, Sharp moved to the Crow Agency in Montana to live in a studio located near the Custer battlefield. Sharp spent a number of months each year, over the course of several years there, painting landscapes and nearly two hundred portraits of Crow, Cheyenne, and Sioux Indians. Eventually, around 1912, he settled in Taos, where he helped found the Taos Society of Artists and lived the rest of his life, renowned for the quiet but frank respect for Native Americans expressed in his paintings.

Around World War I, residents of San Francisco often saw a slender figure in distinctive Western garb on their streets. Sometimes a waiter might call out from a restaurant, "Morning, Mr. Dixon. Cold fog!" "Cold as Christian charity," would be the response as Maynard Dixon (1875–1946) climbed the steps to his studio on Montgomery Street. By then, Dixon, born in Fresno, California, had achieved considerable acclaim as one of the West's leading artists. An authentic, iconoclastic, self-created individual, Dixon had a long, productive life, a work of art in its own right, and the two loves of this life were the great Western landscape and the Native American.

For much of his life, Dixon traveled the arid lands of the West. He discovered a difference between the frontier and the West. The frontier, a historical concept concerned with certain American values, had all but disappeared, while the West itself seemed timeless. Through his paintings, murals, drawings, and poetry, Dixon emerged as a regionalist long before the term was coined, with a confirmed belief in the vitality of the American West.

When wildlife painter Carl Rungius (1869–1959) came to the United States from Germany in 1895 to join a friend on a hunting trip in Wyoming's Wind River Mountains, he decided to stay for good. Rungius specialized in painting big game animals—elk, moose, grizzly bears, mountain sheep and goats, and deer. With bold, fluent brushwork he eventually depicted nearly every North American big game animal, with many of his paintings reproduced in the leading outdoor periodicals of his day. From his studio on Long Island, New York, Rungius made frequent trips to the Yellowstone and Jackson areas, and into Alberta, Canada. A National Academician by the early 1920s, Rungius is considered the greatest wildlife painter of his time.

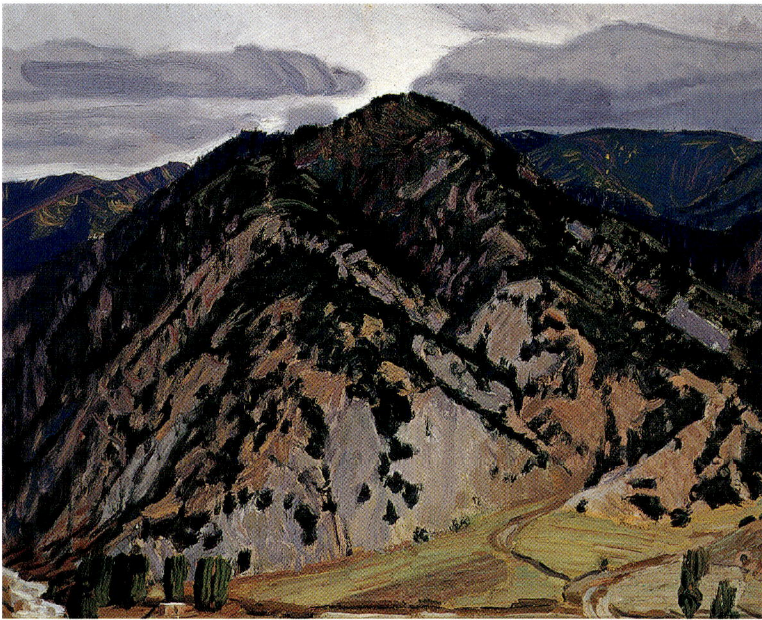

Ernest Blumenschein,
STUDY FOR TAOS, NEW MEXICO,
oil on canvas,
16 by 20 inches, circa 1920.
Photograph courtesy of Owings-Dewey Fine Art and Biltmore Gallery.

Inspired by Joseph Henry Sharp's glowing description of Taos, Ernest Blumenschein (1874–1960) and his friend Bert Geer Phillips made a fabled journey there in 1898. From about 1909, Blumenschein divided his time between Taos in the summer and New York the balance of the year. In 1919 he moved his family to Taos permanently.

A successful illustrator in New York, trained in the finest European academies, Blumenschein abandoned his literal, academic background in Taos to pursue a more intuitive, finely crafted approach to New Mexico's landscapes and native peoples. His canvases are noted for their monumentality, strong design, and Southwestern colors. Blumenschein remained responsive to the art movements of his time and emerged as the best-known member of the Taos Society of Artists.

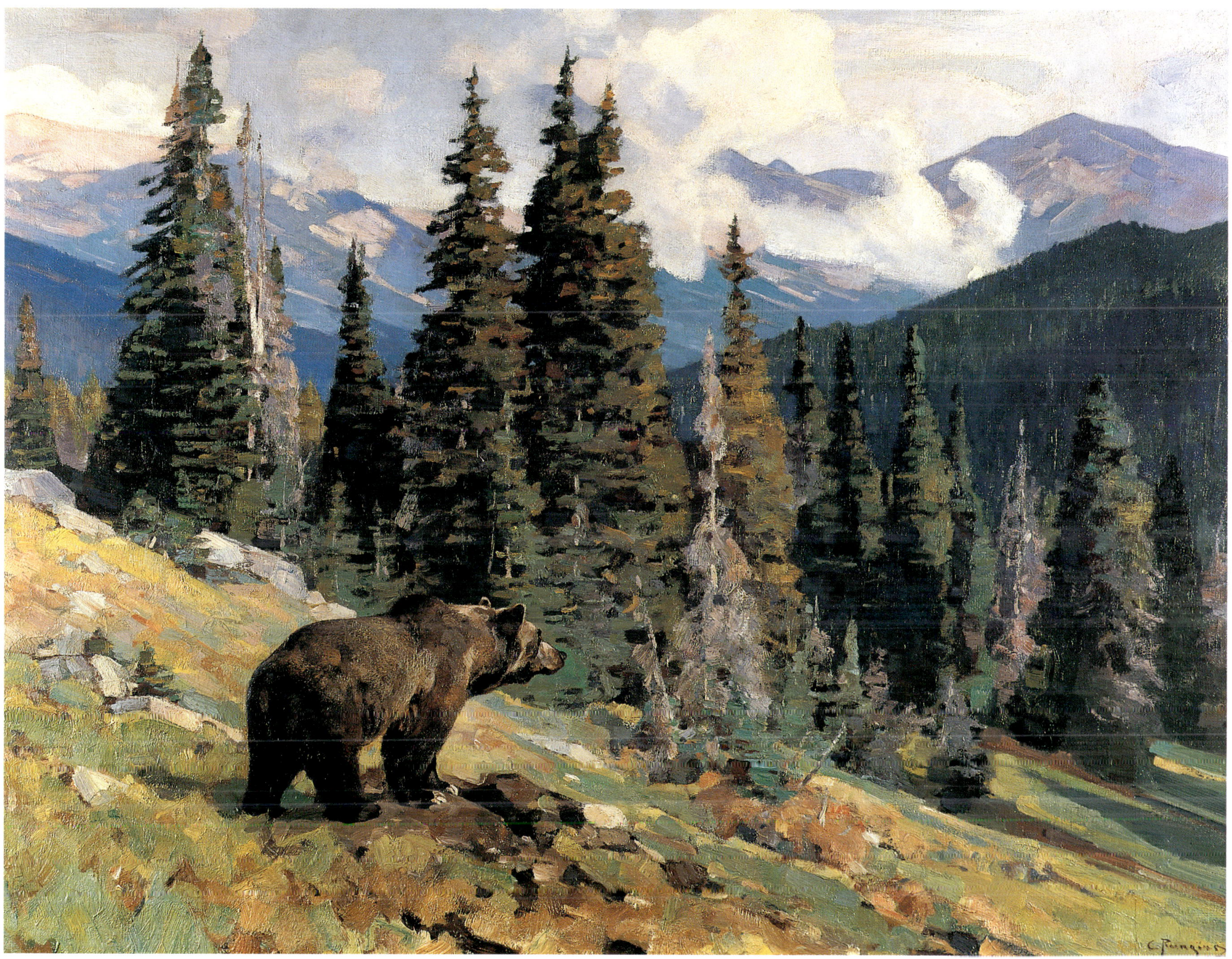

Carl Rungius, LORD OF THE CANYON, *oil on canvas, 30 by 40 inches, no date. Collection of National Museum of Wildlife Art.*

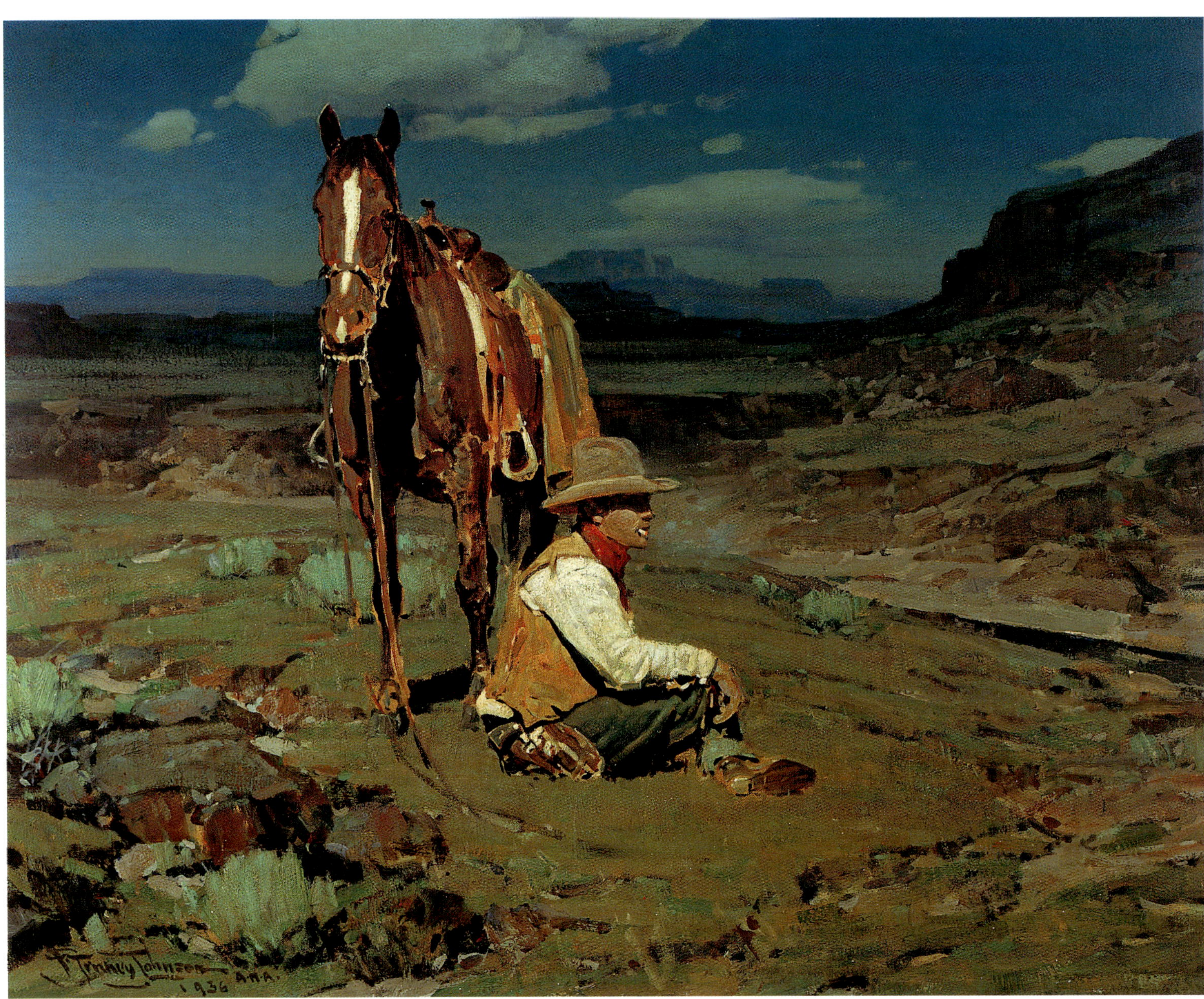

Frank Tenney Johnson, GUARDA DE GANADO, *oil on canvas, 24 by 30 inches, 1936. Photograph courtesy of Thomas Nygard Gallery.*

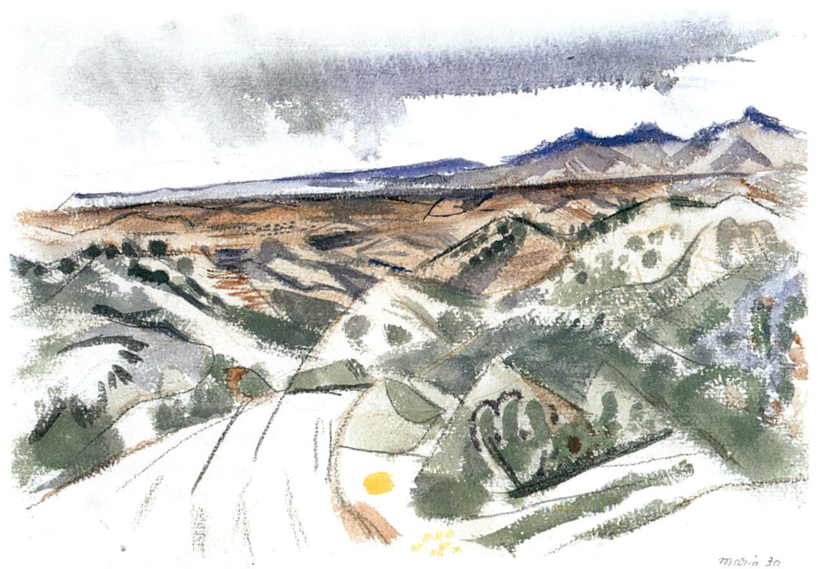

John Marin,
NEARING SANTA FE FROM TAOS,
watercolor, 14 by 20 inches, 1930.
Private collection; photograph courtesy of Owings-Dewey Fine Art.

Some artists encountered the West only briefly, yet left a lasting legacy. Alfred Stieglitz first recognized the uniqueness of the art of John Marin (1870–1953). While the urban city and the seascapes of Maine occupied most of his long career, two summers Marin spent in New Mexico at the suggestion of Georgia O'Keeffe produced some of the most original art drawn from the Western landscape.

In the summers of 1929 and 1930, Marin found a specific pictorial vocabulary in New Mexico's light and austere terrain. Over two hundred of the watercolors from these trips became the subject of a 1936 one-man show at the Museum of Modern Art in New York. Marin brought a modernist vision to landscape painting, his New Mexico watercolors endowed with simplified, geometric forms and a unique perspective.

In the early 1900s, the magazine *Field & Stream* sent Frank Tenney Johnson (1874–1939) to Colorado and New Mexico on assignment. Intrigued with the life of cattlemen, he spent time as a working cowboy and decided to devote his career to Western scenes. He became fascinated with horses, the Western landscape, and the effect of light. In 1905 he met the novelist Zane Grey, and was asked by the author to illustrate his books, which he did for the next fifteen years. Johnson gained considerable fame not only for those illustrations, but ultimately for his nocturne paintings.

By the early 1920s, Johnson's easel paintings had developed a different vision than those of most painters of the West. While other painters' subjects were cowboys, horses, and Native Americans, Johnson portrayed them differently, often outdoors under twinkling stars, bathed in the glow of moonlight. He studied the techniques of painter Maxfield Parrish, whose work he admired, and developed a special underpainting technique to endow his paintings with that special quality of a clear Western night.

Among the many fine landscape painters active in the West between the two World Wars, Edgar Payne (1888–1947) stands out. Born in Missouri's Ozark Mountains, Payne left home at fourteen to pursue art and finally settled in southern California. Payne, who was primarily self-taught, encountered the "other" West when, at the invitation of the Santa Fe Railway, he journeyed to the Navajo Reservation and Canyon de Chelly in 1916. He continued to make frequent pilgrimages to the region until the early 1940s.

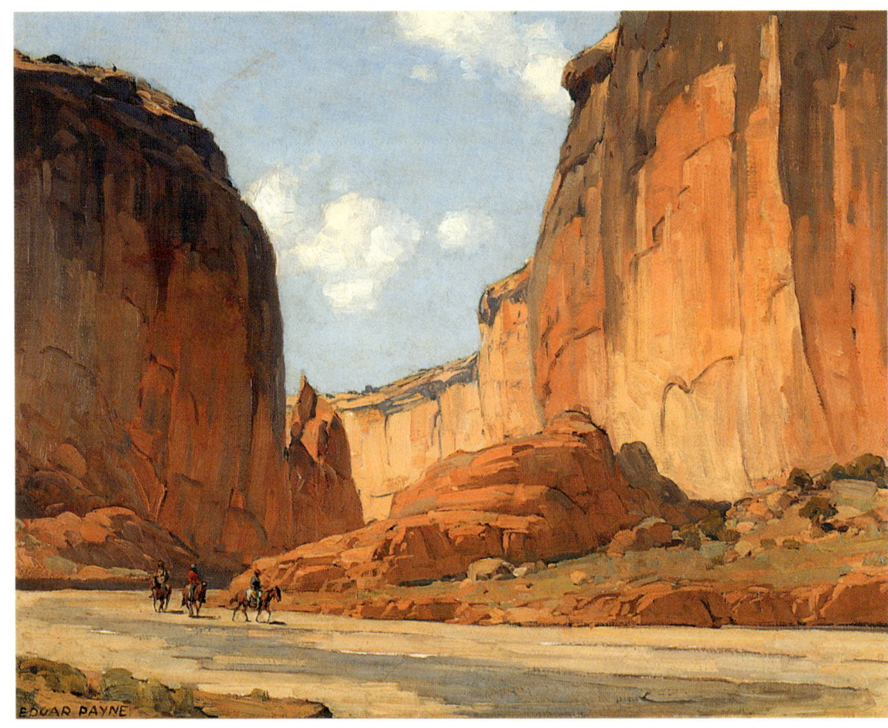

Edgar Payne,
CANYON DE CHELLY,
oil on canvas,
32 by 40 inches, circa 1920.
Collection of Rowena and Charles Simberg; photograph courtesy of Suzanne Brown Gallery.

Artists, Payne believed, must respond to an unpolluted natural world to uncover the animate and inanimate forms around them. In his bold, structured, postimpressionist paintings, soliloquies about light, he celebrated the West's landscapes, from the snow-capped Sierra Nevada to the limitless horizons of Navajo country. The relationship between the Native American and the landscape is a constant theme that runs through Payne's Southwestern work, especially his paintings of Canyon de Chelly.

From Yosemite to the Grand Canyon, Gunnar Widforss (1879–1934) celebrated the West's natural wonders. A native of Sweden, Widforss came to the United States in 1921. Encouraged by Stephen Mather, the first director of the National Park Service, the quiet Swede, as he was known, toured the majestic national parks of the West—Yellowstone, Bryce, Zion, Yosemite, and the Grand Canyon—in search of the spiritual in the landscapes.

From the mid-1920s until the final year of his life, Widforss spent most of his time painting at the Grand Canyon. A superb watercolorist, he brought forth the geology, color, and various moods of the Canyon like no other painter. Widforss pursued images of the Canyon from every angle, from the rim to the canyon floor, and through the change of seasons. After his death, a section of the North Rim was named Widforss Point.

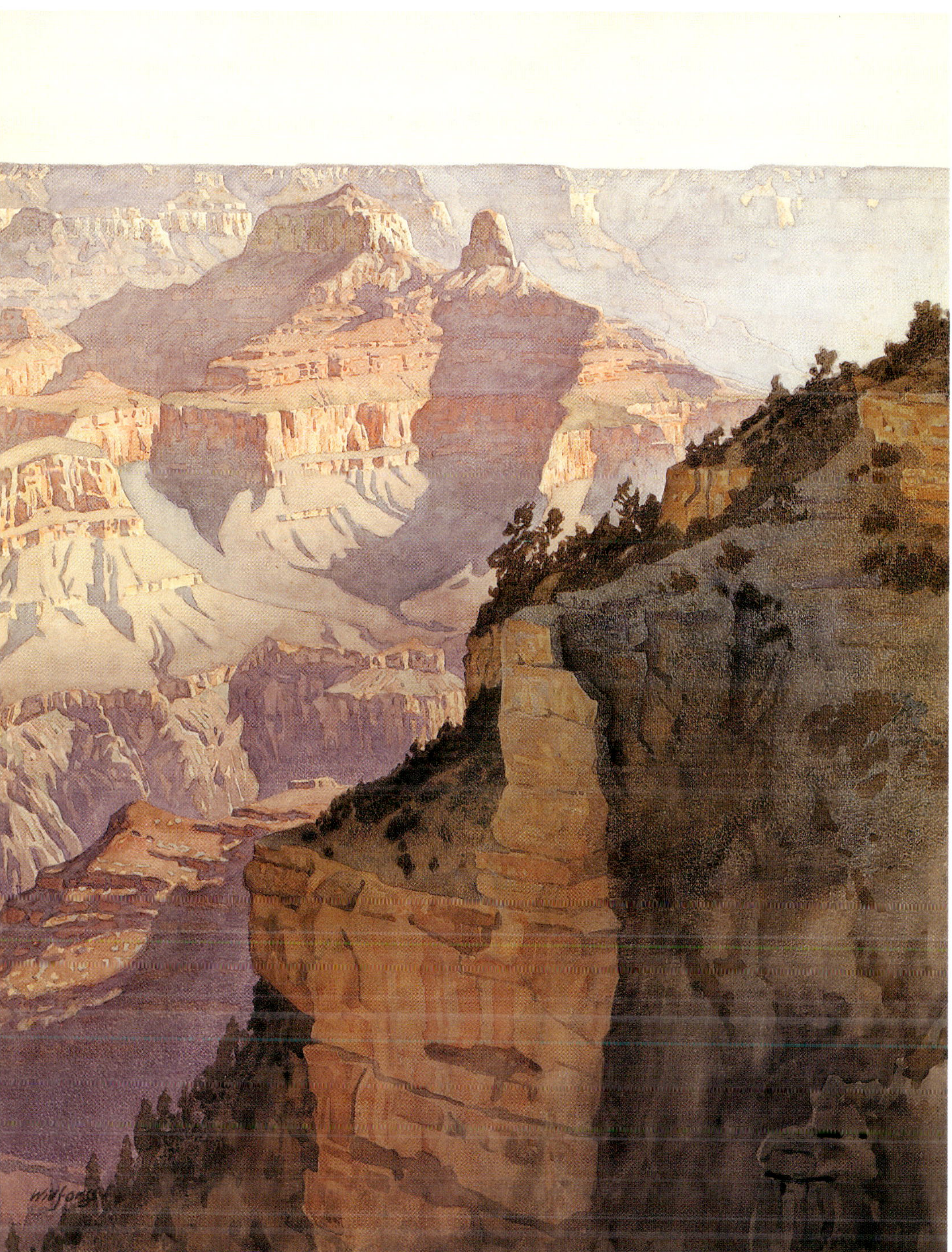

Gunnar Widforss,
GRANDEUR POINT,
watercolor,
25 by 20 inches, circa 1920.
Photograph by Bill McLemore photography,
courtesy of Arizona West Gallery.

Wild West stories fueled the desire of another German-born artist, Winold Reiss (1888–1953) to pursue portraits of Native Americans. After his immigration to the United States in 1913, he became a successful illustrator, muralist, and designer.

In 1919, Reiss traveled to Browning, Montana, to study and draw Blackfeet Indians. From 1919 to the early 1940s, Reiss traveled intermittently to Montana, usually in the summer, to paint striking portraits of Blackfeet men, women, and children, as well as other Westerners. For three decades, starting in 1933, the Great Northern Railway published a large, full-color reproduction of one of his Blackfeet portraits at the top of their annual art calendar. Reiss used pastel almost exclusively because it worked so well in representing his subjects' countenances and the explosive colors of their attire.

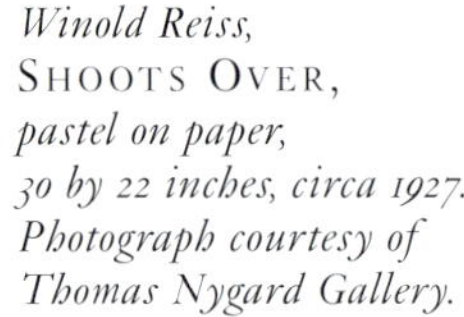

Winold Reiss,
SHOOTS OVER,
pastel on paper,
30 by 22 inches, circa 1927.
Photograph courtesy of
Thomas Nygard Gallery.

Reiss's subjects included portraits of the older Blackfeet, members of the last generation to have lived at the time when the buffalo still roamed free, as well as portraits of children and middle-aged individuals, which revealed a changing culture. In 1943 alone, he painted over seventy portraits. Inspired by his close admiration for and friendship with the Blackfeet, he executed portraits with insight and sympathy. The Blackfeet, in turn, named him Beaver Child because of his great capacity for work. After Reiss's death in 1953, Blackfeet friends scattered his ashes over the reservation.

Canadian-born artist Robert Lougheed (1910–1982) began his interest in animals and wildlife as a youngster, when he drew horses and cattle around his family's farm in Central Canada. After formal study at two Canadian art schools, Lougheed moved to New York in 1935 to continue studies at the Art Students League under Frank Vincent DuMond and Dean Cornwell.

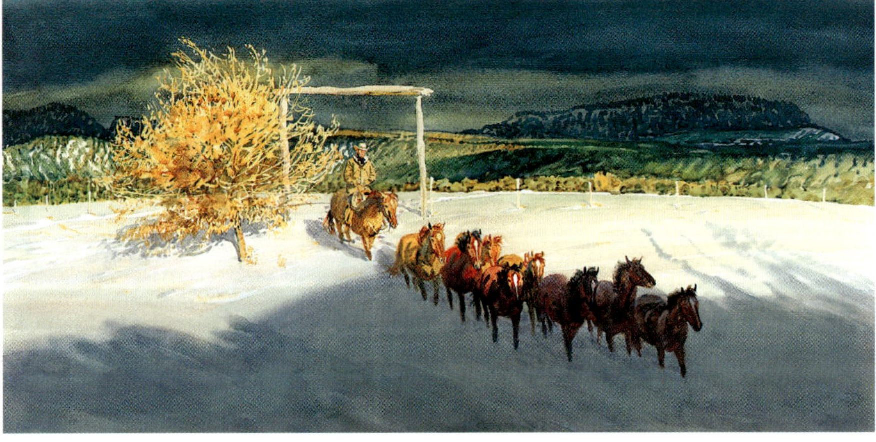

Robert Lougheed,
THROUGH THE GATES OF HOME,
watercolor,
20 by 40 inches, circa 1975.
Photograph courtesy of
Thomas Nygard Gallery.

As a successful illustrator, he created Mobil Oil's flying red horse and illustrations for *Reader's Digest*, *Sports Afield*, and other magazines. After a trip to New Mexico in 1952, Lougheed increasingly spent time in the western United States and Canada. In 1970 he moved to Santa Fe, where he added to his illustration credits a book about the state's famous Bell Ranch. Lougheed devoted years of close study to animals and the landscape, and his knowledge, by all accounts, was encyclopedic, due in part to his dedication to painting plein-air. His work is loose and impressionistic. Lougheed's painting trips took him out of New Mexico, as well, to the Pacific Northwest and Alaska. He is noted for his generosity in assisting young artists with their aspirations, and he was a leader in the Cowboy Artists of America and the National Academy of Western Art.

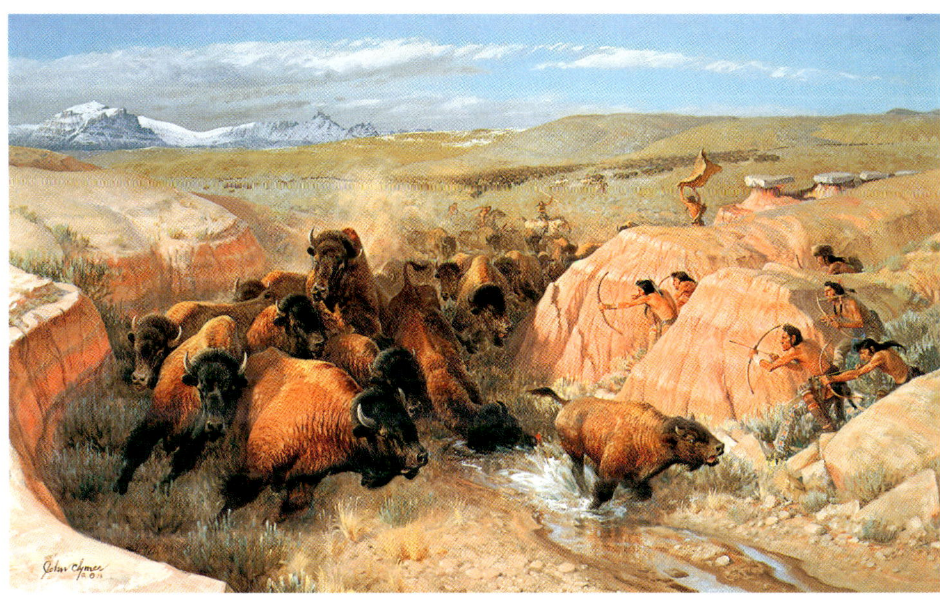

John Clymer,
TRIBAL HUNT,
oil on canvas,
30 by 40 inches, 1973.
Collection of National Museum of Wildlife Art.

John Clymer (1907–1989) was inspired to study the art of the American West by his teachers, Frank Schoonover, N. C. Wyeth, and Harvey Dunn. After forty years as one of this country's most productive illustrators, with more than eighty covers for *The Saturday Evening Post* under his belt, he retired in 1970 to Jackson, Wyoming, in pursuit of the West's history through easel painting. He retraced the steps of Lewis and Clark from St. Louis to the Oregon beach where the epic journey ended. Another expedition took him the entire length of the Oregon Trail. In 1966, Clymer floated down the upper Missouri River, visiting those spots where Lewis and Clark, and later the artist Karl Bodmer, had stopped. Still other excursions saw him trace the Nez Perce and Bozeman Trails. Clymer's primary subjects included the mountain men of 1804–1840, and the Plains Indians of the same period.

Clymer, like his close friend Robert Lougheed a member of the Cowboy Artists of America and the National Academy of Western Art, pursued a strong commitment to history and tradition. Through his visits to real locations and his narrative-realist approach to painting, Clymer's paintings

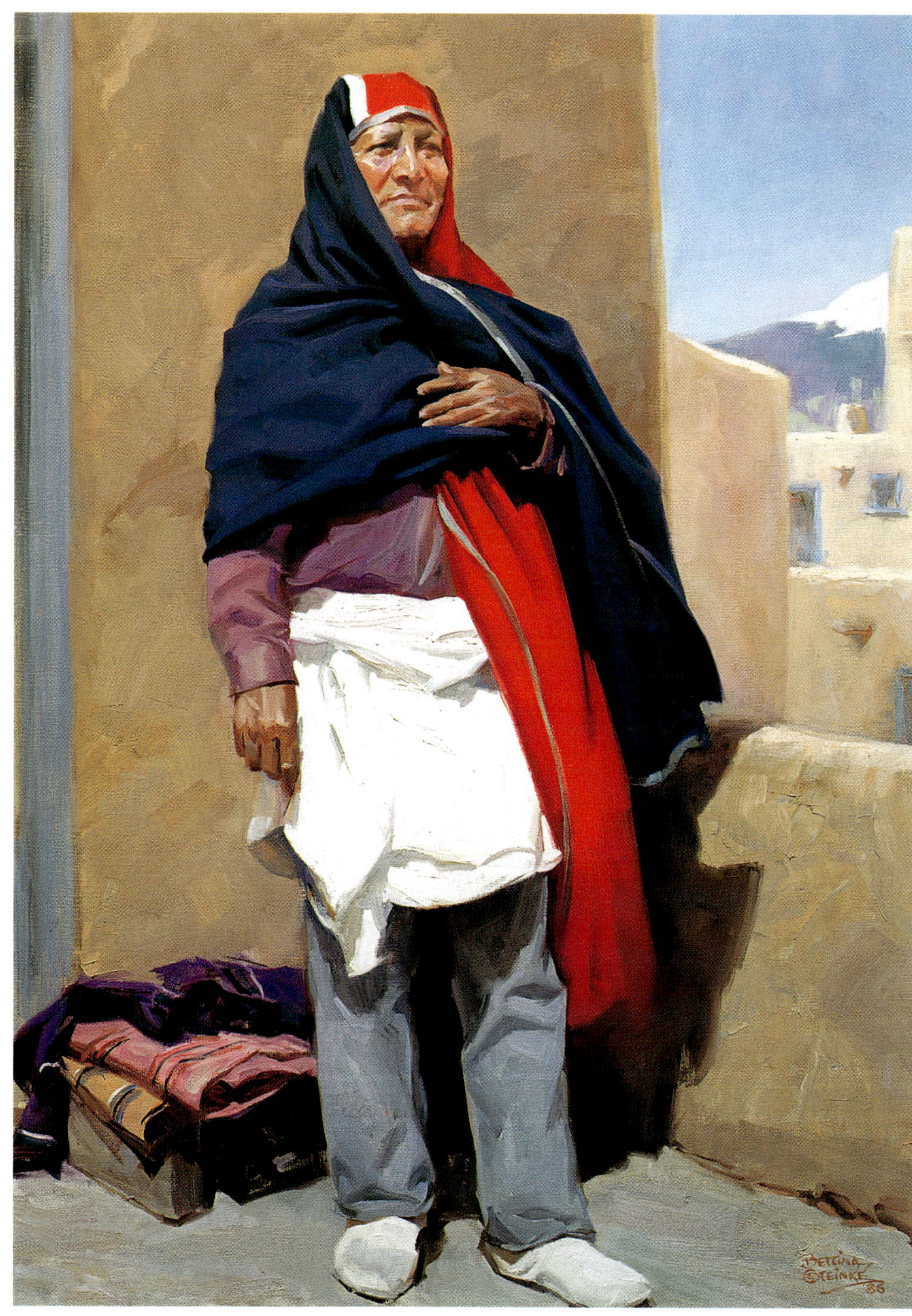

Bettina Steinke,
TAOS WAR CHIEF,
oil on canvas,
41¼ by 29¼ inches, 1986.
Photograph courtesy of National Cowboy Hall of Fame.

invited his viewers back in time. Specific historical locations, times of year, and documented events are embedded in his work. His art has a clear feel for what might have occurred in the past.

Finally, Bettina Steinke (b. 1913), a painter of Native American portraits and related subjects, and a longtime member of the Society of Illustrators, represents the final link that ties Clymer, Lougheed, and others to the current crop of realist artists at work in the West. A native of Maine, Steinke became an illustrator of national repute. Her career as a painter of Western subjects started when she lived in Taos and Santa Fe during 1947. Ten years later she made Santa Fe her permanent home.

Steinke was among the first academicians elected to the National Academy of Western Art in 1973. She is noted for her portraiture of Native Americans, from Southwestern groups to those in the far north of Alaska, and remains an important influence on a new generation of artists.

As Western art grew in importance after World War II, museums formed to collect and interpret this art. There are now a number of museums located throughout the American West that schedule exhibitions, issue catalogs, and otherwise support Western art. The National Cowboy Hall of Fame in Oklahoma City, founded in 1965, hosts an annual *Prix de West Invitational Exhibition and Sale,* and is in the midst of a major expansion. In Tulsa, Oklahoma, each spring the Gilcrease Museum offers the *Gilcrease Rendezvous,* a retrospective for two artists whose subject matter reflects the Western experience. In California, the Autry Museum of Western Heritage plays an active role in historic and contemporary Western art. Recently the Buffalo Bill Historical Center in Cody, Wyoming, constructed the Kriendler Gallery of Contemporary Western Art. The Eiteljorg Museum of American Indian and Western Art in Indianapolis, Indiana, also focuses on contemporary art. From time to time, they present their *New Art of the West* exhibit, a showcase of eclectic painters and sculptors active in the West.

The Heard Museum in Phoenix and the Wheelwright Museum of the American Indian in Santa Fe often present exhibitions of contemporary Native American painters and sculptors. In Wausau, Wisconsin, the Leigh Yawkey Woodson Art Museum hosts two invitationals, *Birds in Art* and *Wildlife: The Artist's View,* that attract some of the West's leading animal and wildlife artists. A new museum, the National Museum of Wildlife Art in Jackson, Wyoming, opened in September 1994, and is already a major force in the world of wildlife art. One gallery is dedicated to the work of Carl Rungius, and another to John Clymer.

Several magazines are active in the promotion of Western art. The premiere one is *Southwest Art,* founded in 1971, a monthly publication with articles on historic and contemporary artists, gallery and museum shows, trends, and a large array of other related subjects. Another one is *Art of the West,* a bimonthly magazine. In addition, *Wildlife Art News* often includes articles on painters and sculptors of Western wildlife and animals.

Since the 1960s, many organizations emerged to further the rising interest in Western art. Probably the most famous, the Cowboy Artists of America, came out of a meeting at Bird's Oak Creek Tavern in Sedona, Arizona, in 1965. Six artists sat down to discuss starting an organization dedicated to standards of quality in Western art. The group held their first exhibition at the National Cowboy Hall of Fame in 1966, and continued annual exhibitions there until 1972, when they moved their group show to the Phoenix Art Museum. Each year the members' exhibition in Phoenix is a major, high-profile event.

After the Cowboy Artists of America departed from their facility, the National Cowboy Hall of Fame, through the assistance of Robert Lougheed and others, instituted the National Academy of Western Art (NAWA), a juried invitational exhibition and sale for the West's leading artists. After the first show in 1973, successive exhibitions awarded the Prix de West for a painting or sculpture, with the winner purchased by the Hall for its permanent collection. In 1995 the Hall decided to continue without the NAWA title, and this important event, now called the *Prix de West Invitational Exhibition and Sale,* still showcases the West's premiere painters and sculptors.

Other organizations dedicated to Western art include the Northwest Rendezvous Group, which holds an annual exhibition in Park City, Utah, and the Artists of America in Denver, Colorado, as well as the California Art Club, American Indian and Cowboy Artists, and the Texas Cowboy Artists Association, to name only a few. Women artists are especially active in the formation of organizations, among them American Women Artists, the Western Academy of Women Artists, and Women Artists of the West.

Artists selected for inclusion in this book should be viewed as "selective fragments," representatives extracted from a much larger array of artists who respond to the American West. As such, they speak for thousands of their colleagues. Most of them profiled here are at the zenith of their careers, or near it. Several include "N.A." (National Academician) after their name, meaning they are recognized by the National Academy of Design for their achievements. Others place "CA" on their paintings or sculpture, reflective of membership in the Cowboy Artist of America. Some of the artists reflect emerging talent, with bright prospects for the future. A few of them, however, ride a solitary trail. They do not belong to art organizations, exhibit in juried, invitational shows, or seek museum exhibitions. There are other criteria for inclusion in this book, certainly technical skill, but also that often overused word, *vision.* These are painters and sculptors who are able to see, and see powerfully. Finally, there are several artists here whose styles venture beyond what might be included within the usual boundaries of Western art, with paths outside conventional imagery.

Most of the artists profiled here live in the western United States, although one lives in Ontario, Canada, one in New Jersey, and another in Connecticut. They reside in large urban centers like Denver, Tucson, and Seattle, and many live in the artists enclaves of Santa Fe, or Loveland, Colorado. Others are scattered in small communities around the West such as Billings, Montana; Point Reyes Station, California; Mason, Texas; South Jordan, Utah; Chimayo, New Mexico; Pawhuska, Oklahoma; and Pinedale, Wyoming.

The subject matter of these one hundred artists reflects a non-urban West, and includes such topics as landscapes, animals and wildlife, women, still lifes, ranch and farm life, cowboys, the historical West, Native American spirituality, and family and community. Of course, there are many painters and sculptors who tackle the challenge of an urban and industrialized West in compelling works, within the language of modernism and the tradition of the sublime. But that is another story.

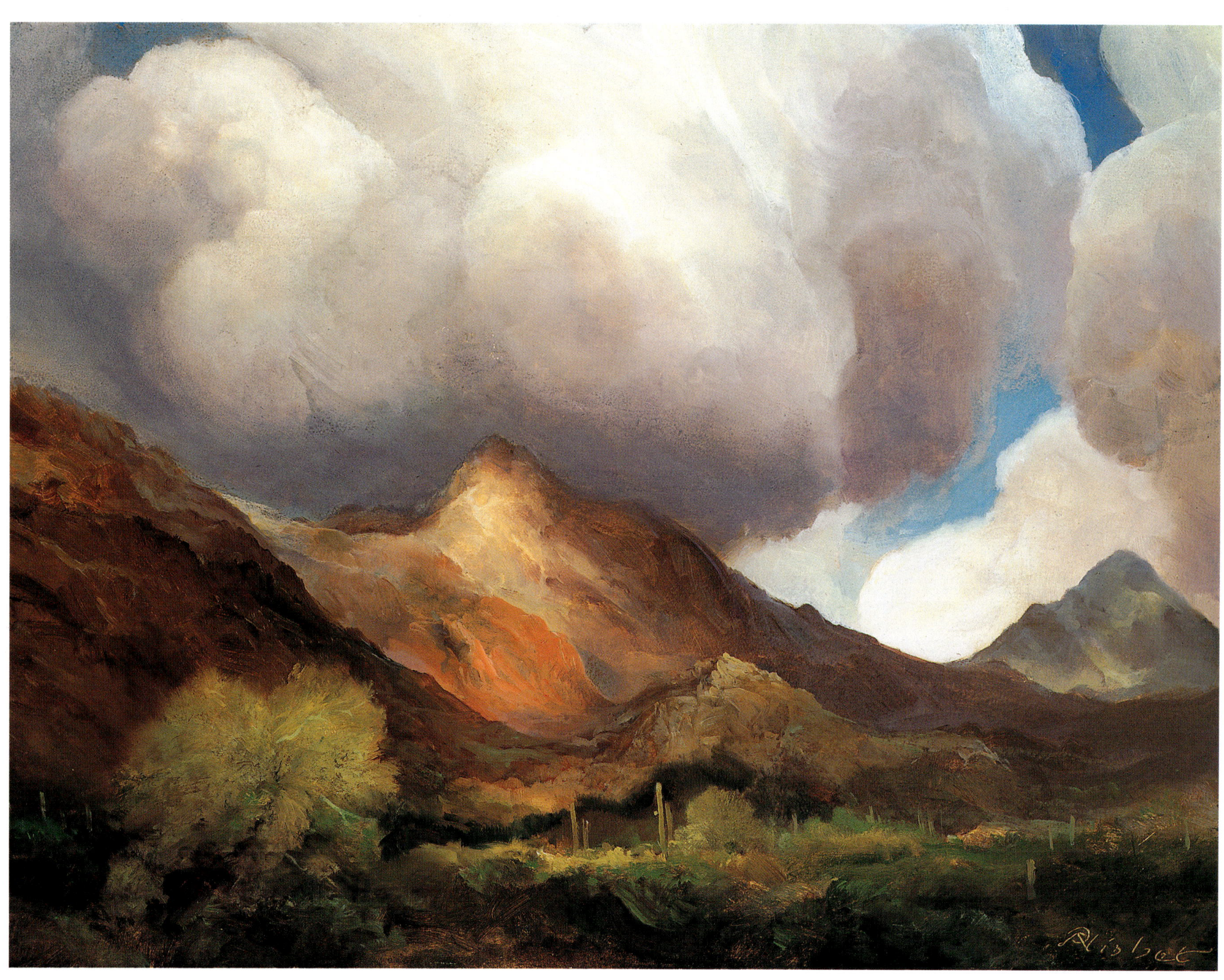

WESTERN LANDSCAPES

The West, the West, Always the West

For contemporary landscape painters of the American West, nature is a starting point. With little commonality in style or subject matter, except for the land, they pursue varied approaches in their painting, and in different media. Many artists find inspiration outdoors with feet firmly planted on the ground, while others discover a rapport with their images in a studio's controlled environment. The majority engage in varied forms of realism, a legible language that they feel can uncover the truth about the West's complex, sometimes ethereal landscapes.

Their art is a meditation about man's relationship to nature, the topographic realities of the West's landscapes transformed into their own private mirages. Some define the land's configuration with exuberant paintings that reflect the breadth and scale of places like the Grand Canyon or the great sweep toward the horizon in Taos Valley, with far-flung skies and clouds. Others, however, depict the ordinary here and now, soft spoken accounts of an aspen grove or a particular rock formation. These are less concerned with the conjuring up of universal truths, and more with the specifics of time and place, and the turning of the earth. Such impressions parallel those of writer D. H. Lawrence, who wrote when he first encountered New Mexico, "The moment I saw the brilliant, proud morning shine high up over Santa Fe, something stood still in my soul, and I started to attend. . . . In the magnificent fierce morning of New Mexico one sprang awake, a new part of the soul woke up suddenly, and the old world gave way to the new" ("New Mexico," *Survey Graphics,* May 1931).

P. A. Nisbet,
Tucson Mountain Park,
oil on board,
12 by 16 inches, 1995.
Private collection.

In most cases, human presence rarely intrudes upon the settings in these paintings. These landscapes are quiet, ageless, unaffected by the hand of man. If there is architecture, or human figures, they remain subservient to the landscape, and never detract from the promise of unspoiled terrain. These paintings take us to places like Canyon de Chelly, the Stillwater River, Truchas, and the Rio Chama, for example, and to places without names. About them hover, it seems, the ghosts of earlier landscape painters attracted to the magnificent land: Albert Bierstadt, Thomas Moran, Maynard Dixon, Georgia O'Keeffe, and Edgar Payne. For the present-day artists, there is a message that the Western landscape is more than an image or a picture—it is more about exploration, about forming a relationship to the "there" out there. As one artist exclaimed about his painting subjects, "The West, the West, always the West!"

Among them is **CLYDE ASPEVIG** (b. 1951). Raised on a small wheat farm near Rudyard, Montana, Aspevig determined he would pursue art at age eleven, a decision that has led him into a lifetime of painting the "out there." Since 1988, Aspevig has lived in Loveland, Colorado. Aspevig paints his light-drenched landscapes from his studio in a remodeled historic church, surrounded by books of art, philosophy, and poetry.

Aspevig has had little formal art training. He has developed his landscape painting over the past two decades through constant application to his craft, and extensive study of such artists as John Singer Sargent, Anders Zorn, and Winslow Homer. Aspevig is known not only for his productivity, but also for the quality and integrity with which he pursues his craft. His paintings, direct perceptions of nature, reflect a sensitive, intense feel for his subjects. Aspevig counts among his numerous awards the Frederic Remington Award and the Robert M. Lougheed Memorial Award, both from the National Cowboy Hall of Fame.

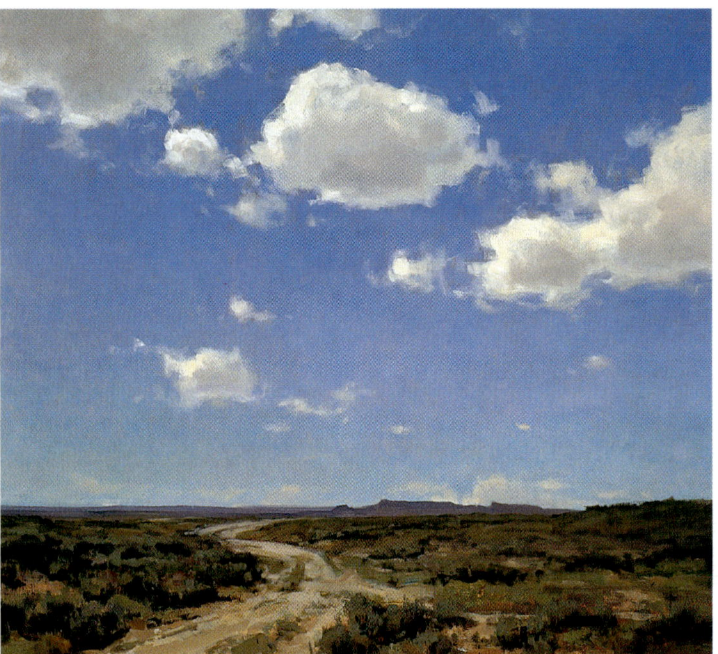

Clyde Aspevig,
WYOMING SKY,
oil on canvas,
36 by 40 inches, 1989.
Private collection.

Aspevig travels extensively to paint, sometimes going to England, Italy, or the Caribbean. However, places in the Southwest and the Rocky Mountain states prevail as inspiration for his art. "After reading about the West in books by Wallace Stegner," he says, "I find myself searching for the ideal motif. Two things stand out as the most essential element in shaping our lives here in the West—space and water."

With impressionistic paintings like *Wyoming Sky,* Aspevig registers the spirit of space and the arid, water-scarce terrain near Rock Springs, Wyoming. Sky, rather than earth, dominates the

I yearn for country that has not been tainted by subdivisions, power poles, billboards, and water slides. I choose to paint my pictures as if I, or the viewer, were the first person to set foot upon the landscape.

—CLYDE ASPEVIG

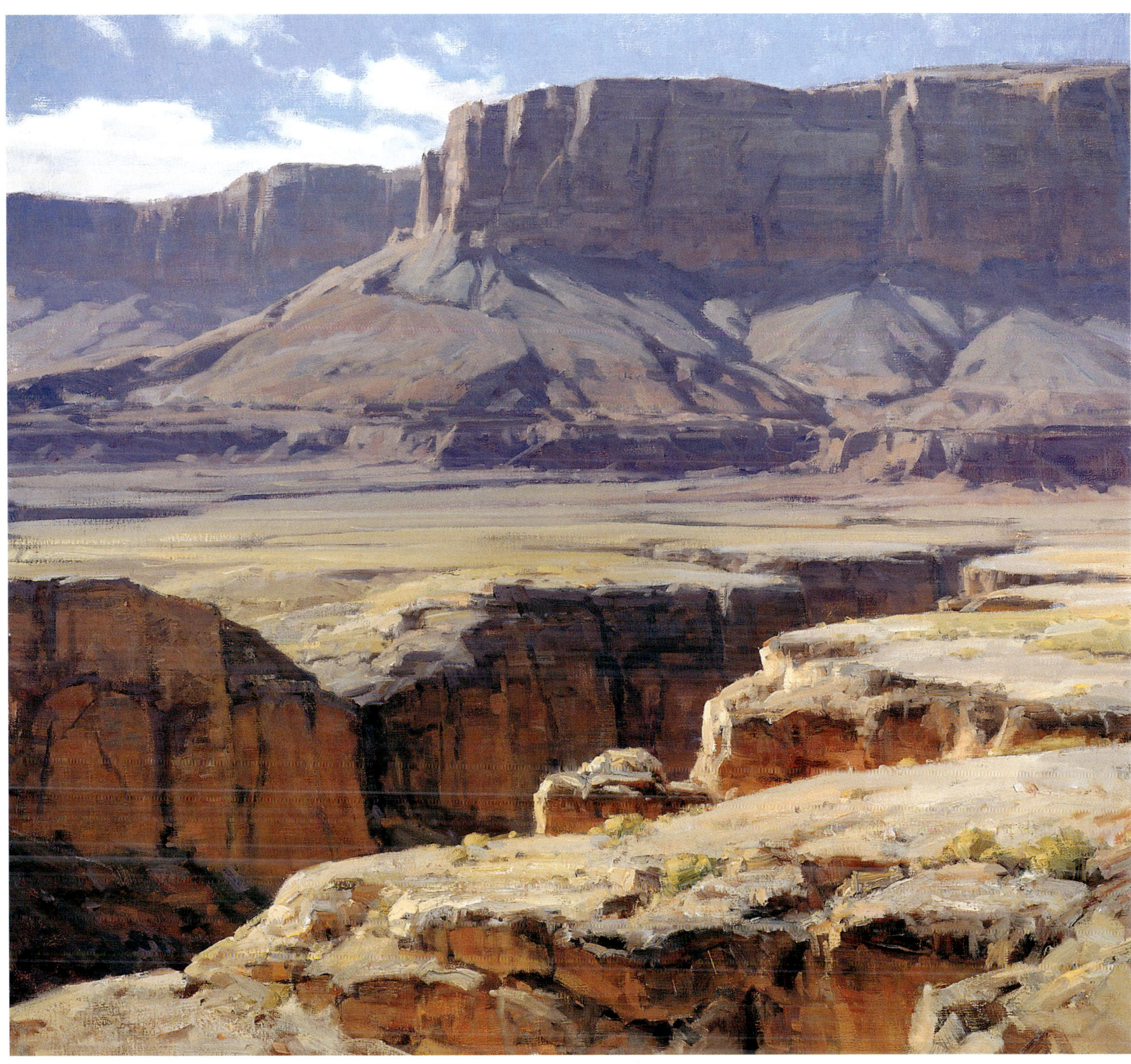

Clyde Aspevig, VERMILLION CLIFFS, *oil on canvas, 36 by 40 inches, 1996. Private collection.*

painting. In another example, *Vermillion Cliffs* (p. 19), profound, elegant forms are captured with soaring light and space, the eye led into the remote reach of the painted distance. “Paintings are a spiritual communion with nature which results in my celebration of life,” he says. “Toward this end, I yearn for country that has not been tainted by subdivisions, power poles, billboards, and water slides. I choose to paint my pictures as if I, or the viewer, were the first person to set foot upon the landscape.”

Ed Mell (b. 1942) grew up in Phoenix, Arizona, but a passion for illustration led him to the Art Center College of Design in Los Angeles. After graduation in 1967, he migrated to New York, where he became an art director for a large advertising agency. Two years later, he founded his own operation, Sagebrush Studios. By this time, Mell's airbrush illustrations, particularly those using angular forms inspired by art deco, had attracted national recognition.

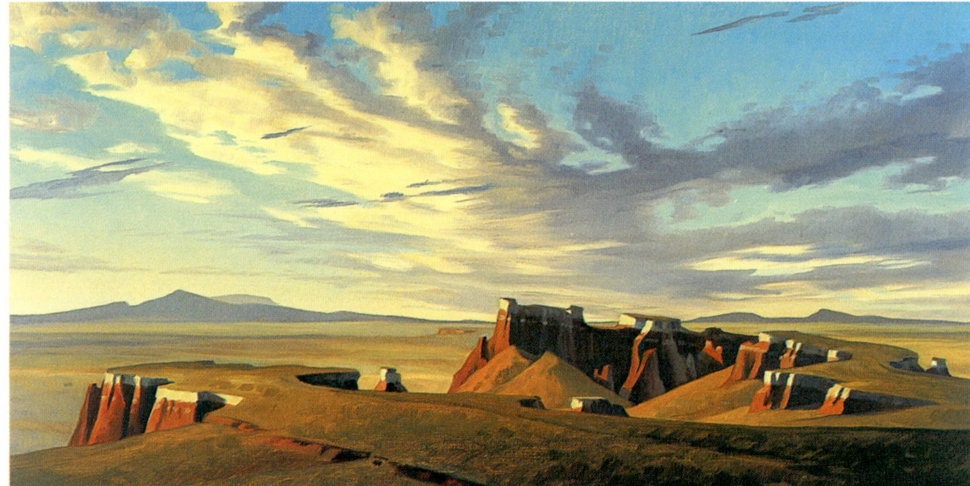

Ed Mell,
View from Ward Terrace,
oil on canvas,
14 by 20 inches, 1996.
Collection of the artist.

Restless, he spent the summer of 1971 on the Hopi Reservation, where he taught art to children and adults. Melodramatic skies, distant horizons, and the Hopi spiritual world pointed him in another direction. He returned to Phoenix in 1973, continued illustration work, and painted landscapes part time; then, in 1978, he made the switch to full-time landscape painter. Besides landscapes, Mell's subjects include longhorn cattle and flowers, and he also creates expressive sculpture. One of his sculptures, *Jackknife,* sits at the intersection of Scottsdale's Main Street and Marshall Way.

No Vibram-soled wilderness hiker, Mell found inspiration for his paintings of the Colorado Plateau from the seat of a helicopter piloted by a friend. For a number of years, Mell hitched rides to such Arizona places as Coal Mine Canyon, Moenkopi Plateau, Lake Powell, Navajo

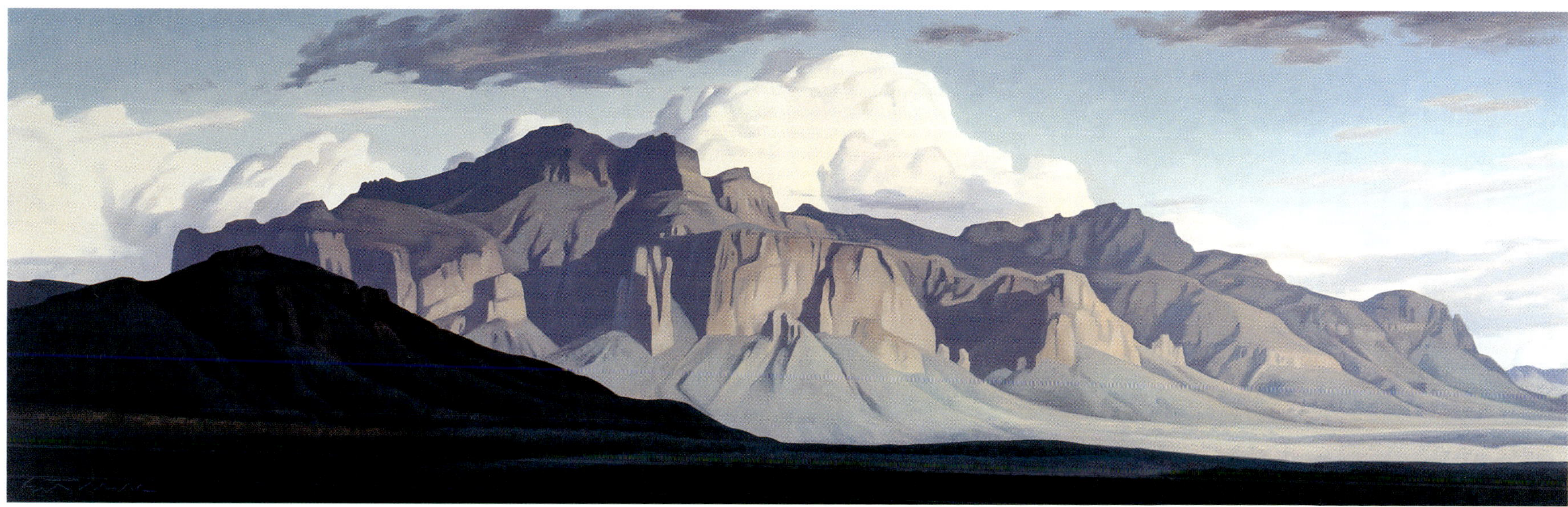

Ed Mell, THE SUPERSTITIONS, *oil on canvas, 20 by 64 inches, 1997. Private collection.*

Mountain, the Painted Desert, and the San Francisco Peaks. From a helicopter seat, the wide-angle horizon perspective is different, the corrugated landscapes and clouds above sharply defined. Mell's sketchbook is a camera. The resultant slides, thousands of them now, serve as visual guides for small oil studies, dress rehearsals for larger canvases. "Windows, I call them," he says.

Initially, the paintings appeared hard-edged and geometric, but as Mell moved between abstract and realistic imagery in the early 1990s, landscape forms became more intuitive. From what he sees, from what he remembers, and from what he invents, Mell captures the poetry of vast distance, as in *View from Ward Terrace.* The location is the Moenkopi Plateau, a landscape marked by ascending shale and sandstone terraces above the Little Colorado River, with boundless vistas, clear light, and aggressive solitude. *The Superstitions,* which portrays a rugged, brooding landmark west of Phoenix, is an exacting synthesis of realism and abstract design, capturing the fleeting qualities of light and atmosphere.

The vision of Montana artist **CHARLES FRITZ** (b. 1955) is grounded in a meticulous method of realist painting based on direct observation of nature and a framework of proven artistic principles. Fritz follows along the path of early twentieth-century artists, like the American impressionists and Russian itinerants, with his plein-air transcriptions of Rocky Mountain and Southwestern landscapes.

After graduation from Iowa State University, Fritz taught third grade in an elementary school. Eighteen months later he decided to pursue full-time painting, and moved to Billings, Montana, in 1981. Fritz received the Lee M. Loeb Memorial Award for landscape painting in 1993 at the Salmagundi Club, and has received two best-of-show awards at the C. M. Russell Museum in Great Falls, Montana. The Denver Art Museum recently purchased one of his paintings for their permanent collection. Fritz has exhibited his work with the National Museum of Wildlife Art, the Gilcrease Museum, the Artists of America, and the National Cowboy Hall of Fame's *Prix de West Invitational.*

The locales for Fritz's paintings are neither grandiose nor sublime, but are quiet places, like the one in *Winter on the Stillwater,* Montana's Stillwater River held in winter's grip. "On some days, the river stays open despite a heavy snowfall overnight," he says. "On those mornings the sound of water seems to be the only appropriate break in winter's silence." From a view he encountered near Shiprock, New Mexico, he painted *Towering Skies at Dusk.* "The land changes at a pace so slow we can barely comprehend, while the sky and clouds swirl and change by the moment," he says. The paintings convey a harmonious, intimate appreciation for the land, a heightened clarity of light, and a sense of specific place. Fritz's paintings are nourished by the earth, his landscape art meditation on the land's spirit.

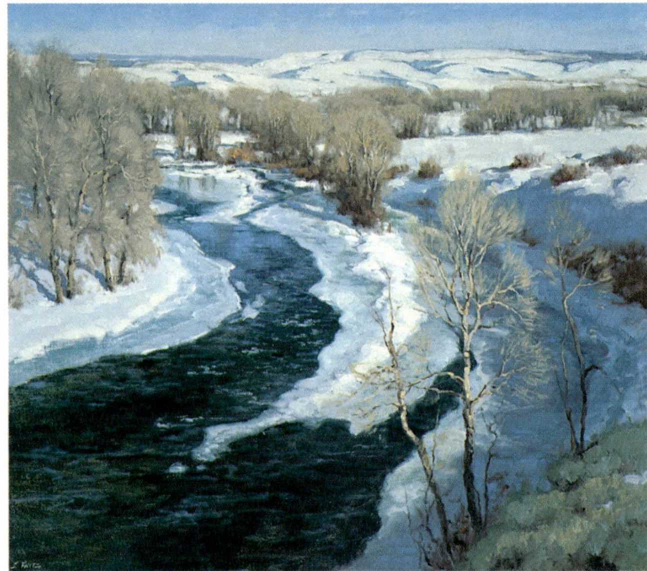

Charles Fritz,
WINTER ON THE STILLWATER,
oil on canvas,
26 by 30 inches, 1994.
Private collection.

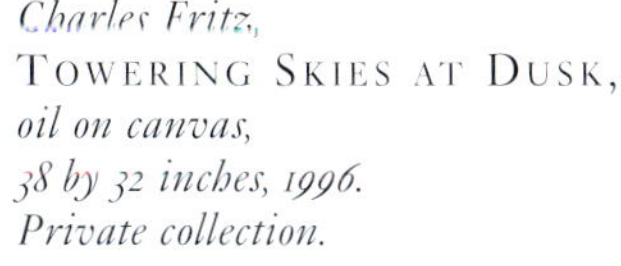

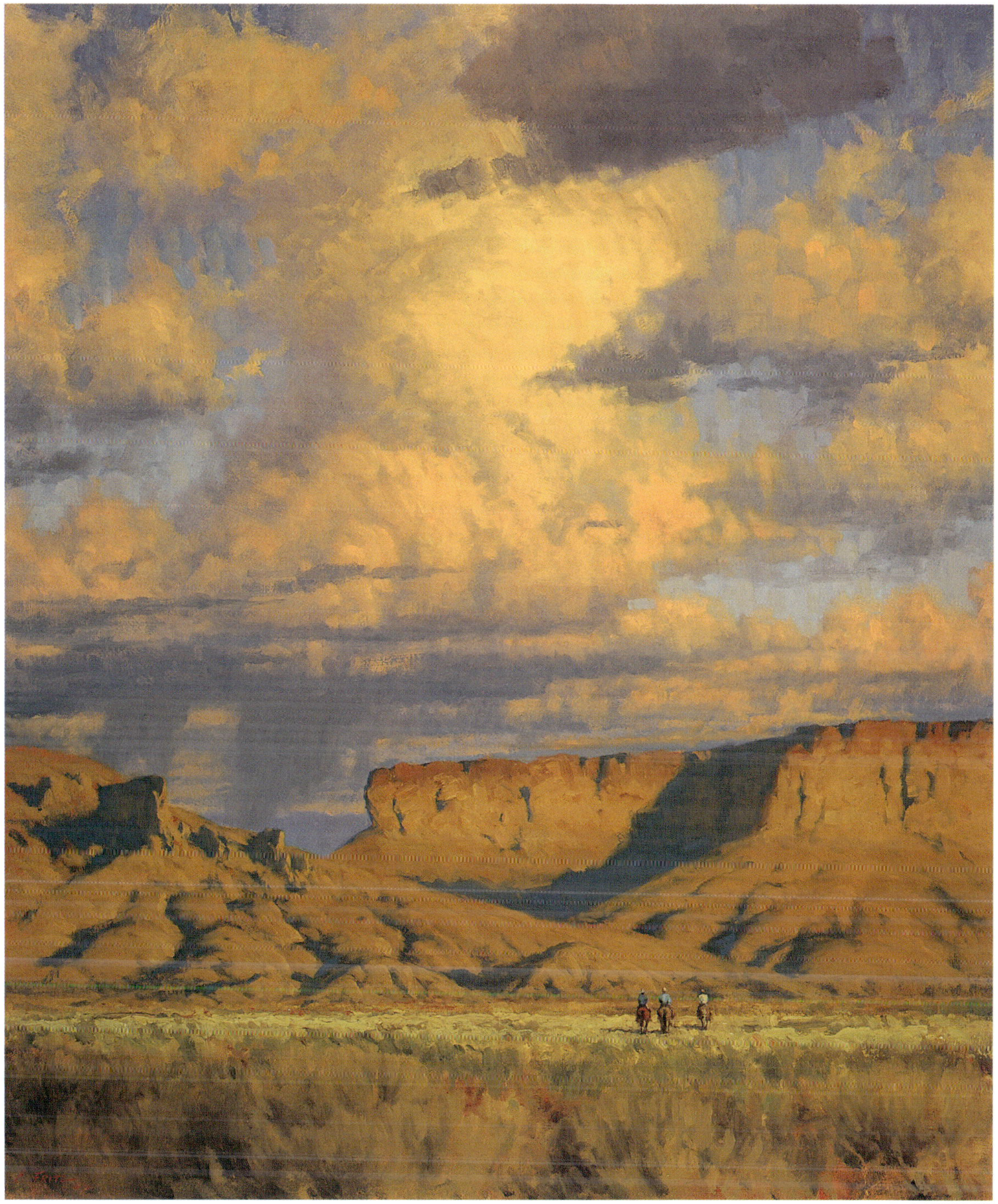

Charles Fritz,
TOWERING SKIES AT DUSK,
oil on canvas,
38 by 32 inches, 1996.
Private collection.

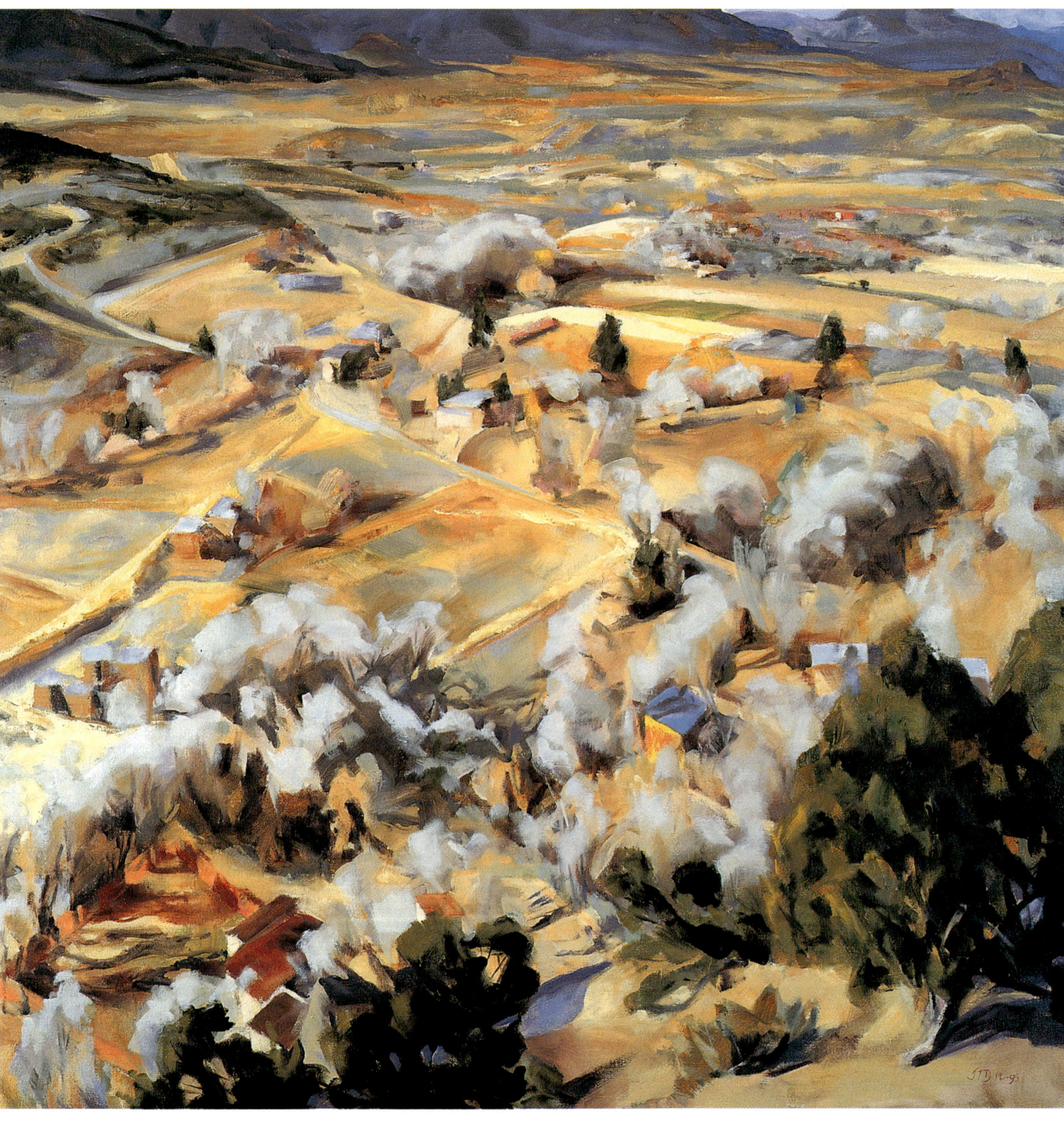

Joellyn Duesberry,
ABOVE TAOS VALLEY,
oil on linen,
40 by 40 inches, 1995.
Collection of Smith College Museum of Art.

Joellyn Duesberry (b. 1944) graduated from Smith College in 1966, then went on to obtain an M.A. in art history at the New York University of Fine Arts on a Woodrow Wilson Fellowship in 1967. For nearly twenty years she worked as an art appraiser, which gave her the opportunity to handle and appreciate beautiful objects.

She started to exhibit her paintings in New York galleries by 1979, then in 1985 she received a National Endowment for the Arts grant, which prompted her to paint full time. That same year, she married a cardiologist and moved to Littleton, Colorado, where the couple purchased property that included a one-hundred-year-old barn, now her studio. The National Endowment grant came in the form of a master course with painter Richard Diebenkorn, conducted at the Institute of Fine Arts in Santa Fe. The class challenged Duesberry's previous assumptions about her art, and shifted her toward the discovery of structural "bones" in her compositions.

Duesberry paints in Maine and New York, and in Italy, Canada, and South America. However, when she was first confronted with the arid expanse of the Western landscape, she groped through virgin territory, rediscovering abstract origins. Challenged by the absolute light and dark extremes of an arid climate, so different from the humid East where everything shares edges, Duesberry responded intuitively. Now she distills Western landscapes into irreducible structural lines and masses, with wide, paint-loaded brushes. The result, for her, flattens quirky landscape shapes into compositions that have little in common with conventional ideas of beauty or realism, as evident in paintings like *Above Taos Valley*. Painting plein-air, she says, assures her the insight a closed studio inhibits. She also contends, "The additional perception is accomplished when I stalk a painting subject, not for its beauty or pictorial qualities, but for resonance with an internal subject which hankers for expression in paint, but eludes me in words."

The art of **Walt Gonske** (b. 1942) is rooted in a romantic-impressionistic tradition, yet handled with a liberal, interpretive approach. A resident of Taos, New Mexico, since 1972, Gonske delights in subjects close at hand—the landscapes and cultures of northern New Mexico. Raised in New Jersey, he studied art at the Frank Reilly School of Art in New York, then pursued a successful illustration career among a handful of artists who specialized in men's fashions. When

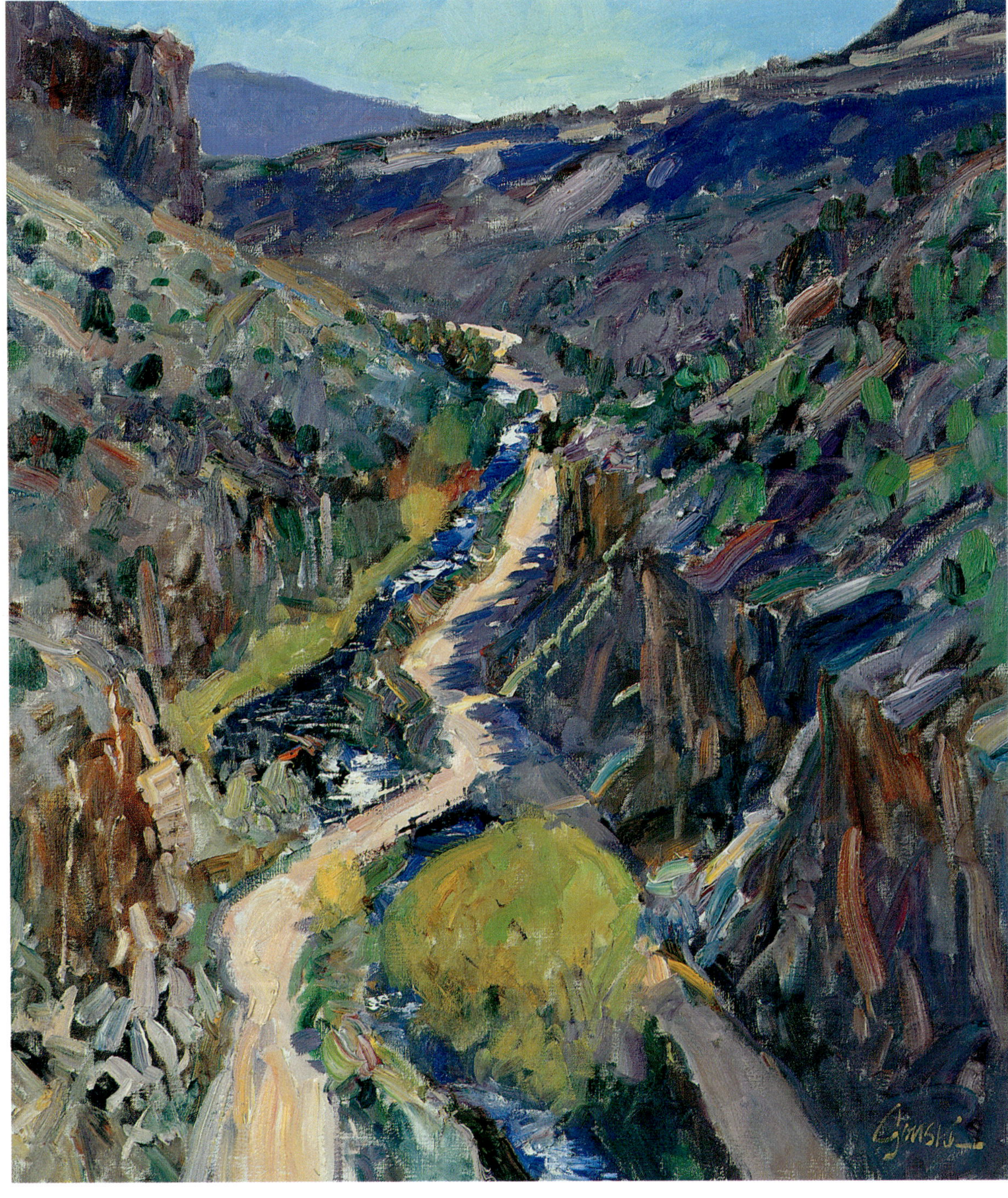

Walt Gonske,
ALMOST TO JOHN DUNN,
oil on canvas,
34 by 30 inches, 1996.
Private collection.

I strive to capture the feelings that this landscape evokes. I allow a certain "letting go" of control to occur and trust my instincts to be my guide.

—WALT GONSKE

Gonske visited Taos in 1971, he found himself struck by the area's beauty, and decided to move there. Since 1972, there have been numerous exhibitions of his work in galleries and museums, among them the National Cowboy Hall of Fame, where he has received gold and silver medals.

Gonske travels to painting locations in his Paintmobile, a 1990 Ford pickup equipped with a customized, fully stocked studio on the truck bed. He might drive up to Colorado for the spring runoff around Ouray and Telluride, or sometimes journey to the California coast. But the allure of northern New Mexico, particularly in the winter months, is what fills his studio-home with glowing canvases. There is a pantheon of places—Ranchitos, Talpa, Los Ojos, Arroyo Seco, Tierra Amarilla, and Vadito—that serve as subjects for his vision. No preconceived formula drives his art, and for him the pleasure in painting is the process. "The doing," Gonske says, "over and over again."

Gonske's paintings are executed with quick, forceful slashes through loosely controlled brush strokes, and they vibrate with color. There is no formula; nothing is calculated. As for colors, well, he loves them all. They are rendered in bold strokes across his canvases, as in *Almost to John Dunn,* a portrayal of the Rio Hondo as it heads toward a rendezvous with the Rio Grande near Taos. "I strive to capture the feelings that this landscape evokes," Gonske says. "I allow a certain 'letting go' of control to occur and trust my instincts to be my guide."

When **Russell Chatham** (b. 1939) approached Livingston, Montana, in 1972, behind the wheel of a battered 1949 Chevrolet pickup, he had only five one-dollar bills in his pocket. No one, probably least of all Chatham, knew whether he and his family would survive. They did, and since then, Chatham has erected a formidable career.

Chatham has had more than three hundred one-man exhibitions, and he is considered one of the world's foremost lithographers. A prolific author, his writings include hundreds of articles, reviews, short stories, and essays about fly-fishing, bird hunting, and conservation, along with pieces on food and wine, for magazines like *Sports Illustrated, Esquire, Outside, Outdoor Life,* and *The Atlantic,* in addition to several books. He also operates several businesses in Livingston, including Clark City Press, a small publisher of literary and artistic books, plus a retail gallery and a production company that issues catalogs, prints, and posters. Recently he opened a restaurant. Top all this off with a passion for fly-fishing, and Chatham is, as someone once described him, a man given to distraction.

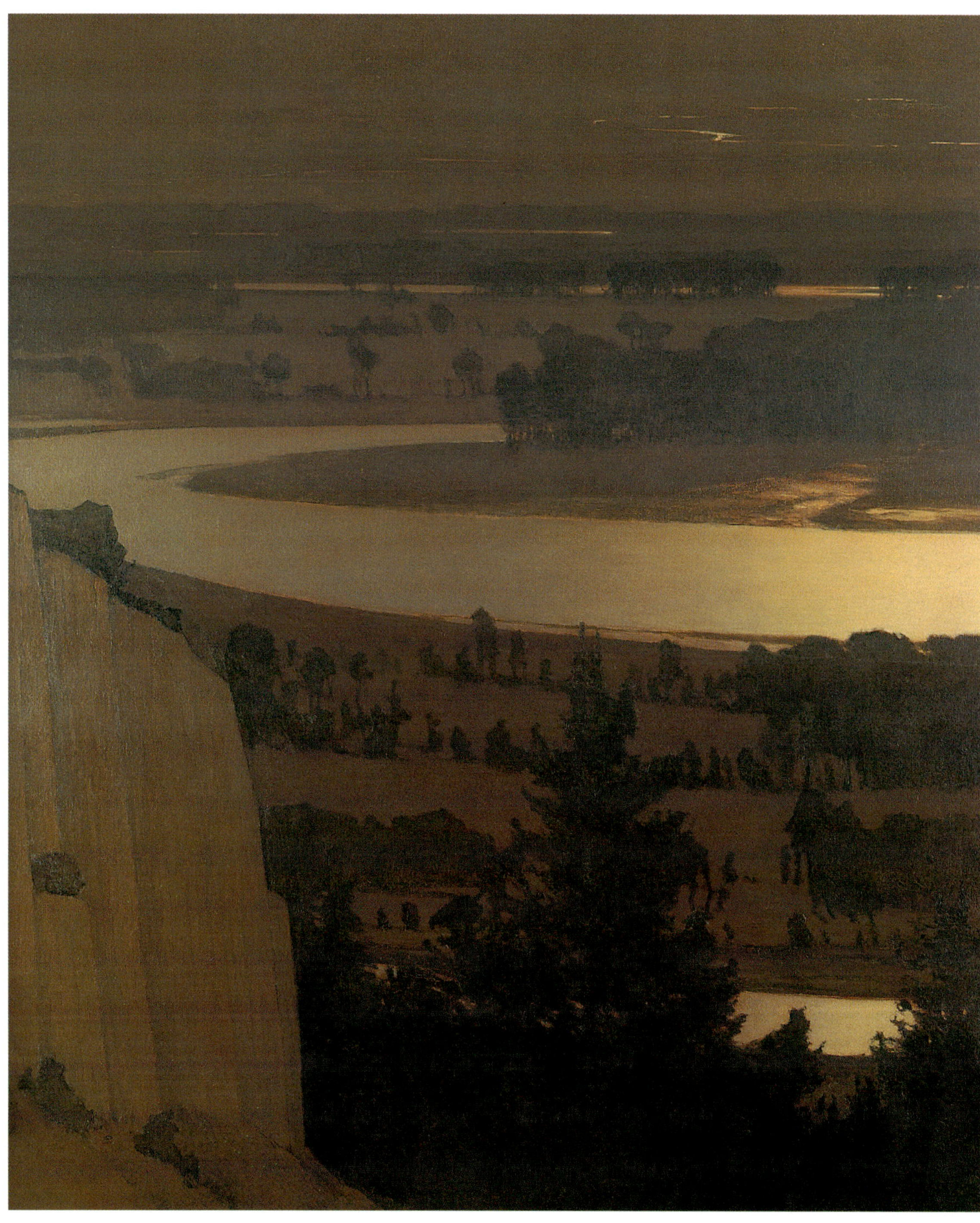

Russell Chatham,
THE SEASONS: THE HEADWATERS OF THE MISSOURI RIVER IN APRIL,
oil on canvas,
14 by 10 feet, 1990.
Collection of Museum of the Rockies.

Chatham's devotion to painting, fishing, and hunting, and his love of the landscape, emerged as he grew up on the family ranch in California's Carmel Valley. Another influence was his grandfather, Gottardo Piazzoni, one of California's leading artists in the early part of the twentieth century, known for his tonalist paintings of northern California landscapes. Chatham still uses the palette, palette knife, sketch box, and easel passed on to him by his grandfather and a great-uncle.

Almost entirely self-taught, Chatham considers himself a maverick, independent and aloof from the contemporary art world. Sometimes he completes only six or seven large paintings each year. His paintings are dark, moody, endowed with moments of transition: winter to spring, or dawn or dusk, when fading light casts a uniform harmony over the landscape. With muted, nearly monochromatic earth tones, Chatham's paintings evoke the silence of landscapes, and for him, spiritual elements. "Creating art," he says, "is an attempt to search for something beyond ourselves." Besides having spiritual overtones, Chatham's landscapes project a nostalgia for wild places, and perhaps a sense of loss.

In 1990, Chatham undertook a commission for the Museum of the Rockies in Bozeman, Montana. He decided to paint twelve paintings, odes to the seasons in Montana. The central image is a large painting titled *The Seasons: The Headwaters of the Missouri River in April,* portraying a pivotal month in the region. The painting is Montana-sized, fourteen by ten feet. He made dozens of investigative trips to study the Three Forks area where the Madison, Gallatin, and Jefferson Rivers unite to form the Missouri River. There is the suggestion of the three seminal rivers in the painting, with leafless willows and cottonwoods fading into a soft, nebulous distance. Time of day is late afternoon, the light dull except where it reflects off distant patches of water, then more forcefully off the Missouri River in the foreground.

Creating art is an attempt to search for something beyond ourselves.

—RUSSELL CHATHAM

For **Lindsay Holt II** (b. 1958), the Southwestern landscape holds the promise of symbolic meaning. His paintings serve as personal metaphors for his outlook on the natural and spiritual world. He is drawn by the feeling of timelessness in the locations he explores, and by a strong desire to embrace the beliefs of the cultures he encounters. Holt was born in El Paso, and returned there after graduation from California's Art Center College of Design in 1982. Several years later, he relocated to the rural villages of northern New Mexico, and he has lived in Santa Fe since 1992. Holt's initial inspiration evolved from the natural light and distinctive landscapes of the region, particularly the vast territory around Abiquiu.

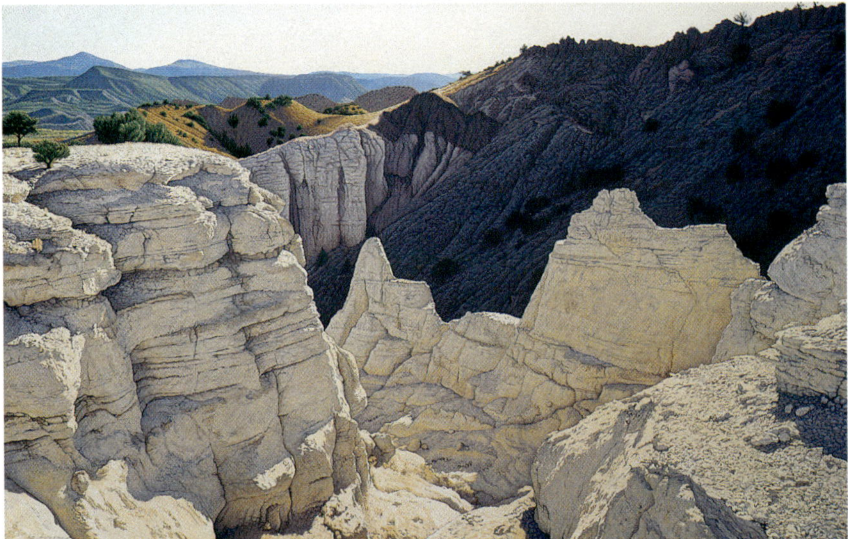

Lindsay Holt II,
LIGHT PLACE/DARK PLACE,
oil on stretched paper,
30 by 46 inches, 1996.
Collection of the artist.

Paintings like *Light Place/Dark Place* often reveal his patient exploration of this diverse landscape. Holt searches for the inherent spirit of the land and the people who have lived there, as did Georgia O'Keeffe, who so well integrated it into her own work and life. Holt's ideal is to paint canyons and mesas with a true realist illusion, yet, at the same time, to create canvases that can be explored on the surface in much the same way as he has traveled the actual terrain.

One painting, *Rio Chama Cottonwood,* represents a solitary cottonwood on the banks of the Rio Chama in early fall. It is a tree that prefers solitude, as does Holt. As he has begun to travel beyond New Mexico to other great scenes of the Southwest, he often finds the spirit of the cottonwood confirming a new location or direction for his work. The Lakota refer to this lovely tree as "the dreaming tree," a place for visions. Perhaps Holt finds future visions and his own personal symbols among the shivering and clattering leaves of the old cottonwoods of the West.

Lindsay Holt II,
RIO CHAMA COTTONWOOD,
oil on linen on panel,
44 by 44 inches, 1996.
Collection of Bob Cowart;
photograph courtesy of the artist.

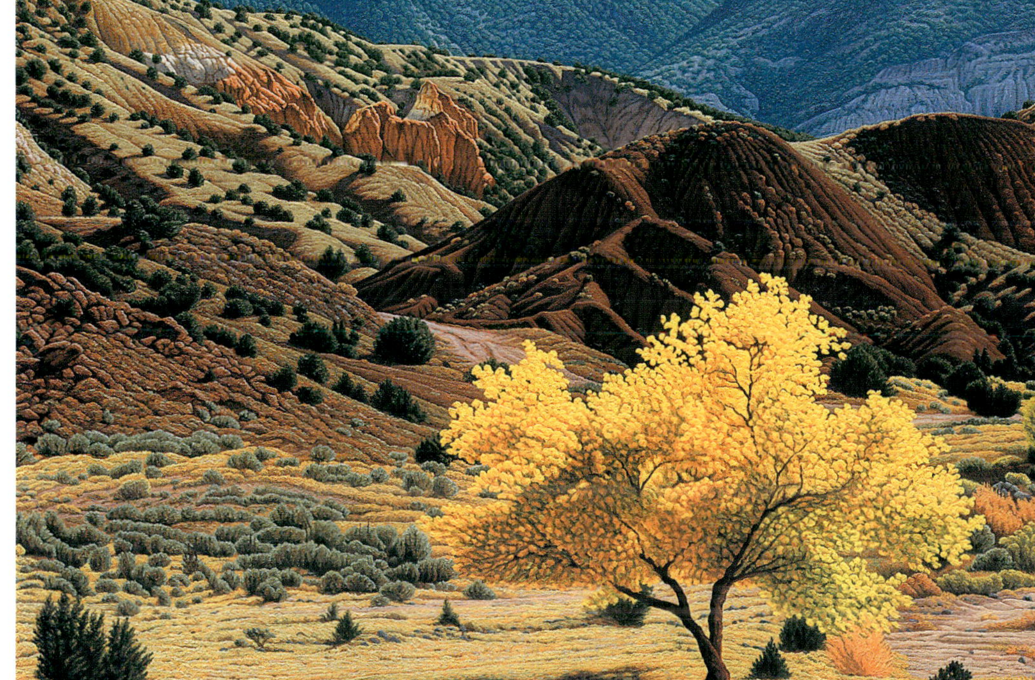

P. A. Nisbet (b. 1948) started to paint at the age of ten. After graduation from the University of North Carolina, he served in the U.S. Navy, including a ten-month tour of duty in Vietnam. During that time the secretary of the navy appointed him to serve as director of art services for the navy's office of information. After discharge from the navy in 1974, Nisbet worked as a free-lance commercial artist. In 1980 he moved to the Southwest and began painting landscapes. Now a resident of Santa Fe, his art is derived from the land surrounding him, rooted in the tradition of nineteenth-century American and European landscape masters.

Nisbet's current work emphasizes the play of light and space as a method of expression for spiritual concerns. Always eager to explore new frontiers, Nisbet was selected by the National Science Foundation to travel to Antarctica during 1995–1996 as part of their Artists and Writers Program. His work is held by the National Aeronautic and Space Administration, Senator John Chaffee, the Duke and Duchess of Bedford, and more than two hundred private collections.

To Nisbet, his paintings are not exclusively about nature, but about his relationship with nature. For him, nature, as embodied in a painting, is often elusive, intellectual, and emotional. Most importantly, though, it is spiritual. His language of paint, as in *Taos Gorge,* and *Tucson Mountain Park* (p. 16), is one derived from the past, since he believes the highest standard of excellence for painting occurred before the onset of the twentieth century. In this work, Nisbet portrays the ragged slash of the Rio Grande gorge that bisects New Mexico's Taos Valley, with transparent, atmospheric light and spiritual force, an image worthy of Frederick Church or Albert Bierstadt.

After more than a decade as an architect, **Morris Rippel** (b. 1930) switched to a career as a painter in 1967. An Albuquerque resident born and bred, Rippel still finds the subjects for his dry brush watercolors and egg tempera paintings in the landscapes of New Mexico and adjacent areas. "I have no need to travel extensively to find new material," he reflected in the 1996 National Cowboy Hall of Fame *Prix de West Invitational* catalog. "There is a mystery about the light in New Mexico, particularly the light of later afternoon in the fall season. I have considered it one of the more difficult subjects to correctly portray the contrast of cool shadows with the warm fall season light on adobe walls."

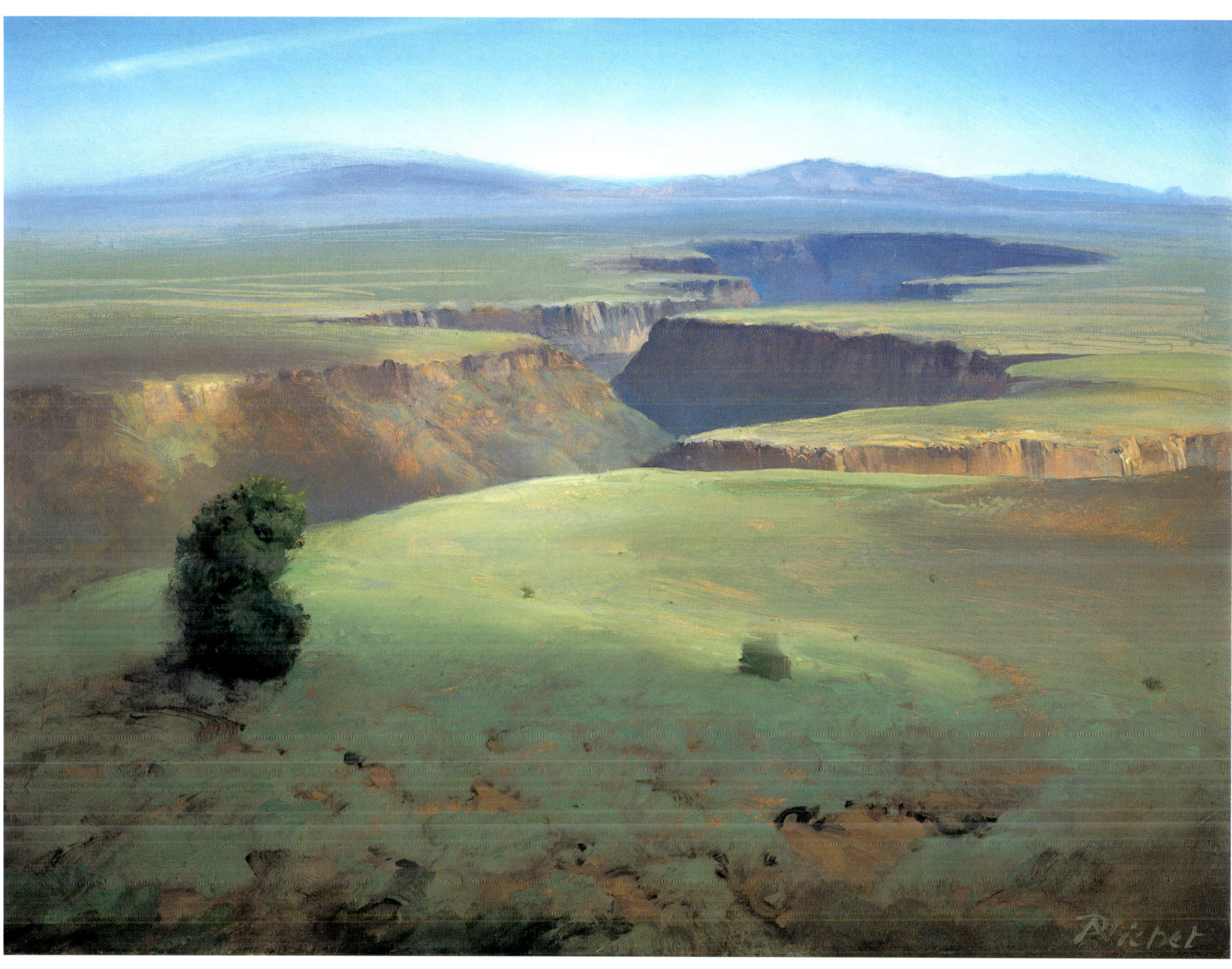

P. A. Nisbet, TAOS GORGE, *oil on board, 12 by 16 inches, 1995. Private collection.*

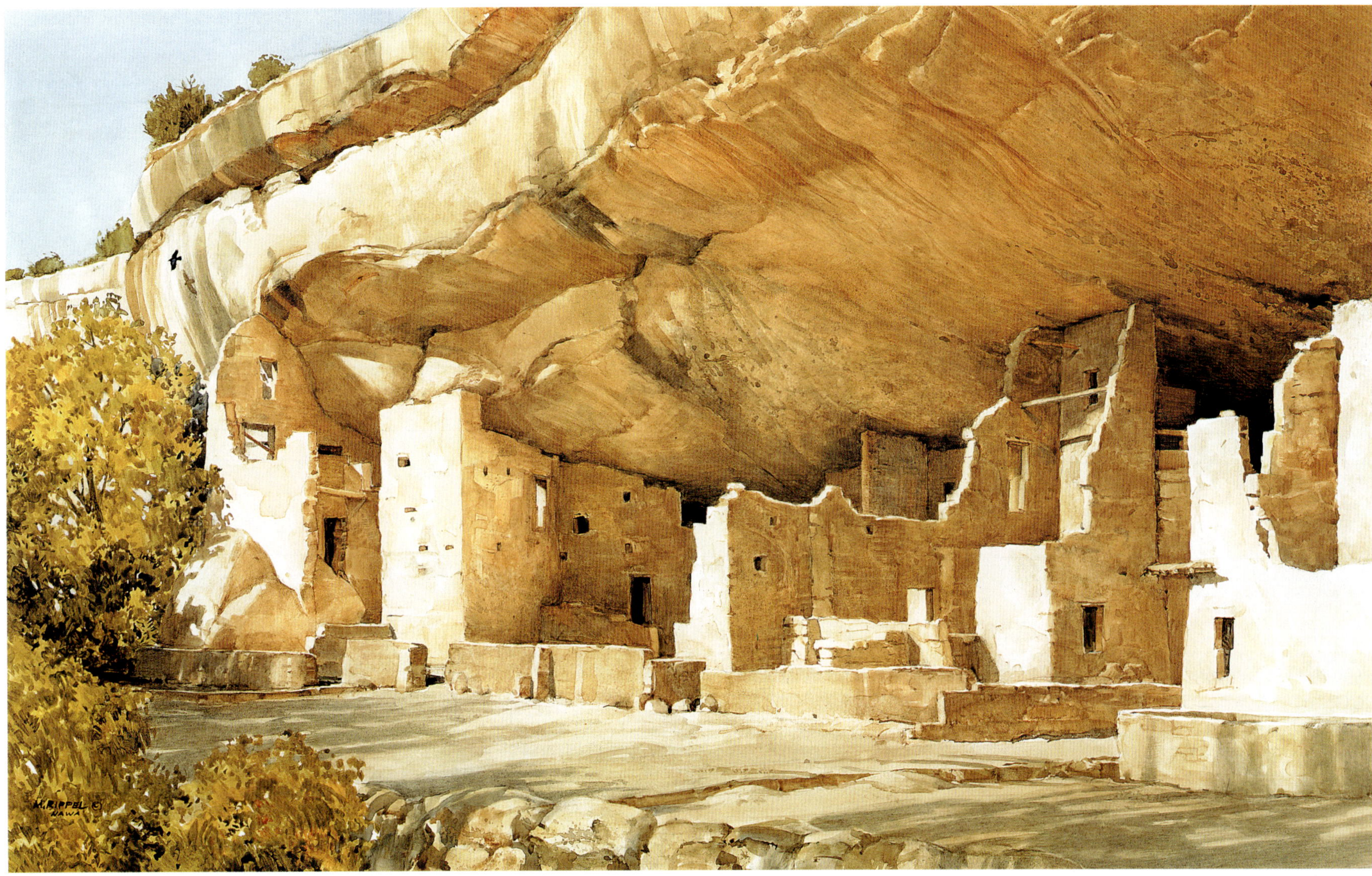

Morris Rippel, ECHOES OF THE ANASAZI, *watercolor, 16 by 26 inches, 1996. Private collection.*

I have considered it one of the more difficult subjects to correctly portray the contrast of cool shadows with the warm fall season light on adobe walls.

—MORRIS RIPPEL

A realist, Rippel neither paints from imagination, nor rearranges, nor exaggerates or distorts views. His watercolors seem reverential as he articulates the sunlight that floods a winding road, the texture of adobe structures, or the golden flame of cottonwood trees. In 1979, Rippel won the Prix de West at the National Cowboy Hall of Fame. The Gilcrease Museum honored him with a retrospective in 1988, while the Royal Watercolor Society in London featured his work in 1992.

One of Rippel's watercolors, *Echoes of the Anasazi,* an image of a Mesa Verde cliff dwelling, was exhibited at the 1996 National Cowboy Hall of Fame's *Prix de West Invitational.* "I have a profound spiritual kinship to the Mesa Verde cliff dwelling complex," Rippel stated in the *Prix de West Invitational* catalog, "and have expressed many different viewpoints both by angle and light conditions. One factor that weaves through me is the embodiment of the Anasazi spirit into the flight of the canyon crow. Its call echoes along the canyon walls almost as though it carries with it the souls of the people of the past."

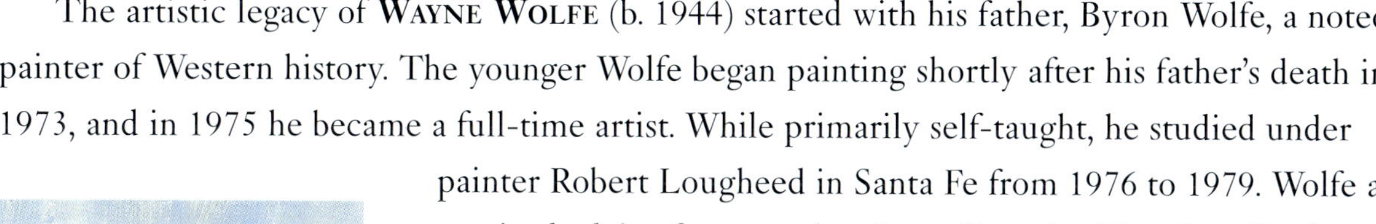

The artistic legacy of **WAYNE WOLFE** (b. 1944) started with his father, Byron Wolfe, a noted painter of Western history. The younger Wolfe began painting shortly after his father's death in 1973, and in 1975 he became a full-time artist. While primarily self-taught, he studied under painter Robert Lougheed in Santa Fe from 1976 to 1979. Wolfe also received advice from another Santa Fe artist, Tom Lovell, whom he credits with the improvement of his knowledge of anatomy.

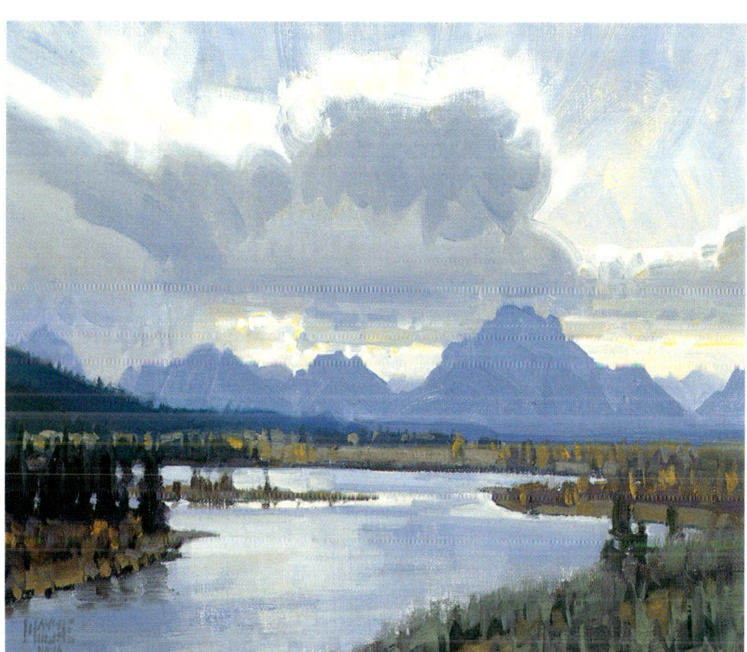

Wayne Wolfe, OXBOW BEND, *oil on canvas, 20 by 24 inches, 1996. Private collection.*

Wolfe has exhibited at the *National Academy of Western Art* at the National Cowboy Hall of Fame, at which he won the top honor in 1982, and at the Hall's *Prix de West Invitational.* Other places he has had work shown include the Gilcrease Museum, the National Museum of Wildlife Art, the Museum of Fine Arts (Santa Fe), and the Artists of America (Denver).

From his home in Loveland, Colorado, Wolfe explores various locations in the West, from Wyoming's Grand Tetons to Colorado's San Juan Mountains. The results are paintings such as *Oxbow Bend,* a

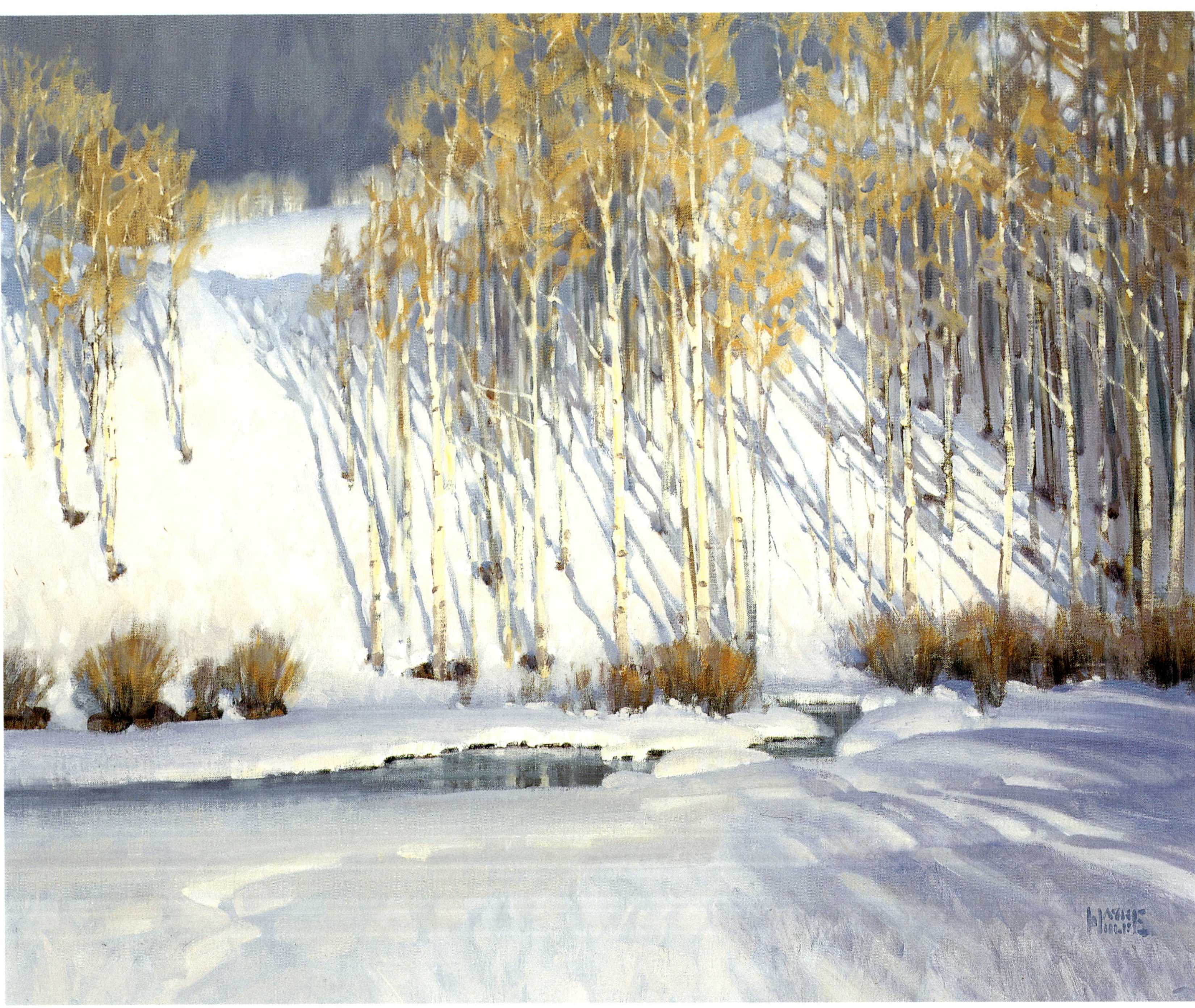

Wayne Wolfe, FIVE O'CLOCK SHADOWS, *oil on canvas, 30 by 36 inches, 1995. Private collection.*

Painting raw landscapes from life, especially a changing mood, is my greatest joy in art, because all of my senses are involved.

—WAYNE WOLFE

portrait of the Snake River and the Grand Tetons, or *Five O'Clock Shadows,* a vision of aspen trees and snow south of Telluride, Colorado, under late afternoon raking light. Small oil studies or charcoal sketches are used to record initial impressions and solve composition problems. The facts in his paintings are as much the properties of atmosphere as they are formations and color.

Wolfe no longer needs to search for the why and how—now he paints the Western landscape with the sure knowledge of someone a part of it. "Painting raw landscapes from life, especially a changing mood, is my greatest joy in art, because all of my senses are involved," he says. "Rodin believed that a sketch allowed the artist to seize the fleeting beauty of a gesture whose fugitive truth would expose deeper and longer study. In other words, capturing essence."

Sketching outdoors is also the foundation of the art of **GREGORY KONDOS** (b. 1923). His home and studio in Sacramento are jammed with pastel, pencil, and pen-and-ink landscape drawings. Drawing for Kondos is the skeleton under the flesh of his paintings; it is where art begins. "It helps to understand the landscape better," he says, "and does not allow the false sense of covering problems in the composition with color."

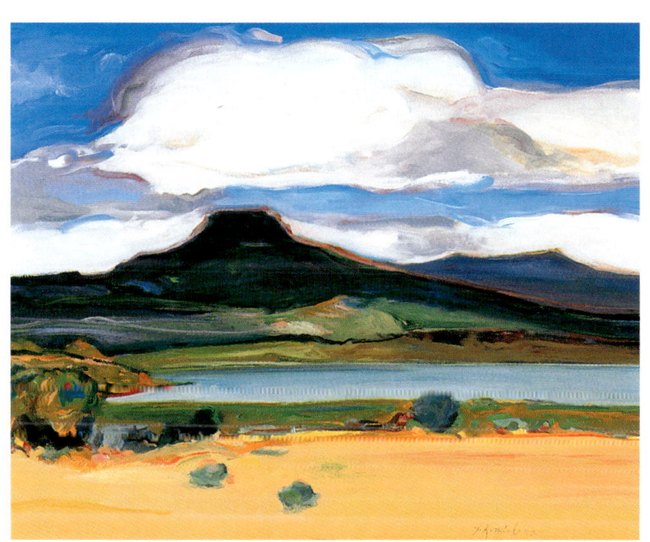

Gregory Kondos, MT. PEDERNAL—A VIEW FROM GHOST RANCH, *oil on canvas, 30 by 36 inches, 1996. Private collection.*

An essayist wrote in the catalog for a recent exhibition of Kondos's Yosemite landscapes, "It is always high noon on a summer day in his landscape paintings." Whether Kondos paints in Greece, in California's Napa Valley, in Yosemite, at the delta where the Sacramento and San Joaquin Rivers converge, or in the Southwest's Chaco Canyon, Canyon de Chelly, Grand Canyon, or Pedernal Peak, his landscapes appear solid and manifest under the bright, sapphire light of day. His longtime friend, painter Wayne Thiebaud, suggests Kondos is somewhat of a classicist: big sky, large areas of evenly applied solid color, and a strong reference point.

Kondos was born to Greek immigrants in Massachusetts. His parents, desirous of a climate similar to their native country, moved to Sacramento, California. There Kondos studied art at Sacramento City College, then obtained bachelor's and master's degrees from California State University, Sacramento. For twenty-seven years, until his retirement in 1982, Kondos taught art at Sacramento City College.

Kondos's initial landscape paintings were influenced by Willem de Kooning and other abstract expressionists. Prompted by Thiebaud, though, Kondos gradually shifted toward painterly realism. He started to win awards in 1962, first at the California Palace of Legion of Honor (San Francisco), then in numerous solo and group museum exhibitions in the years that followed. Important recognition arrived in 1995, when Kondos was elected to membership in the National Academy of Design. Now a vigorous seventy-four-year-old, Kondos delights in the act of painting, and defines his landscapes with clarity and simplicity. Kondos is gregarious, yet nevertheless describes himself as a loner, his gaze fixed on the far horizon.

One oil painting, *Mt. Pedernal—A View from Ghost Ranch* (p. 37), graced with heightened color, fluid brushwork, and an emphasis on the momentary, portrays the polychrome mesa that serves as a spiritual beacon in Georgia O'Keeffe country. When he first saw it, Kondos thought, "That's my Mont Sainte-Victoire," in reference to Paul Cézanne's famous landmark. With deft strokes, Kondos painted Pedernal Peak in the tradition of Georgia O'Keeffe, but did it the Kondos way. He knew the clouds in attendance belonged in the painting, as well. "They seemed to grow out of the ground, and, as a composition in motion, tie into the mesa," he says.

Tesuque, New Mexico, a view from actor Gene Hackman's backyard, is proof of Kondos's proficiency in pastels as well as oils. "Nature is so protective of colors, the artist has to push them and make them recede into space," he says. The image resonates with New Mexico's "sandpaper look," as he terms it, and the horizontal tension between land and sky. In this, and his other landscapes, Kondos eliminates the nonessential, but retains the spirit that gives them significance.

Nature is so protective of colors,
the artist has to push them and make them recede into space.

—GREGORY KONDOS

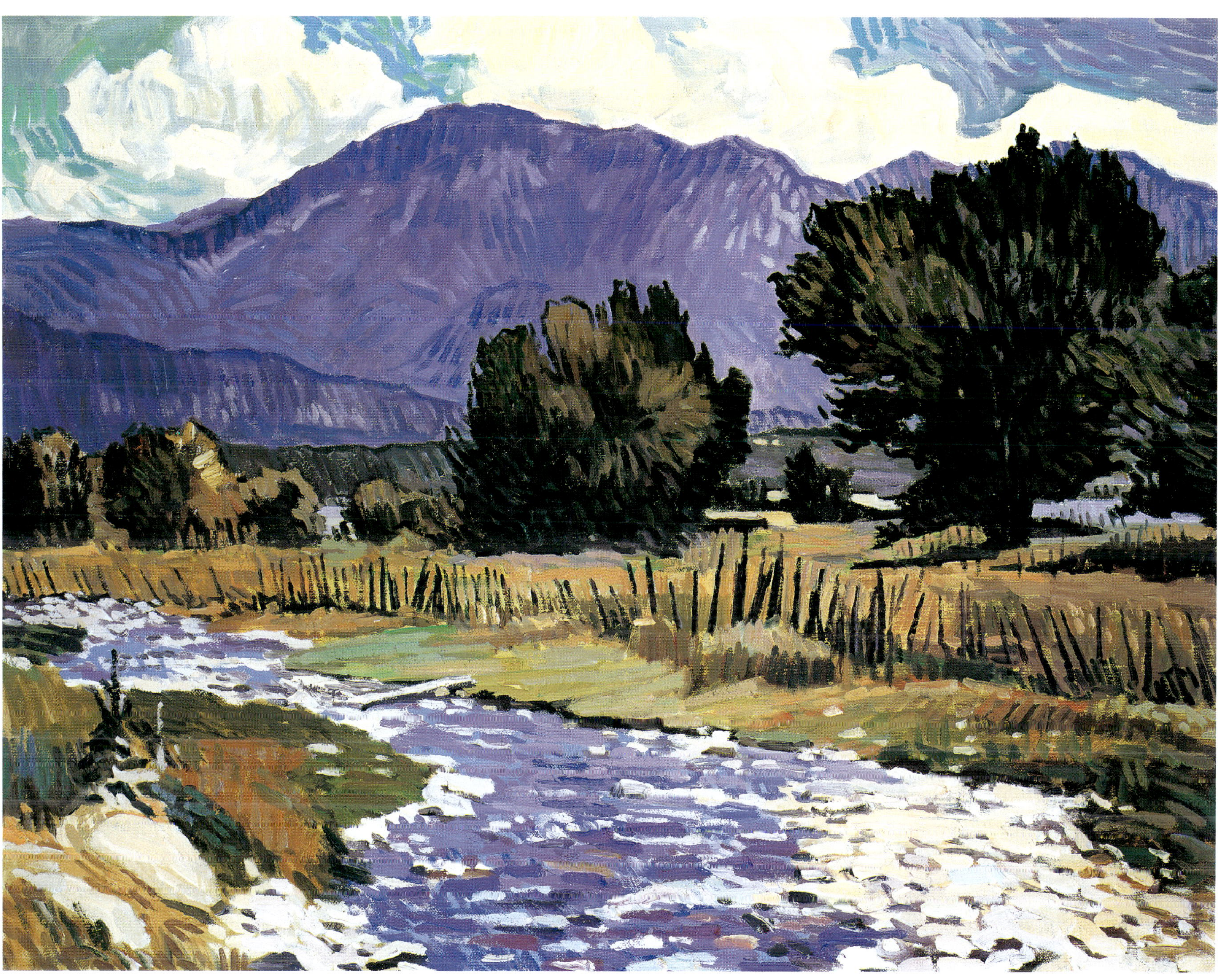

Robert Daughters, RIO HONDO, *oil on canvas, 28 by 36 inches, no date. Private collection.*

Rather than describing himself as an impressionist or expressionist, Daughters says he is a "composist," his term for an artist who creates paintings with color harmony, the contrast of light and dark values, and, above all, structure. He starts a painting like *Rio Hondo* (p. 47) with an organized composition, the image of the sparkling stream and the Sangre de Cristo Mountains created from photographs, charcoal sketches, and small plein-air oil studies. The emphasis is on structure, an orderly arrangement of shapes, tones, and atmospheric effect. "The composition always comes first," Daughters says. "I like to have an important visual point; sometimes it is a structure, and sometimes it might be a color."

On the western edge of the continent, particularly in southern California, a new breed of environmentally conscious artists reminiscent of the early California impressionists has emerged. One of them, fourth-generation Californian **Peter Adams** (b. 1950), started art studies in 1969 in San Miguel de Allende, Mexico. Afterwards, he studied briefly at the Otis Art Institute and the Art Center College of Design, then at the Lukits Academy of Fine Art with Theodore Lukits, who instilled in Adams a reverence for outdoor painting.

Adams's plein-air landscape paintings are drawn from his explorations along the southern California coast, the San Gabriel Mountains five minutes from his home in Pasadena, and the Grand Canyon. Other artistic adventures have taken him to India, Bhutan, China, Tibet, and, in 1987, Afghanistan, making him the only American artist to travel and paint in that war-torn nation.

Adams is trained in bonsai, the Japanese art of shaping trees. The trees in his landscapes, like the California view *Nearing the Bend: La Cañada Flintridge,*

Peter Adams,
NEARING THE BEND: LA CAÑADA FLINTRIDGE,
oil on board,
24 by 22 inches, 1996.
Private collection.

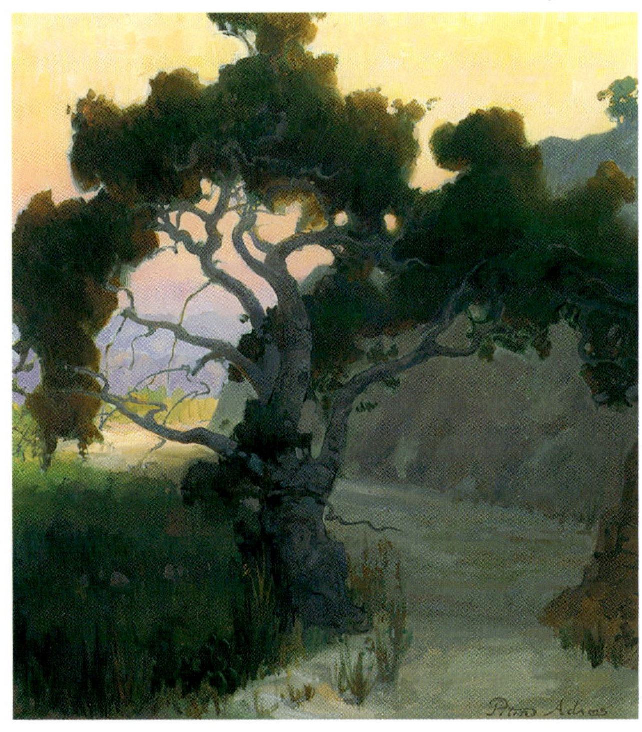

I hope that my landscape paintings remind others of the intrinsic relationships we share with all things.

—PETER ADAMS

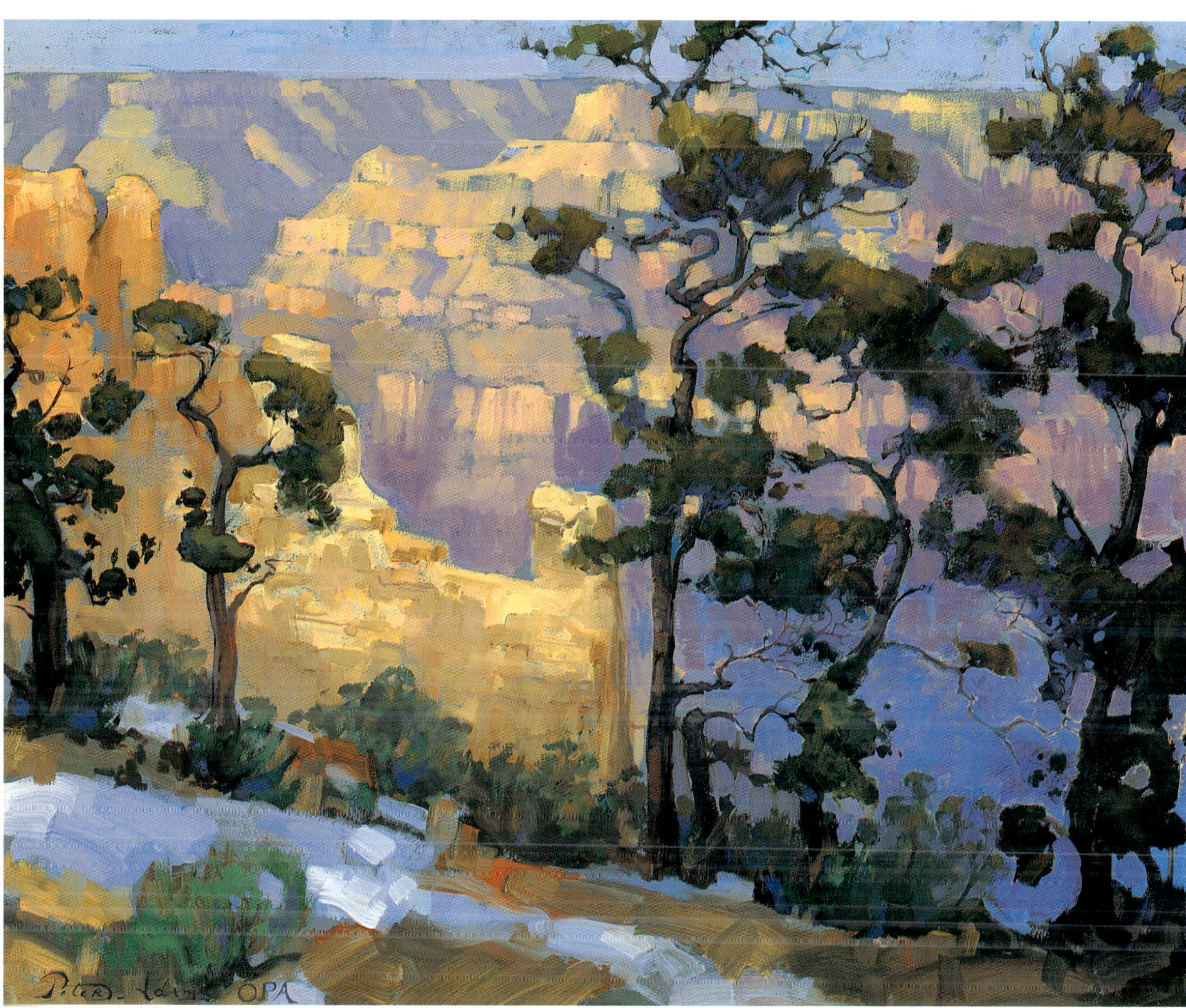

Peter Adams, AFTERNOON SHADOWS AT MARICOPA POINT, *oil on board, 18 by 22 inches, 1995. Private collection.*

or his Grand Canyon painting, *Afternoon Shadows at Maricopa Point* (p. 49) are conscious design statements created out of his editing of forms. Drawn to an Asian philosophy that suggests nature is a centering force within which one can discover peace and calm, Adams's landscapes are serene and meditative. "I hope that my landscape paintings remind others of the intrinsic relationships we share with all things," he reflects. "My best paintings come from the beginning and end of day, when I can capture atmospheric moods. Painting plein-air allows me to record my impressions and feelings at that moment."

Like the art of Peter Adams, that of **MEREDITH BROOKS ABBOTT** (b. 1938) reveals light and serenity, in her case in the land and oceanscapes around Santa Barbara. Artists Carl Oscar Borg, Thomas Moran, Douglas Parshall, and Fernand Lungren came to this region and stayed, enthralled with its beauty. Edward Borein established a studio in Santa Barbara, where he could draw and paint the area's still-vital ranch life.

Meredith Brooks Abbott,
THE FIELD,
oil on canvas,
36 by 40 inches, 1996.
Private collection.

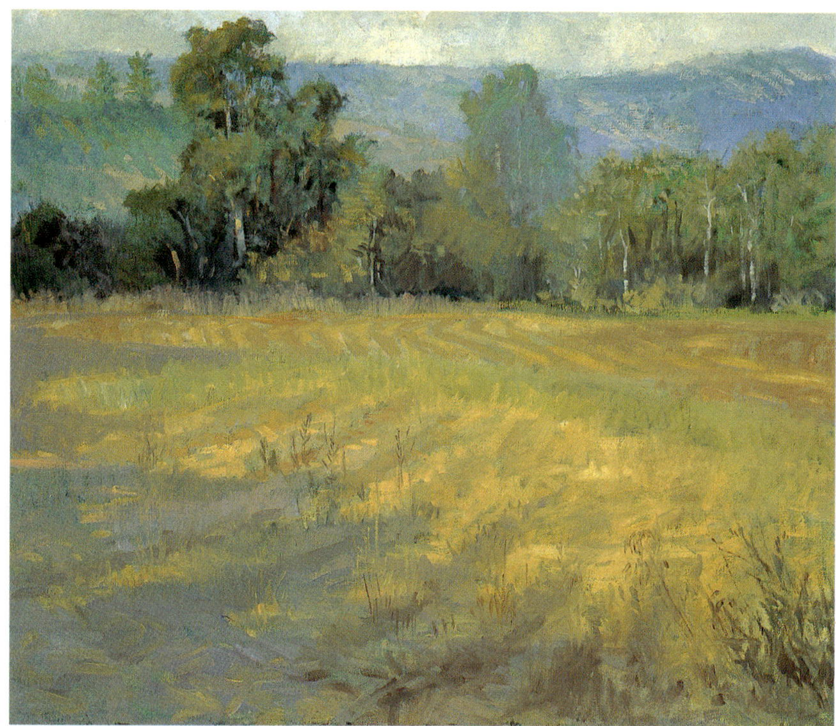

Abbott's work is reminiscent of the early California impressionists. Like them, she has a predilection to paint at specific locales, from real things seen. Abbott was raised on a ranch in Carpinteria, so the concept of painting outdoors proved natural. After graduation in 1964 from the Art Center College of Design, Abbott moved to New York, where she worked for advertising agencies while enrolled in night classes at the Art Students League. Among the artists she has studied with are Parshall, Richard Meryman, and Clarence Hinkle.

I put as much of myself into the landscape as I can.

—MEREDITH BROOKS ABBOTT

When she returned to Santa Barbara, Abbott dedicated herself to plein-air painting; her subjects were the tawny hills of the Los Padres National Forest and the nearby coastline, executed in a solid and authentic manner. Abbott belongs to the twenty-five-member Oak Group, an organization of local landscape artists founded in 1986 to protect and preserve the last remnants of shoreline in the area. Abbott's favorite subjects are the watercourses and hillsides brightened by light. In *The Field,* she revels in the play of light upon the landscape, patterns and contours of the California hills illuminated with clarity. "I put as much of myself into the landscape as I can," she says. "It is important to immerse myself in a scene, to be there, and to paint honestly."

Further north, life among the sensual hills of California's Marin County, and next to Point Reyes National Seashore, has influenced the work of **JERI NICHOLS QUINN** (b. 1939), much as the region did for the early California impressionists. The essences of golden-flanked hillsides, textured wooded ravines, buckeye, and sea mists are distilled in her landscape paintings.

As a teenager, Quinn studied under Raymond Fromes and Frederick Taubes. She pursued additional studies at the University of New Mexico and Baylor University, then graduated from the Art Center College of Design. Afterwards, Quinn worked as a commercial illustrator in New York. In the late 1960s, she and her husband, wildlife painter Thomas Quinn, moved to Point Reyes Station, adjacent to Point Reyes National Seashore.

From her studio, Quinn paints landscapes inspired by the scenes seen as she walks the coastal hills and estuaries. What appears on canvas is a personal response to her observations, captured initially by photographs and field notes. Quinn paints with a fluid technique—splotches, and broad, choppy strokes—visual shorthand that captures the landscape's luminous light and color. The earth-tone palettes in coastal Marin and Sonoma counties are predominant in her canvases.

Sometimes she captures transient wildflowers scattered along hillsides, as in *Lupine Cloak, Rocky Hill* (p. 52), which includes some of the hues that define this region. "I am concerned with colors," she remarks, "and what light does to them." Many of her works are small and spontaneous, but for juried shows and competitions, such as the Art for the Parks, she paints larger ones. One of her paintings ranked among the top one hundred in the 1992 Art for the Parks competition. For Quinn, the spirit of the California landscape is captured through large paint masses, simplified form, and subtle but rich color arrangements.

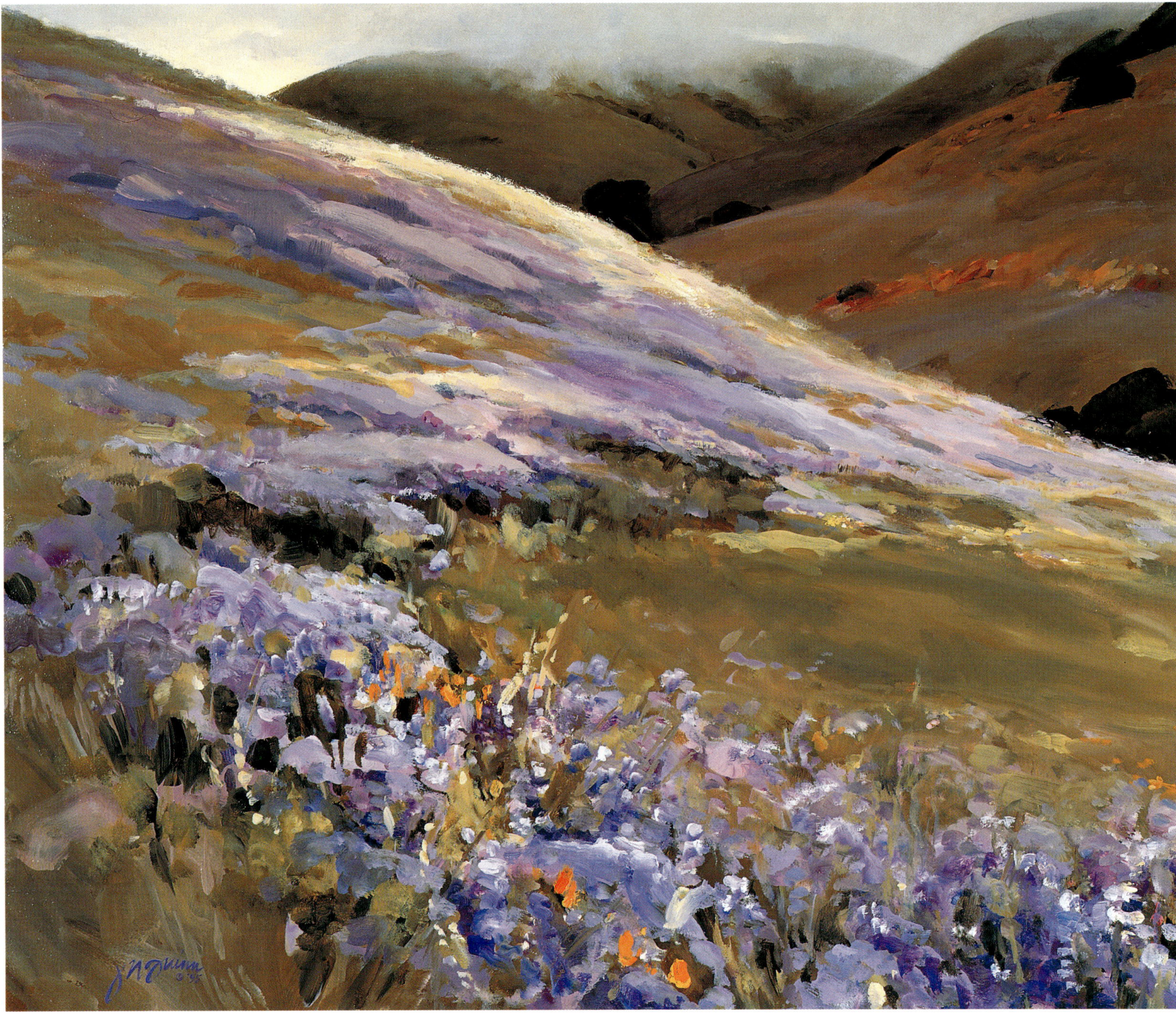

Jeri Nichols Quinn, LUPINE CLOAK, ROCKY HILL, *oil on canvas, 30 by 40 inches, 1995. Collection of Margaret Clark and Philip Silverman.*

The home of **DONNA CLAIR** (b. 1939) in Taos reflects a thirty-year painting span that responds to the beauty of the Taos-Truchas area of northern New Mexico. Known as the High Road, New Mexico Highway 68 meanders through the Sangre de Cristo Mountains, past settlements rich in Hispanic and Native American cultures, places like Placitas, Trampas, Truchas, and Peñasco. This is where she discovered Truchas, a small village that awakened and nurtured her art. Born in Chicago, Clair attended the University of Illinois, the Layton School of Art in Milwaukee, and the Art Institute of Chicago. She lived in Santa Fe for seventeen years, Truchas for three years, and then finally moved to Taos.

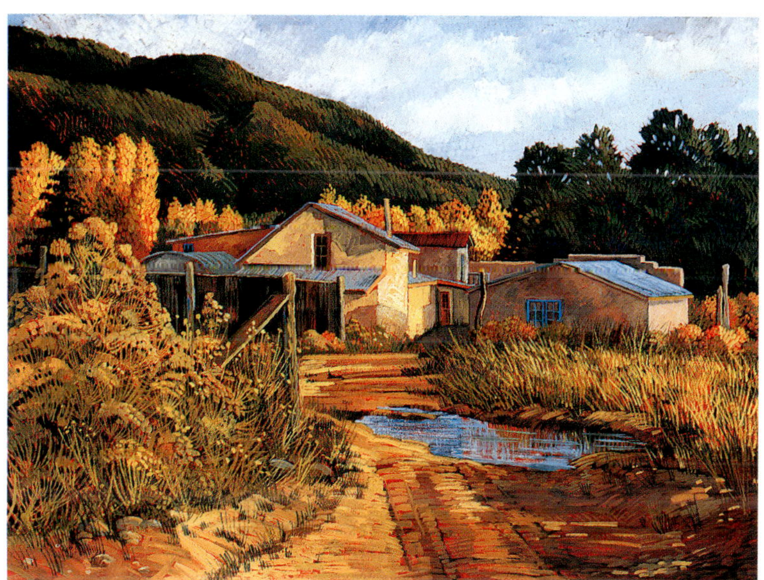

Donna Clair,
ARROYO SECO,
oil on linen,
30 by 40 inches, 1991.
Private collection.

Intrigued by the way colors blend in the eye of the viewer rather than on canvas, and fascinated by the techniques of French artist Georges Seurat, Clair has developed a distinctive painting technique marked by cross-hatched brush strokes, as in *Arroyo Seco.* She works wet-on-wet, layer upon layer onto the canvas, bleeding colors into one another, their vibrancy enhanced by the underpainting. Clair "dances with the easel," having already made emotional preparation with the canvas. "I have learned to follow my instincts," she says.

"There is a peaceful, timeless quality here and life is lived with simple grace and dignity," she continues. "Truchas is my spiritual home and a treasure trove beyond real." One of her paintings of the quiet village is *Last Light on Truchas* (p. 54). Here she has captured remnants of a New Mexico sunset that radiates on the structures scattered along the hillside. "What I paint is the canvas in my head," she reiterates. "This canvas painted itself—fourteen hours a day for ten days—and all I did was sit there and hold a brush. The painting is emotional and personal to me, and pays homage to the place and what it provided to my life."

What I paint is the canvas in my head.

—DONNA CLAIR

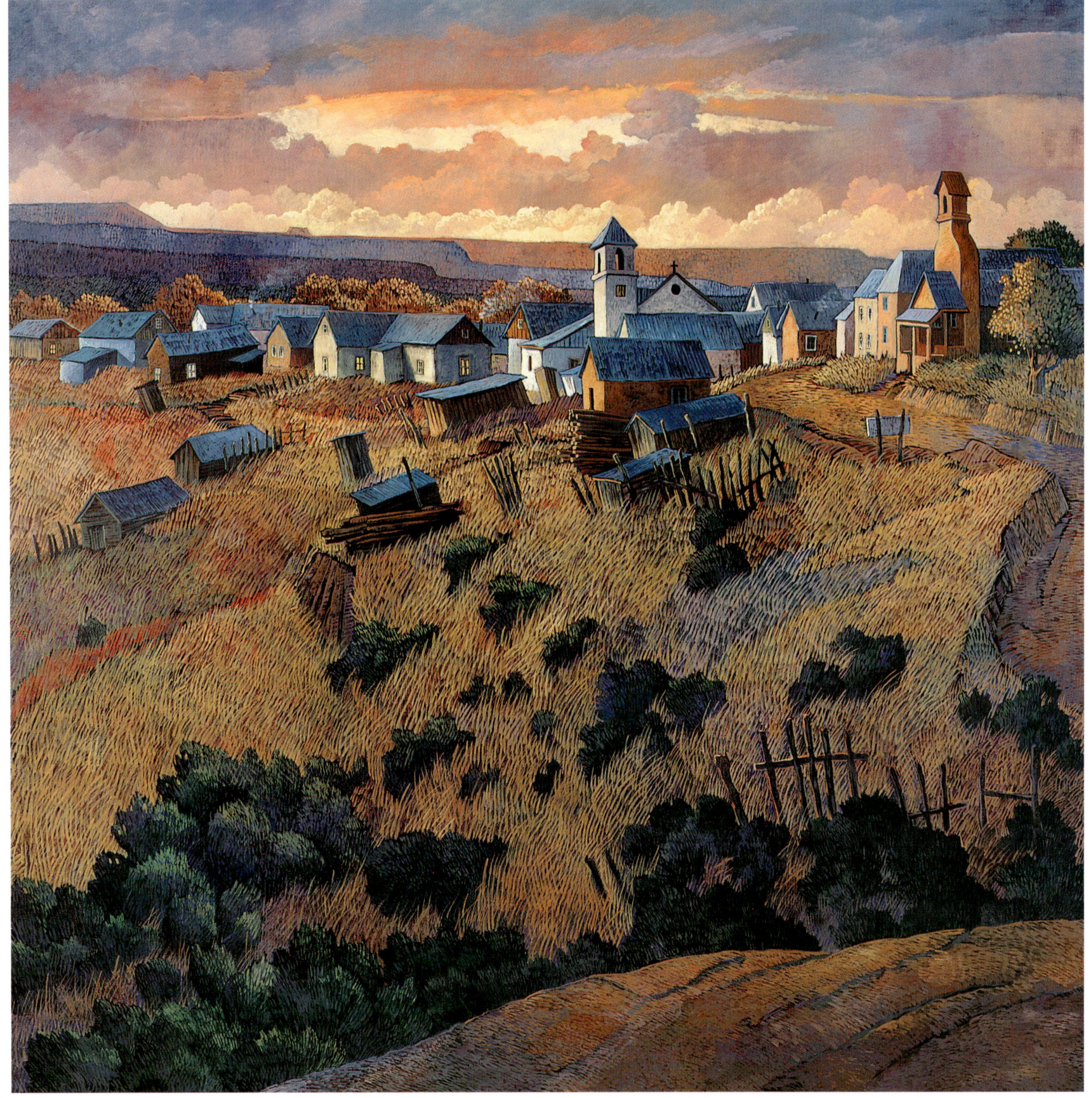

Donna Clair, LAST LIGHT ON TRUCHAS, *oil on canvas, 60 by 60 inches, 1995. Private collection.*

Joan Foth (b. 1930) lives in a small solar home and studio in Chimayo, New Mexico, a historic Hispanic community nestled in the foothills of the Sangre de Cristo Mountains north of Santa Fe. From here she takes painting trips to places in northern New Mexico, like Chama and Abiquiu, but more often she ventures just down the road from her home. Her choice of medium is watercolor, usually rendered on a large scale. Watercolor captures light, shadow, and form in subtle ways, in compositions that invite reflection. "They are landscapes that you can walk through and live in," she says.

Foth earned an art history degree from Barnard College in 1952, then moved to Topeka with her attorney husband in the late 1950s. There she discovered the Kansas prairies vital to her work, with their openness and space. When William Least Heat Moon wrote his acclaimed 1991 book, *PrairyEarth,* one of Foth's watercolors adorned the dust jacket. She considers this and her other landscapes poems to a natural world slowly vanishing. "I think I became a more honest painter living in Kansas, developing the ability to live in that openness," she says. Her work has been a part of exhibitions at the Wichita Art Museum, the National Museum for Women in the Arts, the Rockwell Museum, and the Joslyn Art Museum, and is in corporate and private collections including the Wichita Art Museum, Mobil Oil Corporation, FMC Corporation, and others.

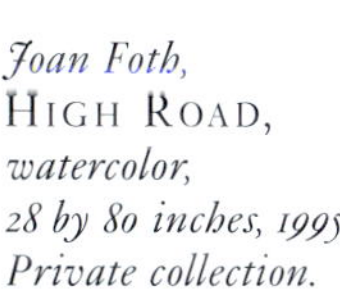

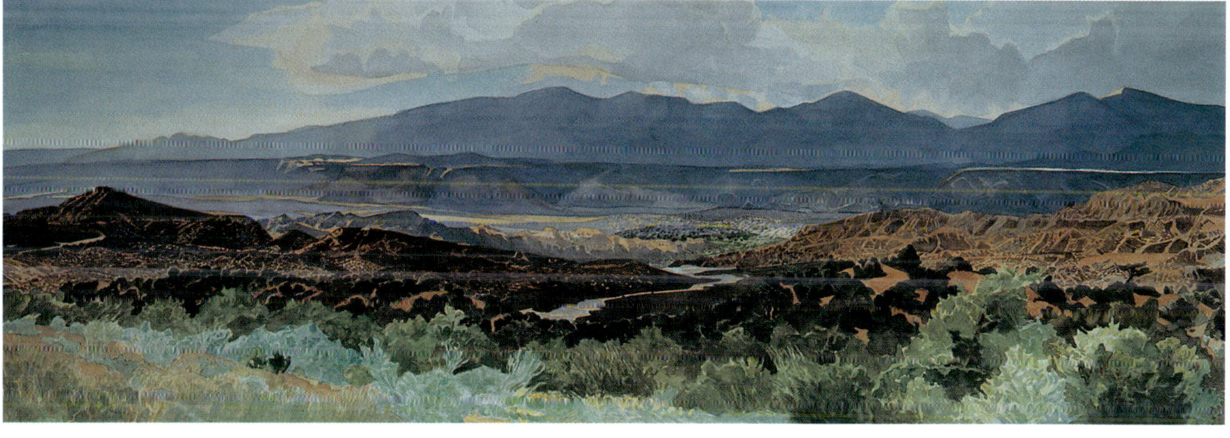

Joan Foth,
HIGH ROAD,
watercolor,
28 by 80 inches, 1995.
Private collection.

I don't want just a part of the landscape, I want the whole thing.

—JOAN FOTH

My work is about responding, not thinking.

—ELMER SCHOOLEY

After her husband died, Foth moved to Chimayo. Her New Mexico landscapes are captured in the transparent brilliance of watercolor, works like *High Road* (p. 55), an image with an imprint of the region's luminescent light and scale. The location in the painting is near Cordova, on the High Road to Taos. The view looks toward Chimayo and out to the Jemez Mountains. "This is one of the great views of the world," Foth says. Not a prolific artist because of the large-size canvases she favors, Foth is influenced by the heroic images of the early Western landscape painters and Chinese scroll painters. "Like them, I don't want just a part of the landscape, I want the whole thing," she says.

The mural-like canvases of **ELMER SCHOOLEY** (b. 1916) illuminate small things in the grasslands and forests of New Mexico. Out of his studio and home in Roswell, New Mexico, emerge large-scale, hand-stretched linen canvases, their surfaces a kaleidoscope of detail and color.

Now eighty-one years old, Schooley taught for thirty years at New Mexico Highlands University in Las Vegas, New Mexico. He gained distinction as a printmaker in the 1950s and 1960s, making prints for such artists as Kenneth Adams and Theodore Van Solen. In 1965, he was thunderstruck by a Pierre Bonnard exhibition in Chicago. "Here is perfection," Schooley thought.

Schooley paints directly on the canvas, without the use of preliminary sketches, and averages perhaps seven eighty-by-ninety-inch paintings every three years. Each consumes three hundred to five hundred hours, and some demand nearly fifteen hundred. Heavy paint, great depth of vision, and a variety of colors are used to construct an Elmer Schooley painting. He does not refer to a conventional perspective nor paint figures in his landscapes. One painting, *Winter Solstice,* is an endless accumulation of detail, and at initial glance his taste for pattern appears as an abstraction. The paintings are religious, Schooley feels, an homage to nature.

Among his favorite subjects are grasses, and he rejoices in their varied forms. "Grass is one of the most successful plant groups ever," he says. With countless strokes, thousands upon thousands of them, he brings to life their graceful structure, as found in *Ferguson's Pasture* (page xvi). Like the rest of his art, this painting is about tiny, insignificant things, ordinary worlds revealed. "My work is about responding, not thinking," Schooley says. "I function between the paint and nature to convey the direction of the painting."

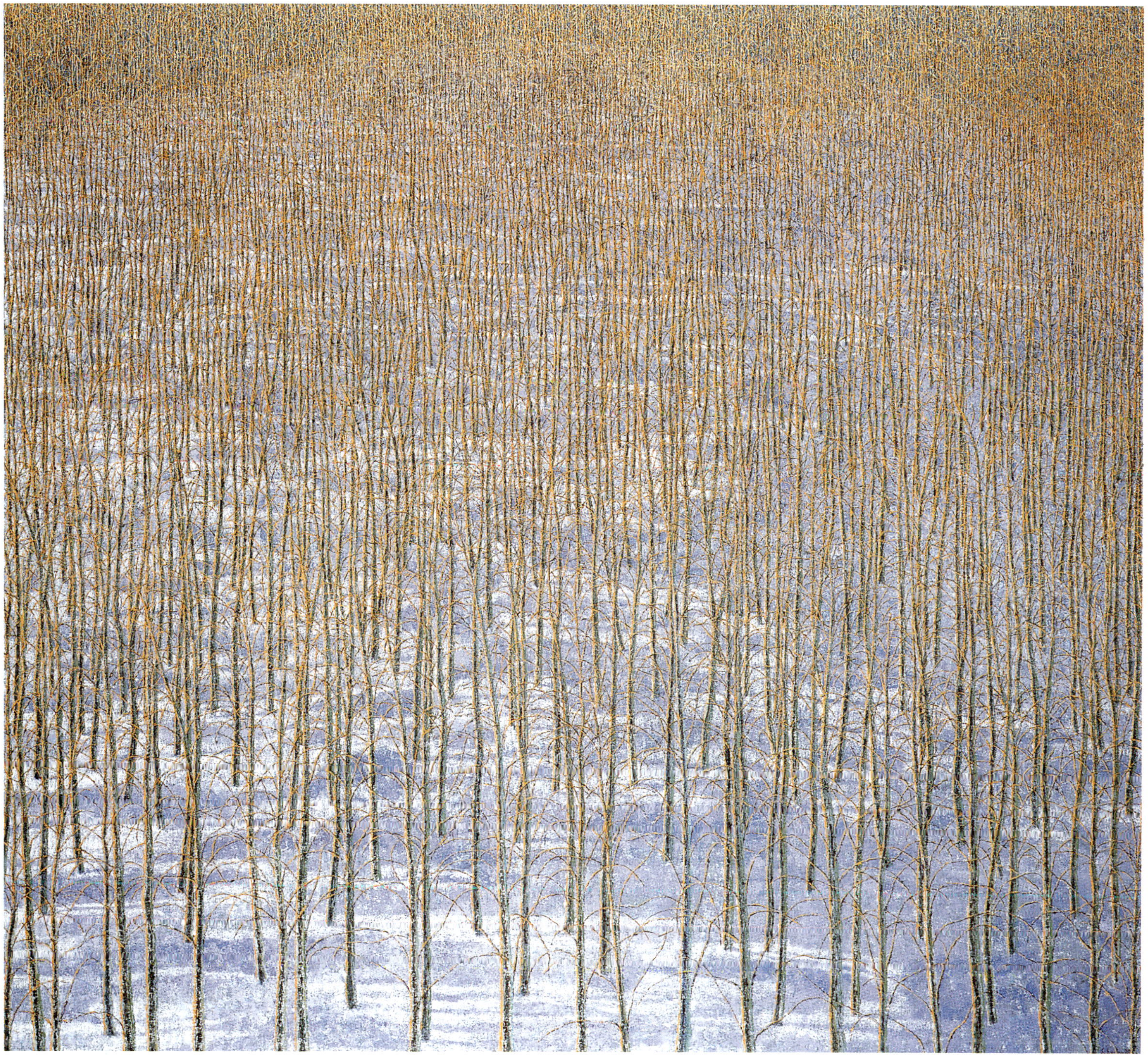

Elmer Schooley, WINTER SOLSTICE, *oil on canvas, 80 by 90 inches, 1987. Private collection; photograph courtesy of Munson Gallery.*

Fidelity to a narrowly framed slice of landscape often marks the art of **PETER HOLBROOK** (b. 1940). Holbrook's approach is derived from photo-realism, although he does not consider himself a strict practitioner of that style. After graduation from Dartmouth College in 1961, Holbrook received a fellowship that permitted travel abroad, then another to study at the Brooklyn Museum Art School. An art teacher told him to focus on content, and style will evolve, which Holbrook still considers good advice.

In his Redway, California, studio, Holbrook paints with the assistance of photographs, referring to them for detail impossible to capture by other means. Confronted by the contradictions of vast landscapes, Holbrook searches for a particular look. Although his paintings seem like traditional photo-realist work, solid and monolithic, their mosaic surfaces break into fragmented color and vanish upon close inspection.

Holbrook has had numerous solo and group exhibitions, most recently a 1996–1997 tour, which originated at the Mesa Southwest Museum, then traveled to two Midwest museums. His work is found in corporate and private collections, and in museums, including the Brooklyn Museum and the Art Institute of Chicago.

Holbrook usually begins a painting with a long drive to find his subject matter, which he considers an abstract search in itself. Then there is the camera and the selection of film and lenses. Back in the studio, he begins another process, which might include several days spent upon the selection of one slide from among hundreds taken on a trip. The camera is a means of wrestling with the awesome in the landscape, a tool to whittle it down to manageable size.

Holbrook often constructs unique perspectives in his work, as in *Spider Woman,* a portrait of famed Spider Rock, painted after a visit to Canyon de Chelly. Artists who paint Southwestern landscapes are often confronted by more sky than earth, but not at Canyon de Chelly, where views are often fragmented. When painting *Spider Woman,* Holbrook selected a particular fragment of the rock-dominated landscape, the top of the eight-hundred-foot-tall monolith, and painted a tightly framed composition.

As Holbrook strives to find meaning in what he sees, he remarks, "Time, perspective, even gravity seems displaced in Canyon de Chelly. Value patterns shift in a moment as sheer walls fall into and out of shadow, revealing hieroglyphics of ancient weather patterns. This is a landscape painter's dream—or nightmare. Canyon de Chelly is a place where traditional conventions are useless and soon abandoned."

Peter Holbrook,
SPIDER WOMAN,
oil and acrylic on canvas,
45 by 30 inches, 1996.
Private collection.

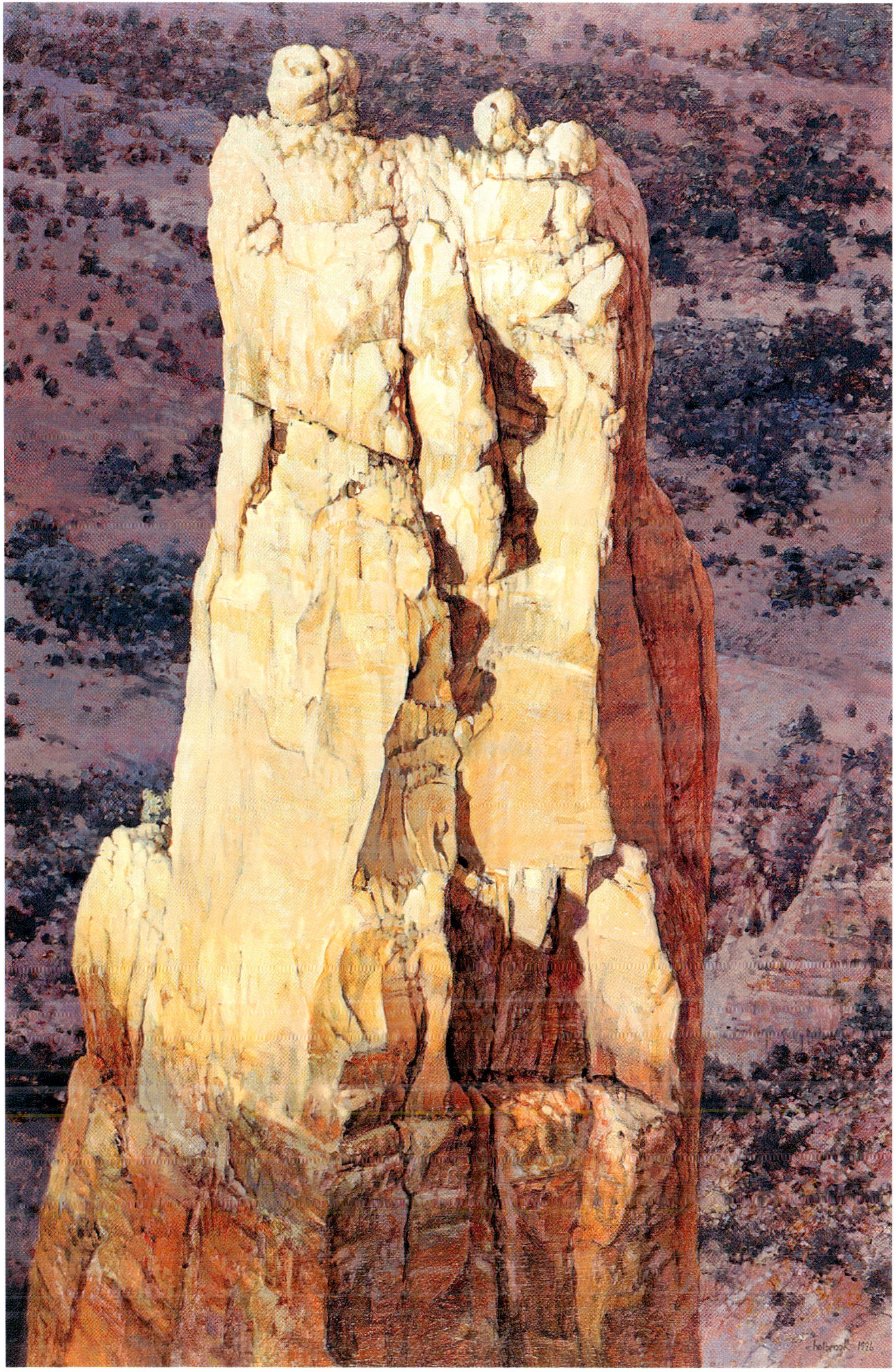

Order and clarity mark the Southwestern paintings of **WILLIAM HOOK** (b. 1948). His affection for the region began in the 1960s while he attended the University of New Mexico in Albuquerque. In 1975, after two years of advanced study at the Art Center College of Design, Hook moved to Denver. There he worked in advertising and illustration, and eventually became a full partner in a prominent agency. Finally, after thirteen years in commercial art, he began to paint landscapes full time in 1987.

Hook now lives and works in Englewood, Colorado, and makes frequent pilgrimages to northern New Mexico. He won the Art for the Parks landscape art award of merit in 1992, and has been the featured artist for the New Mexico Symphony Orchestra. His work is in the collections of Bank One, The Nature Conservancy, the University of New Mexico, the World Trade Center in Los Angeles, and the Denver Art Museum, among others.

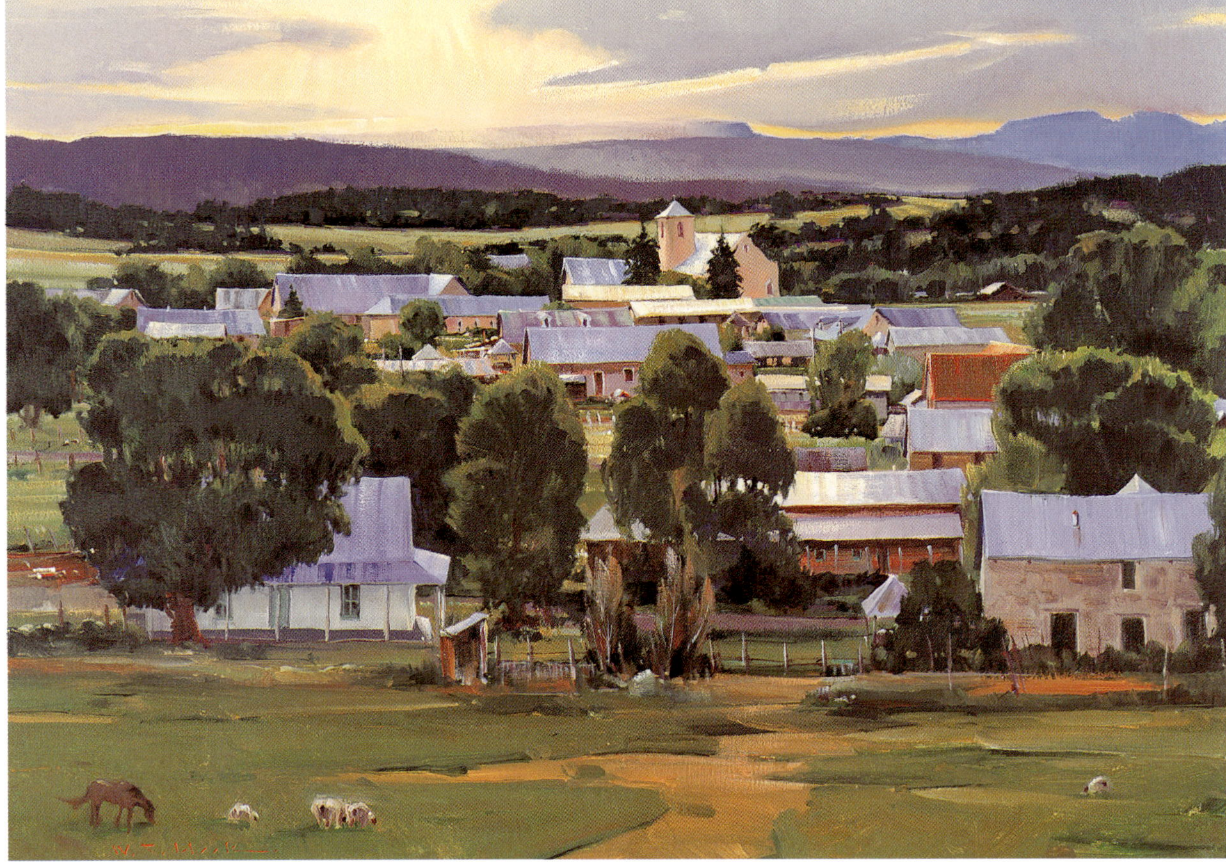

William Hook, SUMMER VILLAGE, *acrylic on canvas, 30 by 40 inches, 1995. Private collection.*

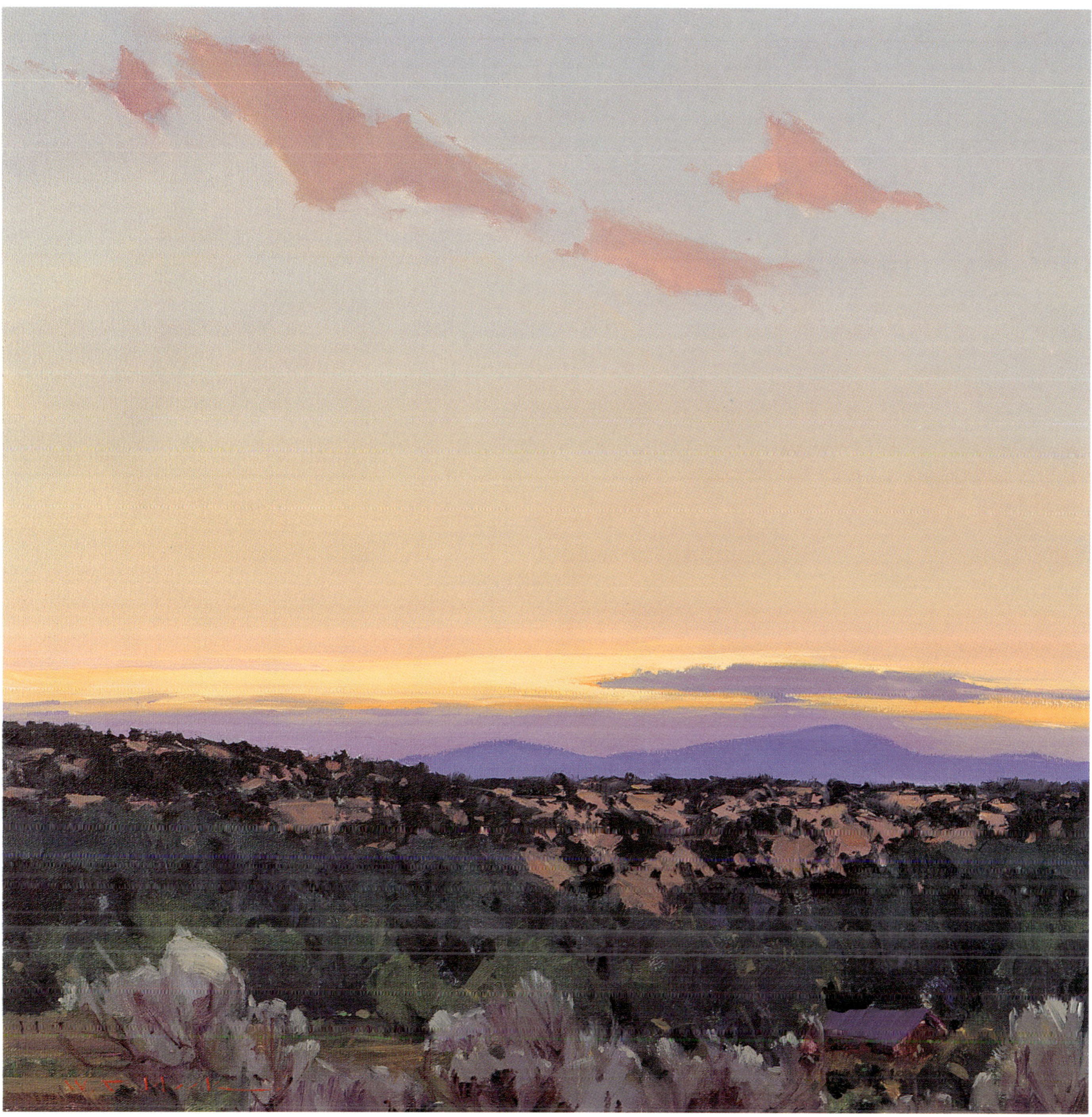

William Hook, FOUR PINK CLOUDS, *acrylic on canvas, 24 by 24 inches, 1994. Private collection.*

Hook's paintings articulate line and form, the result of his training in the graphic and fine arts, yet move assiduously through a variety of images and styles. Hook uses acrylics and works small sections of a painting at a time to manage that fast-drying, water-based medium. Fascinated with Southwestern light, he declares, "It's so essential because the human eye would not see the land forms if light did not make it possible."

Northern New Mexico's magical places attract him—Rio Chama, Mora, Los Ojos, and other favored locales. Hook's paintings celebrate the spirit of these special landscapes. "My first childhood experiences in the desert Southwest still inspire the way I experience the landscapes I paint today," he says. "The excitement of being in a place where the heat of the sun can be heard as it warms the earth is the reason I attempt to paint." In one painting, *Summer Village* (p. 60), a view of Los Ojos, Hook has watched, then embraced a pivotal time when the light is the most memorable. A spirit of place is embedded in this painting and *Four Pink Clouds* (p. 61), supported by a structural composition and bold brushwork.

Much like William Hook, **CURT WALTERS** (b. 1951) calls himself an "observant," a landscape painter who observes nature, especially those moments of time that capture a certain light. Walters, born in Farmington, New Mexico, began painting landscapes at the age of twelve. From his home in Sedona, Arizona, he journeys to the Grand Canyon, Canyon de Chelly, and New Mexico, and along the dramatic coast of California. His paintings are found in collections like the Maytag Foundation, Cummings Oil Company, New Mexico State University, and others. Exhibitions of his work have been held at the Rockwell Museum and the Museum of Northern Arizona.

Several years ago, Walters abandoned studio painting, images derived from photographs and on-site drawings, in favor of painting plein-air. "There is an emotional charge that you get from painting outdoors—an urgency, an immediacy, a rush," he says. Known for his paintings of the Grand Canyon, Walters has painted this great mile-deep abyss for over twenty years, and is still enthralled with its timeless, primal beauty. Nearly a quarter of the hundred or so canvases he paints each year are Grand Canyon landscapes. Furthermore, Walters always discovers a new perspective on the Canyon. "It's the ultimate landscape, with more depth, more color, more size than anything else," he says.

There is an emotional charge that you get from painting outdoors—an urgency, an immediacy, a rush.

—CURT WALTERS

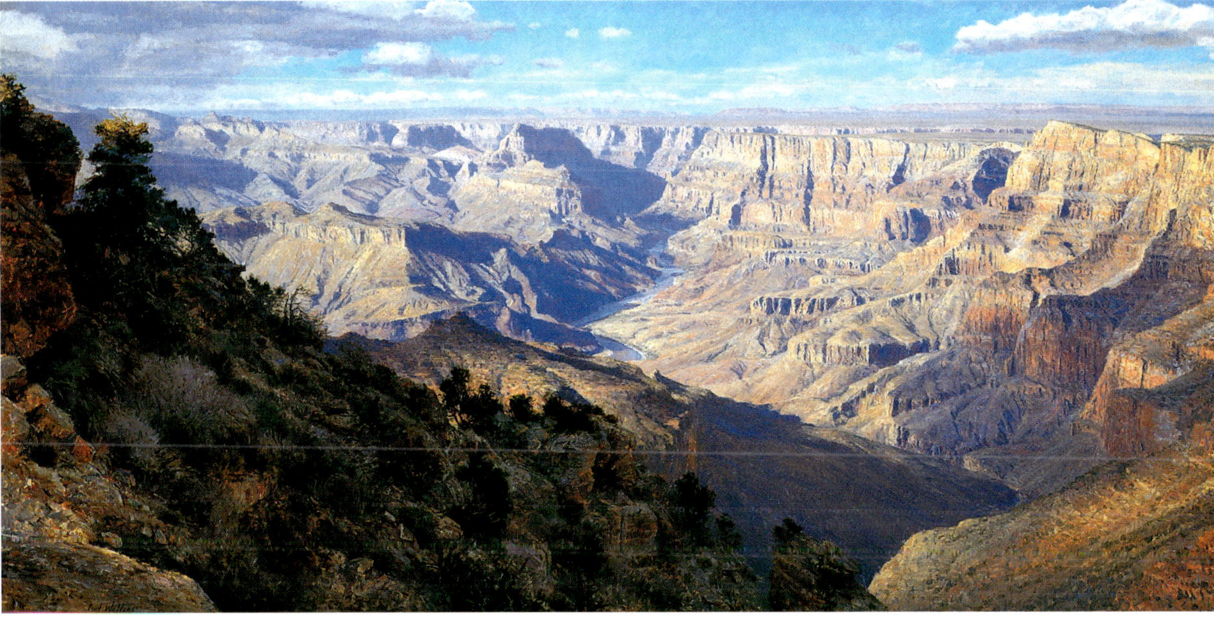

Curt Walters,
PALISADES OF THE DESERT,
oil on canvas,
40 by 80 inches, 1996.
Private collection.

Walters paints the Canyon as he sees it, the labyrinth walls, the sublime color, even the haze caused by air pollution, in an effort to document the different moods. A dedicated environmentalist, Walters is concerned with increased air degradation as the Southwest continues to urbanize and grow in population. Recently he donated one of his large Grand Canyon paintings to the Grand Canyon Trust and the National Park Service, and now he repeatedly allocates portions of proceeds from painting sales to the Trust.

Walters might work on a painting two or three days outdoors, then bring it back to his studio for refinement. He revels in colors, and uses a wide range in his palette. In addition, he utilizes large canvases to capture the Grand Canyon's boundless panorama, layer by layer, as in *Palisades of the Desert.* For Walters, the creation of this painting was an expression of the Grand Canyon as a sacred place, the act of painting itself an aesthetic ceremony.

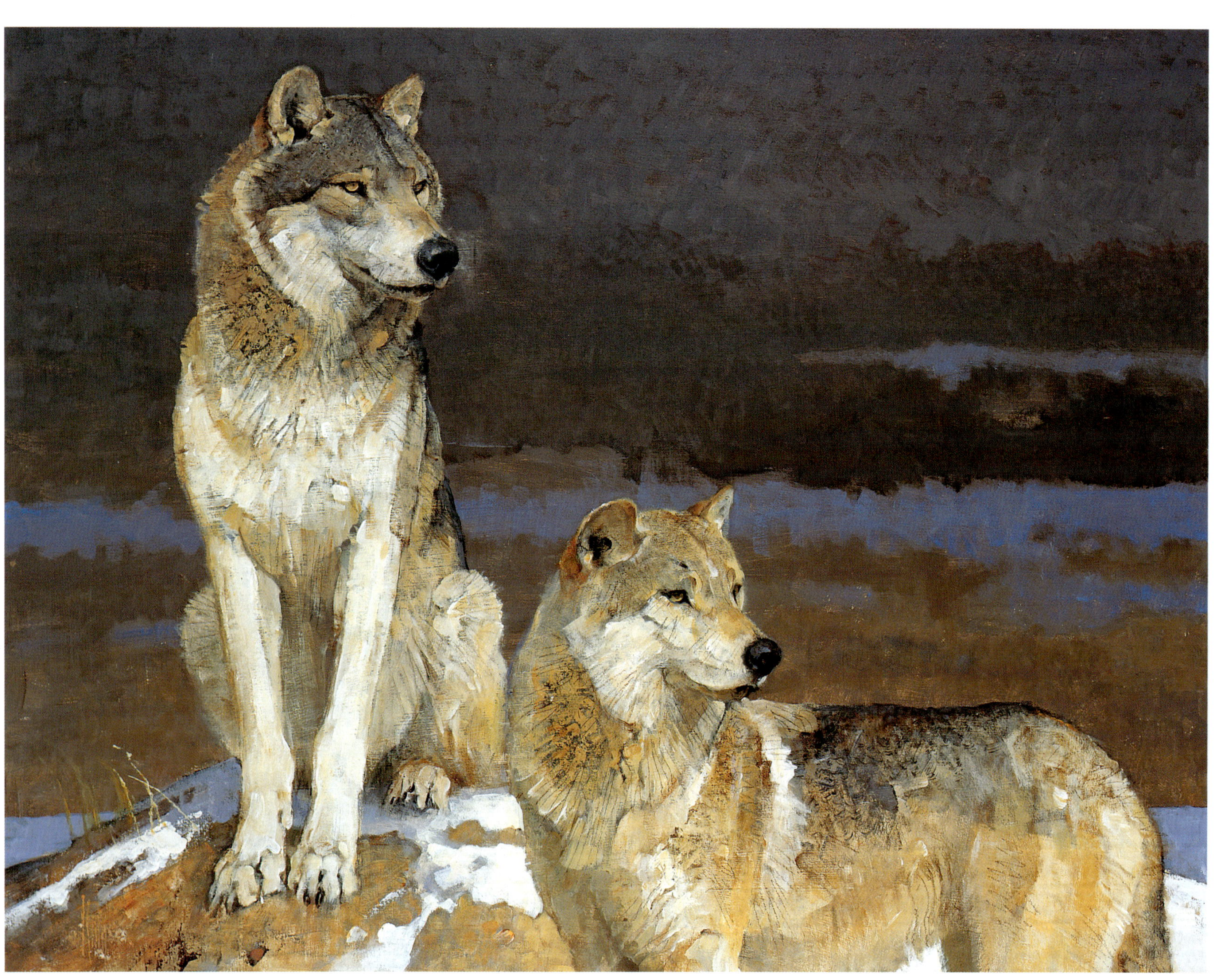

CHAPTER *two*

ANIMALS AND WILDLIFE

Natural Observations

LIKE THE LANDSCAPE ARTISTS PROFILED IN CHAPTER ONE, MANY PAINTERS AND SCULPTORS OF animals and wildlife seek out wild places throughout the American West where they can observe their subjects firsthand, from life, in the animals' own environments. Others, however, utilize zoos, photographs, and videos, concerned mostly with an animal's correct anatomy and personality. Most embrace realism, filtered through their own personal styles and techniques.

Interest in wildlife and animal art has grown enormously in recent years, in part because larger numbers of talented artists want to tackle a broader array of subjects: wild and domestic mammals, birds, fish, even reptiles, amphibians, and insects. This renaissance, along with recognition of the genre as fine art with aesthetic merit, has led many to enter exhibitions at the National Cowboy Hall of Fame, the Leigh Yawkey Woodson Art Museum, and the National Museum of Wildlife Art.

Bob Kuhn,
RETURN OF THE CARIBOU,
acrylic on canvas,
20 by 30 inches, 1995.
Private collection.

Whether they explore wilderness environments or more controlled locales such as zoological parks, these artists bring rich imagination to their interpretive creations. They are executed in various media, including oil, acrylic, gouache, watercolor, or color woodcuts, or shaped from clay, stone, or bronze. Through an endless search for behavior, movement, and form, immersed in the details of living creatures, wildlife and animal artists are devoted researchers, knowledgeable about botany, biology, animal behavior, and ecology.

There is a difference between wildlife artists and animal artists, who portray the behavioral characteristics of specific animals. For the wildlife artists, the painters, habitat is paramount; the paintings must include the right terrain, vegetation, and mood. They are as much landscape painters as they are delineators of wildlife. For other artists, sculptors and realist painters like Tom Palmore, the animal itself is the sole subject, as the artists pursue each creature's personal idiosyncrasies.

One artist who emphasizes the depiction of animals in their natural state is **BOB KUHN** (b. 1920). By the time he turned twenty-five years old, his wildlife illustrations had appeared on the covers of major outdoor magazines. Until 1970, when he left commercial illustration, Kuhn

Understanding animal behavior is at the heart of animal painting.

—BOB KUHN

ranked among the country's premiere wildlife illustrators. Many of the wildlife artists at work today feel they owe their inspiration to Kuhn. Some, like George McLean, consider him a mentor.

Kuhn has been enthralled with painting "critters," as he calls them, since childhood. He studied at the Pratt Institute of Art in Brooklyn and the Art Students League. Thereafter, beginning in 1941, he produced illustrations and covers for books, calendars, and magazines, including *Field & Stream, True, Argosy, Outdoor Life,* and *Reader's Digest.* There have been numerous exhibitions of his paintings, including those at the Boone and Crockett Club, the Royal Ontario Museum (Toronto), and the Gilcrease Museum. Included among his many awards are the 1991 Prix de West from the National Cowboy Hall of Fame, the Rungius Medal from the National Museum of Wildlife Art (1992), and the Elliot Liskin Memorial Award from the Society of Animal Artists (1995).

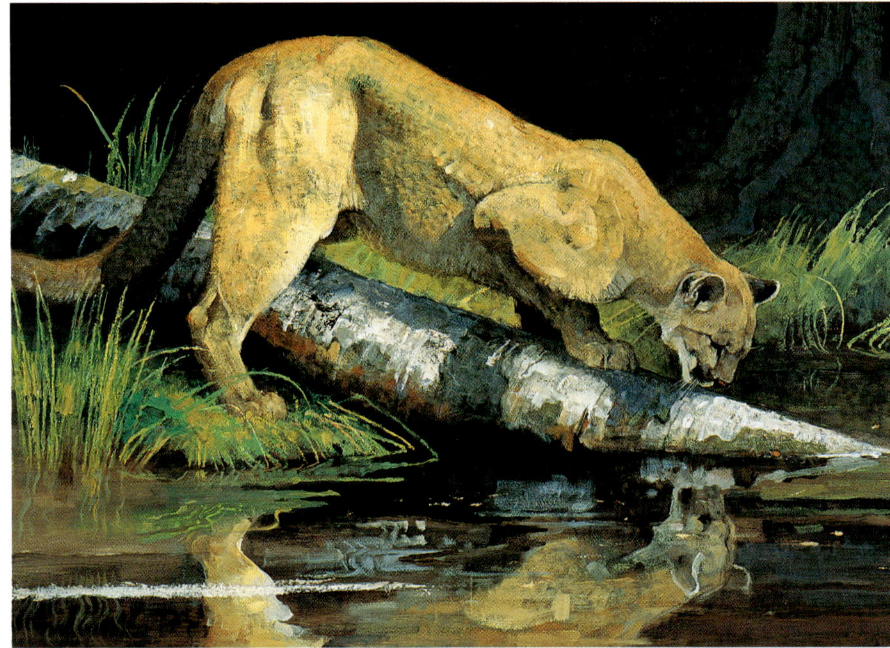

Bob Kuhn,
NARCISSUS,
acrylic on canvas, 22 by 30 inches, 1990. Private collection.

Kuhn has a home in Tucson and makes numerous trips to study animals firsthand, including eleven expeditions to Africa, six to Alaska, and countless forays into eastern Canada and the American West. Frequent visits to zoos offer additional insight. Recognized for his skill at capturing an animal's movements and countenance, Kuhn is also noted for complex compositions that portray them in their natural habitat. Over time, Kuhn's work has gradually shifted from traditional, realistic paintings to ones more impressionistic and painterly.

Solidity of form reigns supreme in Kuhn's acrylic paintings of animals, such as *Return of the Caribou* (p. 64), in which two gray wolves anticipate the arrival of a caribou herd, or *Narcissus,* his interpretation of a mountain lion paused in stride to admire his reflection at a waterhole. Above all, correct gestures in animals are important to him. Kuhn believes wildlife artists must intimately know their animals. "Understanding animal behavior is at the heart of animal painting," he says. "When pursuing the elusive essence of an animal's character, it is imperative that one sees his subject in a wild state. Gesture is a vital consideration in any painting. The right gesture will define the animal's character; it is the key to expressing the essence of the animal."

Like the paintings of Bob Kuhn, the bronze sculptures of **SHERRY SALARI SANDER** (b. 1941) combine realism and impressionism. When Sander observes an animal's form, she knows her eye focuses on a particular spot, while the remainder is less clear. Her sculpture reflects that experience, with the intent that viewers draw their own conclusions.

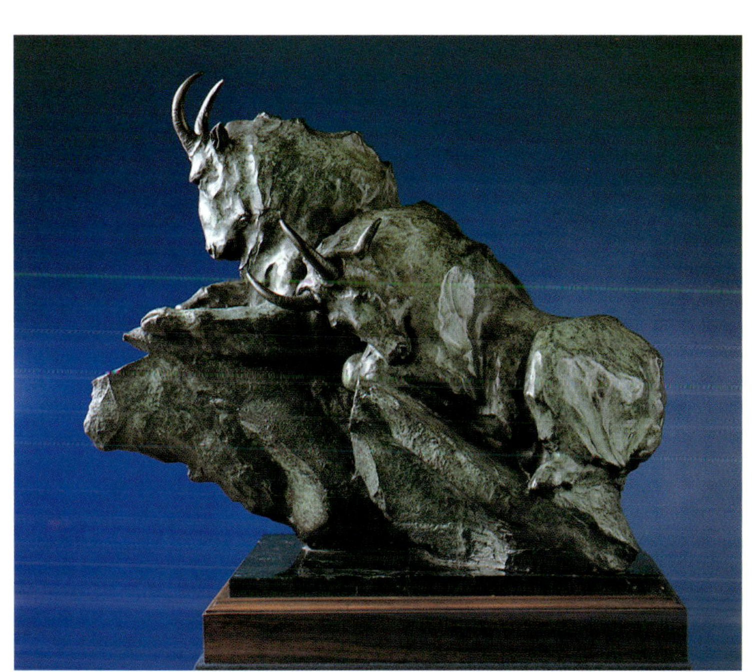

Sherry Salari Sander, GOATS AT REST, *bronze (edition of 35), 15 inches high, 1985.*

Sander's work is found in museums and private collections throughout the world. Among her awards are gold and silver medals from the National Academy of Western Art and the Elliot Liskin Memorial Award from the Society of Animal Artists. She exhibits widely, including national and international tours for the Leigh Yawkey Woodson Museum and the Society of Animal Artists. Some of her commissions include life-size sculptures for the Denver Zoo and the National Museum of Wildlife Art.

Sander and her husband live on a homestead in Kalispell, Montana, where her studio overlooks a dredged pond that attracts numerous wildlife. Besides observing animals around her home, Sander travels frequently to nearby Glacier National Park, and has made additional trips to Africa, Japan, and the Northwest Territories of Canada.

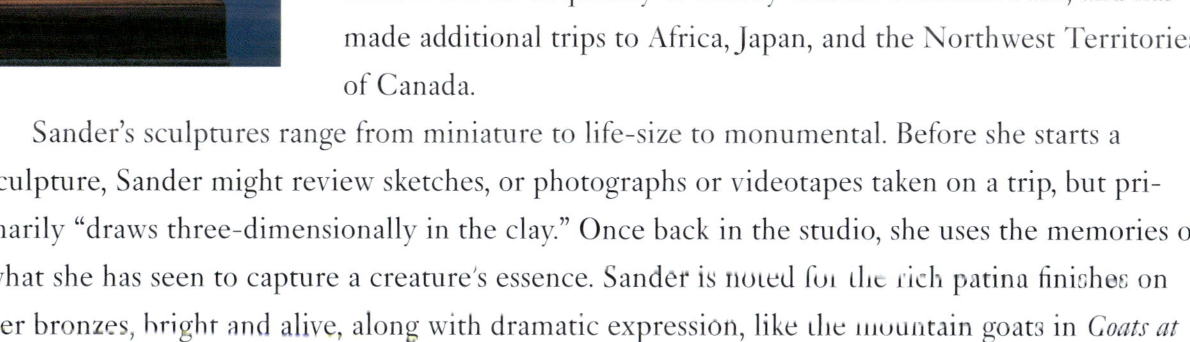

Sander's sculptures range from miniature to life-size to monumental. Before she starts a sculpture, Sander might review sketches, or photographs or videotapes taken on a trip, but primarily "draws three-dimensionally in the clay." Once back in the studio, she uses the memories of what she has seen to capture a creature's essence. Sander is noted for the rich patina finishes on her bronzes, bright and alive, along with dramatic expression, like the mountain goats in *Goats at Rest.* "I am constantly challenged to present animals intimately linked with their environment," she says. "Furthermore, I'm comfortable leaving things unsaid in a sculpture. Saying a lot by doing a little is the hardest aspect of all."

I'm comfortable leaving things unsaid in a sculpture.
Saying a lot by doing a little is the hardest aspect of all.

—SHERRY SALARI SANDER

John Schoenherr (b. 1935), winner of the 1988 Caldecott Medal for children's book illustration, has illustrated over forty books, among them Sterling North's *Rascal,* Jean Craighead George's *Julie of the Wolves,* and Frank Hebert's *Dune.* In recent years, however, he has devoted himself to the study and illustration of wildlife.

Schoenherr grew up in the Sunnyside section of Queens in New York. His parents presented him with his first set of watercolors when he was eight years old. By thirteen, Schoenherr had enrolled in Saturday classes at the Art Students League. Frequent trips to the Bronx Zoo and the American Museum of Natural History furthered a fascination with the natural world. He studied at the Pratt Institute of Art in Brooklyn, and graduated from there in 1956. Afterwards, he carved out a successful career as a book illustrator, in addition to creating art for *Reader's Digest* and *Astounding Science Fiction.* Eventually he turned to wildlife painting.

Schoenherr lives on a farm in rural New Jersey, and has traveled widely, particularly to Alaska, Wyoming, and Montana, in search of large animals. "Art should always come before subject matter," he says. He does not consider himself a wildlife artist, but an artist who paints wildlife to express his thoughts about the natural world. To Schoenherr, animals should be depicted in their element, on their terms.

"My trips are crucial," he explains, "since I have learned that I need considerable exposure to animals in their environment." Bears are his favorite subjects, particularly grizzlies, and he travels to Yellowstone and Glacier National Parks once a year to search them out in their territory. "Bears are solitary, and I'm solitary," he says. "They are single-minded; I am single-minded."

Schoenherr's sketchbook is a camera, although on occasion he makes small oil sketches to work out composition problems. At other times he might draw on the canvas with a brush. Schoenherr's great love is structure, the creation of forms, and in particular, attention to the solid shapes of his monochromatic bears, as in *Summer Snows,* in which a grizzly bear ambles with a purposeful gait down a ridge in Montana's Glacier National Park, the formidable body outlined against atmospheric light generated by the snow field in the background.

Art should always come before subject matter.

—JOHN SCHOENHERR

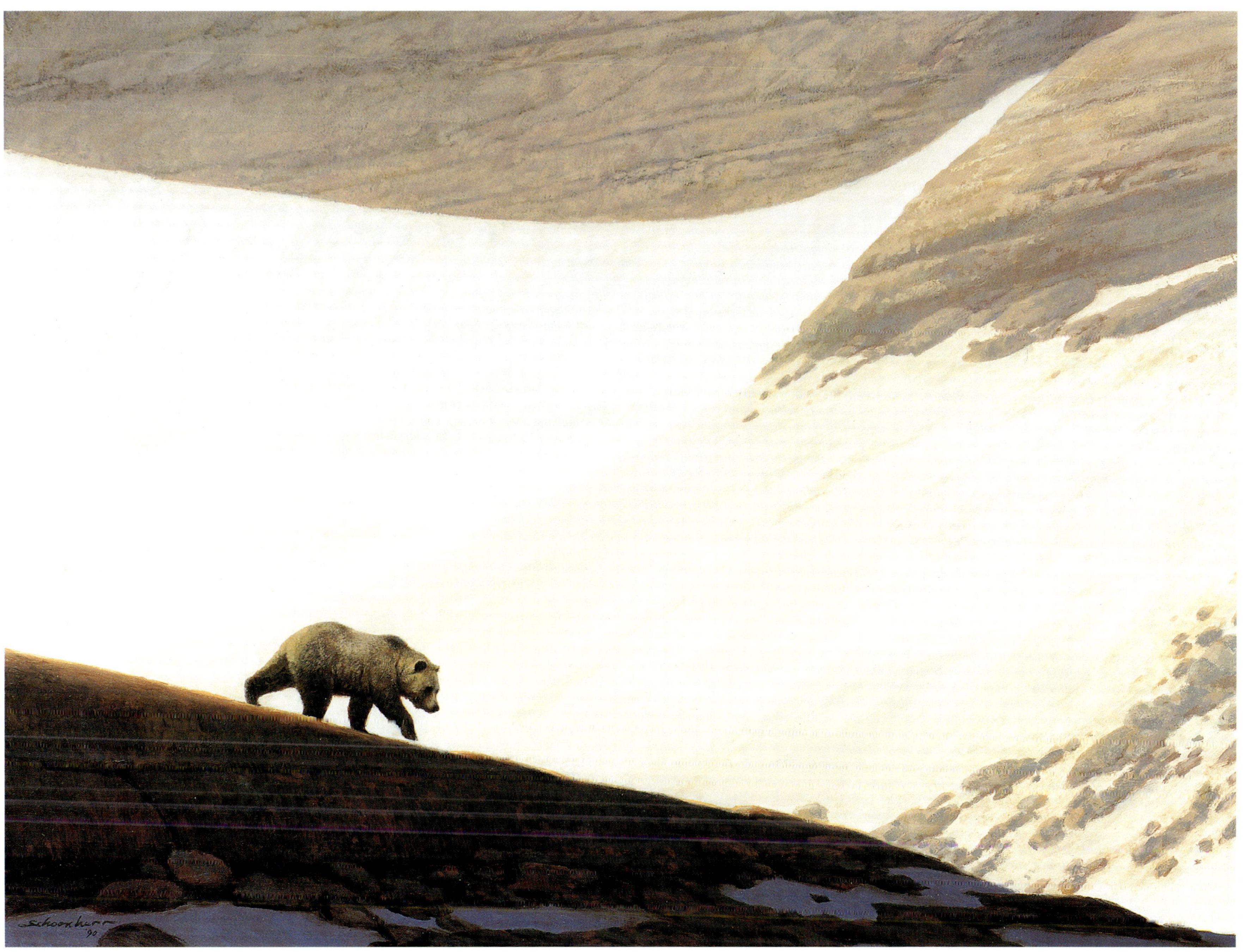

John Schoenherr, SUMMER SNOWS, *oil on canvas, 30 by 40 inches, 1990. Private collection.*

Some wildlife painters express the drama inherent in predator-prey interaction, and among them is **GEORGE MCLEAN** (b. 1939). Born in Toronto, McLean now resides in Bogner, Ontario, in an old fieldstone house surrounded by one hundred acres of forest, most of which he planted. The majority of wildlife and landscapes in his paintings are found within walking distance, but he also travels throughout Canada and the western United States in search of subject matter.

McLean works almost exclusively through commissions; consequently, his painting output is relatively limited each year. He has exhibited his art throughout North America, Britain, and Europe, and in 1995 had an important show at the Suntory Museum in Osaka, Japan, and another in Tokyo. Much of his work hangs in private collections, but some are in museums in Canada and the United States. In 1992, McLean was designated a Master Wildlife Artist by the Leigh Yawkey Woodson Art Museum.

All of McLean's paintings are preceded by an intense period of field observation and research. The winter season offers opportunity for dramatic encounters as in *Ermine,* in which a short-tail weasel searches the fringe of a frozen pond, suspended above the bottom by clear, thick ice.

Like Bob Kuhn and Kenneth R. Bunn, with whom McLean shared an exhibit at the Royal Ontario Museum in 1990, these examples explore animal individuality. As McLean explains: "I always try to express something of an animal's intrinsic nature and undeniable beauty. Capturing the gesture and getting the habitat right are important to me. I don't paint animal portraits. I paint animals where they should be, doing what they naturally do, and that is the essence of animals I capture in my work."

I always try to express something
of an animal's intrinsic nature and undeniable beauty.

—GEORGE McLEAN

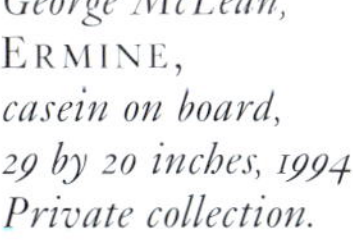

George McLean,
ERMINE,
casein on board,
29 by 20 inches, 1994.
Private collection.

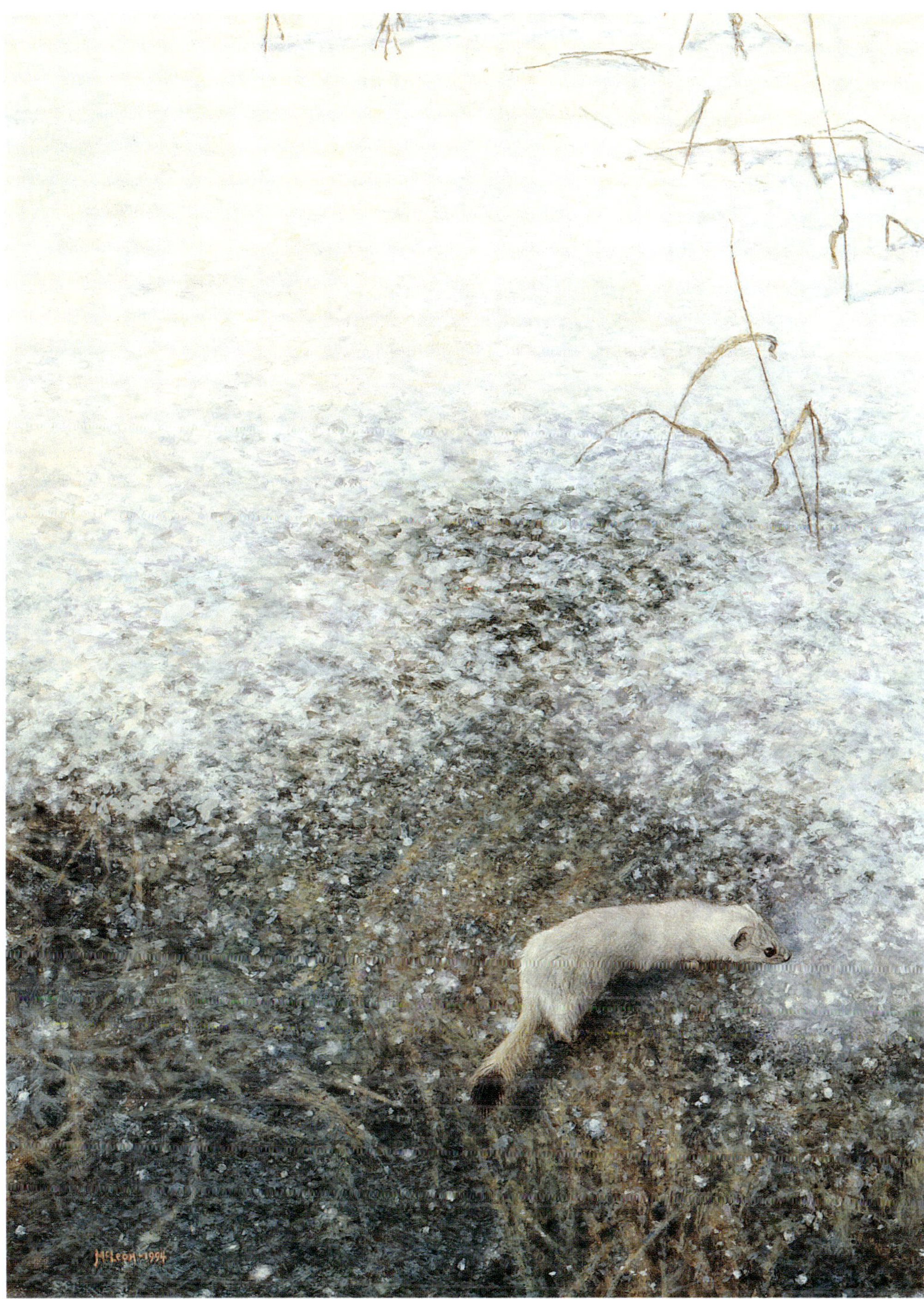

Kent Ullberg (b. 1945), a native of Sweden, studied art at the Konstfack School of Art in Stockholm, then at museums in Germany, France, and the Netherlands. Armed with a degree in museum studies, Ullberg lived for seven years in Botswana, where he served as a safari guide, taxidermist, and curator for the Botswana National Museum.

An invitation from the director of the Denver Museum of Natural History in 1974 led Ullberg to accept a position there for one year. "A stroke of bloody luck," he calls that decision. Since then he has made the United States his home. Ullberg maintains two studios; one on Padre Island near Corpus Christi, Texas, the other in Colorado. His sculptures have met with wide acclaim, and a recent commission of sailfish, the largest bronze wildlife monument in the world, resides at the Broward County Convention Center, Fort Lauderdale, Florida. He has nearly fifty other monumental sculpture commissions located throughout the world, including ones in Sweden, Luxembourg, and South Africa.

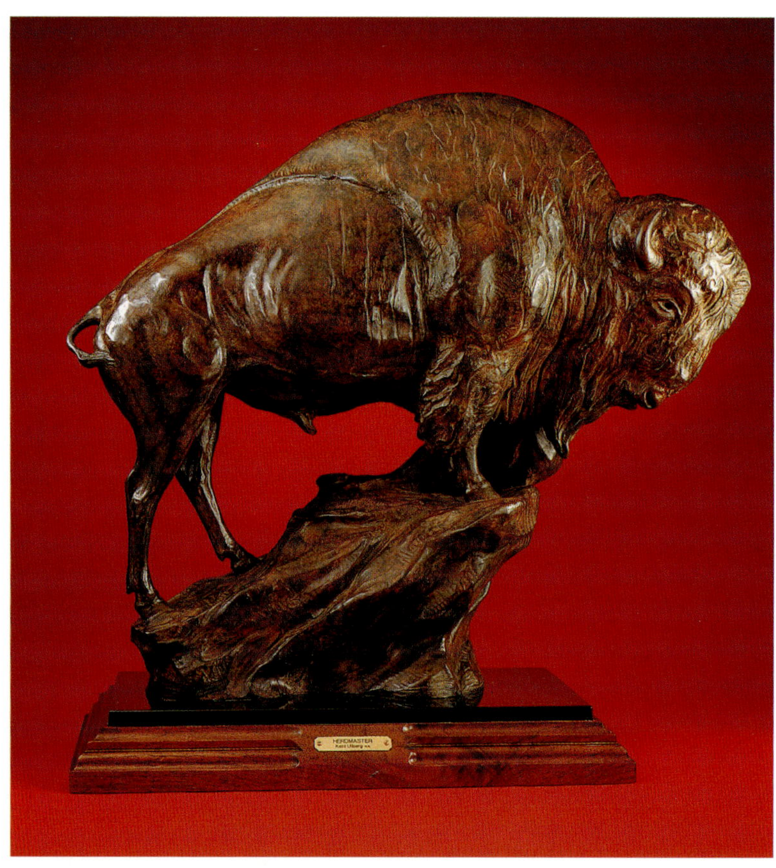

Kent Ullberg,
HERDMASTER,
bronze (edition of 20), 24 inches high, 1995.

Besides holding membership in many prestigious art organizations, Ullberg has been honored with numerous awards, among them gold medals for sculpture from the National Academy of Western Art, and the Henry Hering Medal from the National Sculpture Society. In 1980, he was elected to the National Academy of Design, making him one of the relatively few wildlife artists who are a part of that organization. In 1992, Ullberg was named the official state artist of Texas.

Ullberg feels he "sculpts from the inside out," making use of his observation of animals in the wild and his experience in taxidermy. His sculptures have integrity, derived from the innate structural elements of the compositions. Through long experience and intuition, Ullberg creates an animal shape in wax or clay, then adjusts positions to remain faithful to natural form. The completed model, or *maquette,* is cast in metal and serves as a reference when he works on the final sculpture. Just enough detail is added to a finished work to make it believable, yet retain the elegance.

One example of Ullberg's sculpture is *Herdmaster,* selected for the Frederic Remington Award at the National Cowboy Hall of Fame's *Prix de West Invitational* in 1995. Ullberg strives to communicate the significance of the animal's powerful presence in the bronze sculpture. "There is never as much detail as in nature; instead the spirit of this animal is interpreted and contained," he says.

When **KENNETH R. BUNN** (b. 1935) decided in 1969 to embark on his own full-time career as an animal sculptor after several years as the manager of a commercial sculpture studio, success arrived quickly. Within a relatively short period, the National Academy of Design, the National Sculpture Society, the National Academy of Western Art, and the Society of Animal Artists elected Bunn to their memberships. His sculpture has been exhibited widely, at places like the Royal Ontario Museum, the Colorado History Museum, the National Cowboy Hall of Fame, the National Academy of Design, the Gilcrease Museum, and the National Museum of Wildlife Art. In 1993, the Leigh Yawkey Woodson Art Museum honored Bunn as their Distinguished Wildlife Artist.

For Bunn, the creation of animal sculpture reflects endless study of behavior, shape, environment, and movement. He only sculpts animals he has familiarity with, and expends considerable time around animals that inspire him. "I need to work from life," he says, "in the field, or at a zoo." A regular visitor to the Denver Zoo, he has also made fourteen trips to Africa, in addition to frequent travel to wilderness areas in the American West. From these experiences, Bunn creates small studies focusing on details from his observation of live animals, in search of what he terms "implied action."

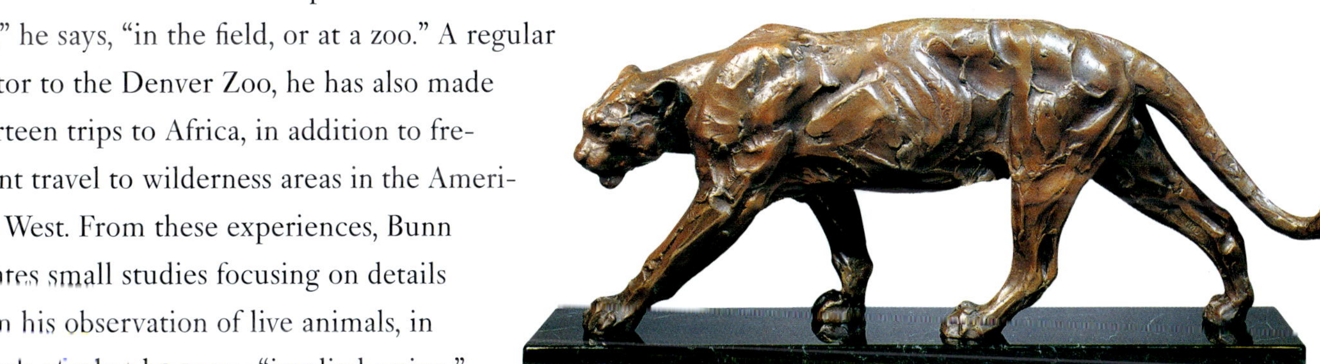

Kenneth R. Bunn, STRIDING COUGAR, *bronze (edition of 21), 10¼ by 23 by 8 inches, 1992.*

I strive for the ultimate satisfaction of creating an animal form that is infused with all the elements of a work of art.

—KENNETH R. BUNN

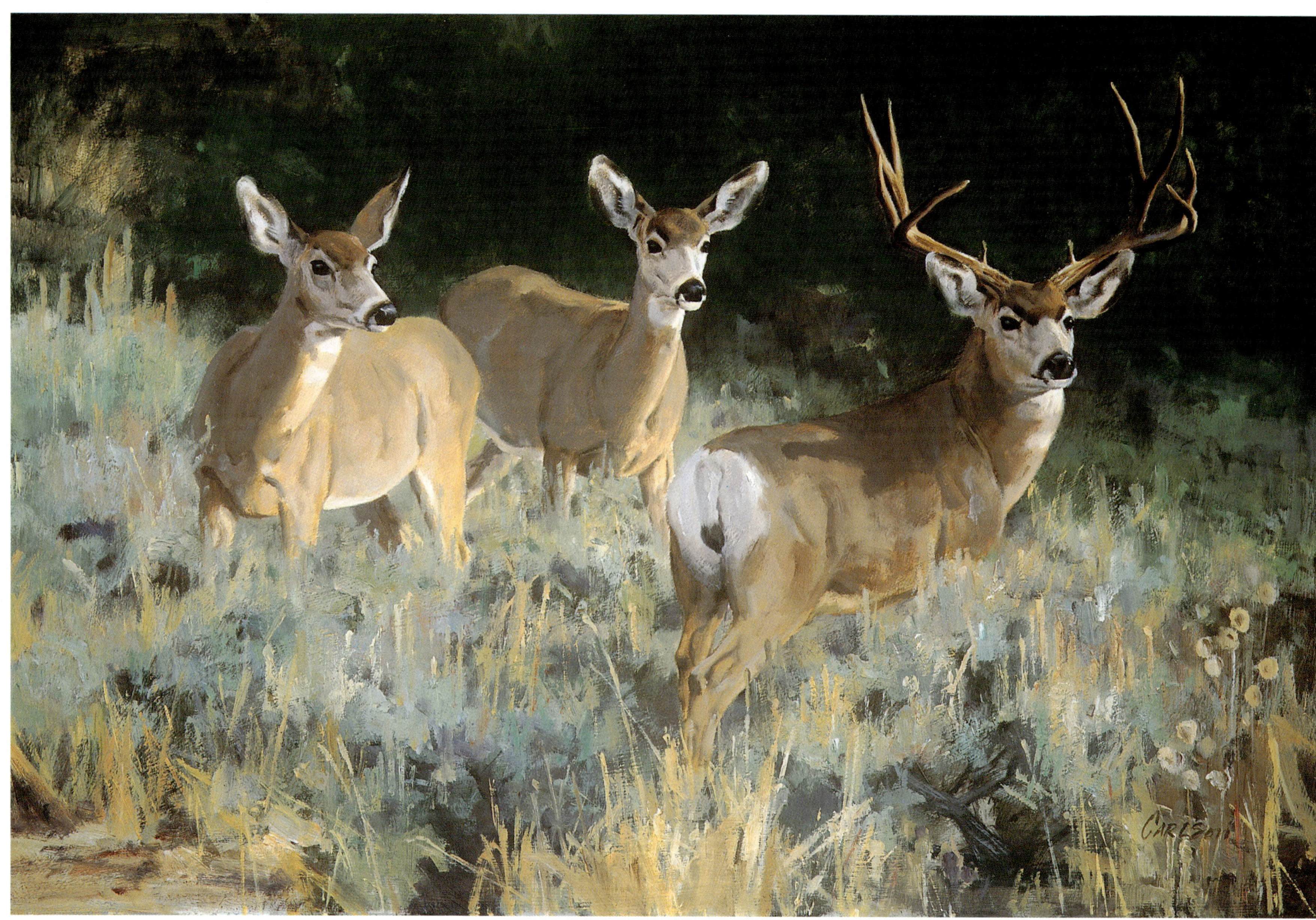

Ken Carlson, EDGE OF THE SHADOWS—MULE DEER, *oil on canvas, 20 by 30 inches, 1996. Private collection.*

Design is as important to Bunn as subject matter. "I strive for the ultimate satisfaction of creating an animal form that is infused with all the elements of a work of art," he explains. Bunn reshapes the anatomy of his subjects, suspends motion, and explores situations that redefine reality, like his bronze sculpture of a mountain lion, *Striding Cougar* (p. 73). "When we are aware of an animal's individual behavior," Bunn says, "then we have greater sense of it as a living thing."

Ken Carlson,
SEASON OF CONQUESTS,
oil on canvas,
24 by 36 inches, 1994.
Private collection.

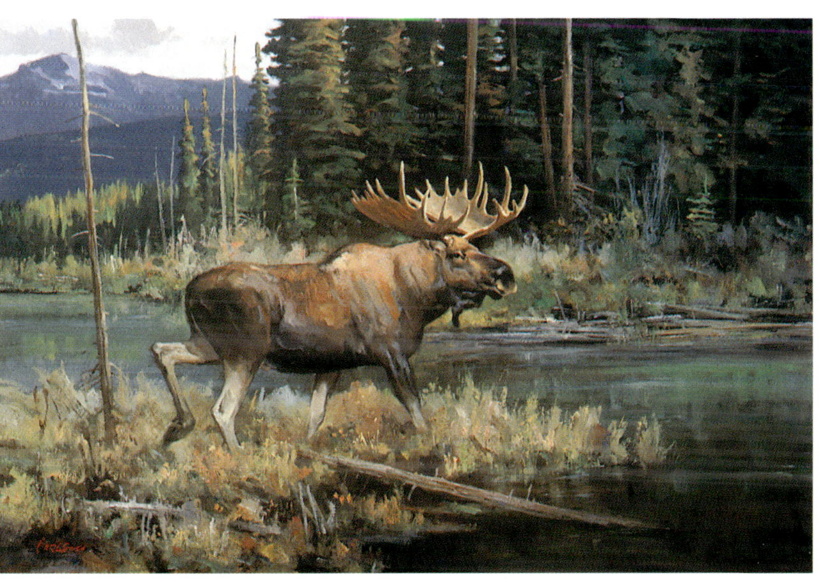

Born and raised in rural Minnesota, **KEN CARLSON** (b. 1937) won a contest at age fifteen to study art at the Minneapolis School of Art. The director of the school, a freelance artist for *Sports Afield,* took a personal interest in him, which Carlson acknowledges taught him the value of first-hand observation. Carlson often visited the local zoo, and for further insight studied the works of important wildlife painters, particularly Carl Rungius and Bob Kuhn, and their approaches to form, character, design, and structure.

Carlson worked in commercial art as a freelance illustrator for over a decade, then switched to wildlife painting in 1970. While detail remains important, he eventually developed a painting style that emphasizes loose brushwork, with animals often projected against abstract backgrounds and executed with bold technique and strong colors.

Carlson has exhibited at the National Academy of Western Art events for several years, and most recently at the National Cowboy Hall of Fame's 1996 *Prix de West Invitational.* In 1996, Carlson was designated as a Distinguished Wildlife Artist by the Leigh Yawkey Woodson Art Museum. Since 1981, he has lived in the scenic hill country near Kerrville, Texas. He often paints deer, and needs only look out his studio window for reference material. A major trip every autumn to Alaska, Wyoming, or Canada secures other subject matter.

If a painting doesn't sing with emotion
and doesn't suggest a mood, you have failed.

—KEN CARLSON

The search for a particular mood drives Carlson's art. "If a painting doesn't sing with emotion and doesn't suggest a mood, you have failed," Carlson reflects in a January/February 1995 article for *Sporting Classics.* Lighting is also crucial, as is his emphasis on a loose, painterly style. Often his paintings elaborate dramatic narratives, as in *Edge of the Shadows—Mule Deer* (p. 74), in which three mule deer have paused, their gaze fixed on some unseen object. One painting, *Season of Conquests* (p. 75), prompted by a visit to Alberta, is a singular portrait of a bull moose, lord of the northern forest. Carlson knows early autumn is fighting time for bull moose, when they battle other males over females. This one stands firm in the middle of a pond, ready to take on any challenger.

Jim Morgan (b. 1947) paints with the goal of engaging viewers emotionally, along with increasing awareness for often overlooked aspects of nature. Inspired by the work of Bob Kuhn, Morgan studied art at Utah State University. After graduation in 1970, he worked for Wurlitzer Piano in Logan, Utah, painted after work and on weekends, then became a full-time painter in 1980. Morgan has participated in numerous exhibitions since then, at museums and shows like the National Academy of Western Art, the Northwest Rendezvous, and the Leigh Yawkey Woodson Art Museum. Among his awards is the 1994 Robert M. Lougheed Memorial Award from the National Academy of Western Art.

Jim Morgan,
SILENT AS WINTER,
oil on canvas,
24 by 36 inches, 1996.
Private collection.

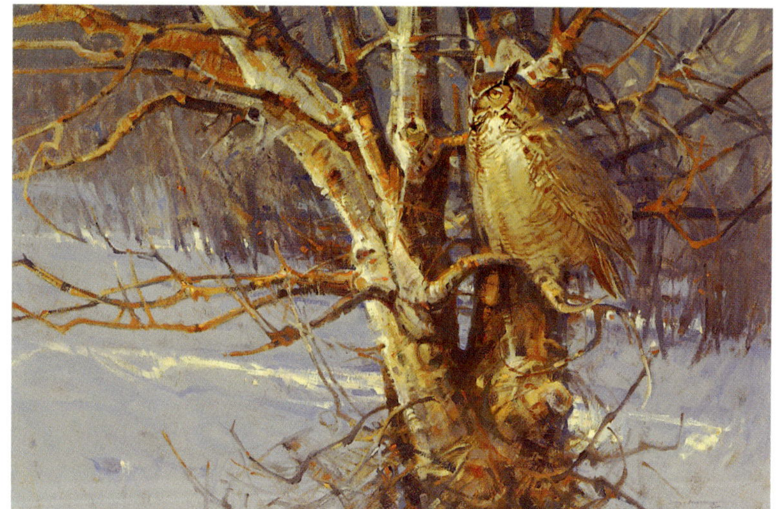

From his home in Utah's Cache Valley, Morgan ventures into the nearby Wasatch Mountains, along marshes around the Great Salt Lake, and to other places throughout the Rocky Mountain West in search of "a little section of landscape"; a pattern of animal tracks in the snow, or the way a small stream curves through a quiet meadow. Morgan orchestrates a balance between subject and environment in his paintings through the sensory play of light, shadow, and subtle color changes. "In my work," he says, "I am concerned with accuracy, but not so much with detail." He seeks certain events, usually at early morning or evening, with low light, long shadows, and rich hues. His art begins with an impression, along with openness to possibilities. "If I go out specifically to get an idea for a painting, it usually ends up as a painting that doesn't work," he said in a recent article for *Wildlife Art News.*

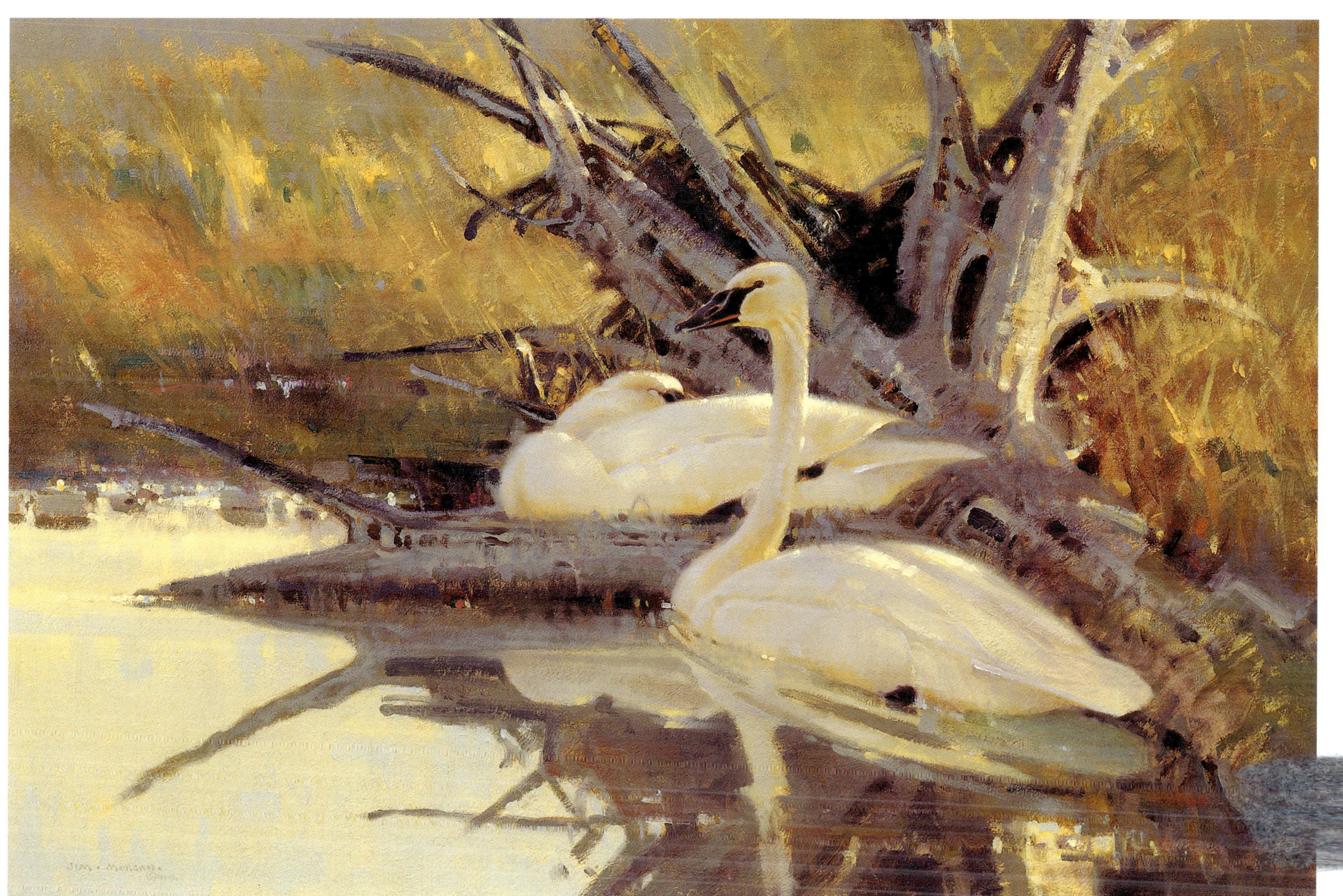

Jim Morgan, BACKWATER SANCTUARY, *oil on canvas, 20 by 30 inches, 1995. Private collection.*

One of Morgan's favorite times to paint is somewhere between winter and spring, coupled with the selection of tranquil, transitory moments. In *Silent as Winter* (p. 76), a great horned owl, that notable predator of the night, immobile as stone, perches on a small tree. Morgan encountered the spot only one-half mile from his home. Another painting, *Backwater Sanctuary* (p. 77), portrays two trumpeter swans at rest beside a felled tree along Wyoming's Snake River. An early September light illuminates the regal birds with a golden glow, their white forms the centerpiece in the painting.

As **LANFORD MONROE** (b. 1950) grew up in Bridgewater, Connecticut, she was prompted to an early interest in art by her father and mother, both artists, along with family neighbors Bob Kuhn and John Clymer. Influenced by Kuhn and Clymer, she created her first commercial illustration at age six. Later she was awarded a Hallmark Scholarship in Fine Art, and attended the Ringling School of Art in Florida. Discouraged by the emphasis on non-representational art, she left to pursue her own path.

Lanford Monroe,
BREAK OF DAY,
oil on canvas,
28 by 40 inches, 1995.
Private collection.

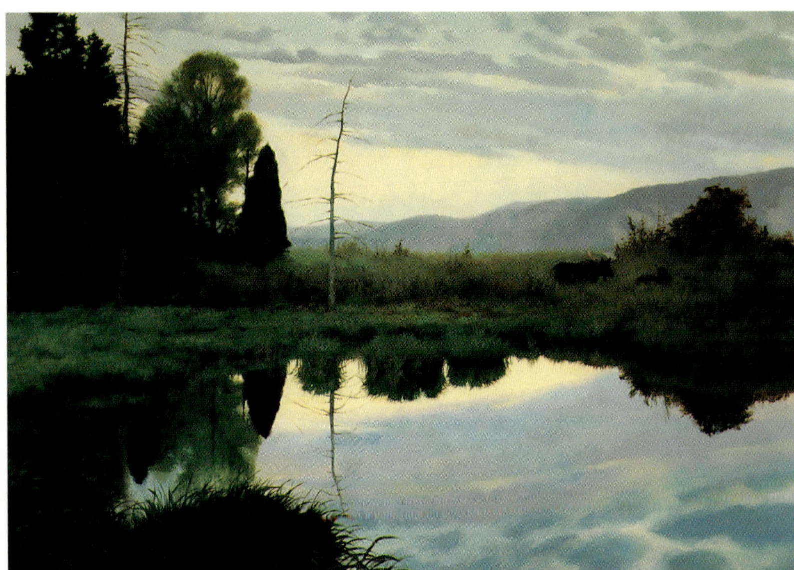

Monroe is known for the light and atmosphere in her somber landscapes, which often include animals set in their natural habitat. Her paintings, in fact, blur the boundary between landscape art and wildlife art. Her numerous awards include the Society of Animal Artists Award of Excellence, the American Academy of Equine Art Popular Prize and Landscape Award, and the *U.S. Art Magazine* Award of Merit in the Arts. Among her exhibitions are the National Cowboy Hall of Fame's *Prix de West* events.

A resident of Taos, New Mexico, Monroe schedules regular painting trips throughout North America and Europe, but one of her favorite haunts is the Yellowstone–Grand Teton National Parks region. Her work there reflects tranquil, intimate scenes, with animals in her paintings half-hidden, still as stone. In *Break of Day*, two moose pause

The mood is the most important thing.
It's what I want to communicate to the viewer.

—LANFORD MONROE

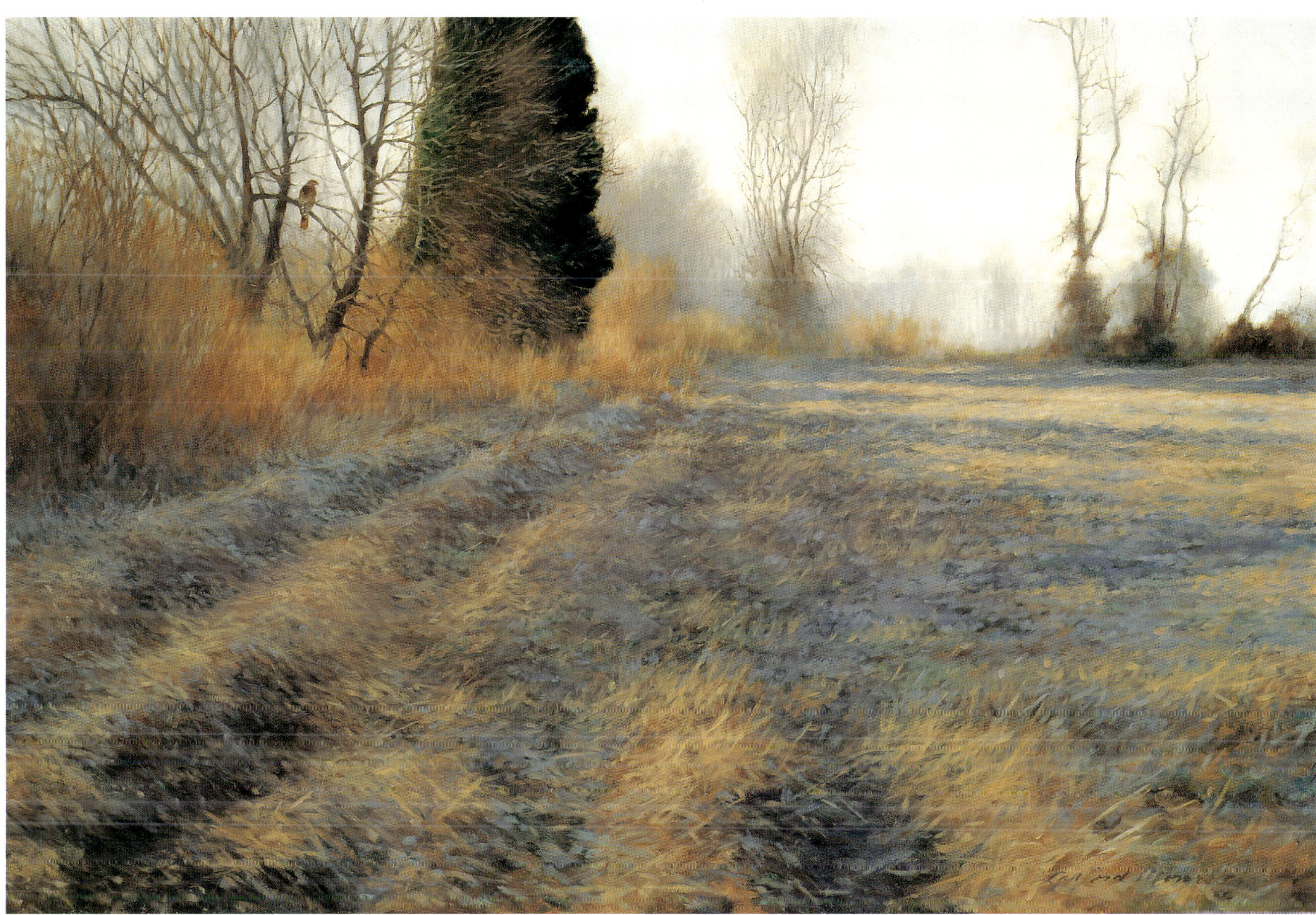

Lanford Monroe, MORNING FROST, *oil on canvas, 24 by 36 inches, 1995. Private collection.*

along the tangled underbrush beside the Snake River, their forms nearly indistinguishable in the glimmer of light reflected on the thick vegetation. "The mood is the most important thing. It's what I want to communicate to the viewer," Monroe says. Her studio paintings, like *Morning Frost* (p. 79), are a composite of field studies, photographs, and being there at the right moment.

From his studio in Point Reyes Station, California, near Point Reyes National Seashore, **THOMAS QUINN** (b. 1938) explores the region's diverse natural beauty. His focus is on local fauna—mammals, raptors, waterfowl, shorebirds, and songbirds. Quinn has an intimate familiarity with the chaparral-and-redwood covered hillsides, quiet tidal estuaries, and remote coastal beaches.

Born in Honolulu, Quinn graduated from the Art Center College of Design, then headed east for New York and a career in graphic design. However, a near-fatal confrontation with a liver disease in 1966 led him to consider another career. After he recovered, Quinn and his wife, Jeri Nichols Quinn, moved to Marin County in California, he to paint wildlife, she to pursue landscape painting. His work has been exhibited at the Field Museum of Natural History, the California Academy of Sciences, the New York Museum of Natural History, and the Leigh Yawkey Woodson Art Museum. He won a gold medal in watercolor at the 1994 *National Academy of Western Art* exhibit.

After thirty years, Quinn has mastered an intimacy with wildlife—and a distinctive style in his watercolor and gouache paintings. "Less is more" seems evident in Quinn's art, through the shape of negative space and what is left unsaid in the image. Quinn's work reflects the approach of Chinese painters of the Sung Dynasty, or nineteenth century Japanese landscape artists. "In painting," he says, "I don't believe undeveloped space must be viewed as a disappointment, but perhaps a place of stillness, a pause that

Thomas Quinn,
BLUE COUGAR,
watercolor,
14 by 16 inches, 1996.
Private collection.

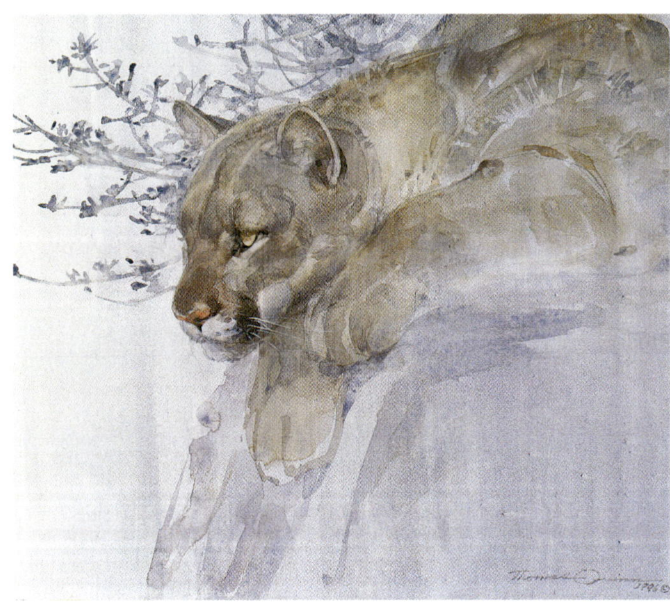

I don't believe undeveloped space must be viewed as a disappointment, but perhaps a place of stillness, a pause that may accompany some surprise of color, some revelation.

—THOMAS QUINN

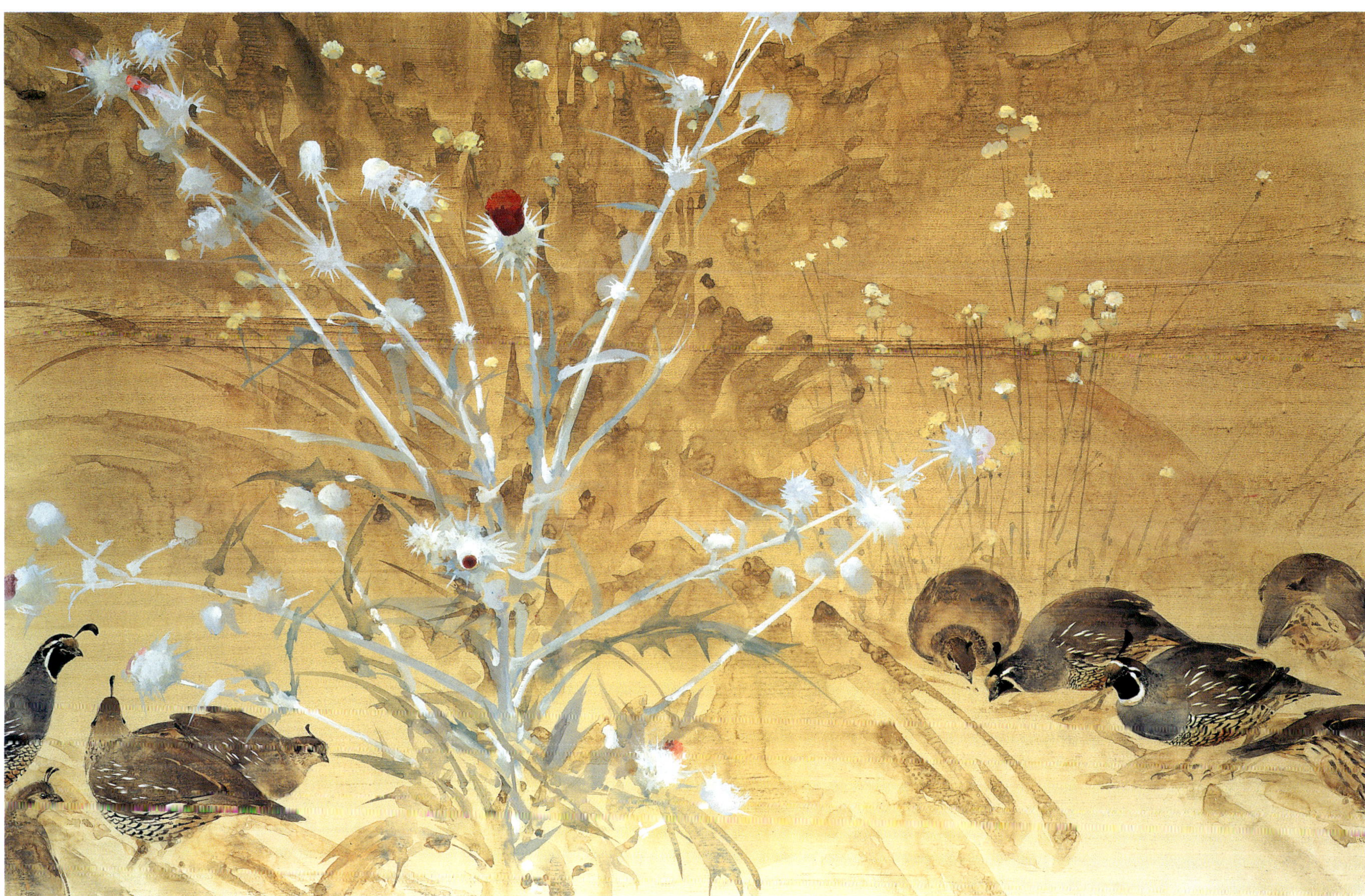

Thomas Quinn, SILVER FOUNTAIN, *watercolor, 25 by 39 inches, 1993. Private collection.*

Serendipity is one of the pleasures of carving stone.

—TONY ANGELL

may accompany some surprise of color, some revelation. To me, painting is about what is implied and what is left unsaid."

Quinn's subjects are sometimes predators, like the resting mountain lion in *Blue Cougar* (p. 80). But more often, he elaborates quiet scenes, as in *Silver Fountain* (p. 81), in which a group of California Quail scratch around the base of a thistle, the plant's dramatic silver coloration and red flower a center device for the picture.

Sculptor **TONY ANGELL** (b. 1940) is driven to carve form on stone, model works for bronzes, or draw and paint the natural world by his surroundings at his home in Seattle and at his studio located on one of the San Juan Islands. Salmon run up the creek near the studio, while birds and animals flit or tiptoe around the perimeter of both places.

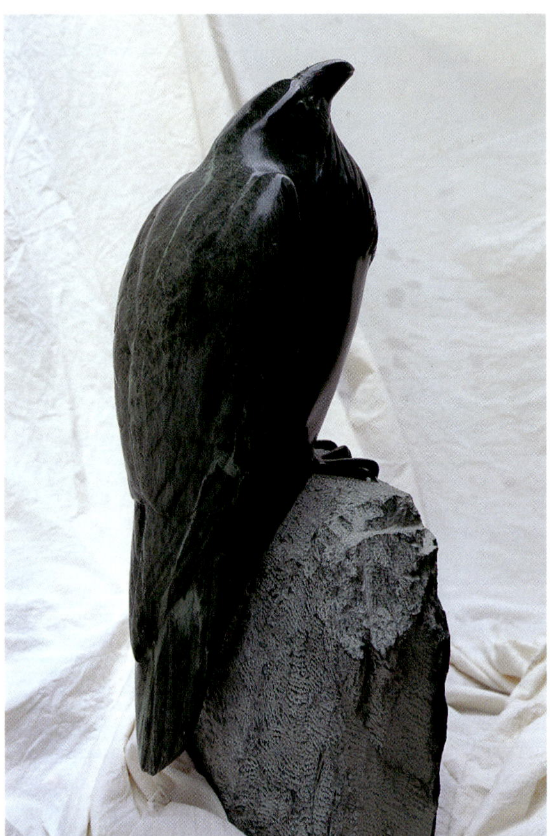

Tony Angell,
TRANSFORMATION,
limestone,
24 inches high, 1987.
Private collection.

Writer Ivan Doig has suggested Angell is the Remington or Russell of Washington's regional art. Angell has created a body of work—drawings, paintings, and particularly sculpture—that explores his vision and passion for the Pacific Northwest's birds and mammals. Years of dedication to his craft has given Angell a feel for the shape and texture of alabaster, marble, and steatite. His sculpture has been exhibited at the National Cowboy Hall of Fame's *Prix de West Invitational,* and at the National Academy of Design.

He is the interpreter, the creator of a form from stone or bronze. He works on several sculptures at once. "Lighted fuses," he calls them. Angell believes his art articulates the balance and integrity within nature, and marches to Thoreau's advice, "simplify, simplify."

"Beneath the exterior of a rock," he says, "lies a personality." Liberation of stone spirits by chisel.

The subjects for Angell's sculptures may include mammals, even fish, but it is birds that most attract him—murrelets, tundra swans, loons, owls, hawks, and especially ravens. To Angell, the voice of the raven "is familiar, more an exclamation than a song," he says, "and in wild places the raven is a shy and elusive ambassador inviting me in." One of Angell's raven sculptures, *Transformation,* is shaped from metamorphic rock obtained from the north Cascade Mountains. The rock, which slowly changed from jade green to ebony black as he carved it, seems appropriate for a raven. "In Native American culture, the raven is trickster skilled at changing itself, in one way or another, to achieve its desires," Angell says. "There may have been some of the trickster at work when I sculpted this piece. I had no idea that the stone changed color until the work was polished. Serendipity is one of the pleasures of carving stone."

Tucker Smith, WYOMING RANGE, *oil on canvas, 20 by 30 inches, 1995. Private collection.*

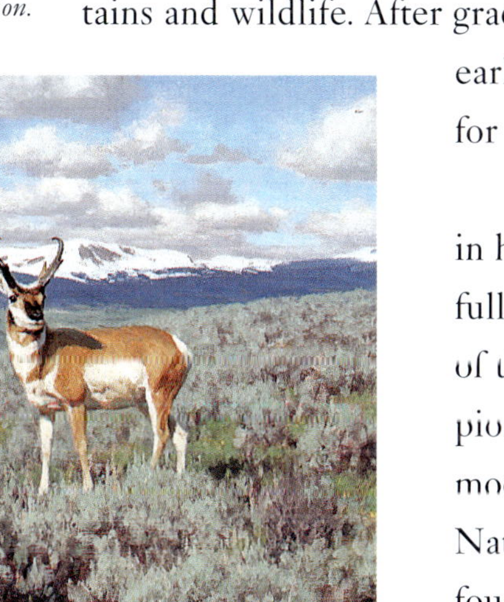

TUCKER SMITH (b. 1940) and his family moved to Pinedale, Wyoming, when he was twelve years old, and as a youngster he worked on the local ranches, surrounded by the shining mountains and wildlife. After graduation from the University of Wyoming in 1963, he did not have early goals of becoming a full-time artist, but he thought he might work for a number of years and then pursue art.

While employed by the Montana Highway Department, Smith painted in his spare time. Eventually, after eight years, the desire to become a full-time artist surfaced, and he started to paint professionally at the age of thirty-one. Smith's art follows the line of classic Western wildlife art pioneered by Carl Rungius, with big game animals such as antelope, elk, moose, and mule deer as subjects. Among his awards for painting is the National Academy of Western Art's 1990 Prix de West. He is also a founding member of the Northwest Rendezvous Group, and regularly exhibits with that organization.

Smith now lives thirty miles north of his childhood home of Pinedale, on the eight-thousand-foot-high rim of Wyoming's Hoback Basin, adjacent to the Wind River Range and other mountains, where large mammals are abundant. Several miles south of his home, Smith painted *Wyoming Range,* a portrait of several pronghorn antelope set in a vast sagebrush

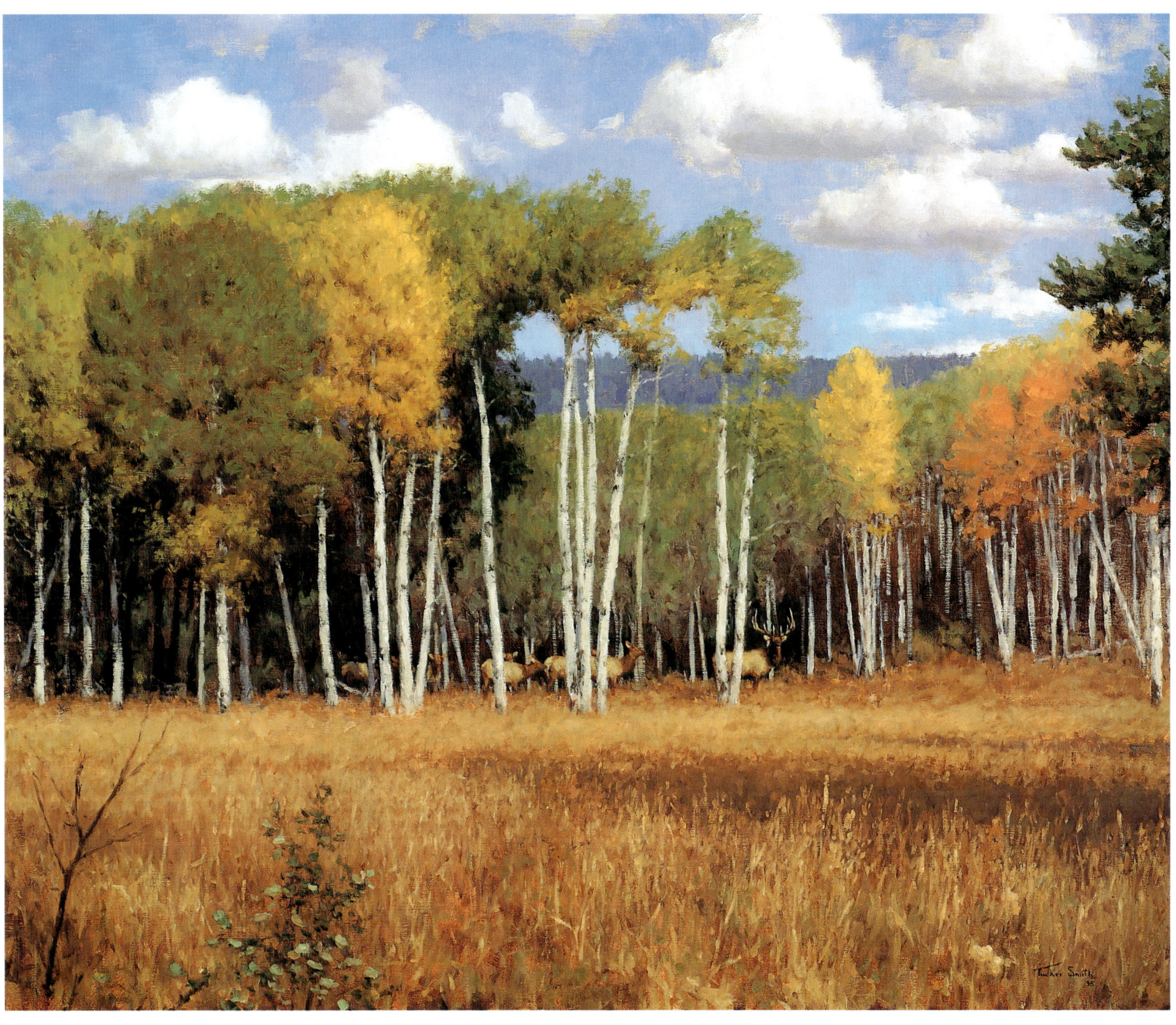

Tucker Smith, AUTUMNAL EQUINOX, *oil on canvas, 30 by 36 inches, 1995. Private collection.*

ocean, overseen by the distant ramparts of the Wyoming Range. The time is early June, remembers Smith, and "the color and clarity of light, everything so fresh," prompted the painting.

Smith's paintings center on light and color, the result of the light in Wyoming's vast landscapes, particularly in the fall months. Autumn arrives early in this high country, and Smith searches for pockets of bright color in the aspen groves. In his painting, *Autumnal Equinox,* a group of elk pause along the edge of an aspen grove, a rest area on their migration to lower elevations as the threat of snow chases them from the high meadows. "The shapes of these aspens echoed in the clouds made this a scene I had to paint," Smith says.

Tom Palmore, JACKRABBIT, *oil on canvas, 52 by 40 inches, 1995 Private collection.*

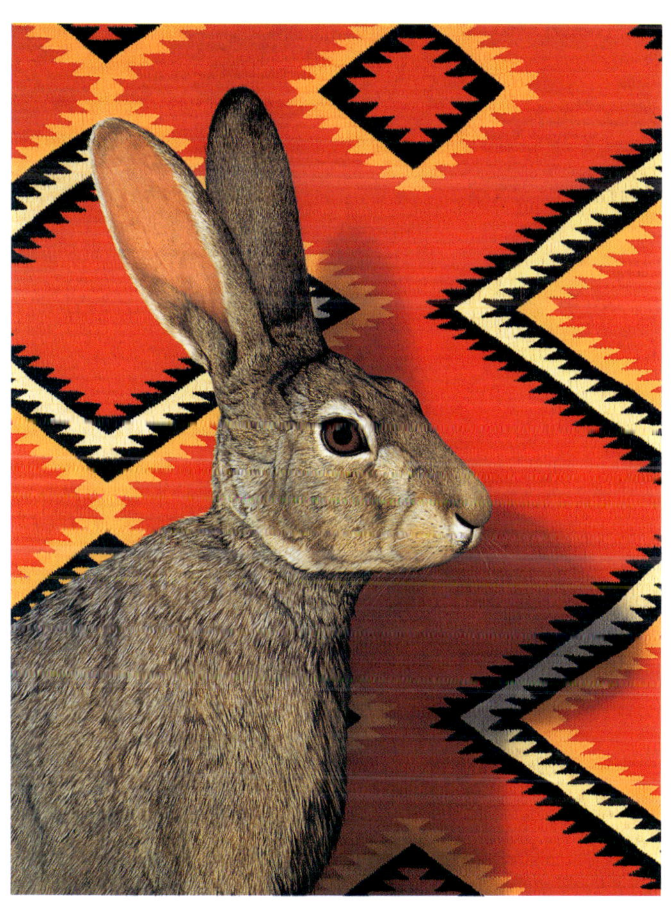

Unique among animal artists, **TOM PALMORE** (b. 1945) of Wister, Oklahoma, takes animals of the American West and presents them in paintings endowed with the attributes of formal portraits. Palmore was born in Ada, Oklahoma, was raised in Texas, and studied at the Pennsylvania Academy of Fine Arts. He started to paint animals in 1969, and since then has earned an international reputation for portraiture that seems to probe beyond his subjects' appearances. Among the institutions that own his art are the Whitney Museum of American Art, the Buffalo Bill Historical Center, and the Smithsonian Institution. Numerous solo and group exhibitions of his work have been held throughout the United States, Japan, and Europe.

Animals have intrigued Palmore ever since his childhood in Oklahoma. His technique, a form of complex theater, emerged when he began to paint gorillas at the Philadelphia Zoo in 1969. Now wild and domestic animals, often posed against incongruous backgrounds, appear as if they might fly, step, or gallop out of the canvas. The ironic contrast of subject and background is used to project the animal's image further into the consciousness of the viewer. Palmore has visited every major zoo in the United States. Usually he is accompanied by a professional photographer, whom he hires to capture the likeness of a particular animal.

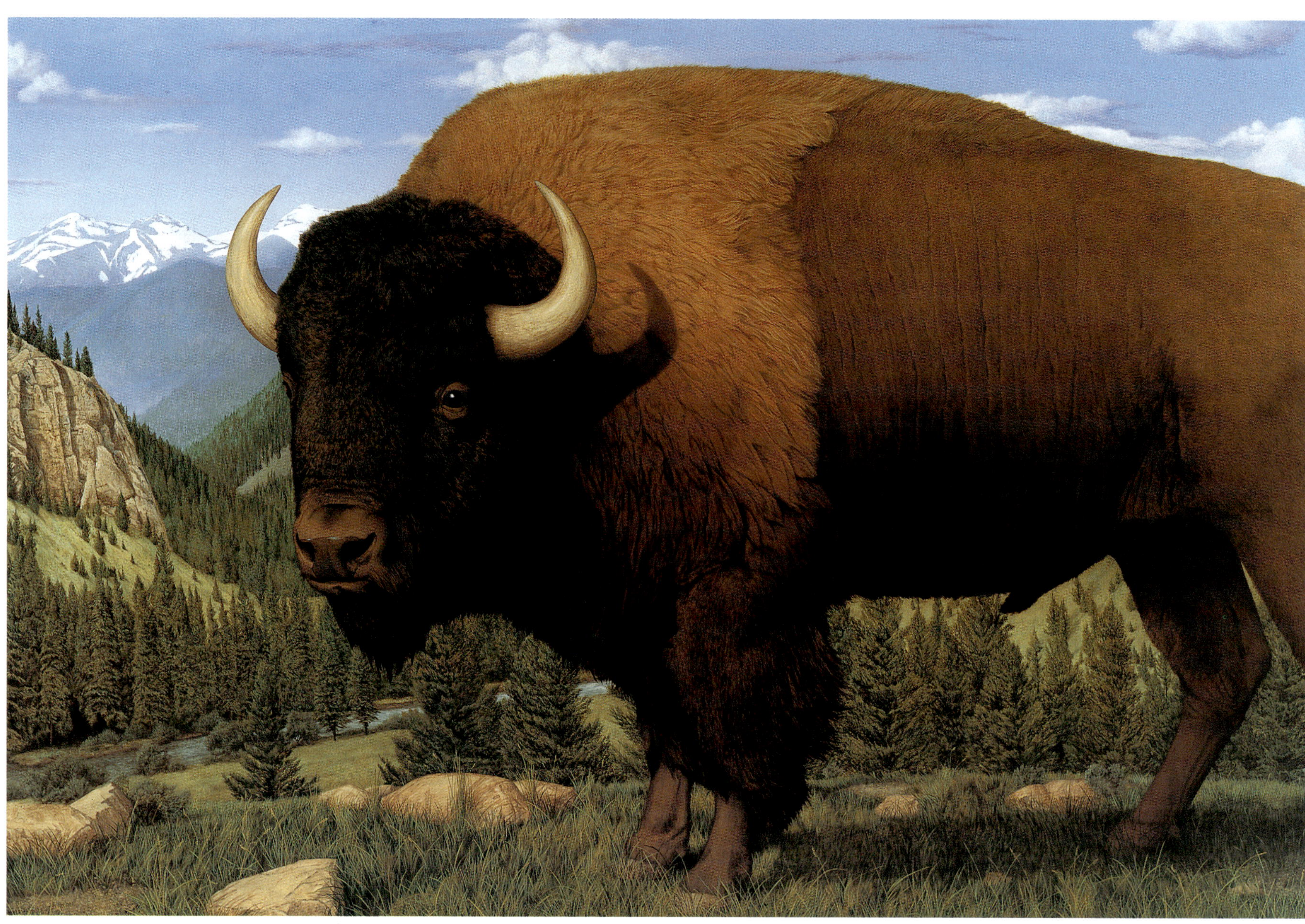

Tom Palmore, GUNSMOKE, *oil on canvas, 72 by 96 inches, 1995. Private collection.*

Palmore explains, "I feel the animals ask me to do their portraits. It seems they request how they would like to be painted." The photographs serve as initial inspiration for him, yet do not dictate the actual painting of the animal. When he paints a subject, the photographs fade at a certain point, and the animals emerge on the canvases, as if in close collaboration with the artist. Palmore wants his animals to appear alive—enjoyable, memorable, educational, and provocative.

One of his paintings, *Jackrabbit* (p. 85), presents that ubiquitous animal of the American West posed in front of a colorful Navajo blanket, the textile's red color and geometric design a counterpoint to the serenity of the creature. Palmore works on a large scale: Many of his canvases are five by six feet or even seven by nine feet. One example is *Gunsmoke,* a portrait of a bison done for a client in Montana. The animal, named Gunsmoke, belonged to a friend at a ranch in Oklahoma, but the background is what Palmore considers descriptive of a Montana landscape.

GERALD BALCIAR (b. 1942) has a love of animals, much like Palmore's, that was fostered by life around Wisconsin's north woods and rural farms, where he avidly observed wildlife along the local rivers. After graduation from high school, Balciar worked for a local taxidermist, then migrated west to Denver, where he found employment with Jonas Brothers, a large taxidermy company that specialized in big-game trophies. Balciar stayed with them for eleven years.

Balciar first started to sculpt animals in clay, then eventually turned to stone and bronze. His career blossomed, and he received the National Academy of Western Art's Prix de West in 1985. Other awards have come from the National Sculpture Society and the Northwest Rendezvous. Balciar has exhibited at the Gilcrease Museum, the Denver Museum of Natural History, the C. M. Russell Museum, and the National Academy of Design, among others.

Nowadays, this self-taught artist works in a large studio near Parker, Colorado, twenty-five miles southeast of Denver. Efforts are divided between bronze and stone, and he lets both subject and composition dictate which medium is selected. "Some animals are made for marble, while others

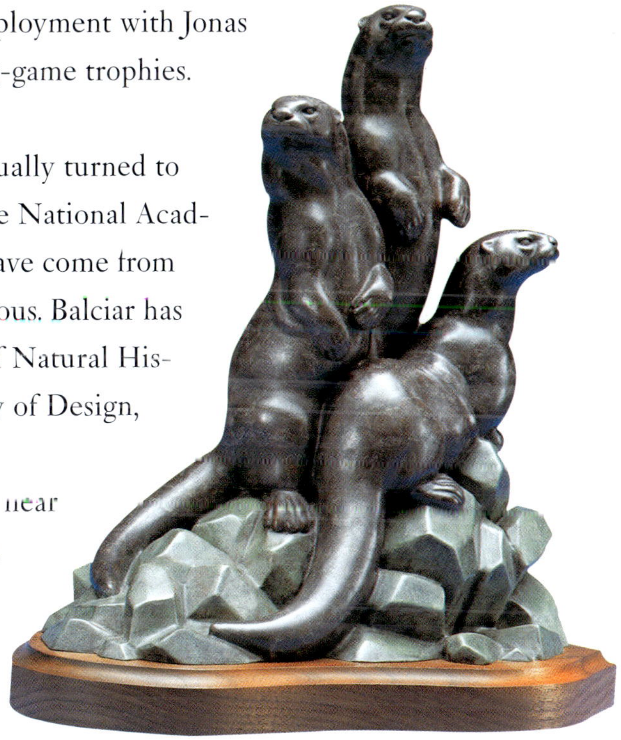

Gerald Balciar,
RIVERSIDE,
bronze (edition of 45),
16 by 14½ by 9½ inches, 1996.

look better in bronze," he says. Over time his style has evolved from realistic to more impressionistic and expressive. He strives to discover the behavior, emotion, and the intelligence of animals, in search of their serenity.

Balciar's sculptures are noted for their rounded curves, flowing lines, and gentle expressions. Besides anatomical accuracy and composition, Balciar stresses personality in his animals, and looks for the completed sculpture to possess strong form. He consults an extensive library—which includes photographs, magazine articles, books, and study casts—along with live models. When Balciar was commissioned to sculpt a fourteen-foot-tall bronze elk in 1982, he devised an innovative method that revolutionized traditional enlargement processes for sculpture. More often, though, Balciar prefers to sculpt the smaller, more sensitive animals, such as river otters, like the three elegant, intelligent, and inquisitive creatures in *Riverside* (p. 87).

Now twenty-seven, **LUKE FRAZIER** (b. 1970) wasted little time in establishing himself as a promising wildlife artist. Born in Provo, Utah, Frazier remembers he always drew pictures as a youngster. During his senior year in high school, he took an oil painting class that furthered his interest in art. Eventually, he earned a B.F.A. in painting, then an M.F.A. in illustration from Utah State University.

Luke Frazier,
WHEN WOLVES SPEAK,
oil on board,
9 by 12 inches, 1996.
Collection of National Museum of Wildlife Art.

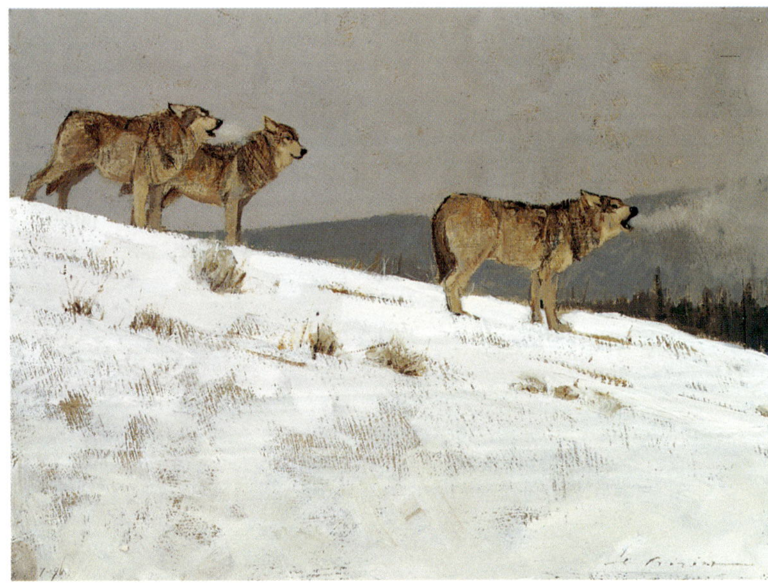

He won his first competition as a college freshman in 1989. More recently, ten of Frazier's paintings have been selected for inclusion in the prestigious annual Arts for the Parks top one hundred paintings. Two paintings won the 1994 and 1996 Wildlife Art Awards and earned a place on National Parks stamps. In addition, Frazier's art has appeared in *Field & Stream, Reader's Digest,* and *Alaska* magazine.

Frazier, who lives in Utah's Cache Valley, often spends one day a week at the Logan Zoo. He visits in the late afternoon, after the facility closes and the animals are fed, in search of ideas. At other times, he may view an extensive video collection of animals, or hike through the Wasatch Mountains doing small, quick field studies. Sometimes he ventures over to his friend

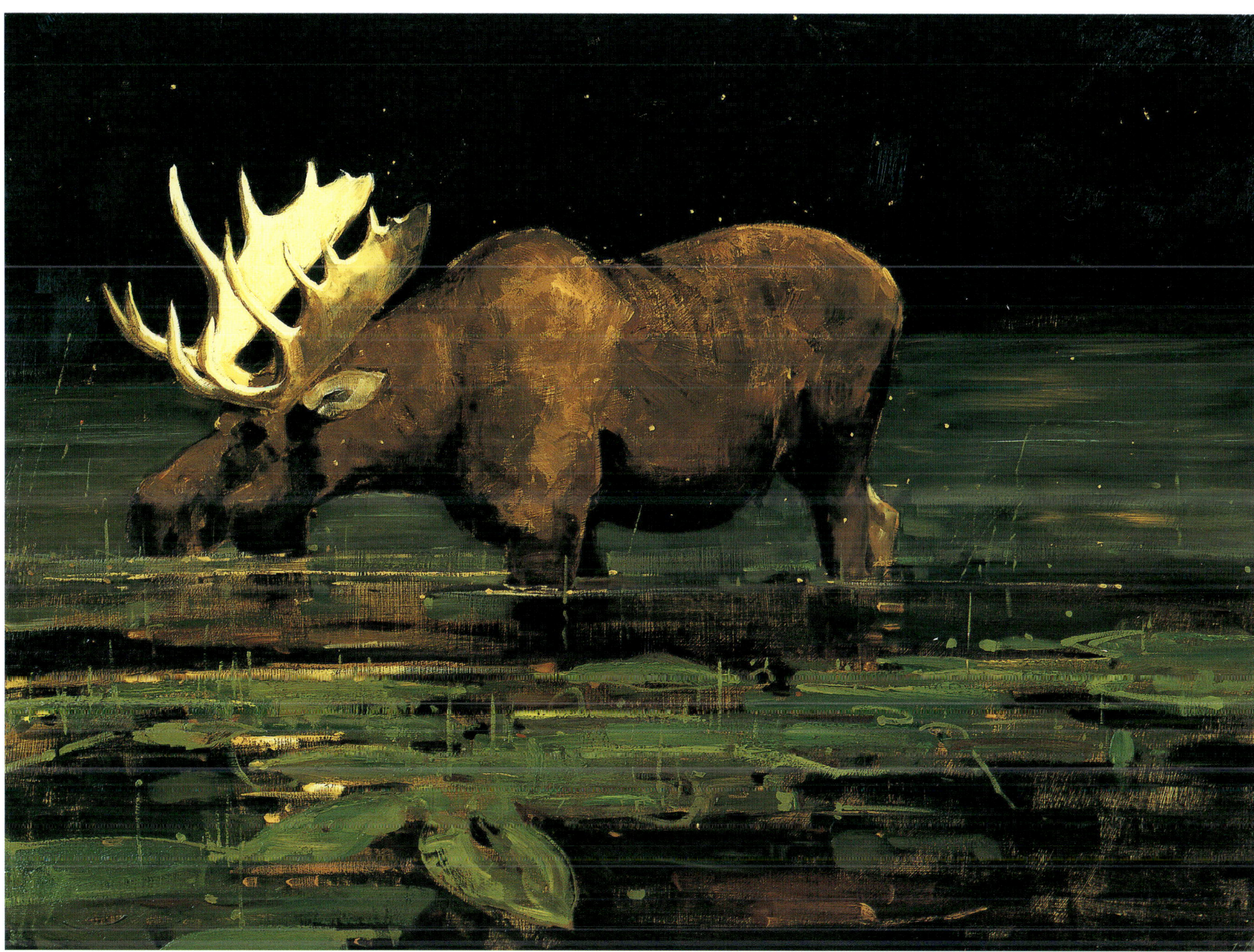

Luke Frazier, DARK WATER BECKONS, *oil on canvas, 30 by 40 inches, 1996. Private collection.*

Doug Seus's place in Heber Valley. Seus owns Bart, moviedom's famous brown bear, star of *Call of the Wild,* and a dozen wolves. There, Frazier made a small oil sketch, *When Wolves Speak* (p. 88), his interpretation of communicative wolves in the wild.

"My infatuation for painting wildlife has helped me cultivate and develop my art," he explains. "Experiencing the outdoors and having a chance to see elusive creatures functioning is amazing. I want to share with others what I feel when I see a starving bobcat leaping after a hare in a snowy meadow, or a brown bear snatching salmon out of frigid water. I try to capture them in their moments of repose, regality, and at times when they are physically at their best." His painting of a moose, *Dark Water Beckons* (p. 89), illustrates this emphasis on body form and musculature. The rich color of the moose's velvet-brown coat contrasts with the dark tones of the water and vegetation.

Finally, some wildlife and animal artists utilize media they think express their subject matter in a special manner. One such artist, **ANDREA RICH** (b. 1954), creates color woodcuts of birds and animals and their environments. An earlier practitioner of this craft was Gustave Baumann, who celebrated the natural world and indigenous cultures of the Southwest in color relief printing.

A resident of Santa Cruz, California, Rich graduated from the University of Wisconsin, Whitewater, with a degree in art education. Her color woodcuts have been exhibited in solo and group shows at the Leigh Yawkey Woodson Art Museum, Eastern New Mexico University, the California Society of Printmakers, Minot State University, Louisiana State University, and the Society of Animal Artists. Among her awards is the 1996 Award of Excellence from the Society of Animal Artists. The Fine Arts Museums of San Francisco, 3M Corporation, and Mills College are some of the institutions that collect her work.

Andrea Rich,
PILEATED WOODPECKER,
color woodcut (edition of 20), 16 by 20 inches, 1996. Collection of the artist.

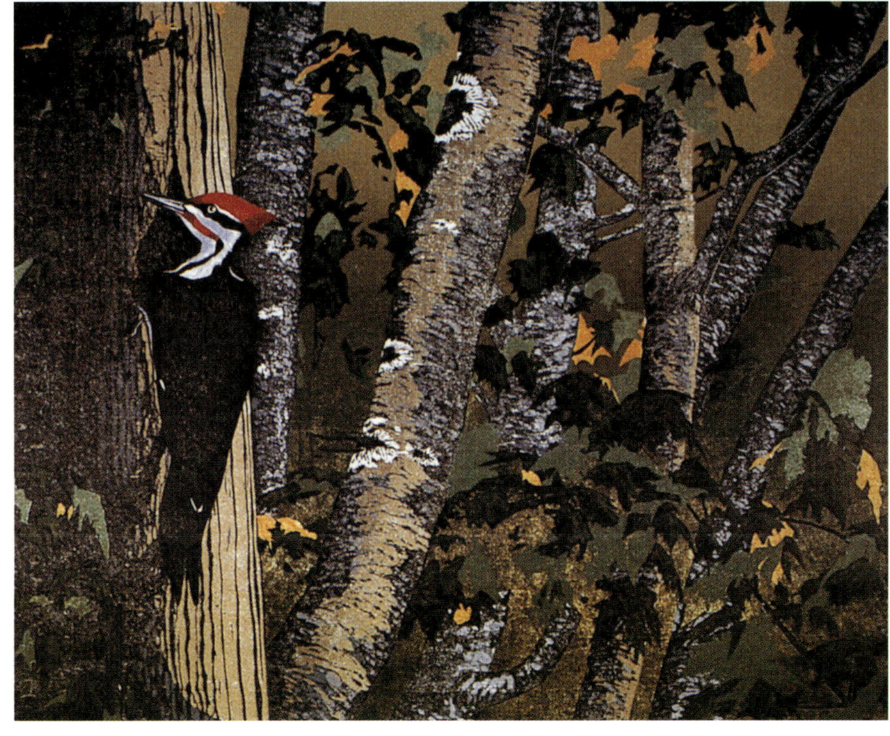

A multicolor woodcut is an image that is printed, usually in a small edition, from the carved surface of woodblock. The process, from the initial design to carving on the block to the final printing, is complex and labor-intensive. Generally it takes Rich nearly a month to complete one woodblock, and the edition might range from twenty to thirty prints. One of her color woodcuts, *Pileated Woodpecker,* illustrates the richness obtainable in wood-block prints. The handsome, crow-sized bird, a species that can be found throughout much of the western United States, is perched on a branch, adjacent limbs festooned with colorful gray, green, and yellow patches of lichen, complimentary to the bird's black and white plumage.

The artists profiled here celebrate the West's startling beauty and its animals in images marked by meaning and depth. In a calling once dominated by an emphasis on scientific illustration and a limited choice of subject matter, artists today search for inspiration from the natural world and the animal kingdom, conveying a wide range of behavioral emotions through expressive styles and techniques. Their dynamic work is driven by a reverence for nature, filtered through their hearts and minds.

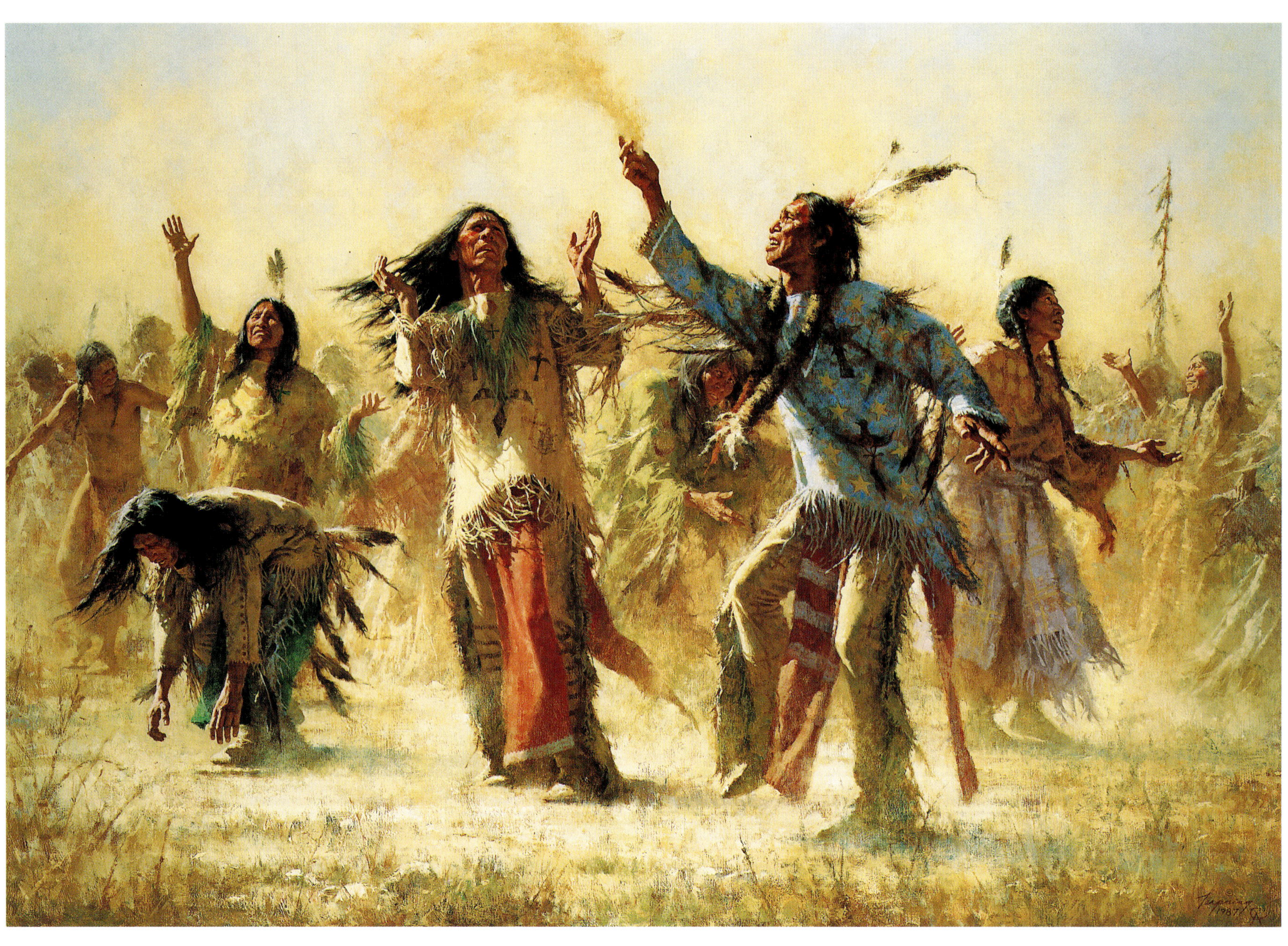

THE ROMANTICIZED WEST
Storytellers

Howard Terpning,
HOPE SPRINGS ETERNAL—
THE GHOST DANCE,
oil on canvas,
44 by 62 inches, 1987.
Private collection; photograph courtesy of The Greenwich Workshop.

THERE IS A VERITABLE ARMY OF PAINTERS AND SCULPTORS WHO TAKE FROM THE PAST AND replicate persistent, overtly Western motifs—cowboys, soldiers, mountain men, settlers, pioneer women, and Native Americans. Often these artists are interpreters of the past first, and painters or sculptors second. For them, story transcends the medium. They are conduits through which the vital myths, legends, and history of the American West are perpetuated and sustained.

These artists envision themselves as purveyors of the Western myth, of heroes, heroines, and heroic events; they are the keepers. They digest the past's cultural experiences, then conjure those experiences onto paper and canvas, or fashion them with stone and bronze, and each creation is like a fly in amber, a slice of time frozen. It transports viewers back to another time and place. Their work reflects commitments to narratives from history and tradition, and attempts to engage viewers in specific stories or anecdotal moments. Many of them pursued earlier careers as illustrators, picture-makers, thorough craftsman who honed their techniques from years of labor.

The work of all of these artists is "Western"—the Old West of cattle ranges, wild mustangs, mountain men, cowhands, frontier soldiers, and proud, breechcloth-clad Indians. While the geographical and cultural realities of the Old West have faded, the idea of the frontier, with its individualism, free enterprise, and romance continues to maintain a presence in this art. For many, Indian warriors, fur trappers, or cowboys are the heroes, nature's anarchists, solitary individuals unaffected by urban civilization, endowed with toughness and honesty. They use this and many other examples of the great mythical sagas of the nineteenth century to comment on what is useful for today.

Other artists in this genre seek their inspiration from different sources; for example, Ted Rose turns to historical railroads to inspire his watercolors, and Star Liana York and Glenna Goodacre portray women and children in their sculptures. Their work, and that of others, may not reach far back in time, but instead draw images from the present. Nevertheless, their paintings and sculpture project a feel for storytelling and the storied past.

One successful illustrator, **HOWARD TERPNING** (b. 1927), took his friend Don Crowley's advice and started to paint Western historical scenes in 1975. By 1977, after twenty-five years in commercial art, he severed those connections and moved to Tucson. Terpning had always known he would be an artist, and after military service he had studied at the Chicago Academy of Fine Arts and the American Academy of Art, also in Chicago. His rise in the world of illustration art had been meteoric. He created art for more than eighty movie posters, for such films as *The Sound of Music, The Guns of Navarone,* and *Cleopatra.* He also produced covers for magazines like *Reader's Digest, Time, Newsweek,* and *Ladies' Home Journal.*

Noted for their emotional, spiritual content, Terpning's paintings address the historical lifeways of the Plains Indians. One of them secured the Prix de West at the National Cowboy Hall of Fame in 1981, and another received the Hall's Frederic Remington Award in 1992. In 1979, Terpning joined the Cowboy Artists of America, and he has exhibited at their annual events. The Gilcrease Museum gave him a one-man show in 1985. The Hubbard Museum (Ruidoso, New Mexico), now the Museum of the Horse, awarded him their Hubbard Award of Excellence in 1990.

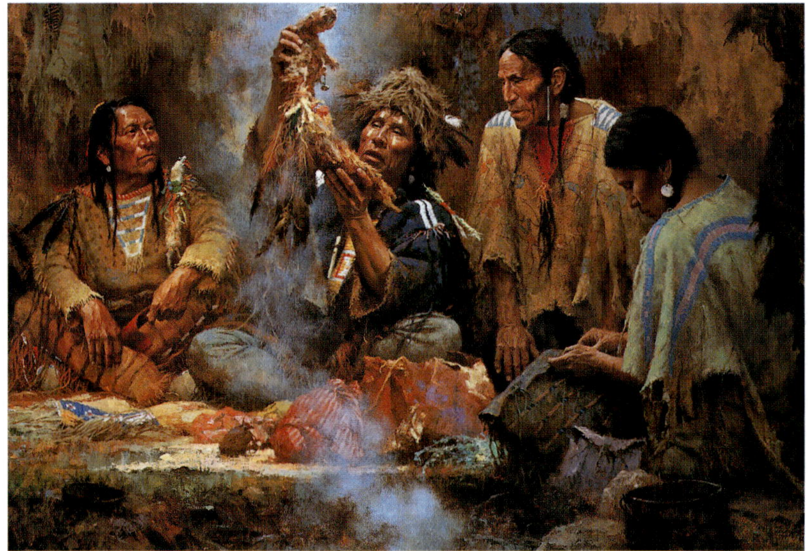

Howard Terpning,
OPENING OF THE SACRED BUNDLE,
oil on canvas,
38 by 56 inches, 1994.
Private collection; photograph courtesy of The Greenwich Workshop.

Terpning tries to capture, with an almost theatrical approach, the moment and mood of the subjects in his paintings, as in *Hope Springs Eternal—The Ghost Dance* (p. 92). The time is around 1890, and the Ghost Dance has swept through the Plains tribes, particularly the Lakota and Cheyenne. Some Plains Indians, a few attired in Ghost Dance clothing, dance frenetically, imploring the spirits of the departed to return. Another one of his works, *Opening of the Sacred Bundle,* reflects the meditative, symbolic mysticism of Plains Indian life.

KENNETH RILEY (b. 1919) had always had an interest in art, fueled by parents and teachers. After he graduated from high school, Riley attended the Kansas City Art Institute, where one of his teachers was Thomas Hart Benton. He went on to the Art Students League and the Grand Central Art School in New York, where he studied with Harvey Dunn and Frank Vincent DuMond, among others.

Riley embarked upon his distinguished career as an illustrator in 1947, and for twenty-five years his work appeared in *The Saturday Evening Post, Life, National Geographic,* and *Reader's Digest.* His interest in the West and Western history prompted a move to Tucson in the early 1970s.

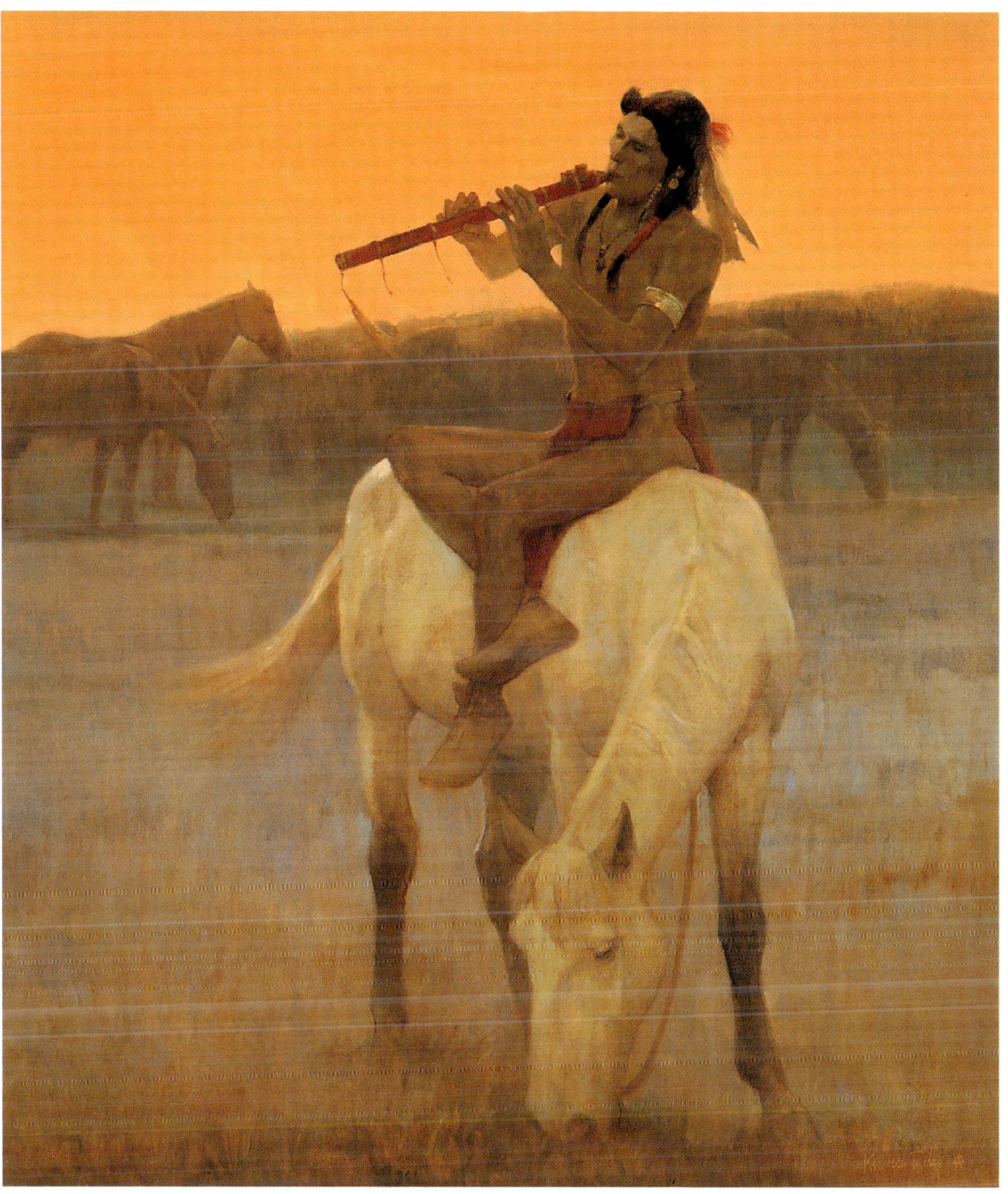

Kenneth Riley,
THE RED FLUTE,
oil on canvas,
24 by 28 inches, 1996.
Private collection.

Most of Riley's subjects involve episodes from Native American history. Events drawn from the Apache Wars appeared in his early paintings, but eventually he turned to the Plains Indians.

The Cowboy Artists of America invited Riley to join their membership in 1982, and he has exhibited in their annual shows since. Riley's paintings are included in the collections of the White House, the West Point Museum, the Smithsonian Institution, and the Air Force Academy. In 1995, he received the Prix de West from the National Cowboy Hall of Fame.

When Riley commenced painting in the early 1970s, he brought his love for the figure and an illustrator's approach to the work. His paintings rely on written accounts, especially diaries. "Original journals are inspirational, since they are not watered down through successive interpretation," he says. Riley filters his research on Plains Indian cultures through his own personal revelations about harmony and perfection in art. The painting *As One,* (page xiv), for example, shows a painted warrior, attired in his finest clothing and personal adornment, posed next to his horse, who is equally adorned in a tapestry of beadwork. Another painting, *The Red Flute* (p. 95), is a portrait of a young Indian man astride his horse, playing a flute. Both of these paintings project a somber, mystical feel. They are momentary stories, but they also say something about Riley's composition and arrangement. In other words, his design tools. As he says, "The value of my paintings is not in the external image but in what I have brought to the two-dimensional surface in terms of light, line, color, and other combinations."

The value of my paintings is not in the external image
but in what I have brought to the two-dimensional surface
in terms of light, line, color, and other combinations.

—KENNETH RILEY

Much as Kenneth Riley does, **TOM LOVELL** (b. 1909) recreates, on an epic scale, paintings that respond to the drama of the nineteenth-century American West. As author Byron Jones wrote in *Southwest Art,* "His paintings are rooted in history, they tell the story of the past; they speak of peoples and places and character of the land; they tell of faith, greed, ambition, and leadership; they picture drama and danger, exploration and conquest; most of all they make the past vibrant and dynamic, they make it come alive."

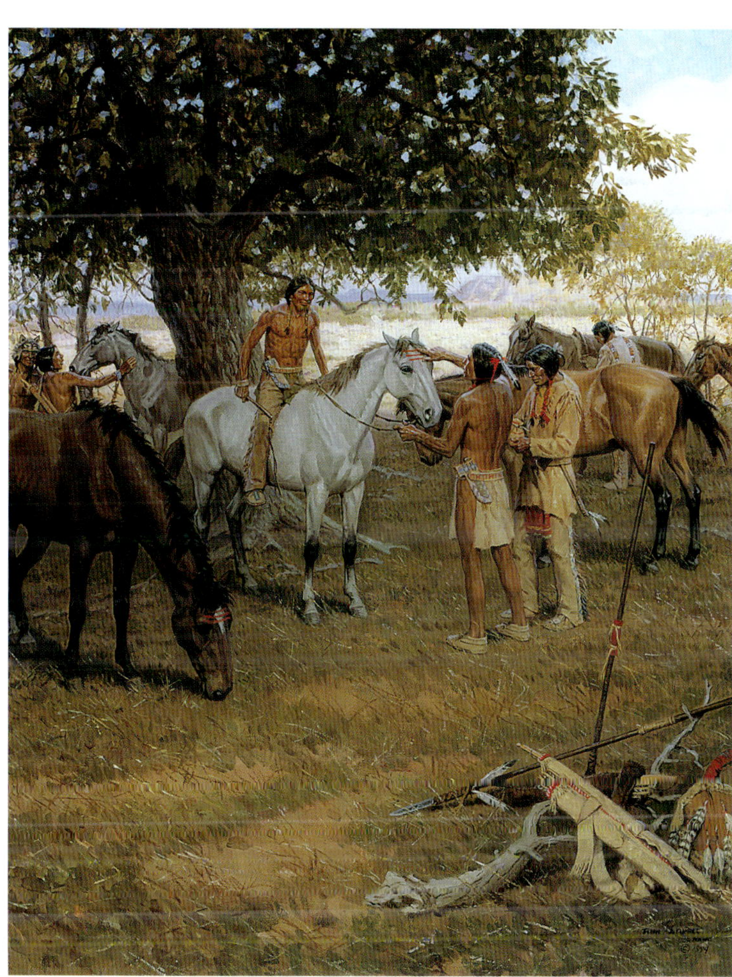

Tom Lovell,
PAINTING THE STOLEN HORSES,
oil on canvas, 36 by 28 inches, 1994.
Private collection.

Lovell's early career included work as an illustrator for magazines such as *Collier's, Life, National Geographic,* and *Time.* He also illustrated novels by Sinclair Lewis and Edna Ferber. In recognition of his contributions to the field of illustration, the Society of Illustrators elected him to their Hall of Fame in 1974. The National Cowboy Hall of Fame awarded him their Prix de West in 1974, then again in 1986. In 1992, they honored Lovell with a retrospective of his art, along with their Lifetime Achievement Award.

Noted for meticulous detail and historical accuracy in his paintings, Lovell attempts to absorb everything about the historical scene he intends to paint. Artifacts, photographs, and other materials are studied carefully for their insight and knowledge. Lovell's intent is the creation of an imaginative art that relates to the human experience, mostly of Plains Indians, and the Western heritage.

Viewers are placed in a "you are there" perspective, as in, for example, *Painting the Stolen Horses.* "Horses were wealth to the Plains Indians, and horse raids were a dangerous and rewarding part of a warrior's life," says Lovell. "Here, after a successful foray, a returning party stops outside of their village to clean themselves and their ponies before entering in triumph. They are painting horizontal red stripes on the foreheads of the captured horses to mark them plainly for the home folks."

PAUL CALLE (b. 1928), like Tom Lovell, is often considered a visual historian, known as an artist who chronicles the American past, specifically mountain men and fur trappers, in tightly controlled, sensitive drawings and paintings. He completed high school at fifteen and graduated from the Pratt Institute of Art in Brooklyn by nineteen. One of his most noted accomplishments is the first-man-on-the-moon postage stamp, which he designed for the U.S. Postal Service in 1969. In fact, Calle sees a parallel between space exploration and the Western experience.

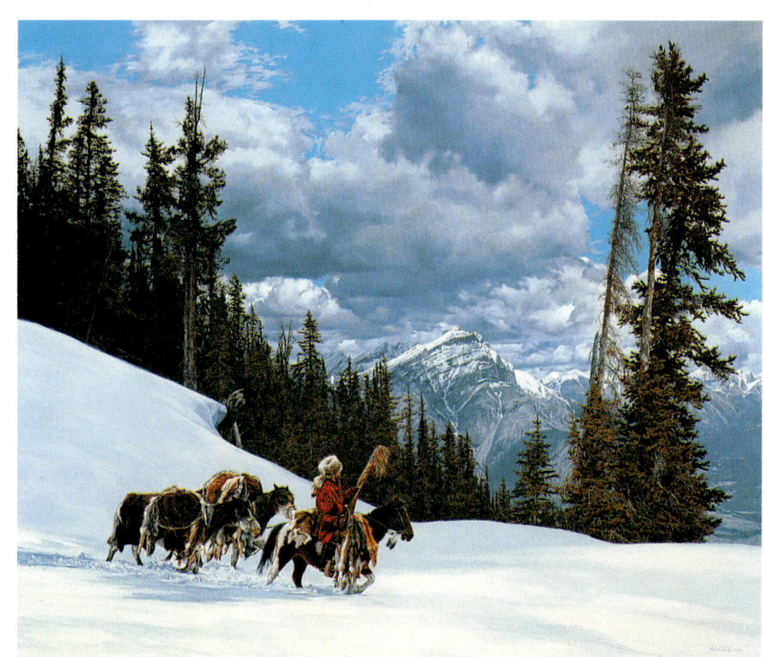

Paul Calle,
INTO THE GREAT ALONE,
oil on panel,
42 by 48 inches, 1987.
Private collection.

Calle has received the Franklin Mint Gold Medal for Distinguished Western Art, and a silver medal from the National Academy of Western Art. At the first National Cowboy Hall of Fame *Prix de West Invitational* in 1995, Calle received the Buyers Choice Award. The Gilcrease Museum held a retrospective of his work in 1991. His paintings and drawings have been exhibited at a wide range of institutions, including the National Air and Space Museum, the U.S. Department of the Interior, the Phoenix Art Museum, the National Gallery of Art, and the Autry Museum of Western Heritage.

The fur trade era, a relatively brief span of American history in the early 1800s, is Calle's passionate pursuit in art. He creates paintings that portray rugged fur trappers and their grandiose dreams, indulging in conjecture, depicting the history of these individuals as "what might have been." An avid researcher, Calle often attends annual rendezvous held in Canada and the western United States. As he traces the trails where fur trappers walked or camped, Calle muses, "When I'm in the meadow or woods, watching elk, buffalo, eagles, and beaver, I see in my mind's eye the mountain men at work. For those moments I'm with them."

"If I had to state a goal," Calle continues, "a hope pertaining to my work, my aim would be to help keep alive that huge reservoir of our past, to draw strength and sustenance from it, to build upon it in ways that are new and different, but not reject it." As an example, consider his painting, *Into the Great Alone,* in which he depicts the singular fortitude and bravery of the mountain man, or *In the Beginning . . . Friends,* where a fur trapper and an Indian stand beside each other, at the moment bonded through their mutual goals of wrestling a livelihood from the wilderness.

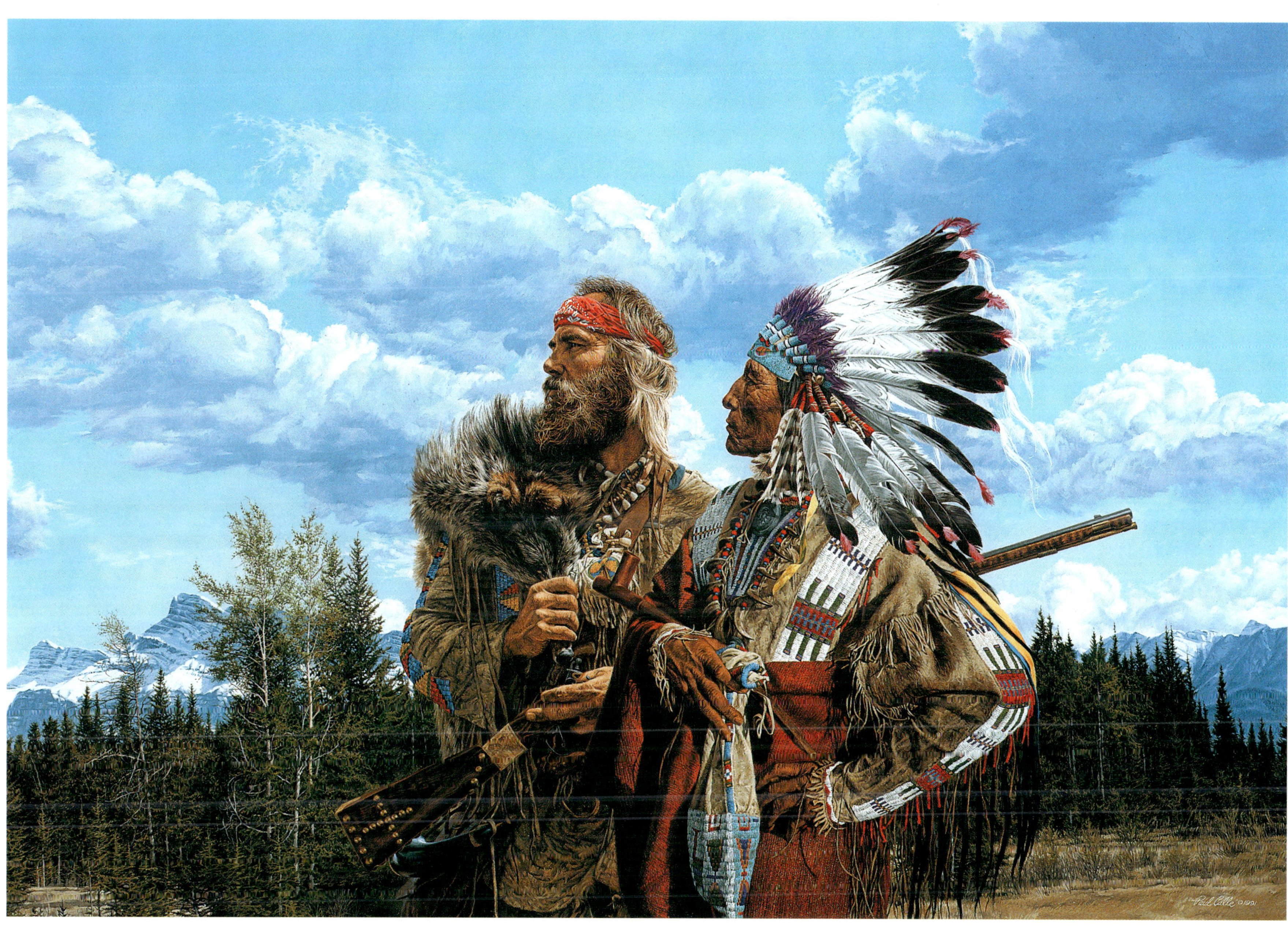

Paul Calle, IN THE BEGINNING . . . FRIENDS, *oil on panel, 33 5/8 by 48 7/8 inches, 1991. Private collection.*

Roy Andersen (b. 1930) knew from an early age that art would be an eventual career. While still in elementary school, he enrolled in courses at the Art Institute of Chicago, then later, during high school, in drawing classes at the Field Museum of Natural History. There, Andersen became interested in the museum's magnificent Native American collection, and began to sketch the artifacts on display.

Andersen went on to attend the Chicago Academy of Fine Arts and the Art Center College of Design in California. Afterwards he worked as a professional illustrator. Some of his artwork appeared as covers on *Time, Sports Illustrated,* and *National Geographic,* in addition to movie posters and book jackets. Andersen also has more than a dozen U.S. postage stamps to his credit. Elected to membership in the Cowboy Artists of America in 1989, he has acquired both gold and silver medals in several of their annual exhibitions.

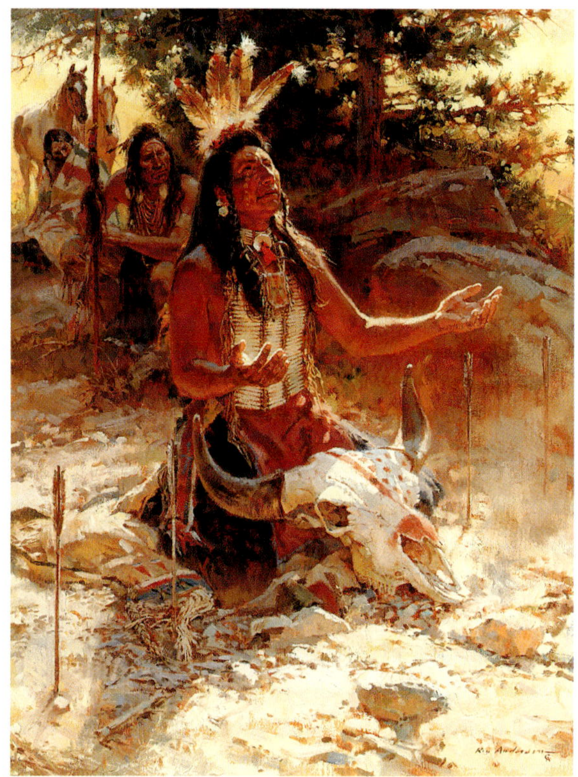

Roy Andersen,
SONG OF THE BUFFALO CALLER,
oil on canvas,
40 by 30 inches, 1992.
Private collection.

Andersen's painting subjects center on stories drawn from the historic American West, especially ones that involve the Crow, Cheyenne, and Apache Indians. Empathy is the dominant factor in his paintings, which are endowed with spirit and emotion, visual mythologies of a vanished West. With narrative realism, Andersen brings to life Native American history and tradition, as in *Song of the Buffalo Caller,* his idea of what might transpire when Plains Indians attempt to access the spirits associated with the buffalo. Another painting, *When Ponies Need Grass,* portrays a Plains Indian group forced to move on in search of new grazing ground for their pony herd. With the sure grasp of an illustrator, anchored with an impressionistic painting technique, Andersen captures the visual grandeur of the past in these canvases.

Sculptor **Richard Greeves** (b. 1935) first encountered Fort Washakie on the Wind River Reservation in Wyoming at the age of fifteen. Several years later he returned to make his home there. Primarily self-taught, Greeves has produced an important body of bronze sculpture centered on Native Americans, particularly the Shoshone, Arapaho, and other Plains tribes. For Greeves, the goal is to discover the character and spiritual undertones of the region's inhabitants.

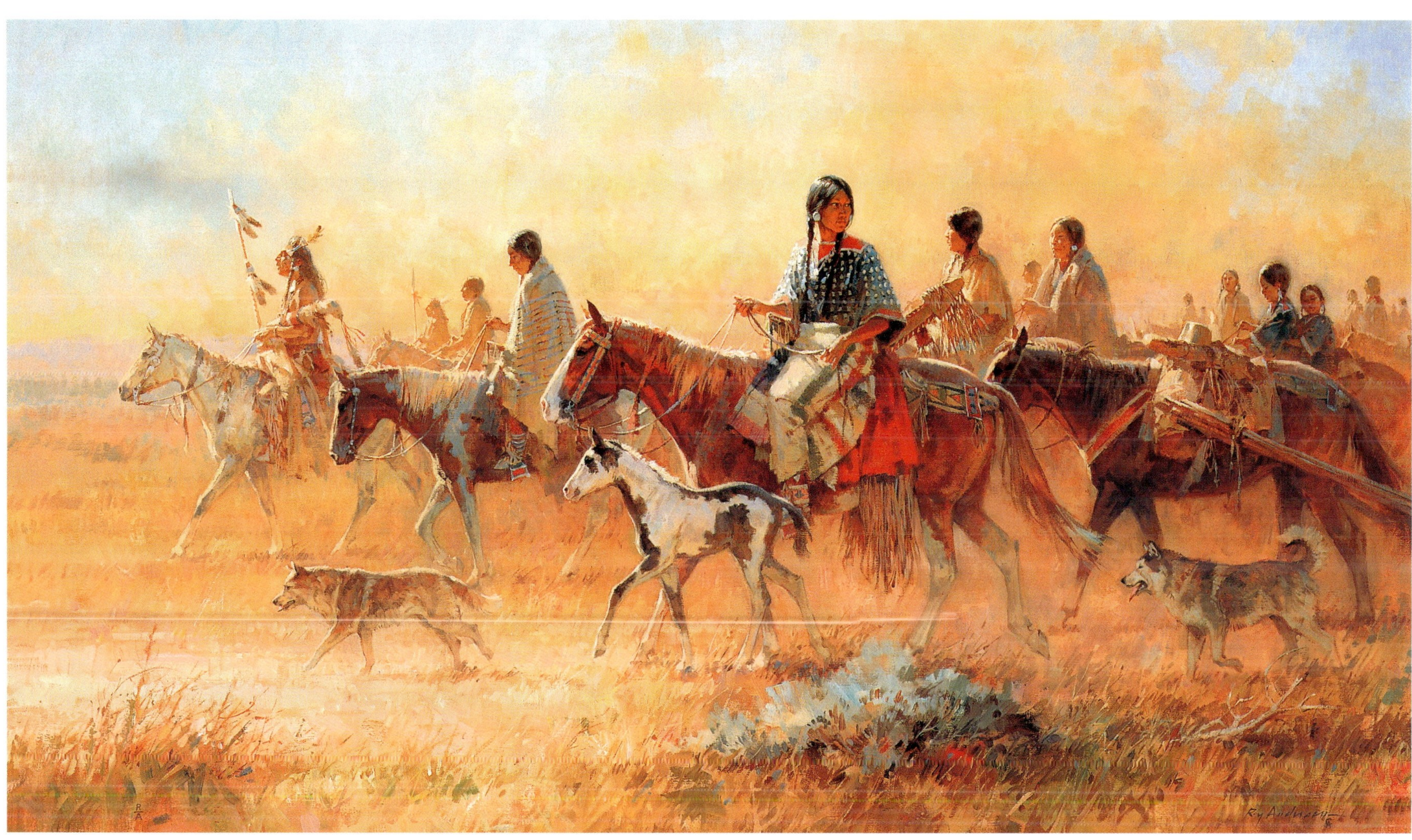

Roy Andersen, WHEN PONIES NEED GRASS, *oil on canvas, 30 by 50 inches, 1995. Private collection.*

Greeves resides along the eastern fringe of Wyoming's Wind River Range, amidst the people he selects as subjects for his art—the Shoshones and Arapahos of the Wind River Reservation. Since 1969, Greeves has exhibited his work at museums like the National Cowboy Hall of Fame, the Wyoming State Museum, the Buffalo Bill Historical Center, and the High Plains Heritage Center. Among his awards are gold and silver medals from the National Academy of Western Art. His sculptures are located in various collections, among them the National Cowboy Hall of Fame, the Indianapolis Art Museum, the Wyoming State Museum, and the Buffalo Bill Historical Center, where his monumental bronze, *The Unknown,* greets visitors.

While Greeves will portray the trapper, trader, and cowboys of past eras, his favorite subjects are Native Americans. He feels his mission as an artist is to tell a story, and to communicate thoughts about what is important. "I'm just trying to bridge these cultures with ones that come after us," he says. Greeves's bronze sculptures are direct and forceful, like *Pawnee.* The Pawnee, he explains, as with a number of Indian tribes, translate their name as *the People.* "I tried to sculpt into this portrait the interpretation that he views his enemy and most of the world as being a level beneath himself," Greeves says.

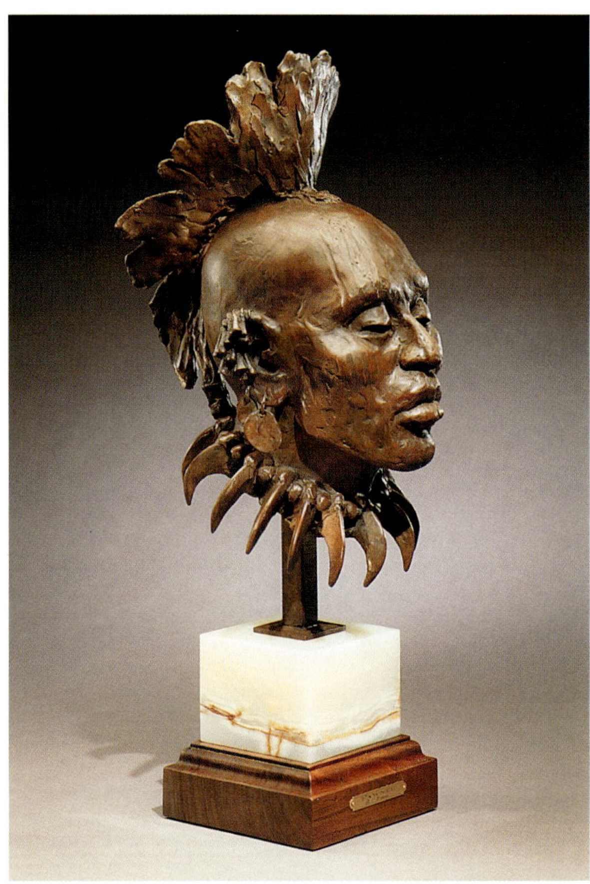

Richard Greeves,
PAWNEE,
bronze (edition of 10),
21 by 10 by 8 inches, 1996.

Born in Edmonton, Alberta, Canada, **HARLEY BROWN** (b. 1939) grew up in Moose Jaw, Saskatchewan, then attended the Alberta College of Art in Calgary, Alberta. Eager for a change, he bought one-way tickets to England for himself, his wife, and their young son, and studied art at England's Camberwill School of Art for two years. His career as a portrait painter started with a commission to paint Winston Churchill. Churchill had recently died, though, which forced Brown to work from photographs to complete the assignment. Afterwards, he specialized in portraits of entertainment and political figures, among them Ronald Reagan.

When he returned to Canada in 1966, Brown decided to paint portraits of Native Americans on reservations along the United States–Canada border. In recognition of this work, the Montana

If you allow yourself to relax and not tell some big story, great things come from small, inconsequential moments.

—HARLEY BROWN

Historical Society hosted a one-man show for him in 1973. Several years later, Robert Lougheed invited Brown in to submit some of his work to the National Cowboy Hall of Fame. The Hall awarded him a gold medal for drawing in 1977, followed by the Robert M. Lougheed Memorial Award in 1990.

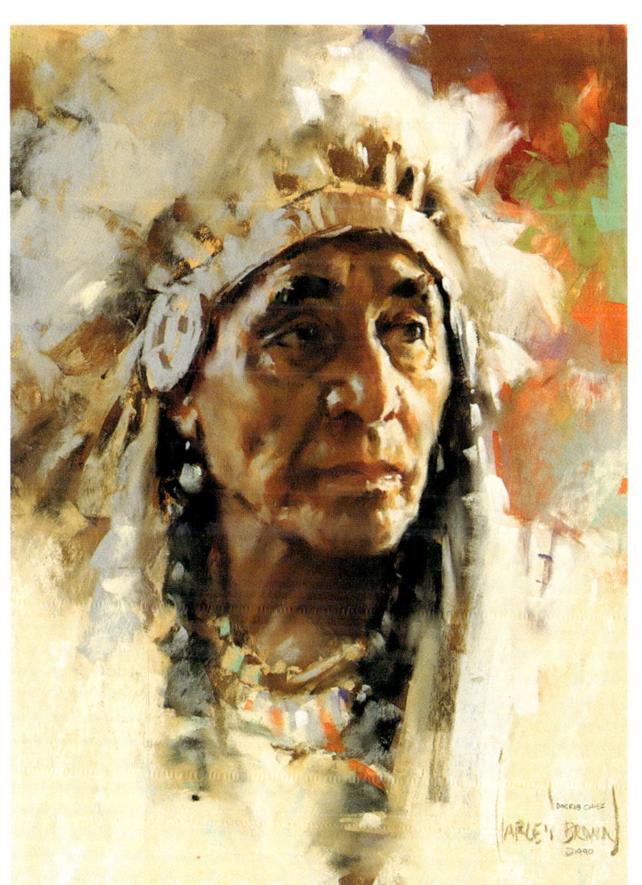

Harley Brown, DOG RIB CHIEF, *pastel on paper, 17 by 14 inches, 1990. Private collection.*

Brown typically uses pastel, a medium he feels captures the expressiveness of his subjects' faces. Now living in Tucson, Brown travels from Mexico to Canada's Northwest Territories in search of his subjects. "In particular," Brown explains, "I don't try to tell a story that is not already there. If you allow yourself to relax and not tell some big story, great things come from small, inconsequential moments."

And what does Brown search for in his portraits? "The face," he says, "the aura," like the one in *Dog Rib Chief.* As Brown recalls, "I met this man in the barren wastes of Canada's Northwest Territories, near the Great Slave Lake. He couldn't be more happy with his lot, as he sat in a very sparse one-room cabin. He put on his ceremonial bonnet and sat for me. A solitary bulb lit one side of his face, and a cool north light from a window lit the other side. To me, there is nothing on earth to match the structure of the human face."

The art of **FRANK C. MCCARTHY** (b. 1924) seethes with action, celebrating the life and conflicts of a nineteenth-century heroic West, in which massed groups of fierce men adorned for war, and their horses, thunder down hillsides; cavalrymen, strung out in line across the landscape, gallop headlong into battle; and Indian hunters ride amongst frenzied bison.

McCarthy studied summers with George Bridgeman and Reginald Marsh at the Art Students League in New York, then attended the Pratt Institute of Art in Brooklyn. In 1948 he established his own studio. Inspired by N. C. Wyeth's colorful illustrations and Will James's horse and cowboy books, McCarthy proceeded to paint hundreds of illustrations for magazines, advertising, and movie posters (including some for James Bond movies) for two decades.

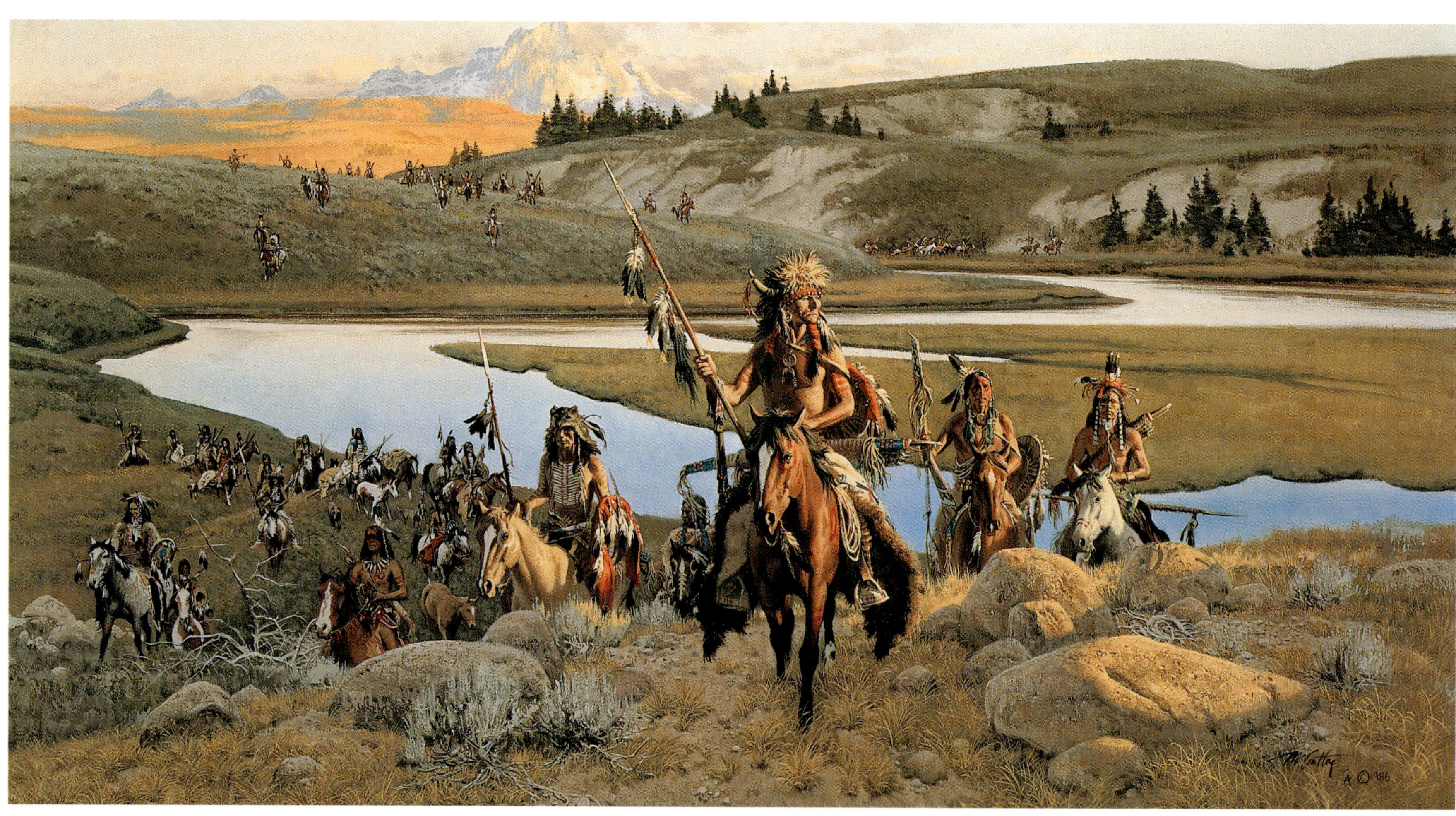

Frank C. McCarthy, AFTER THE COUNCIL, *oil on canvas, 16 by 30 inches, 1986. Private collection; photograph courtesy of The Greenwich Workshop.*

*My approach to painting is not to do a historical document.
It is more a portrayal of an event or scene that has transpired
many times in many places in the West.*

—FRANK C. McCARTHY

In 1969, McCarthy started painting Western subjects for galleries, and received such an immediate response that he left commercial work in 1971. Since then, his career has focused on Indians, mountain men, cavalry, and cowboys, with an epic feel that pulls viewers into an action-filled scene. McCarthy has had numerous one-man and group exhibitions, and regularly shows at annual Cowboy Artists of America events, which he joined in 1975. Retrospectives of his work have been held at the Gilcrease Museum, the Museum of the Southwest, and the R. W. Norton Art Museum. Over one hundred of his paintings have been published so far as limited-edition prints through collaboration with the Greenwich Workshop.

Dramatic and flamboyant, McCarthy's paintings move with the classic feel of John Ford's Western films. They embody energy, bravery, the menace of conflict, and sometimes potential death. A realist painter, McCarthy strives for veracity in his work, with details in the subjects and landscapes carefully transcribed. Each painting is executed with attention to the clarity of light and the feel of space. "My approach to painting is not to do a historical document," he says. "It is more a portrayal of an event or scene that has transpired many times in many places in the West. I give the scene visual impact. The details are as accurate as I can make them." One of McCarthy's paintings, *After the Council,* illustrates his pictorial approach. The painting is McCarthy's story about bands of Lakotas who disperse toward individual camping grounds after conclusion of a tribal council. Designated warriors take the lead while others serve as outriders, guarding the flanks along the Yellowstone River.

Herb Mignery,
THE HUNGRY LOOP,
bronze (edition of 20),
23 by 17½ by 11 inches, 1990.

In contrast, the sculpture of **HERB MIGNERY** (b. 1937) is drawn from memories of his childhood on the family cattle ranch near Bartlett, Nebraska, inspired by the strength of ranchers and farmers who work and stay on the land. Mignery senses beauty in the quiet stamina of these people, and his bronze sculptures remind viewers of another part of the West's history. After Mignery completed a two-year tour of duty as an illustrator in the U.S. Army at the end of 1963, he briefly worked in a number of art-related jobs and played guitar in a band. Primarily self-taught, he was employed as a commercial artist in Hastings, Nebraska, until 1973, when he cast his first bronze and decided to pursue a career as a sculptor. The only award Mignery says he ever really desired is the vote of the Cowboy Artists of America that brought him into their ranks in 1984. The organization elected him president nine years later. Mignery has exhibited at the National Academy of Western Art, the Joslyn Art Museum, the Museum of the Horse, and others. In 1994, the Academy of Country Music commissioned Mignery to create a life-size sculpture for their Pioneer Award. Another monumental sculpture was produced for the one hundedth annual Cheyenne Frontier Days.

In the studio behind his home in Estes Park, Colorado, Mignery creates bronze sculptures that capture the mood and common everyday experiences of the rugged cowboy and the hard-working farmer. One example is *The Hungry Loop* (p. 105), portraying an African-American cowboy and his horse, both burdened by hard times. The man and his mount's quiet stoicism are reflective of their hard life.

TED ROSE (b. 1940) has a passion for railroads, which started when he took his first train ride in 1949 to a railroad fair in Chicago. Then, in the mid-1950s, a teenaged Rose traveled throughout the United States and Canada, photographing and sketching in watercolor what he sensed was the twilight of the steam locomotive.

After receiving a B.F.A. from the University of Illinois in 1962, Rose served in Vietnam, and upon his return settled in Chama, New Mexico. In 1966 he moved to Santa Fe, where he opened a graphic design business. In 1983 he started to paint watercolors full time, with a nostalgic focus on the days when steam ruled the railroads. Rose is a signature member of the New Mexico Watercolor Society and a member of the American Watercolor Society. Recently *New Mexico Magazine* honored him as their Distinguished Artist for 1997.

Ted Rose,
THREE BELOW AT MONERO,
watercolor,
22 by 30 inches, 1995.
Collection of the artist.

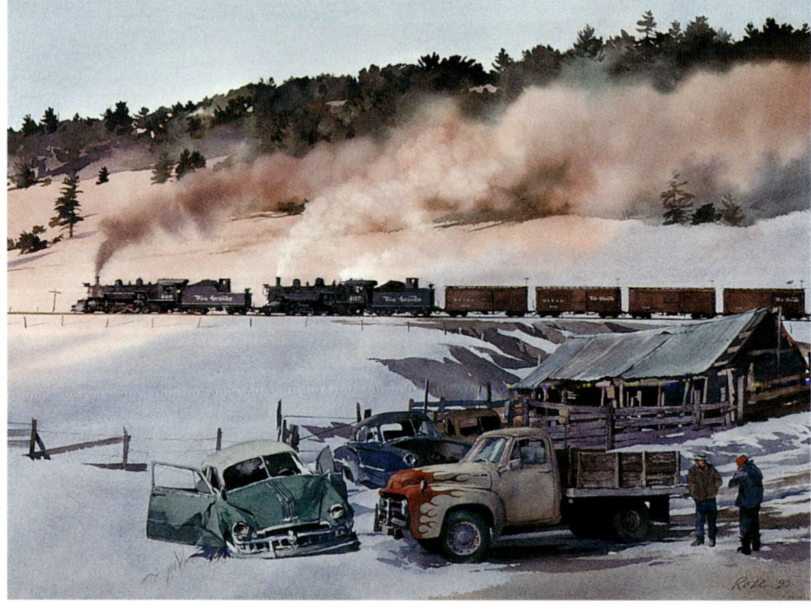

I try to show the Indian philosophy of life.

—STAR LIANA YORK

Rose finds watercolor offers greater options than oil, and is more malleable. "Watercolor is direct; there is almost no complexity in the preparation of the painting aspects of it," Rose says. First he visualizes a prospective painting, then he sketches reference points to understand if what he imagined works on paper. His camera is the sketchbook, but he rarely creates one of his almost photographic watercolors from a single image. Often he searches for illustrations by Depression-era photographers Dorothea Lange and Walker Evans for background material, and even consults old timetables to ensure he is accurate about the exact time of a train's departure from a depot.

One of his watercolors, *Three Below at Monero,* is a memory from the time he lived in Chama, presents the last vestiges of the Denver and Rio Grande Railroad's narrow gauge operations in New Mexico during the mid-1960s. Two locomotives struggle with a freight through Monero and up the grade toward Chama. On this frozen early morning, there is indeed an end of the line ahead, for abandonment looms in 1968.

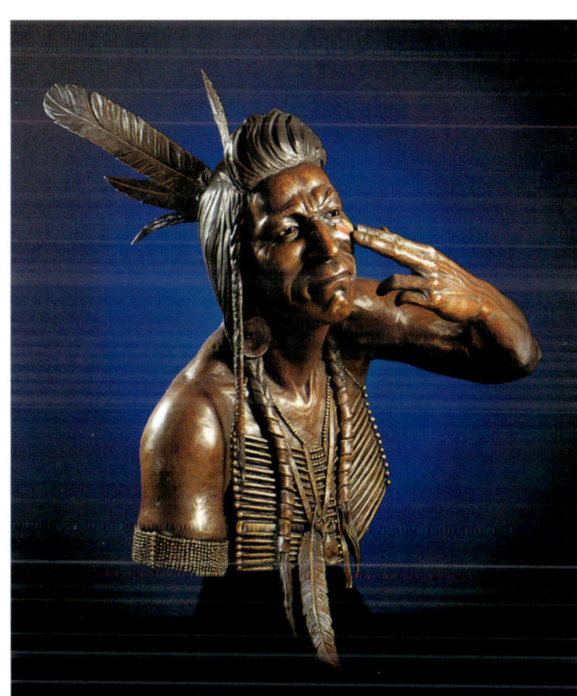

Star Liana York,
WAR MAGIC,
bronze (edition of 30),
28 inches high, 1989.

When **STAR LIANA YORK** (b. 1952) moved to the Southwest in 1985, she felt immediately drawn into the landscape of contemporary American culture, particularly the mythic, heroic aspects of traditional Western lifestyles. York, raised in Washington, D.C., found her creativity nurtured by her mother, a ballerina, and her father, who built the sets in front of which her mother performed. She attended the University of Maryland, then worked as artist-in-residence at a community college in Maryland, where she taught classes in metal design and lost-wax processes. In addition, she fabricated figures for display at the Smithsonian Institution, and for sale through mail-order companies.

As York encountered the Native Americans and other residents of the Southwest after she moved to New Mexico, her work shifted from illustrative, detailed narrative to more emotionally charged interpretations. Stories told by old-time Westerners, or an invitation to observe a private coming-of-age ceremony for a Navajo girl, led York to understand the personal gestures and expressions in prospective subjects. She began to create sculpture that probed an individual's emotions, to communicate those characteristics that make each subject unique. "I try to show the Indian philosophy of life," York says.

York focuses on three-dimensional "people portraits" and wildlife subjects. In her studio, located near Abiquiu, New Mexico, York creates bronze sculptures noted for their imaginative moods. There is no reliance on preliminary sketches, nor models, and she rarely uses photographs. The sculpture is assembled in her mind as she searches for ideas that make people or animals real. When the idea arrives, as with *War Magic,* she begins with clay, shapes the form until ready for a silicon mold, then finally casts the image in bronze. York utilizes various patinas, from polychrome and golden brown to occasional swaths of color.

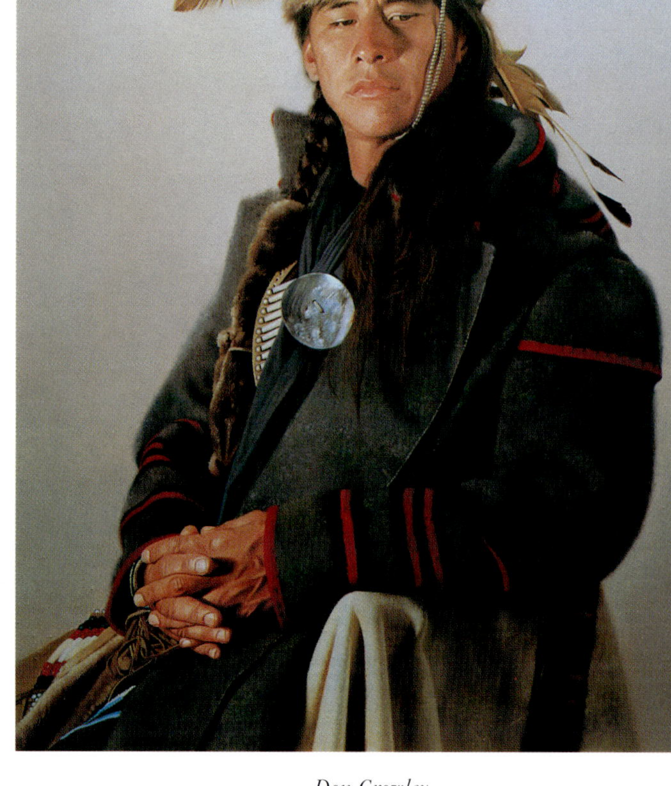

Don Crowley,
WINTER COAT,
oil on canvas,
30 by 24 inches, 1991.
Private collection.

In his art, **DON CROWLEY** (b. 1926) focuses on Native Americans—Paiutes, Pimas, Apaches, and Shoshones. Born in Redlands, California, Crowley served in the merchant marines and the U.S. Navy for four years. After military service, he attended the Art Center College of Design in Los Angeles. He moved to New York in 1953 and worked for the Charles Cooper Studios, where he produced portraits for *Reader's Digest,* covers for Dorothy Sayers mysteries, and posters for a cruise line, among other assignments. He worked at Cooper Studios for seven years, then pursued freelance illustration.

A fellow illustrator moved to Wyoming in the early 1970s and started to paint Western subjects. This encouraged Crowley to consider a similar change, so in 1974, he and his wife moved to Tucson. There, in his large studio, he creates paintings with precise, photographic detail and complex

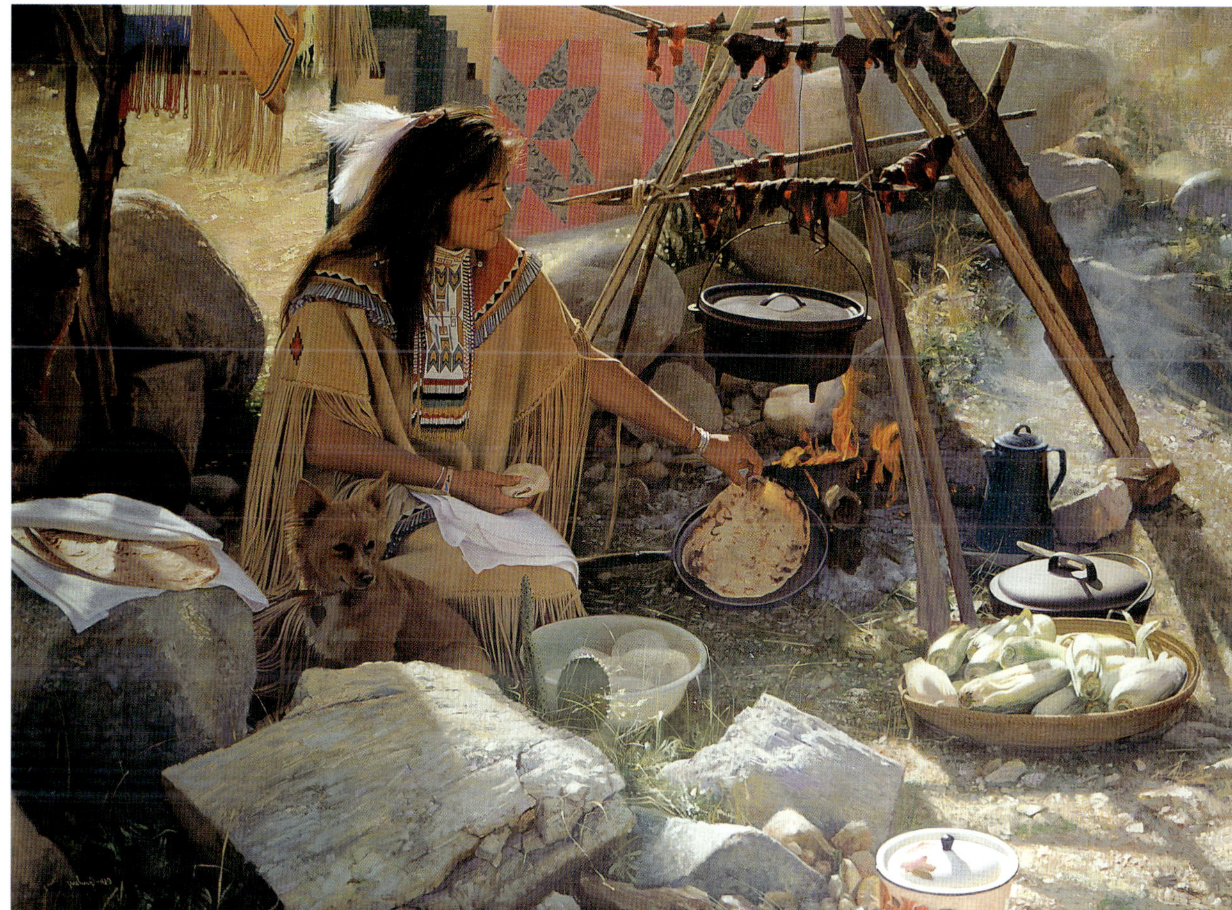

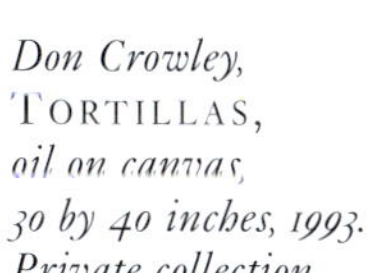

Don Crowley,
TORTILLAS,
oil on canvas,
30 by 40 inches, 1993.
Private collection.

design that chronicle the attitudes, costumes, and traditions of Native Americans. A member of the Cowboy Artists of America since 1994, Crowley walked away with every major award, including the award for best overall work, in that organization's 1996 exhibition at the Phoenix Art Museum.

While Crowley has worked with one family from the San Carlos Reservation for nearly two decades, other models come and pose for him. He positions them, then photographs the individuals in color to record the details of their costumes. He also draws from an extensive collection of photographs of various Indian groups and artifacts, and visits museums.

Fascinated with detail, Crowley determined early in his career that he preferred to paint subjects posed in front of him, rather than the reincarnation of historical scenes. Each painting narrates a personal story. One of them, *Winter Coat* (p. 108), depicts a young man attired in a wool coat, almost reminiscent of the nineteenth century. "When this young Shoshone boy came to pose for me, he brought this wool winter coat he was in the process of making," says Crowley. "I was interested in his strong features and the dignity of his bearing. The coat made a perfect prop to enhance those qualities." Another example of his work, *Tortillas* (p. 109), captures the noble bearing of a Native American woman, surrounded by the intricate detail of cooking utensils, textiles, and other objects.

Garland A. Weeks,
COW BOSS,
bronze (edition of 20), life size, 1990.

In 1971, **GARLAND A. WEEKS** (b. 1942) started to create small sculptures in wax, an experience that eventually shaped his career as a sculptor. Weeks grew up around Wichita Falls, Texas, and before he became an artist, held a variety of jobs. At one time, Weeks was a rodeo champion at Texas Tech University, and after graduation rode professionally. He intimately knows cowboys, their horses, and the other features that surround ranch and farm life.

Weeks studied briefly at an art school in Chicago, and privately with a number of prominent American sculptors. In addition, he examined the works of sculptors such as Daniel Chester French, Alexander P. Proctor, and others, in search of the four attributes he believes sculpture must possess: design unity, compact form, simplicity of outline, and nobility of concept.

Now a resident of Mason, Texas, Weeks's bronze sculptures of Western men and women have brought him membership in the National Sculpture Society, the Texas Cowboy Artists Association, the National Academy of Western Art, and the British Art Medal Society. The Texas state legislature designated Weeks the official state sculptor of Texas in 1995. He has done commissions for the Mercedes Boot Company, the National Cattlemen's Association, Texas Tech University, and Cutter Laboratories, among others.

As a productive sculptor, it is my duty to keep within the modern grasp a spiritual legacy inherited from earlier cultures, not by imitating past work, but by keeping alive their values.

—GARLAND A. WEEKS

As a sculptor who works within a traditional, figurative mode, Weeks's bronzes portray the quieter, intimate, and more introspective side of Western life. He sculpts with the realization that not everyone in the West rode bucking horses or pursued stampeding cattle. One of his bronzes, *Cow Boss,* is an example. "As a productive sculptor, it is my duty to keep within the modern grasp a spiritual legacy inherited from earlier cultures, not by imitating past work, but by keeping alive their values," he says.

When **EDWARD J. FRAUGHTON** (b. 1939) discovered he had won first place for crayon art, judged by a panel of nationally famous artists, he felt thunderstruck. His drawing of the Park City, Utah, train depot had won the Milton Bradley Company's 1949 "America the Beautiful" crayon art competition, judged the most outstanding in the state of Utah among fourth-grade students. He was inspired to pursue his interest in art.

Edward J. Fraughton,
THE COWBOY,
bronze (edition of 20),
29 by 34 by 18 inches, 1988.

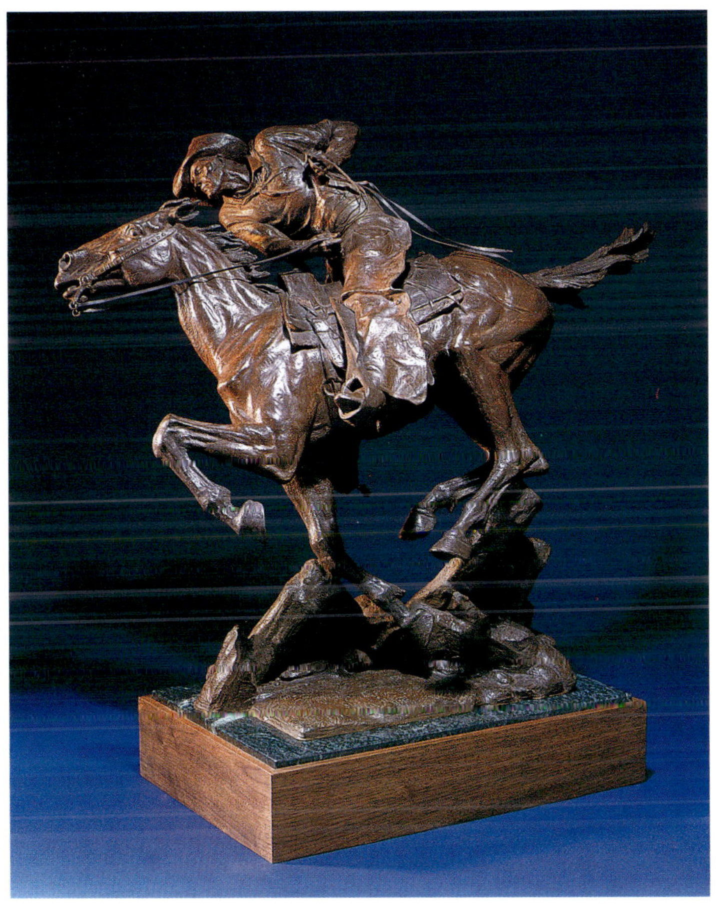

Fraughton, raised in Park City, graduated from the University of Utah with a B.F.A., then pursued further graduate studies. Attracted to sculpture, he studied four years with the noted Utah sculptor Avard Fairbanks, a former student of James Earle Fraser. Only six years after graduation, in 1968, Fraughton received his first important commission, the Mormon Battalion monument on top of Presidio Hill, in Old Town San Diego. Another monumental bronze, the fourteen-foot-high *Spirit of Wyoming,* is installed on the state capitol grounds in Cheyenne. Fraughton, a longtime member of the National Sculpture Society, is also a founding member of the National Academy of Western Art, and won a gold medal for sculpture at the group's 1973 and 1975 National Cowboy Hall of Fame exhibitions. His sculpture has also been featured at the Gilcrease Museum and the Northwest Rendezvous Group.

Done as a prospective monumental sculpture for a competition, one of his bronzes, *The Cowboy,* illustrates Fraughton's interest in cowboys and horses. Fraughton wanted a sculpture that symbolized a cowboy on a running horse, an almost universal image in the saga of the American

West. "The cowboy comes closest to being a Greek centaur, man and horse working together almost as one body," he says.

The term *trompe l'oeil* means "to fool the eye." While **WILLIAM ACHEFF** (b. 1947) admires the work of William Harnett and other nineteenth-century American practitioners of this style, he feels his own trompe l'oeil pieces go further. After Acheff moved to Taos, New Mexico, in 1973, he discovered those objects that are now arrayed in his jewel-like canvases—prehistoric and historic Native American pottery, Hispanic and Navajo textiles, beadwork, and old photographs. Their varied shapes, colors, designs—and New Mexico's pristine light—present a challenge, to which Acheff responds in paintings endowed with the mysticism of vanished cultures.

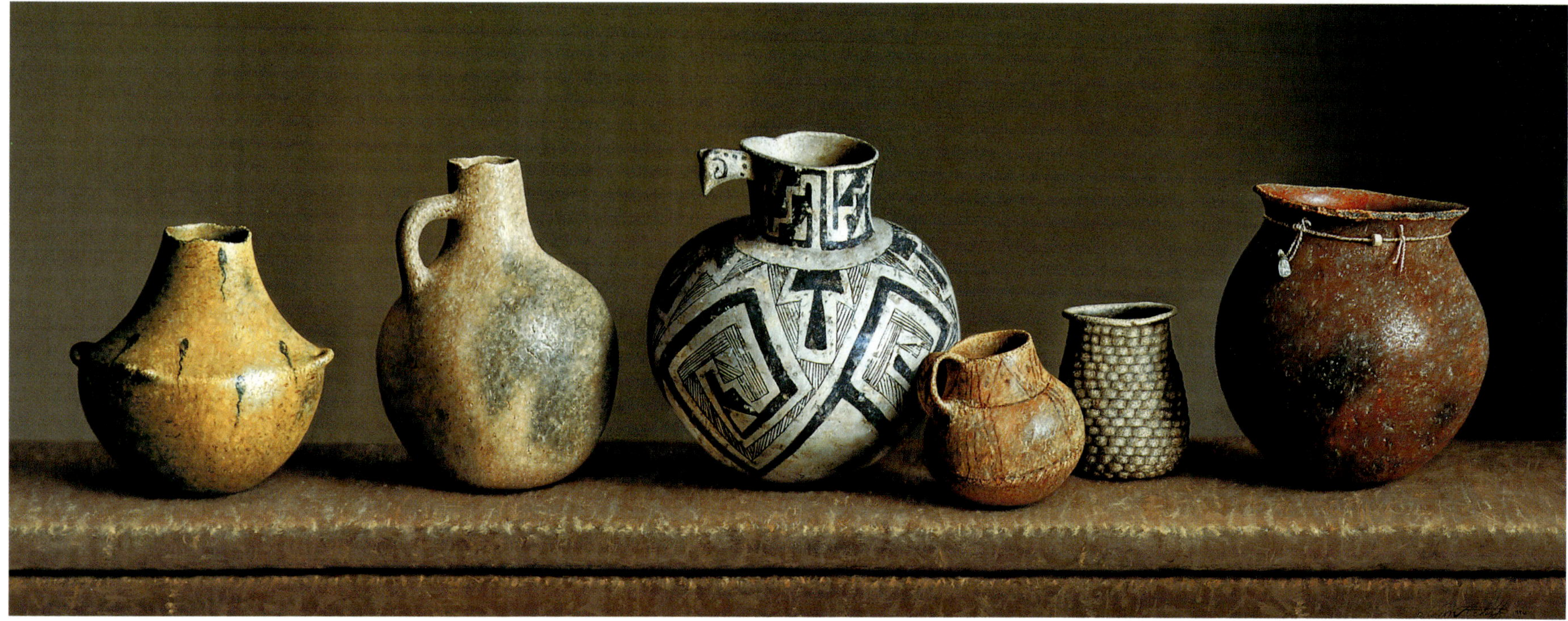

William Acheff, OLD FRIENDS, *oil on linen, 14 by 35 inches, 1996. Private collection.*

William Acheff,
CATCHER OF EAGLES,
oil on linen, 30 by 20 inches, 1996.
Private collection.

Raised in the San Francisco area, Acheff worked as a barber after graduation from high school. By chance, a well-known Bay Area artist, Roberto Lupetti, stopped by for a haircut one day. Lupetti invited Acheff to visit his studio, and "something clicked" for Acheff. Since he started his career in the early 1970s, Acheff has exhibited in many solo and group events, and among his awards is the National Academy of Western Art's 1989 Prix de West.

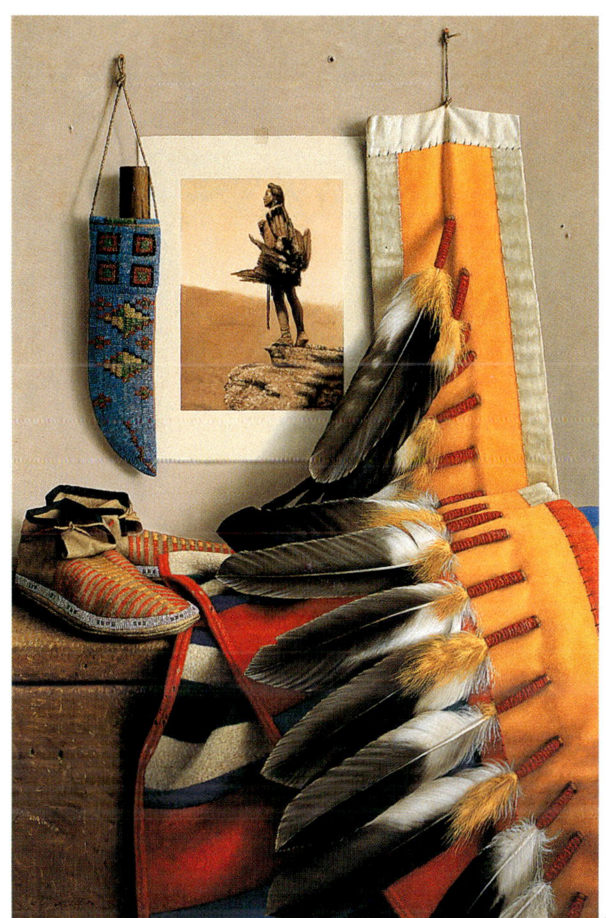

Acheff, who is of Athabascan heritage, assembles, studies, and arranges objects, then paints them not as they appear, but as he wishes them to be. Friends supply him with *santos, bultos,* Plains Indian artifacts, and prehistoric pots. As for the photographs, Acheff searches for them in books, then "ages" them through bent corners and discolored margins. The result can be a painting like *Catcher of Eagles.* Often he creates a painting with tabletop arrangements of the objects. "I once read that the trompe l'oeil painter cannot make an object on a table look as real as a flat object on a wall—and I thought, 'Yes, I can.'" As an example, in *Old Friends,* Acheff developed spatial arrangements that suggest the objects are three-dimensional. For Acheff, his goal as an artist is to stretch the boundaries of vision, and thus respond to the outer and inner image with greater clarity.

I once read that the trompe l'oeil painter cannot make an object on a table look as real as a flat object on a wall—and I thought, "Yes, I can."

—WILLIAM ACHEFF

Sculptor **VERYL GOODNIGHT** (b. 1947) has an interest in the West that includes flying over historic trails with her husband, a retired commercial airline pilot. One of the trails they traced is the Goodnight-Loving Trail, named for her great-great-great-uncle, the famous Texas cowman Charles Goodnight.

Goodnight's sculpture reflects the pre-1900 era of the American West, in particular, stalwart pioneer women and their animal companions. Born in Denver, Goodnight eventually turned in 1982 to sculpture, prompted by her interest in horses and anatomy.

She now works in a two-thousand-square-foot studio at her home north of Santa Fe. There she did the preliminary work for her largest sculpture so far, a monumental seven-ton image of five horses sailing over the broken remnants of the Berlin Wall. Titled *The Day the Wall Came Down,* the sculpture is installed at the George Bush Presidential Library Center at Texas A&M University.

Known for her sculptures of pioneer women, many of them life-size, Goodnight portrays the viewpoints of Western women, often with the animals in their lives. Some of these monuments are displayed at places like the National Cowboy Hall of Fame, the Houston Astrodome, and the Pro-Rodeo Hall of Fame. She participates annually in the Artists of America exhibition in Denver; the Northwest Rendezvous Group in Park City, Utah; and the *Governor's Invitational* in Cheyenne, Wyoming.

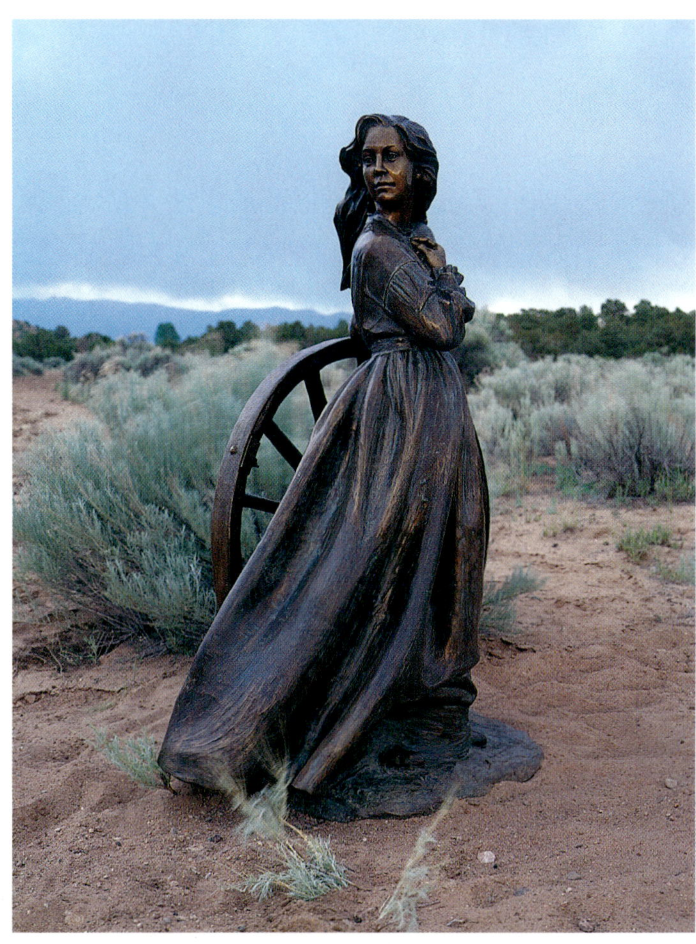

Veryl Goodnight,
NO TURNING BACK,
bronze (edition of 15),
66 by 52 by 28 inches, 1995.

I see a widespread interest in the softer side of the West. Many people seem to have recently discovered that the prairies and mountains were not solely a man's domain.

—VERYL GOODNIGHT

One of her bronzes, *No Turning Back,* part of her Women of the West series, pays homage to the pioneer women who ventured westward on the various trails. Goodnight feels a deep kinship with those women who lived in the West more than a century ago. "I like being a woman, and I like the woman's point of view," she says. "Besides, beyond my personal interest, I see a widespread interest in the softer side of the West. Many people seem to have recently discovered that the prairies and mountains were not solely a man's domain."

Born in Chicago, **Tom Darro** (b. 1946) grew up in a family of artists. His mother performed opera and his father, an accomplished painter and sculptor, taught young Tom to paint. After graduation from high school, Darro worked in New York for a period, then joined the Navy. After his discharge, he moved to Los Angeles, where he lived for thirteen years. There he worked in movie production, and, whenever possible, studied color theory, drawing, and composition, often with live models, to build a solid foundation for his art.

Darro paints Native Americans in pursuit of their daily lives, focused on fundamental issues that surround family—survival, love, cooperation, child rearing, labor, and spiritual faith. The richest, most tender, most significant moments in human lives are conveyed through his art, each painting a response to his own emotional and spiritual life.

Darro begins each painting with the sketch of an idea, then collects artifacts, searches for suitable locations, and finds models. He uses a camera to record the assembled scene. Once he views the models and props in an appropriate setting, the painting takes on a life of its own. Besides the Native American emphasis, Darro's personal style stresses diffused light and rich

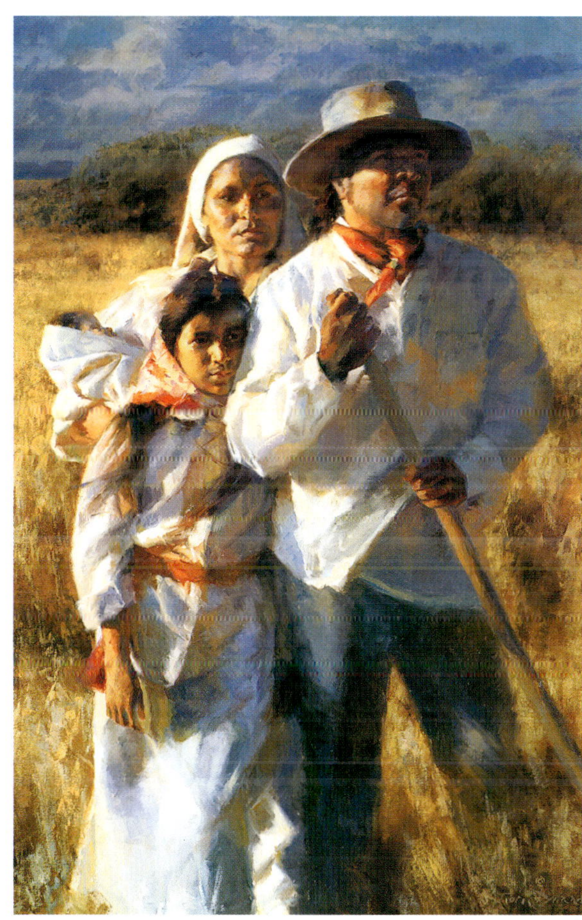

Tom Darro,
THE GREAT SOUTHWESTERN FAMILY,
oil on canvas,
54 by 36 inches, 1993.
Private collection; photograph courtesy of Overland Gallery of Fine Art.

color. "I am painting the composition and essential values within that moment, and I build upon that," he says. For Darro, the elements of the scene—excitement, beauty, exhilaration—are vehicles for his impressionistic art, as in *The Great Southwestern Family* (p. 115). The subjects are arranged in harmonious closeness, supported by a romantic landscape. This, and his other paintings, are suffused with a life-giving spiritual presence that combines distance and intimacy.

The sculpture of **Doug Hyde** (b. 1946) reflects the spirit of his Nez Perce, Assiniboine, and Chippewa ancestors, and the Southwest's Native groups. In high school a passion for sculpture unlocked within him; then, when he moved to Santa Fe in 1972, he discovered an environment supportive of his native heritage.

Hyde began studies at the Institute of American Indian Arts in Santa Fe in 1963. His work netted him a scholarship to the San Francisco Art Institute; however, tenure there was interrupted by service in the U.S. Army and two tours in Vietnam. Seriously wounded, he was discharged in 1969 with a Purple Heart. Afterward, Hyde secured a job making tombstones, and at night worked on his own sculpture. Finally, he entered some of his sculpture for a show sponsored by the Northern Plains Indian Museum in Browning, Montana. When his work sold out, he decided Santa Fe might be an appropriate place to pursue his art. There, he taught at the Institute of American Indian Arts, but left in 1973 to devote himself to sculpture full time. Since then, Hyde has been a part of numerous exhibitions at institutions such as the Gilcrease Museum, the Amon Carter Museum, the Heard Museum, the National Cowboy Hall of Fame, and the Kennedy Center for the Arts. In 1996, the Santa Fe Rotary Foundation awarded him its Distinguished Artist Award.

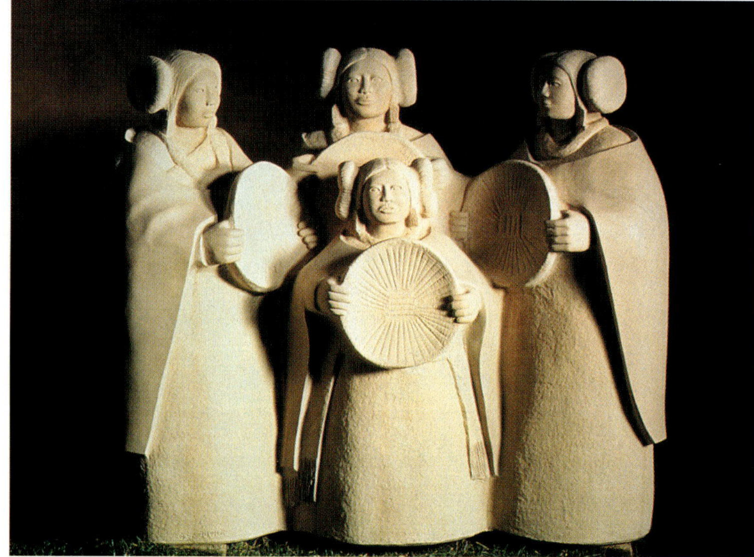

Doug Hyde,
HOPI BASKET DANCERS,
limestone, 5 feet high,
Collection of Colorado Springs Fine Arts Center.

Sometimes the material itself inspires me,
the stone, the shape of it, its color and matrix.

—DOUG HYDE

My work is continually evolving—it is becoming more representational or realistic all the time.

—ORELAND C. JOE

As a sculptor, Hyde utilizes bronze, marble, onyx, limestone, and alabaster, often in monumental size. "Sometimes the material itself inspires me, the stone, the shape of it, its color and matrix. I pursue an idea only when I can visualize the finished sculpture in my mind," he says. The sculptures might represent the stories of his culture told to him when he was a young boy, or portray historical events. For example, *Hopi Basket Dancers* portrays three Hopi women, each with a highly prized yucca basket, as participants in the basket dance.

In 1993, sculptor **ORELAND C. JOE** (b. 1958) became the first Native American artist elected to membership in the Cowboy Artists of America. Joe grew up on the Navajo Reservation near Shiprock, New Mexico, of Navajo and Southern Ute descent, in a family that inspired and understood his creative talents. When Joe visited Paris in 1978 as a member of an Indian dance troupe, he toured Versailles. Later, he recalls, "while chipping away with a kitchen knife and a screwdriver on a piece of stone, my mind went back to those stone sculptures. Something just clicked for me. It all came together."

Oreland C. Joe, MORNING LIGHT, *alabaster, 17 by 17 by 8 inches, 1995. Private collection; photograph by Dale W. Anderson*

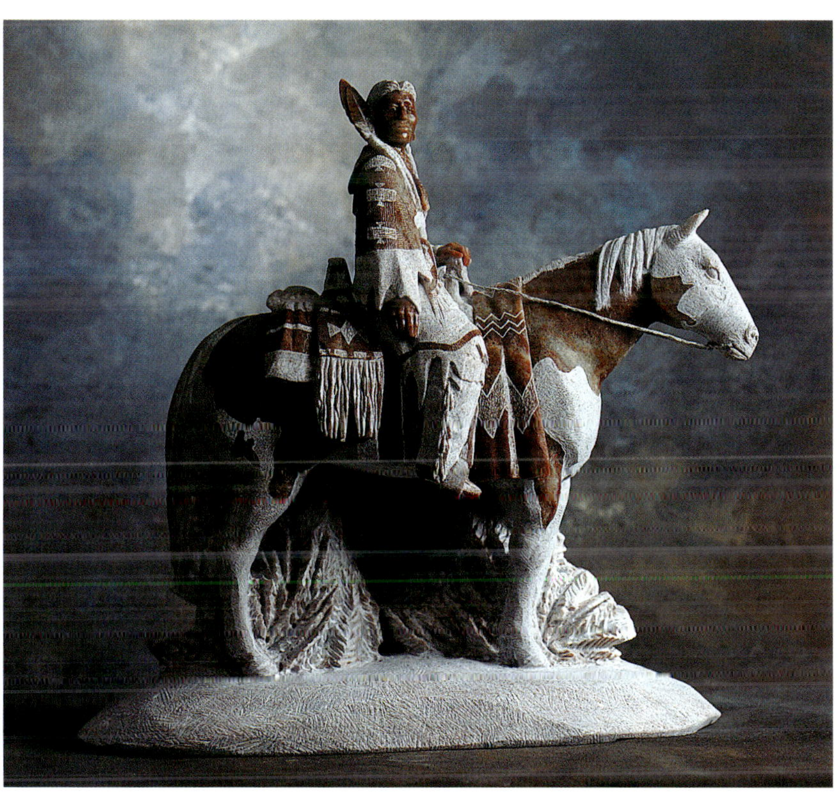

Joe is primarily self-taught, and often invents special tools needed to create the desired effects on his marble and alabaster works. His stone and bronze sculptures, such as *Morning Light,* focus on Navajo and Southern Ute history, legends, and culture, and the influence of traders, mountain men, and soldiers in the period between 1830 and 1920.

Joe's work is in many private and corporate collections, including the Arizona Public Service Company and the Northern Navajo Medical Center in Shiprock, New Mexico. Recently, he designed and sculpted a twenty-two-foot-high bronze statue of a famous Ponca chief for the Ponca Tribe in Oklahoma. "My work is continually evolving—it is becoming more representational or realistic all the time," Joe says.

I paint each person as he or she is, not as I wish them to be.

—RAY SWANSON

The Navajo, Hopi, Apache, and Zuni Indians are inspirations for the art of **RAY SWANSON** (b. 1937). Swanson believes he has a responsibility as an artist to honor the tradition and culture of the people he paints. The subjects in his paintings are real, found in real places. An interest in art came to Swanson early, at the age of twelve, when he saved eight dollars to purchase his first set of oil paints. Before he began to paint professionally, Swanson served in the Air Force, then proceeded to obtain a degree in aeronautical engineering from the Northrop Institute in California. Afterwards, he worked as an engineer for several years. When Swanson inherited his grandfather's paint box, the feel and history of it prompted him to embark on his career in art.

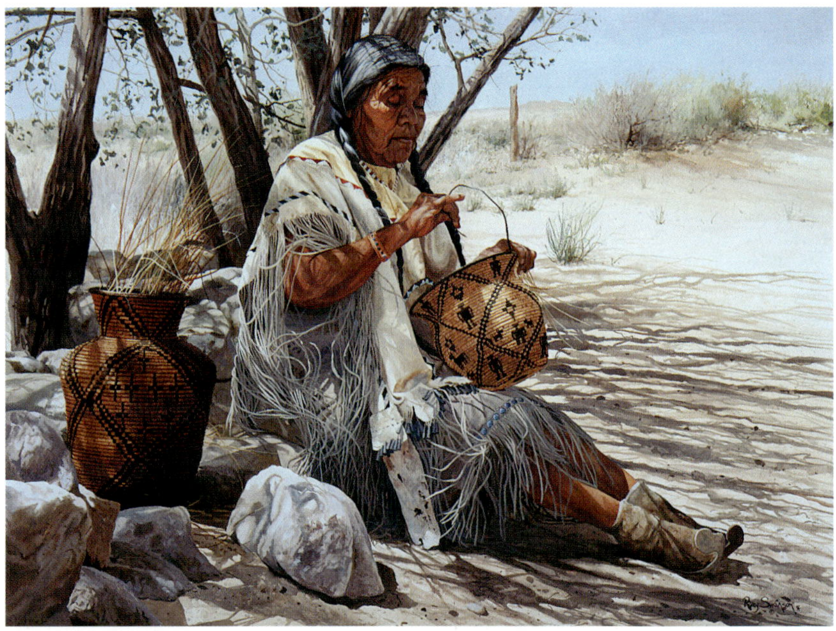

Ray Swanson,
WEAVING A TRADITION,
watercolor,
30 by 40 inches, 1994.
Private collection.

Since the mid-1960s Swanson has painted among the Native Americans of the Southwest, especially the Navajos, and he is acclaimed for his technical accuracy. His many exhibits include the George Phippen Museum, the Artists of America, the *Royal Western Watercolor Exhibit,* the Northwest Rendezvous Group, and the National Cowboy Hall of Fame. In 1986, Swanson joined the membership of the Cowboy Artists of America, and won their Artists' Choice Award in 1994.

During his many years among the Navajos and other groups, Swanson says he received the most pleasure from his observation and recording of the older generation. He was attracted by their lives and personalities. "I paint each person as he or she is," he remarks, "not as I wish them to be." One of his recent paintings, *Weaving a Tradition,* winner of a gold medal at the 1994 Cowboy Artists of America show, illustrates the old basket-weaving tradition of the Apache. Swanson painted a woman at the San Carlos Reservation; the old-style buckskin dress she wears came from Swanson's own extensive collection. Another painting, *Man of the Dineh,* is a portrait of an elderly Navajo man. "I used to see him around Tuba City," Swanson says. "Then later I noticed him at powwows in Flagstaff. For me, he represents the pride in being a Navajo."

"The goal in these paintings, and all my art, is to show how strong and good these individuals are, regardless of their economic circumstances," he says.

Ray Swanson,
MAN OF THE DINEH,
oil on linen,
38 by 26 inches, 1996.
Private collection.

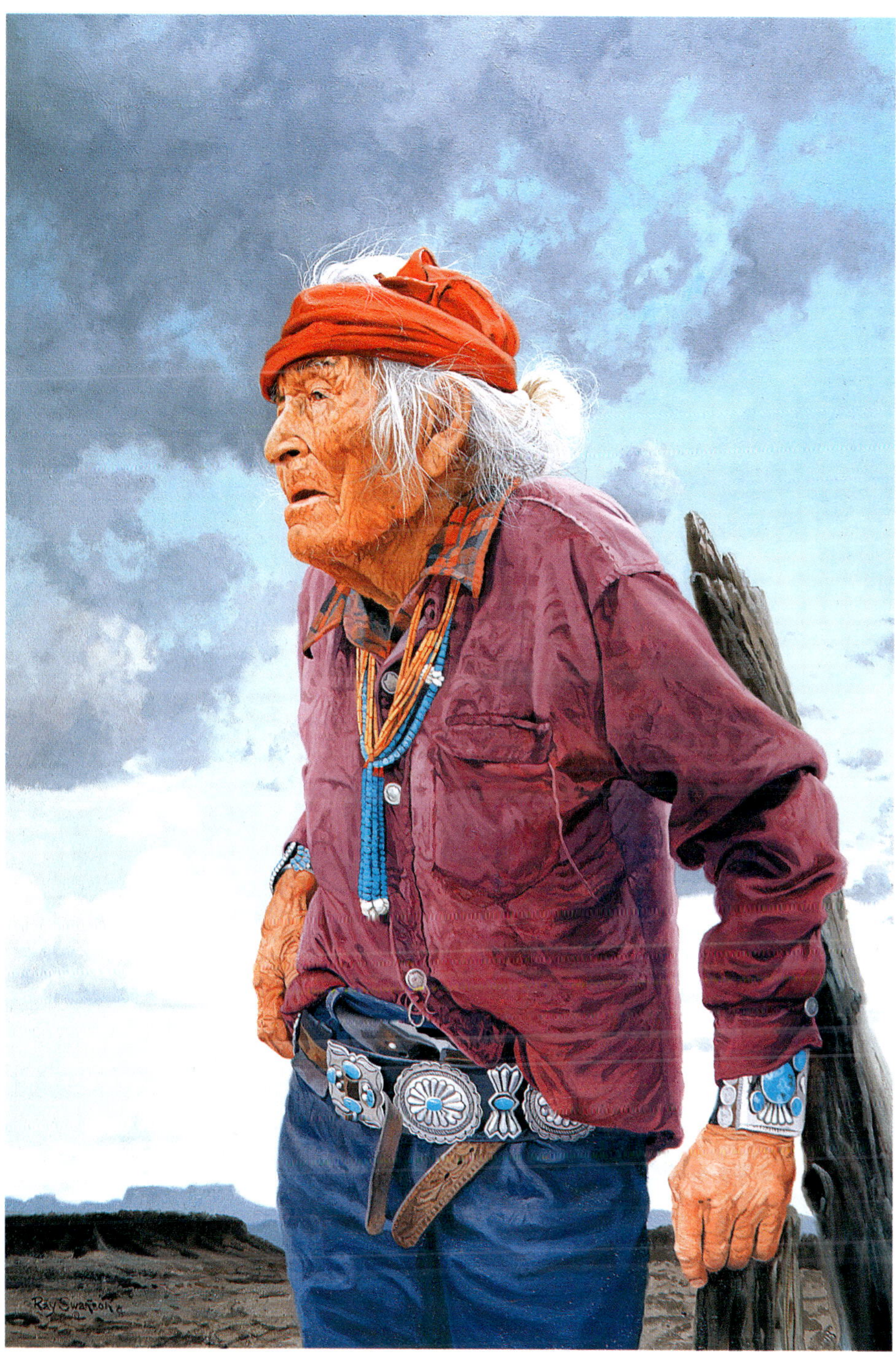

Located on the National Mall in Washington, D.C., is is the best-known work of **Glenna Goodacre** (b. 1939), a seven-foot-tall sculpture called *The Vietnam Women's Memorial,* which was unveiled on Veteran's Day in 1993. Goodacre has always been attracted to people, particularly their faces and forms. She did not start to sculpt until thirty years old, in 1969, when a Santa Fe gallery owner gave her some wax and insisted she work with it. Finally, with a toothpick and bobby pin, Goodacre created a small ballerina and had it cast in bronze. Since then, she has specialized in expressive, sensitive portraits, with an emphasis on composition. Her bronzes are in many public, private, corporate, and international collections.

Born in Texas, Goodacre graduated from Colorado College, then studied at the Art Students League in New York. Since 1983 she has lived and worked in Santa Fe. In 1993 she received the Knickerbocker Artists' Gold Medal for Distinguished Achievement in American Art, and in 1994 the National Academy of Design elected her a member of their ranks. In 1995 Texas Tech University honored her with a retrospective exhibition.

Ideas for Goodacre's sculpture come from her observation of things seen, perhaps a photograph, or a particular scene. Then a small clay model, or maquette, is developed. "I sketch mostly in clay," she says. "I need to work out my sculpture in the round, to make it inviting for people to walk around." When Goodacre commences to work on a final sculpture, such as *Waterbearers,* she uses live models. She relishes the opportunity to work on these monumental sculptures. "My modeling is looser, the surface is more tactile and less static," she says. For her, there is nothing like the human form, with its infinite interpretations.

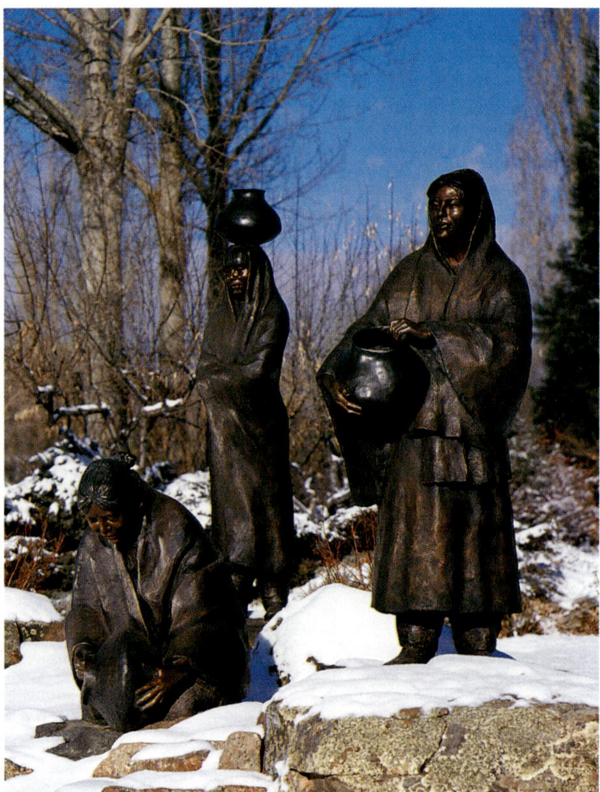

Glenna Goodacre,
WATERBEARERS,
bronze (edition of 12),
7½ feet high, 1986.
Collection of State Capitol Building, Santa Fe, New Mexico; photograph by Jane Hill.

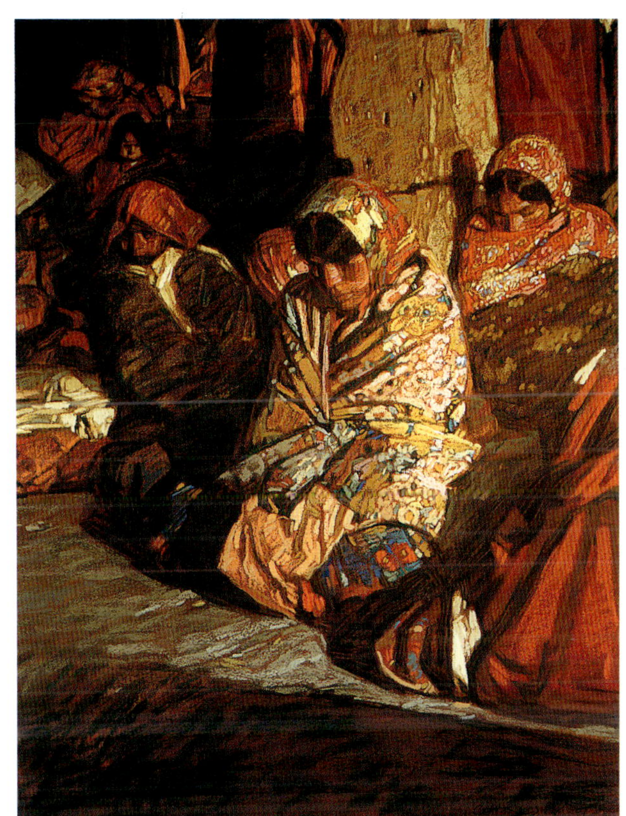

George Carlson, IN SILENCE, *pastel on paper, 28 by 21¼ inches, 1987. Private collection.*

Subjects such as Native Americans, muscular draft horses, and ballet dancers find expression in the sculptures and pastels of **GEORGE CARLSON** (b. 1940). Born in Illinois, Carlson studied art at the American Academy of Art in Chicago and the Art Institute of Chicago, and cultural anthropology at the University of Arizona. He has exhibited at the Denver Museum of Natural History, the National Academy of Design, the Phoenix Art Museum, and the Smithsonian Institution. His work was the subject of a retrospective at the Gilcrease Museum in 1994. Carlson won the Prix de West at the National Cowboy Hall of Fame in 1975, followed by the Robert M. Lougheed Memorial Award in 1989. Recently, he received the 1996 Idaho Governor's Award for Excellence in the Arts. Some of his sculpture commissions include portraits of Bill Cosby and Paul Robeson, and outdoor sculpture for the Eiteljorg Museum and the Colorado Springs Fine Arts Center.

Carlson's career was shaped in part by his experiences among the remote Tarahumara Indians of Mexico's Sierra Madre Mountains in the early 1970s. Carlson would stay there for several months at a time, creating wax sculptures, later refined as bronzes in his studio, and oil and pastel paintings. Intrigued by the vivid red-and-white Tarahumara clothing, Carlson constructed intricately designed pastels, like *In Silence,* a tapestry of Tarahumara figures and colorful clothing.

Carlson's other medium, sculpture, joins the representational with the abstract, the goal to reveal the inner life force of his subjects, as, for example, *Boy and the Eagle II.* Earlier in his career he started to sculpt as a self-help tool for his drawing. "I was convinced then," he says, "that if I knew what the other side of a man's head looked like, I could better draw it." Carlson is fascinated with the human figure, and particularly the inner spirit. "The spirit is the river and the subjects are the tributaries," he says.

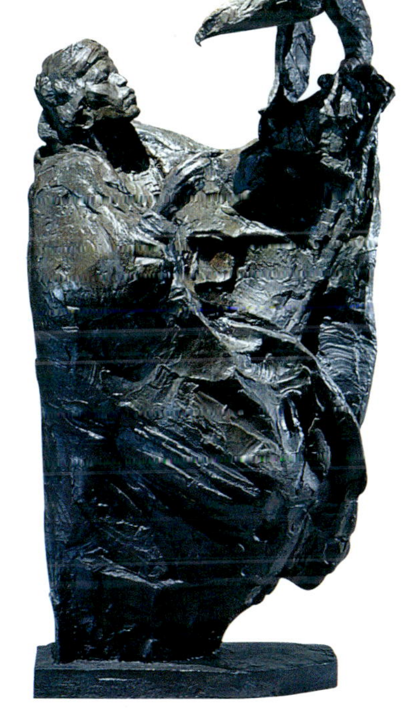

George Carlson, BOY AND THE EAGLE II, *bronze (edition of 12), 58 inches high, 1989.*

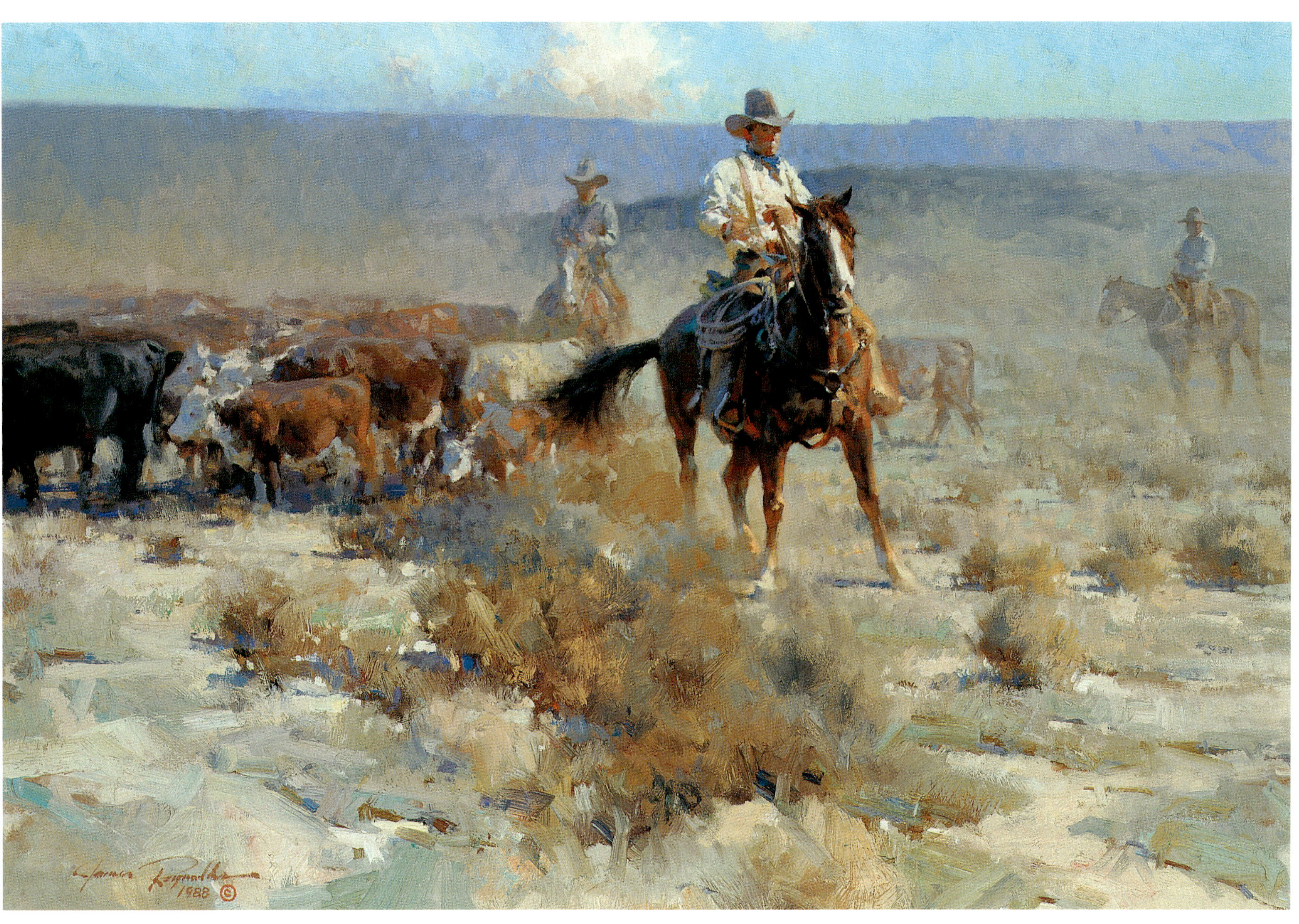

COWBOYS AND RANCH LIFE

Home on the Range

THE PAINTERS AND SCULPTORS WHO PORTRAY THE AMERICAN WEST'S CONTEMPORARY COWBOY, cowgirl, and ranch life usually present what on the surface appears to have little pretense or embellishment, yet the universal myths created by cowboy imagery, past and present, are embedded in their work. Cowboys created the myths; then the myths brought life to the cowboy, and continue to do so. These artists' paintings, drawings, and sculpture articulate respect and reverence for the cowboy's West. They live in the West, love the West, and paint or sculpt work that reflects the Western experience. Versed in the life and trappings of cowboy and horse cultures, some recreate in oil and bronze the quiet moods of range life, while others present the modern-day activities of ranch operations. A few artists have actually worked as cowboys, and some still do.

Some left behind distinguished careers as commercial illustrators, many claim a formal art education, and a few are self-taught. Whether members of the Cowboy Artists of America, or solitary riders on an artistic trail, they have attempted to lasso images of the cowboy spirit in their art. For most, like Bill Owen, Joe Beeler, Gary Niblett, and Gordon Snidow, their goal is strict authenticity, their art an honest reflection of reality. To them, and for many others, the American cowboy rides forever, a paradigm of ideals, values, and aspirations. And for some, like Donna Howell-Sickles, with her laughing, joyful cowgirls, and Bill Schenck, who debunks stereotypical images with a pop art approach, there are other kinds of truths.

James Reynolds,
ACTIN' UP,
oil on canvas,
26 by 36 inches, 1988.
Private collection.

One of these artists, **JAMES REYNOLDS** (b. 1926), won his first painting award in 1949 at twenty-two, in a competition that included some of the top watercolorists in Los Angeles. Upon his release from service in the U.S. Navy after World War II, Reynolds studied at two art schools in the Los Angeles area. After several years of doing freelance illustration and teaching watercolor classes, he embarked on a career as a production illustrator and designer in the film industry. During this time, he worked on many Western films, including *The Tall Men*, *The Comancheros*, *Warlock*, *The Bravados,* and *The Searchers.*

I simply want to interpret, in my way, what I see,
in a manner that is both pleasing and harmonious.

—JAMES REYNOLDS

In 1968 Reynolds retired and moved to Sedona, Arizona, to pursue painting the working cowboy. Now a resident of Scottsdale, Arizona, he has amassed many awards for his art. During his tenure with the Cowboy Artists of America, which he joined in 1969, he accumulated gold and silver medals, two Colt Awards, and several other awards before the organization voted him emeritus status. In 1991, the National Academy of Western Art awarded him a gold medal, and in 1992 he became the first artist ever to win three major awards from them in one year: the Prix de West, a gold medal for best oil painting, and the Buyer's Choice Award. Reynolds was honored with a retrospective at the Gilcrease Museum in 1993.

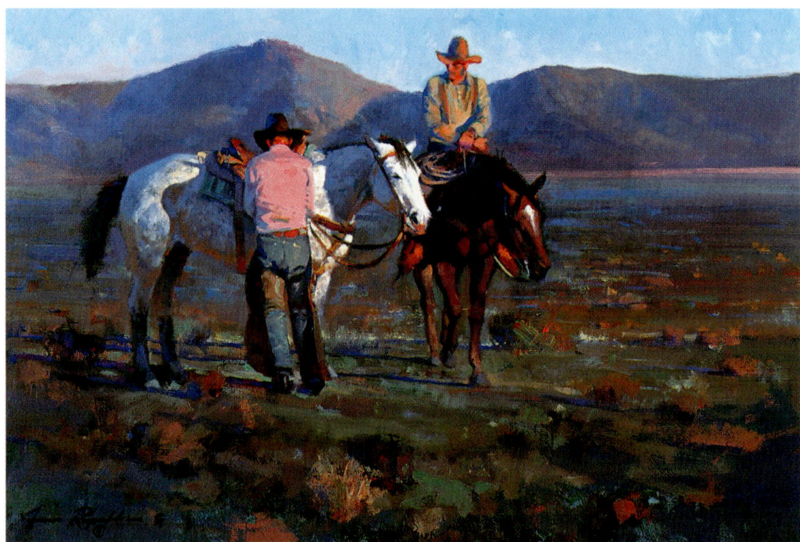

James Reynolds,
A BREAK,
oil on canvas,
20 by 30 inches, no date.
Private collection.

As an artist, Reynolds considers himself a realist with leanings toward impressionism. His favorite artists include John Singer Sargent, Joaquin Sorolla, William Merritt Chase, and some of the early California impressionists. Reynolds says, "I find it easier to express myself in paintings rather than verbally. Some artists expound on the spiritual aspects of their work, their quest for immortality or how they were led by some unseen force to produce the ultimate masterpiece. I lay claim to none of this nonsense. I simply want to interpret, in my way, what I see, in a manner that is both pleasing and harmonious. My reasons for what I do come down to a few basic things—my love of nature, my appreciation for beautiful things, and my training."

These three influences are found in the painting, *Actin' Up* (p. 122), a canvas marked by aggressive light, draftsmanship, and harmonious balance of color and values. Another example of his impressionist work is *A Break,* an image of a cowboy dismounted to tighten the cinch on his saddle. Both paintings surge with an almost incandescent light, endowed with strong, sustainable contrasts.

GARY NIBLETT (b. 1943) was raised in Carlsbad, New Mexico, an area where the American West is not a myth, but is embedded in everyday life. It was there that local ranchers paid young Niblett for portraits of their horses. After graduation from high school, he attended the Art Center College of Design, then spent eight years with Hanna-Barbera Studios as a background artist for television shows like *The Jetsons* and *The Flintstones.* In 1973, Niblett left commercial art to focus on Western painting. Three years later, in 1976, the Cowboy Artists of America voted him into their organization. His paintings of cowboy life have been exhibited at the annual Cowboy Artists of America events; in France, Germany, China, and Taiwan; and with the Royal Watercolor Society in London. He has been honored as *New Mexico Magazine*'s Distinguished Calendar Artist in 1990, and was the recipient of the Santa Fe Rotary Foundation's 1989 Distinguished Artist Award.

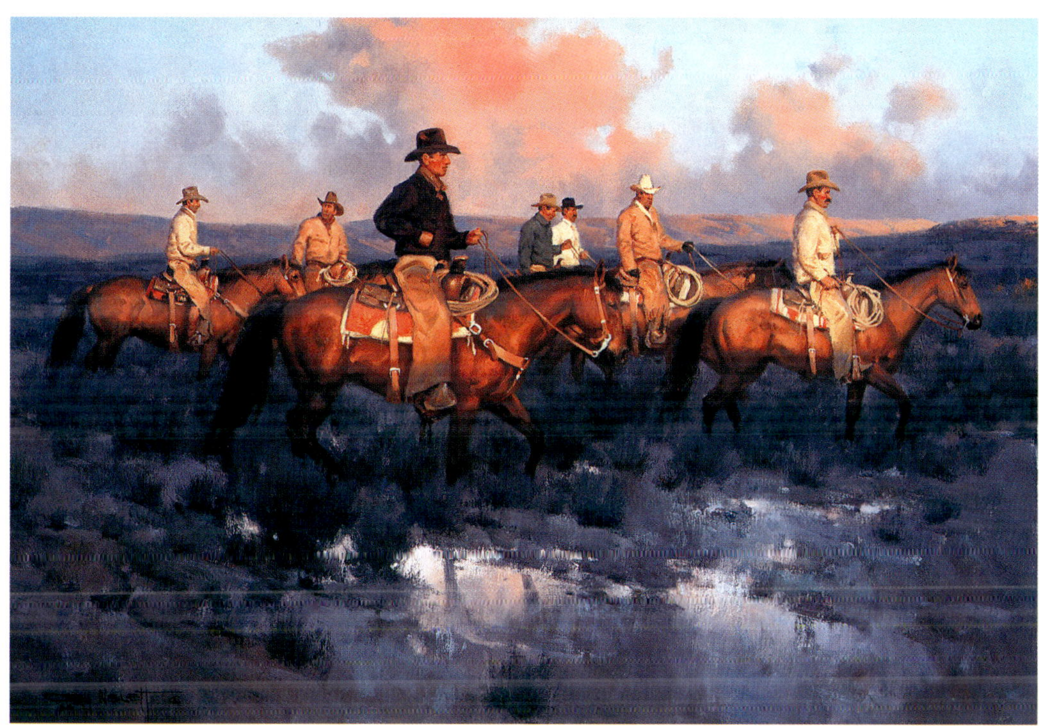

Gary Niblett,
FIRST LIGHT OVER TEXAS,
oil on canvas,
28 by 40 inches, 1996.
Private collection.

Niblett's primary medium is oil, but he also paints watercolors. The primary subject found in his art is cowboy life, although occasionally he reaches back in time for inspiration. In *First Light Over Texas,* Niblett portrays a group of cowboys from the legendary 6666 Ranch on their way out to a roundup, the dawn light cast upon their figures as they ride through the sagebrush. Another painting, *Riders of the Pitchfork* (p. 126), shows cowboys clustered around the famous Pitchfork Ranch red chuck wagon, with white horses and dark, threatening skies a contrast to the light reflected on the men and horses in the foreground.

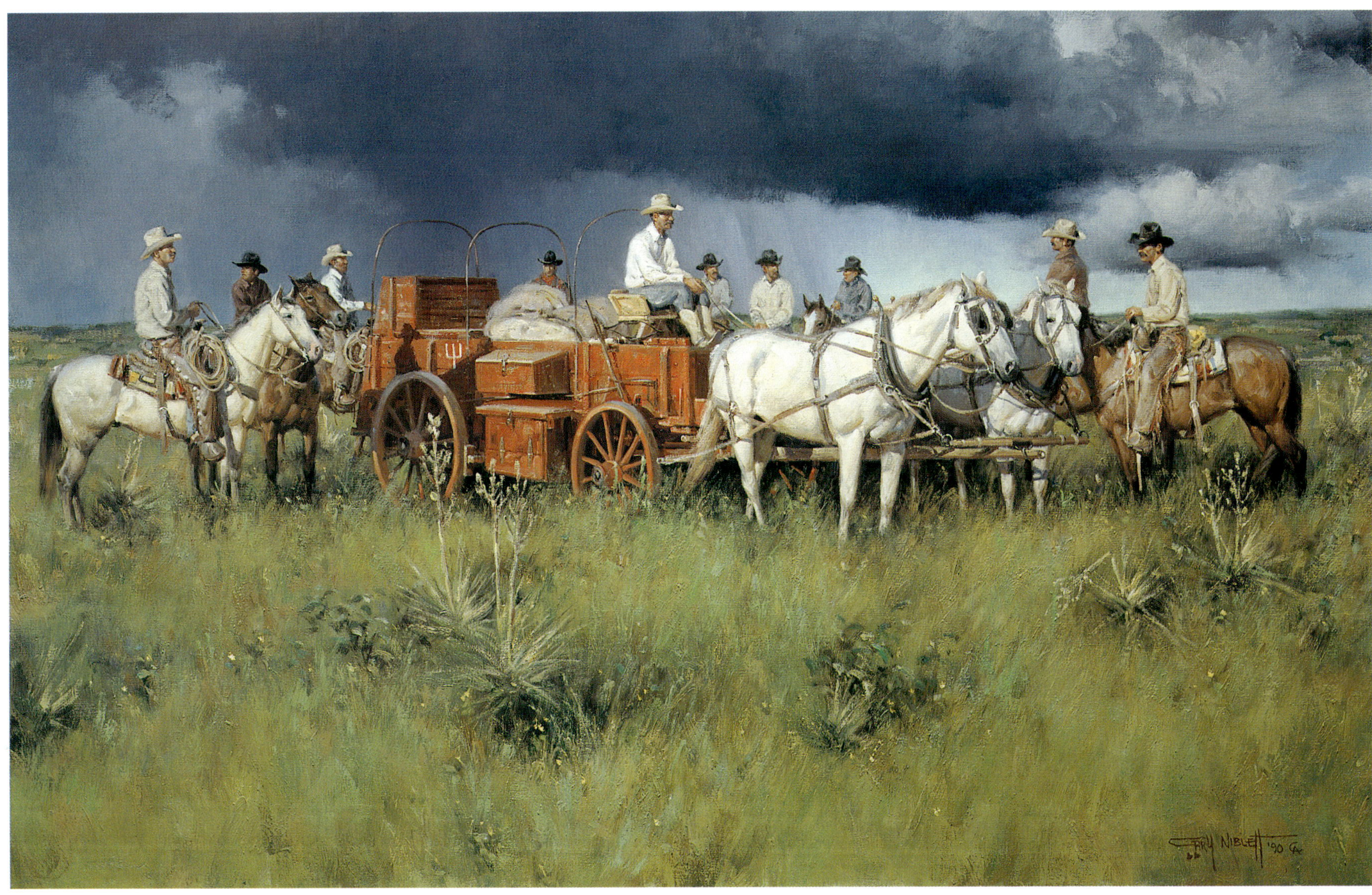

Gary Niblett, RIDERS OF THE PITCHFORK, *oil on canvas, 36 by 56 inches, 1990. Private collection.*

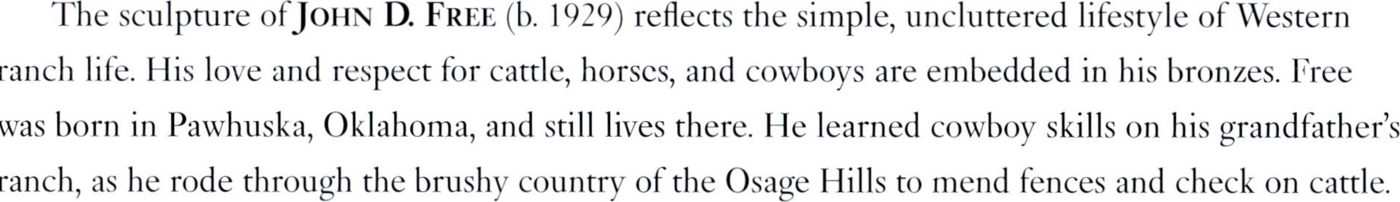

The sculpture of **John D. Free** (b. 1929) reflects the simple, uncluttered lifestyle of Western ranch life. His love and respect for cattle, horses, and cowboys are embedded in his bronzes. Free was born in Pawhuska, Oklahoma, and still lives there. He learned cowboy skills on his grandfather's ranch, as he rode through the brushy country of the Osage Hills to mend fences and check on cattle.

John D. Free,
ROUGH EDGES,
bronze, (edition of 100), 14 inches high, 1984.

Free's early exposure to art came from Winchester calendars and the covers of pulp Western magazines. Will James's book *Big Enough* got him interested in drawing. After college and a hitch in the U.S. Army, Free settled on his father-in-law's ranch near Pawhuska. Painting and sculpture occupied his free time until he finally decided to pursue a full-time art career.

In 1971, Free participated in his first one-man exhibit at the National Cowboy Hall of Fame, followed by another in 1984 at the Woolaroc Museum in Bartlesville, Oklahoma. Elected to the Cowboy Artists of America in 1972, Free often exhibits in their annual events. Among his awards is a silver medal from the National Academy of Western Art. He has completed numerous commissions, including a life-size bronze sculpture of a mare and colt in 1995 for the American Royal Association in Kansas City, Missouri.

"My subject matter is simple, and I try to convey it the very best I can," Free says. Whether portraying cattle or a cowboy astride a frenzied horse, as in *Rough Edges,* his realistic, lean, elemental sculptures reflect a dedication to his craft and a love for the ways of the West.

Known for his paintings of cattle, cowboys, rodeo arenas, and ranch life executed with a unique aerial perspective and sun-drenched hues, **Howard Post** (b. 1948) is an impressionist who portrays the contemporary West in a modern fashion. Post, a native Arizonan, was born and raised on a ranch near Tucson. Perhaps not surprisingly, he gravitated toward the life of the cowboy. The family ranch raised rodeo stock, and as Post gained experience, he started to enter rodeo competitions. In time, he became an Arizona High School All Around Rodeo Champion, a member of the University of Arizona rodeo team, and, eventually, a competitor with the Professional Rodeo Cowboys Association. After Post completed bachelor's and master's degrees in fine art at the University of Arizona, he taught there for two years.

Post worked as a commercial artist until 1980, when he decided to paint what he knew best, Arizona's ranch traditions. His oils and pastels have been included in numerous exhibitions throughout the United States. Many of his paintings are represented in public, corporate, and private collections, including the Smithsonian Institution, Bank of Texas, AT&T World headquarters, and United Airlines.

Viewers of Post's oils or pastels respond to a bird's-eye view of cattle clustered in a corral, cowboys perched on fence rails, or a distant ranch house. This higher perspective endows people and animals in the paintings with stronger shapes and patterns. "I love to take common, overlooked images and bring out the qualities that make them visually exciting," says Post. "I'm fascinated by the shapes and patterns created when several animals crowd together in a holding pen or truck. It's almost as if I sculpt found objects." Post draws from a collection of several thousand slides for imagination, then starts a canvas without preliminary sketches. Up to six colors might be used, painted over a dark background. His work is defined by orderly, strong shadow patterns cast by the figures of cattle, cowboys, trees, or fences, as in, for example, the pastel *High Pasture,* or his oil painting *Cattle Drive.*

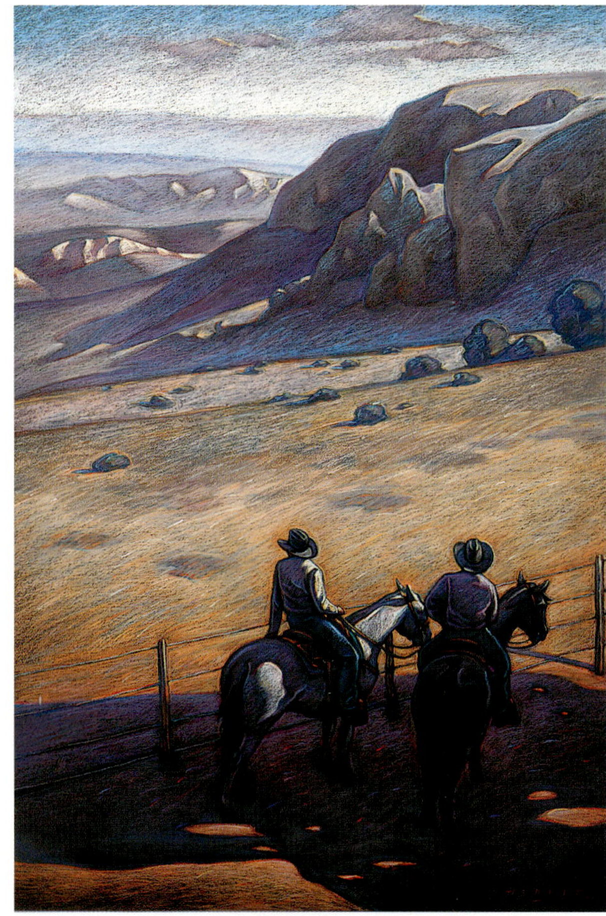

Howard Post,
HIGH PASTURE,
pastel on paper,
44 by 30 inches, 1990.
Private collection.

WILLIAM MATTHEWS (b. 1949) discovered the subjects for his art—cowboys—when he accompanied his friend, photographer Kurt Marcus, to the first Cowboy Poetry Gathering in Elko, Nevada, in 1985. For Matthews, contemporary cowboy culture is the last hurrah of genuine old-style rural values and tradition in America. He has painted

I love to take common, overlooked images
and bring out the qualities that make them visually exciting.

—HOWARD POST

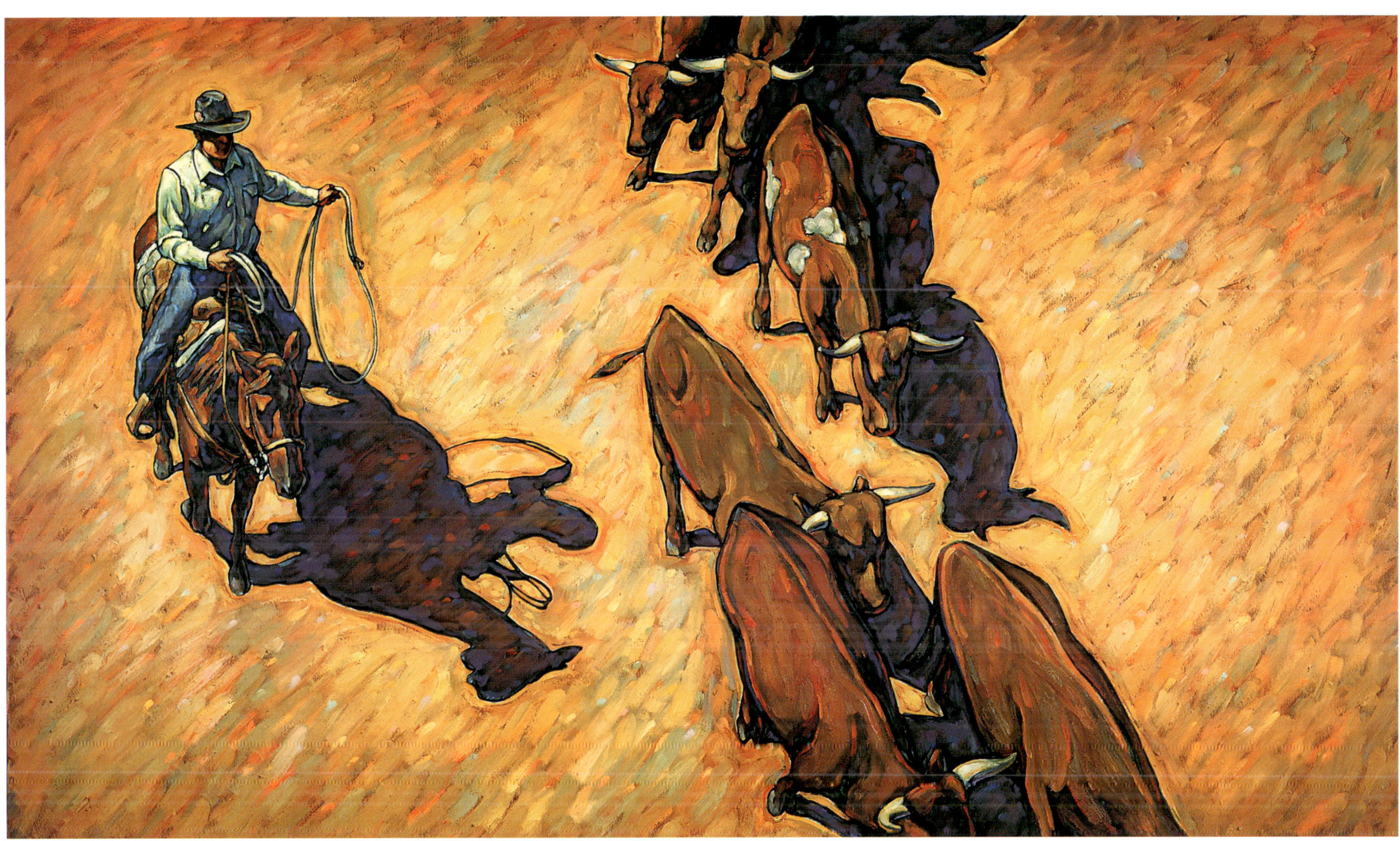

Howard Post, CATTLE DRIVE, *oil on canvas, 42 by 72 inches, circa 1980. Private collection*

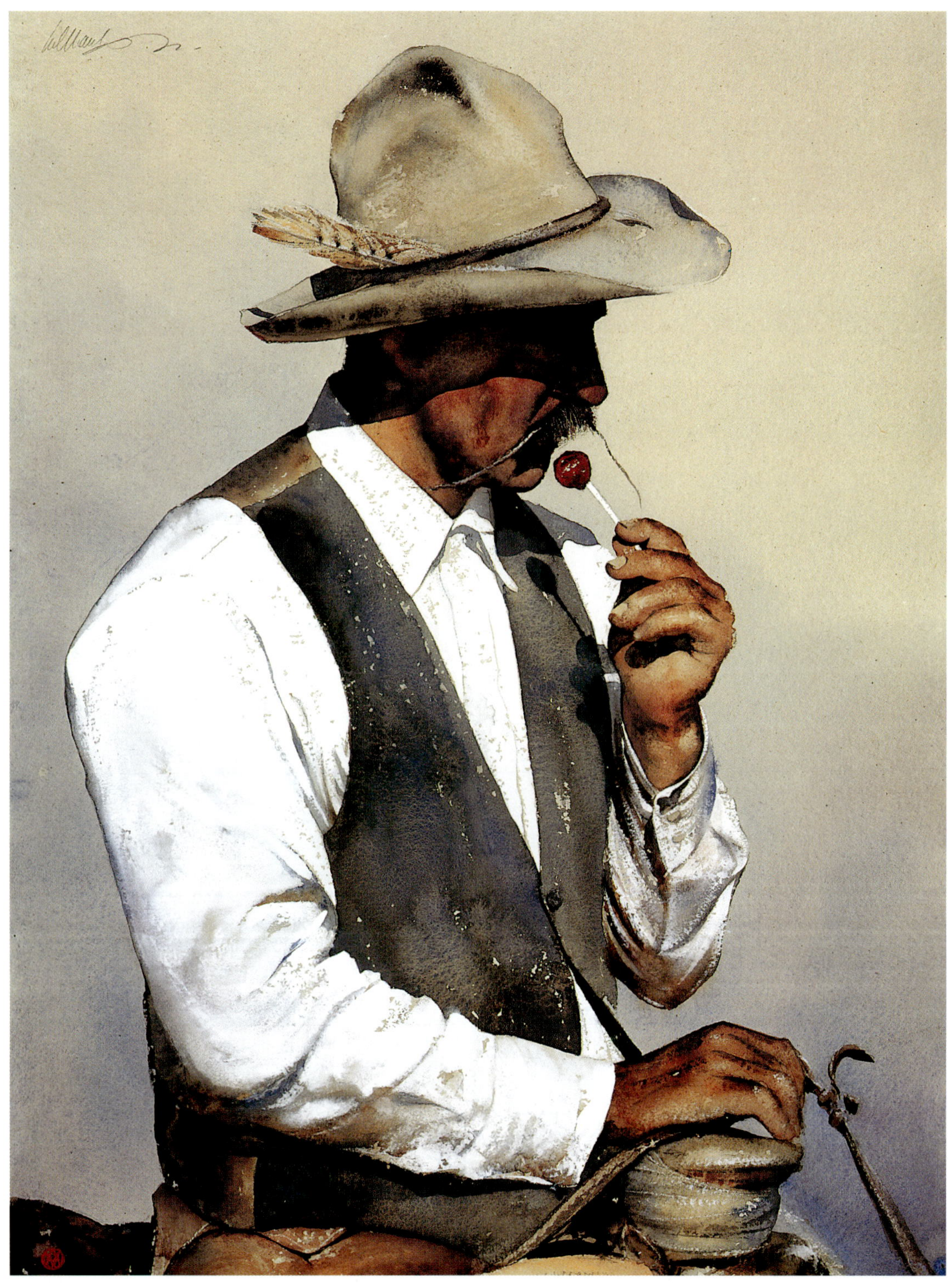

William Matthews,
HARD CANDY,
watercolor,
22 by 29¼ inches, 1995.
Collection of Bace Industries, Denver; photograph courtesy of William Matthews Gallery.

Ranch people are interesting and charged with purpose.
I record their details, often overlooked in the day-to-day confusion.

—WILLIAM MATTHEWS

throughout the world, but his interest centers on the buckaroos who work on the ranches of northern Nevada and southern Oregon. Matthews started painting Western subjects after the cowboy poetry event, but only when he felt comfortable with the cowboys and their life. "Cowboys are intensely private people," he says. "I'm attracted to their way of life, and their culture."

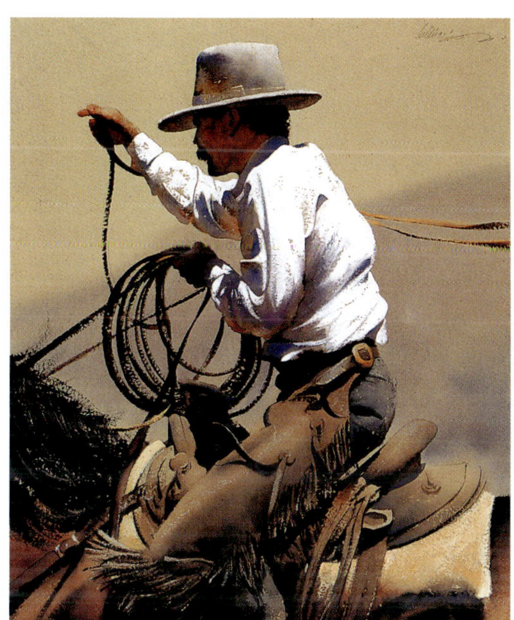

William Matthews,
FREE FLIGHT,
watercolor,
23 by 28¼ inches, 1995.
Collection of Graeme and Norah Bretall;
photograph courtesy of
William Matthews Gallery

Born in New York, Matthews moved to San Francisco with his family in the late 1950s. After twelve months of art school in San Francisco, Matthews left for Los Angeles, where for several years he designed album covers for Capitol Records. Nowadays, he still creates covers for his friend, singer Michael Martin Murphey, and for other artists on the Warner Western label.

Between 1975 and 1980, Matthews traveled throughout Spain, North Africa, Egypt, Great Britain, and Ireland. Matthews says his own art has grown in confidence from absorbing the cultures of different countries. After he returned from his travels abroad in 1980, Matthews decided to settle in Evergreen, Colorado. One of those artists who cuts his own trail, Matthews does not belong to any watercolor society, seldom participates in invitational shows, and does not teach workshops. As a watercolorist, he credits his mother for initial influence, while other inspiration comes from early American and English practitioners of that medium.

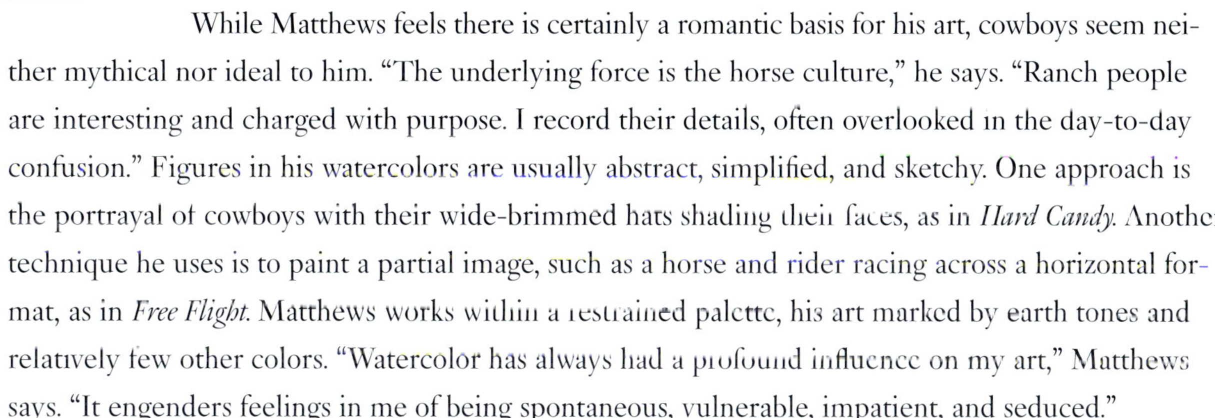

While Matthews feels there is certainly a romantic basis for his art, cowboys seem neither mythical nor ideal to him. "The underlying force is the horse culture," he says. "Ranch people are interesting and charged with purpose. I record their details, often overlooked in the day-to-day confusion." Figures in his watercolors are usually abstract, simplified, and sketchy. One approach is the portrayal of cowboys with their wide-brimmed hats shading their faces, as in *Hard Candy.* Another technique he uses is to paint a partial image, such as a horse and rider racing across a horizontal format, as in *Free Flight.* Matthews works within a restrained palette, his art marked by earth tones and relatively few other colors. "Watercolor has always had a profound influence on my art," Matthews says. "It engenders feelings in me of being spontaneous, vulnerable, impatient, and seduced."

Martin Grelle (b. 1954) was born in Clifton, Texas, and still resides in that community. Elected to membership in the Cowboy Artists of America in 1995, Grelle knew Clifton residents Melvin Warren and James Boren, early members of the organization, both now deceased. Boren and Warren encouraged young Grelle to pursue art, and convinced him he could carve out a career as a Western artist. Grelle's paintings are based on historically accurate locations and subjects. At first, he attempted to reproduce every detail on each canvas, but eventually learned to loosen his brushwork, emphasize the light more, and experiment with different color combinations.

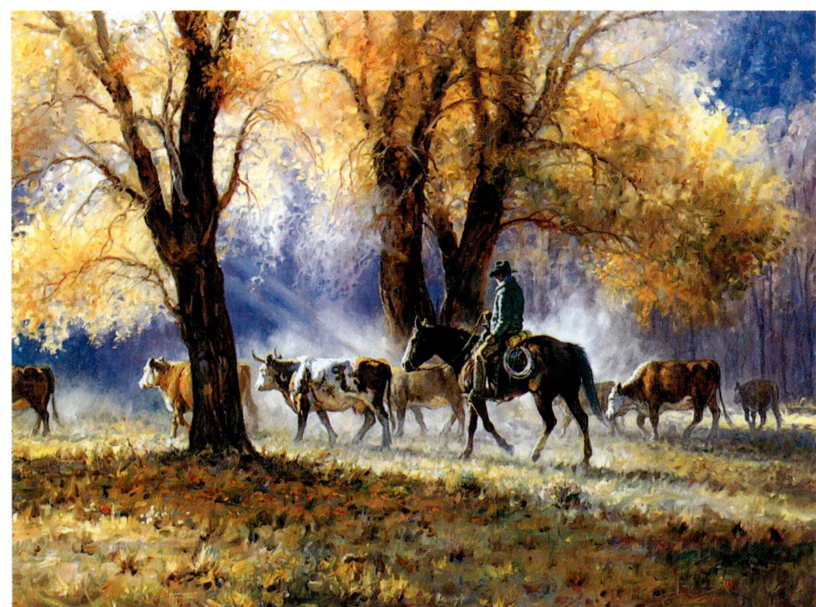

Martin Grelle,
AUTUMN'S GATHER,
oil on canvas,
30 by 40 inches, 1996.
Photograph by Bill McLemore Photography, courtesy of Overland Gallery of Fine Art.

His work has been exhibited at the National Cowboy Hall of Fame's *Prix de West Invitational* and the Cowboy Artists of America annual exhibitions. In addition, Grelle has painted covers for *The Western Horseman* and the *Santa Gertrudis Journal.*

Grelle's work depicts contemporary cowboy life and images drawn from the romance of the Old West. Authenticity is important for his subject matter, and he often finds inspiration from the stories and landscapes of central Texas. Horses, and there are almost always horses, are important components in Grelle's paintings. Overall, his compositions stress a mixture of landscapes and figures, as in *Autumn's Gather.* Intrigued with light, Grelle fills the landscapes in his loose, impressionistic paintings with it, a response to what he encounters at a specific location. "I try to get the feeling of light and atmosphere of a place," he says, "so people looking at my work can feel what I've felt."

In June 1965, **Joe Beeler** (b. 1931) was among several artists gathered at Bird's Oak Creek Tavern in Sedona, Arizona, to discuss the concept of an organization dedicated to standards of quality and authentic representation in contemporary Western painting—the Cowboy Artists of America. Born in Joplin, Missouri, Beeler grew up around the stories told of his pioneer and Cherokee ancestors.

Above all, I have to be honest.
When I paint, I have to be in tune with my work.

—JOE BEELER

The Korean Conflict and his Army service interrupted Beeler's studies at Tulsa University in 1953. When he was released from the Army, Beeler and his new bride moved to Kansas, where he attended Kansas State College. Afterwards, he pursued further study at the Art Center College of Design in Los Angeles, then returned to a cabin on the Oklahoma-Kansas state line, where he worked on cowboy and Indian paintings. Beeler had his first one-man show in 1959 at the Gilcrease Museum in Tulsa, Oklahoma.

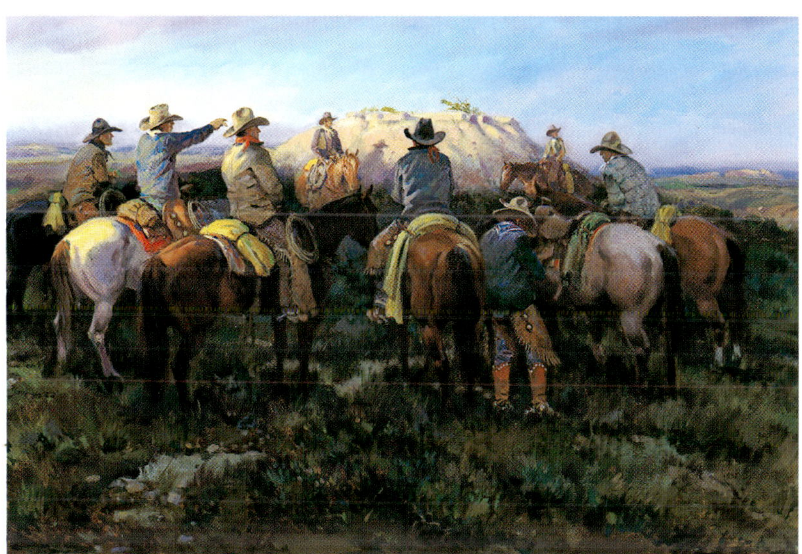

Joe Beeler, SCATTERING THE RIDERS, *oil on canvas, 24 by 40 inches, no date. Private collection; photograph by Peter L. Bloomer, Horizons West.*

Beeler realized he needed a close proximity to the marketplace for Western art, and relocated to the redrock country of Sedona, Arizona, in 1961. Through his role in the development of the Cowboy Artists of America, Beeler emerged as a leader in contemporary Western realism, noted not only for his paintings, but also for his bronze sculpture. He has been recognized with exhibitions at the Gilcrease Museum, the Buffalo Bill Historical Center, the C. M. Russell Museum, and the Montana Historical Society.

In some of the Cowboy Artists of America events, Beeler has won both gold and silver medals. In 1995, he was designated an Arizona History Maker by the Arizona Historical Association, followed by the Living Legend Award from Canada's Cowboy Conference and Arts Council in 1996. Most recently, Beeler won an award for his contributions to art at the 1996 Cowboy National Symposium.

Beeler understands and empathizes with cowboys and their lives, and his paintings, like *Scattering the Riders* or *Mountain Cow Camp* (p. 134), describe not only their spirit, but the honesty of the artist. "Above all," Beeler reflects, "I have to be honest. When I paint, I have to be in tune with my work. Sometimes this doesn't come easy. Occasionally I have to saddle up and go on a long ride before I get lined out. Seeing it, through my own experience, or careful research, relating to it with feeling and imagination; retaining the inspiration, and then putting it down with as much talent and sensibility as I can are all a part of my work."

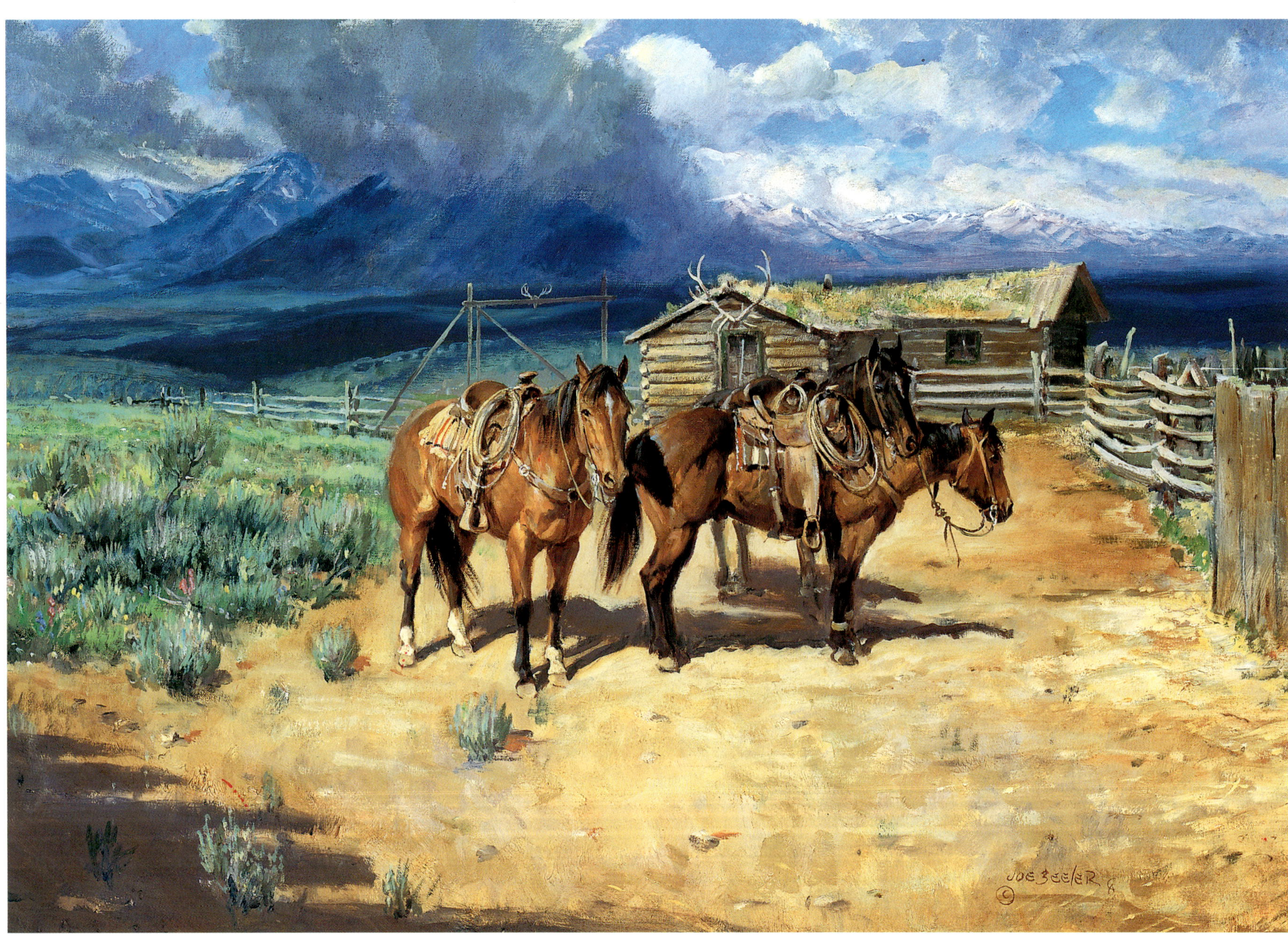

Joe Beeler, MOUNTAIN COW CAMP, *oil on canvas, 24 by 36 inches, 1992. Private collection; photograph by Peter L. Bloomer, Horizons West.*

Another early member of the Cowboy Artists of America, **GORDON SNIDOW** (b. 1936), encountered original paintings by Charles M. Russell and Frederic Remington at the Gilcrease Museum when he was only twelve years old. He immediately knew that he wanted to be an artist. After graduation from the Art Center College of Design in 1959, Snidow worked as an artist at Sandia National Laboratory in Albuquerque, and pursued Western art in his spare time.

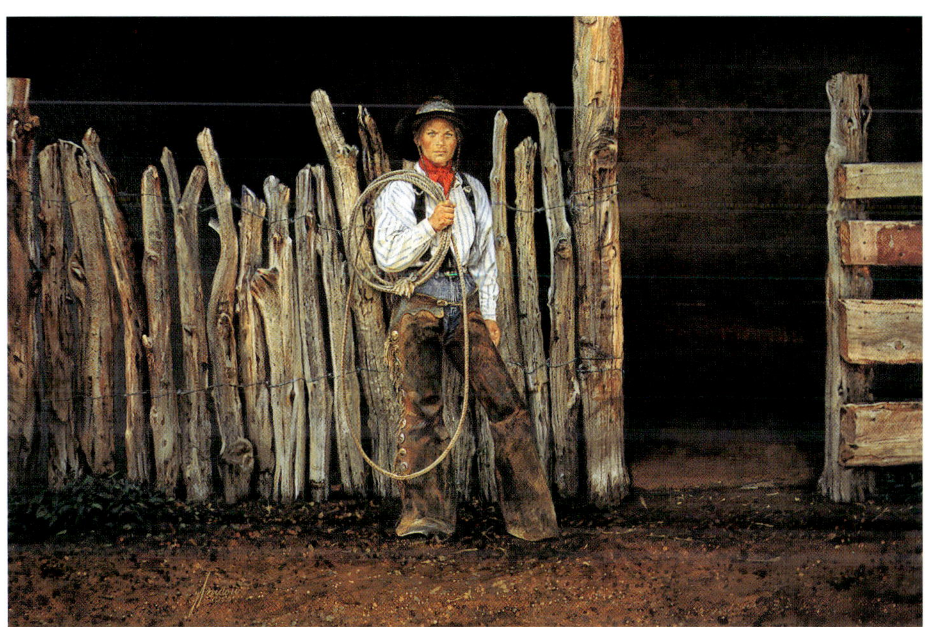

Gordon Snidow, I CAN DO IT ALL, *gouache, 32 by 48 inches, 1993. Private collection.*

Now known as one of the foremost chroniclers of the contemporary American cowboy, Snidow paints the personality of individuals, a psychological portrait of the ordinary made extraordinary, and is considered a master of gouache painting. Snidow joined the Cowboy Artists of America as a charter member, and served as president three times. In addition, he is the recipient of twenty-seven gold and silver medals from the Cowboy Artists of America, and was the organization's top award-winner when he retired from competition in 1989 as an emeritus member.

Snidow has shown his paintings at numerous exhibitions, including those at the Gilcrease Museum and the National Cowboy Hall of Fame, and some in Paris, Beijing, Moscow, Calgary, and London. In 1995, Snidow had a major retrospective of his work at the Museum of the Horse, located in Hollywood Park, California. Besides this active exhibition schedule, he also found time to create the famous Coors Cowboy Collector's Series.

In his art, Snidow includes the contributions of women to Western life. Snidow selected a single model, Carol, and has used her in a series of paintings to represent the modern ranchwoman. In Snidow's painting *I Can Do It All,* Carol stands in her corral, lariat in hand, and looks straight

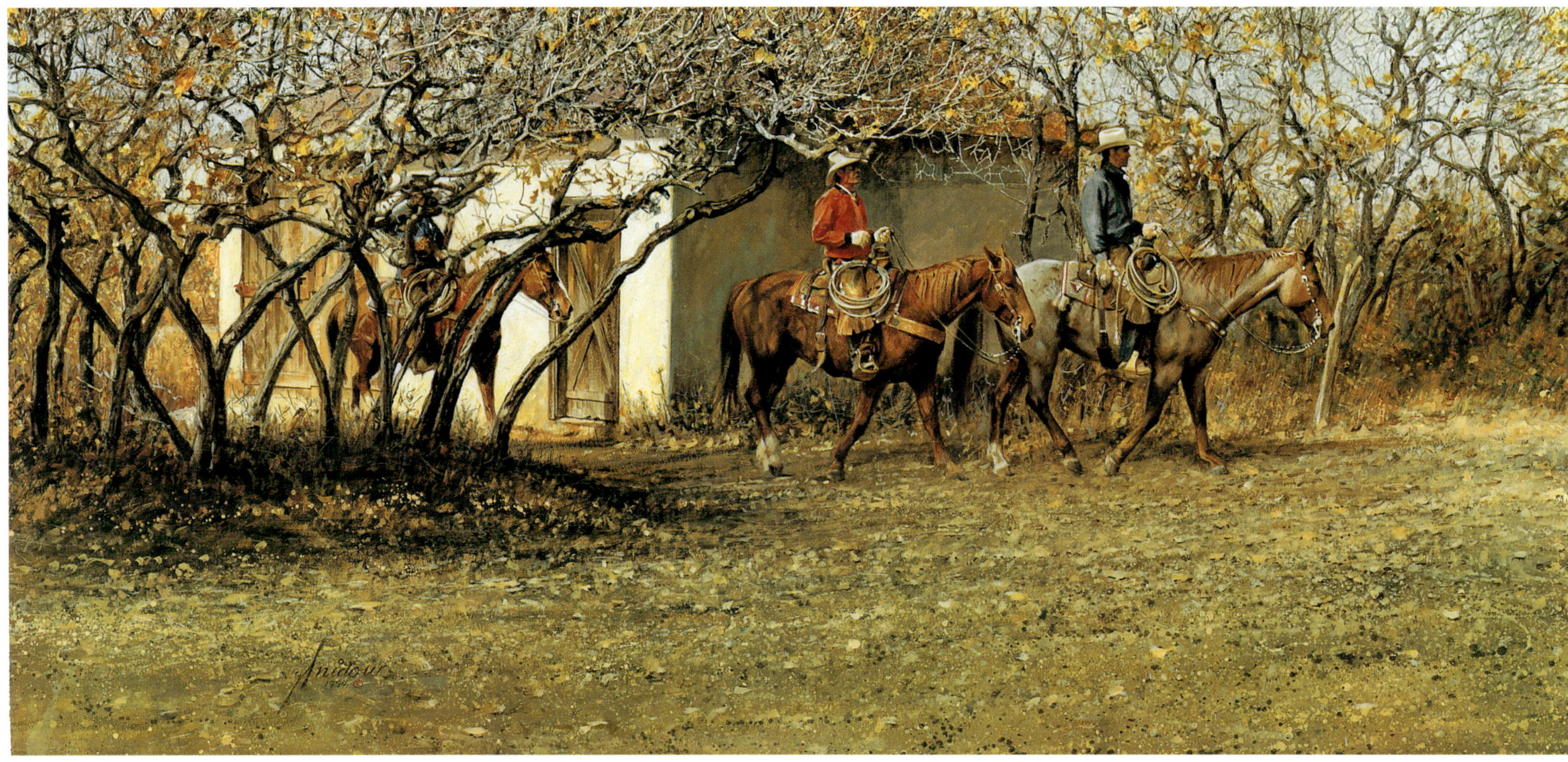

Gordon Snidow, THE RIDERS OF THE GRANDE CAMP, *gouache, 18 by 38 inches, 1994. Private collection.*

out of the image, calm and resolute. "Though I've depicted Carol as a ranch hand wearing men's clothing," Snidow says, "she represents my concept of today's independent woman, the 'can do' attitude of women that I admire." An intricate mosaic marks another one of Snidow's paintings, *The Riders of the Grande Camp,* an image of three cowboys who ride along an abandoned ranch structure. Snidow has drawn attention to the central figure in the red shirt, but overall the vegetation patterns provide an eclectic, abstract feel to the image.

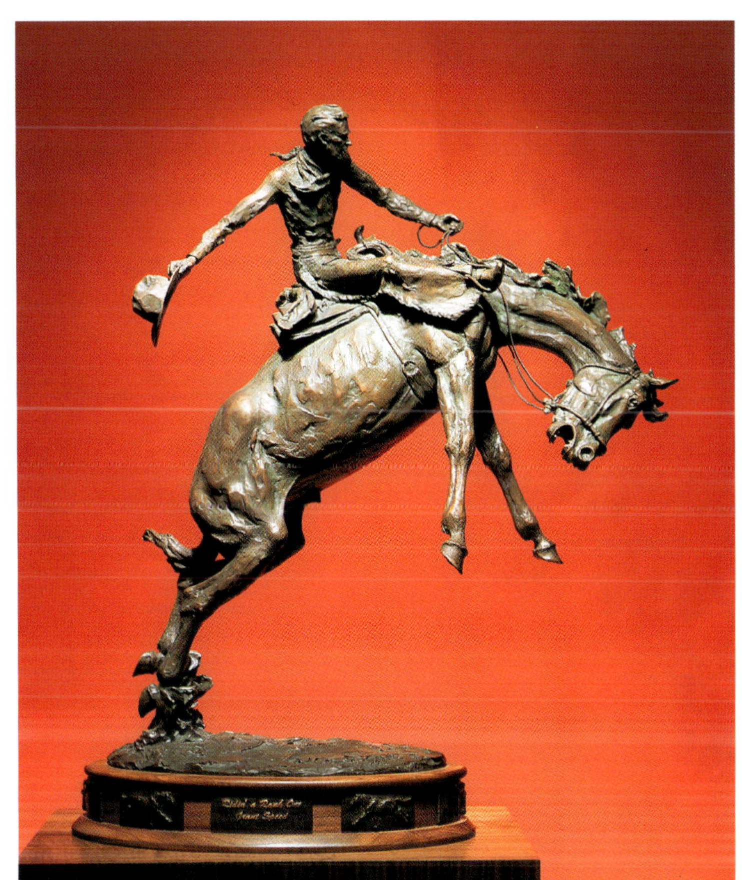

Grant Speed,
RIDIN' A RANK ONE,
bronze (edition of 30),
34 inches high, 1994.

By the time he reached twenty-two, **GRANT SPEED** (b. 1930) had worked as a cowboy on more than fifteen ranches in Texas, Arizona, and Wyoming. He never forgot those impressions. When he graduated from Brigham Young University in 1958, he accepted a position as an elementary school teacher. However, the allure of art tugged at him, and he enrolled in night sculpture classes at Brigham Young University. In 1966, he created his first bronze sculpture.

That year, Speed heard rumors about the formation of the Cowboy Artists of America, and traveled to Arizona to meet with John Hampton, one of the founders. Shortly thereafter, Speed became a charter member, and eventually served three terms as president. His bronze sculptures have been exhibited widely, including at the National Academy of Western Art, where he won the Prix de West in 1994. Speed exhibits with the Cowboy Artists of America, and other shows include the Buffalo Bill Historical Center and the Cowboy Artists of America Museum.

Most often, Speed sculpts cowboys and their horses. To him, horses have personalities as varied as humans: from mean, domineering, and bossy, to laid-back, even comical. One of his bronzes, *Ridin' a Rank One,* winner of the National Academy of Western Art's Prix de West in 1994, illustrates the struggle between a rider and horse in the early 1900s. Speed explains, "I used the lure of action to show the ultimate power the horse can generate, and then added the element of conflict by showing the opposing power the rider has to exert to be able to stay on the bucking horse. This horse is an athletic, snorty bronc with a short fuse that just plain lives to buck."

On the exterior of the National Cowboy Hall of Fame's west wing addition is *The Remuda,* five monumental bas-relief silhouette panels by **TOM RYAN** (b. 1922). The mural depicts the roundup of thirty galloping horses shadowed by two cowboys, one in the lead, the other riding drag. In recognition of the nearly forty years Ryan has chronicled working cowboys, the National Cowboy Hall of Fame awarded him their Lifetime Achievement Award in 1996.

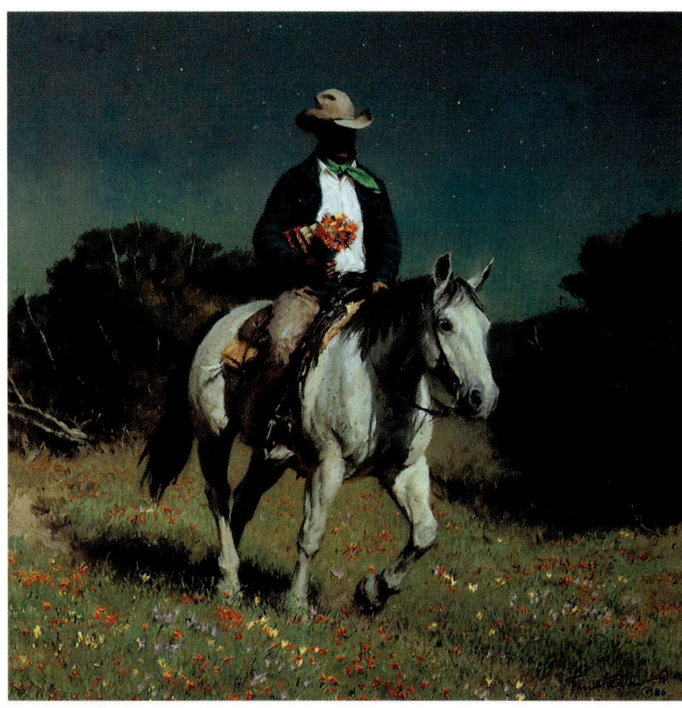

Tom Ryan,
SIX PACK SATURDAY NIGHT,
pastel,
32 by 32 inches, 1986.
Collection of Phoenix Art Museum.

A resident of Midland, Texas, Ryan studied art at the Saint Louis School of Fine Art before service in World War II, then attended the American Academy of Art in Chicago. To further his education, he moved to New York, where he enrolled in the Art Students League and eventually became an assistant to Dean Cornwell. In 1954, he relocated to Lubbock, Texas, and painted Western scenes for book jackets and national calendars. In 1967, Ryan joined the Cowboy Artists of America. Now an emeritus member, he accumulated a number of medals in their annual exhibitions, along with their George Phippen Memorial Award. Ryan's paintings have been collected by the Phoenix Art Museum, the National Cowboy Hall of Fame, and other museums throughout the West.

A 1963 visit to the famous 6666 Ranch in Guthrie, Texas, prompted Ryan to start a quest painting the West's contemporary cowboy and ranch life. Since then, he has painted realistic interpretations of cowboy and ranch culture with force, clarity, and nobility. "The cowboy way of life is singular," he says. "When you think about it, cattle still look like cattle and cowboys still look like cowboys. And they still work like their fathers and grandfathers did. They still spend long hours on the back of a horse. They still rope and brand, still watch the animals and the land."

In *Six Pack Saturday Night,* the week's work is done, and a cowboy rides in search of companionship and good times. Another painting, *The Long Day*, represents a group of cowboys riding into camp after a long, hard day on the range. That cook wagon below them is a welcome sight. Ryan, who is skilled in other media, such as pastel, also celebrates the hard-working cowboy at play.

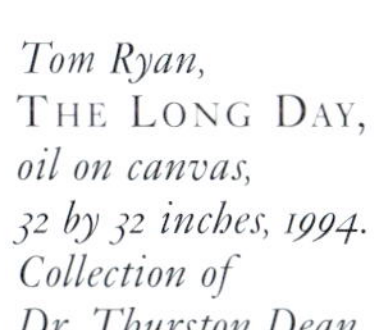

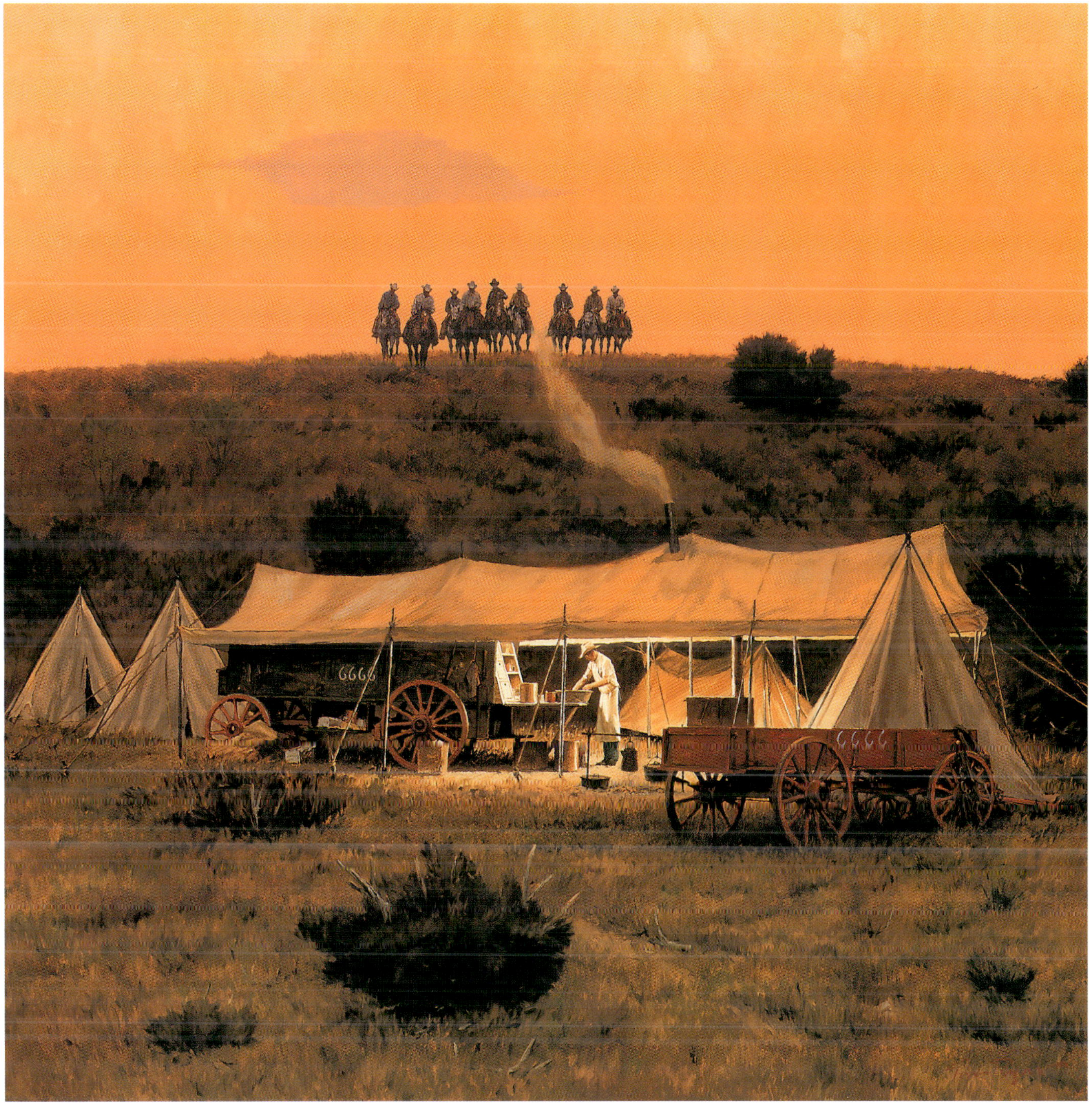

Tom Ryan,
THE LONG DAY,
oil on canvas,
32 by 32 inches, 1994.
Collection of
Dr. Thurston Dean.

Bill Owen (b. 1942) discovers a new experience in each painting of cowboys and ranch life. Owen knows the paths of cowboy life, having worked high-school summer vacations on a ranch in Arizona. He grew up alongside cowboys, and, while still young, started to draw them and their horses. Through the 1960s and the early 1970s, Owen, with no formal art training, practiced painting. In 1970, he started to exhibit his work at a gallery in Sedona.

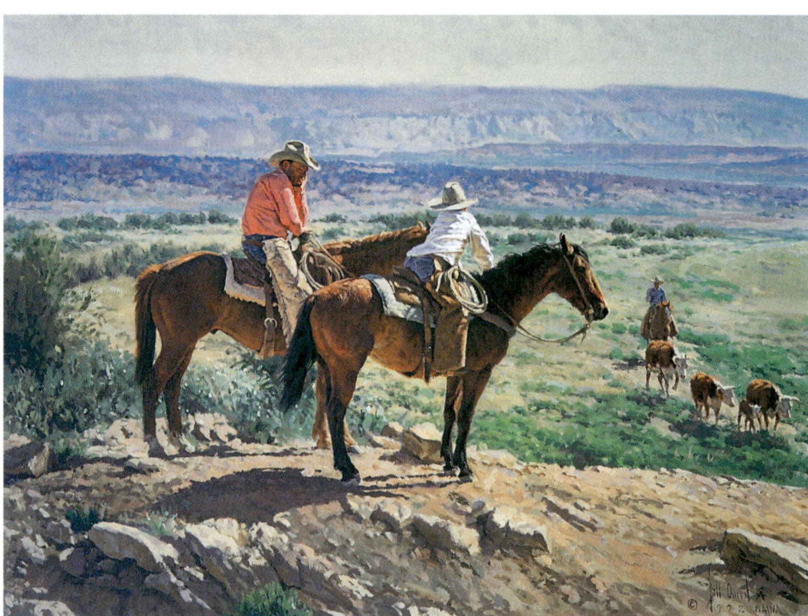

Bill Owen,
BORN TO THIS LAND,
oil on linen,
22 by 30 inches, 1992.
Private collection.

In 1973, Owen joined the Cowboy Artists of America, the youngest member at that time voted into the organization. Elected president twice, Owen also has received several gold and silver medals from them for his oil painting and drawing. The Gilcrease Museum honored Owen at their annual Rendezvous in 1996. His work has been exhibited in Beijing, and at the Grand Palais in Paris. In 1991, he joined the National Academy of Western Art. Three years later one of his paintings won their Frederic Remington Award.

Owen's paintings are a response to the present-day life of cowboy and ranch traditions, and are noted for their accurate detail, color, and light. Each man and horse he paints is real, and Owen writes a description on the reverse of the canvas that includes actual names of the cowboys and their horses. In addition, he often writes the story of the scene. The big ranches are disappearing, Owen feels, thus his paintings, like *Born to This Land,* record the present for history. His research centers around his involvement in the lives of his subjects. "Cowboys are watchers, aware of what transpires around them," he says.

Owen paints small field sketches to capture sunrise or sunset colors, and carries a camera on his saddle to photograph the terrain and action. For Owen, neither authentic nor abstract elements can stand by themselves, and his role as an artist is to bring them together. One of his canvases created for the Gilcrease Rendezvous, *Noon Change on a Big Outfit,* is the largest work he has painted so far. The painting illustrates the daily ritual of cowboys who wait for their horses to be roped out of the remuda. In the foreground, a cowboy brushes his horse before the saddle is

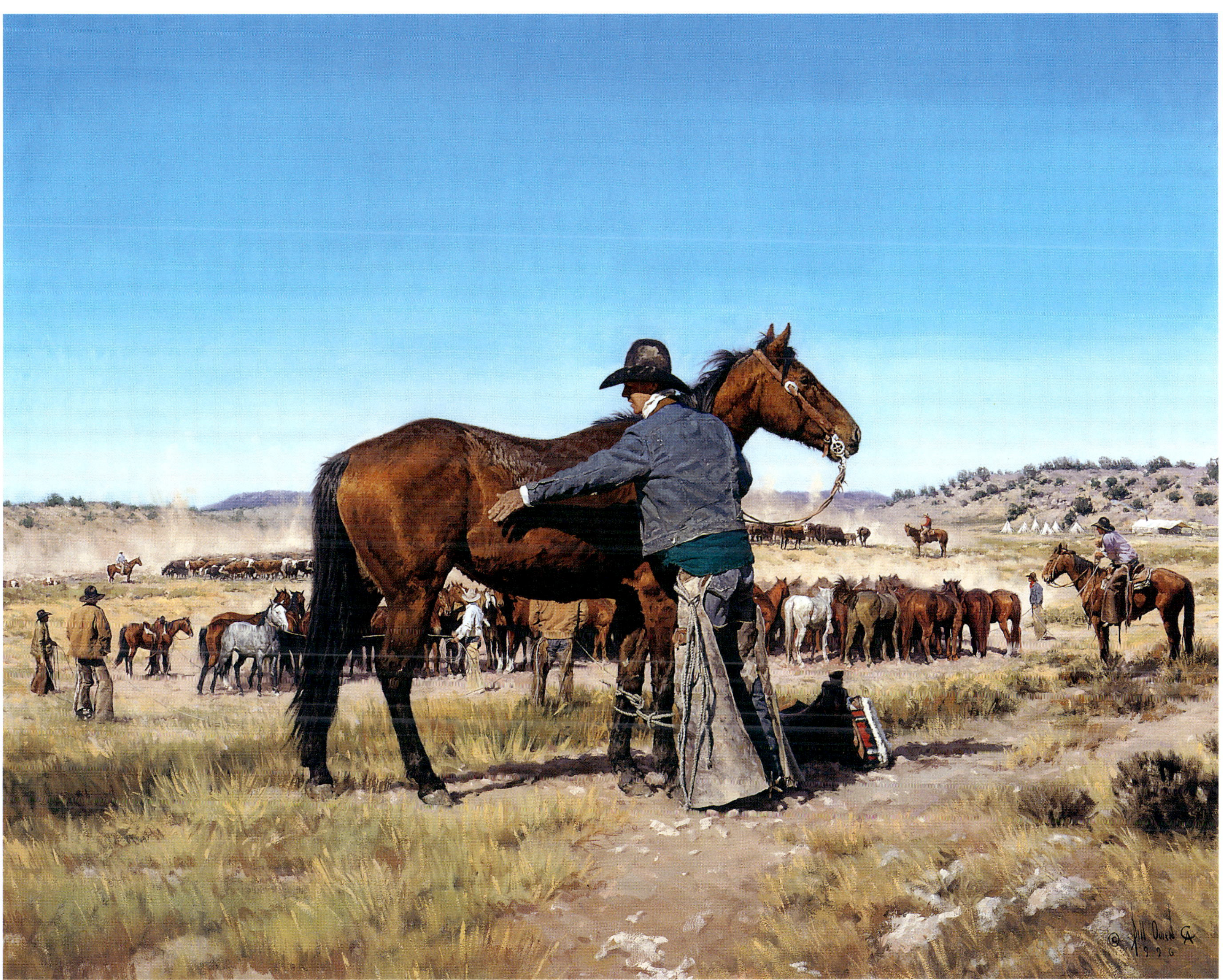

Bill Owen, NOON CHANGE ON A BIG OUTFIT, *oil on linen, 48 by 60 inches, 1996. Private collection; photograph by Bill McLemore Photography.*

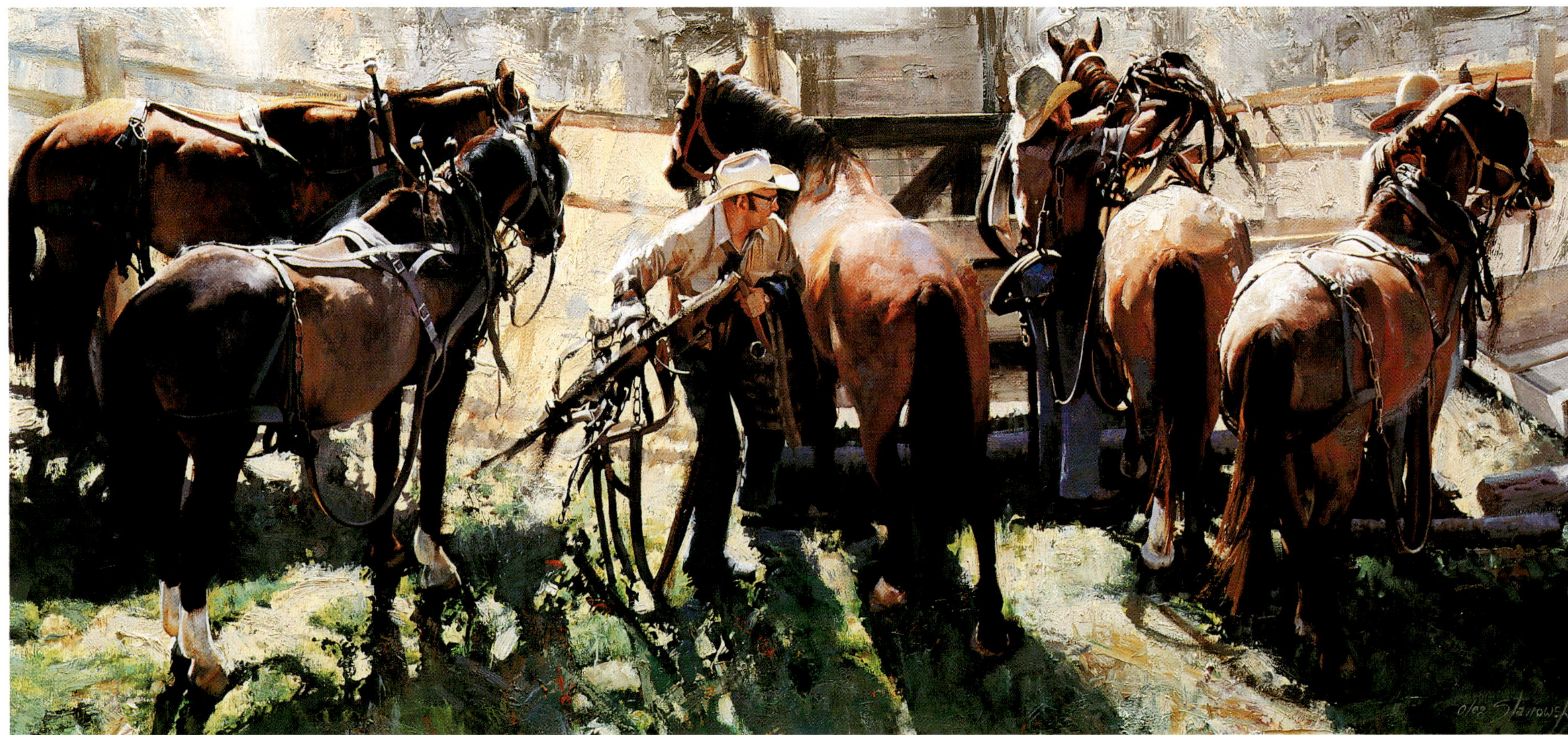

Oleg Stavrowsky, THE HARNESSERS, *oil on linen, 34 by 72 inches, 1996. Private collection.*

placed on his back. "This is a daily event during the fall work that you could see out on the range," Owen says. "Each cowboy has a group of six or seven horses only he rides. You could never call out a horse that wasn't yours."

The work of painter **OLEG STAVROWSKY** (b. 1928) also presents scenes of ranch life, especially cowboys and their horses. Nearly twenty-five years ago, Stavrowsky encountered Western paintings at the National Cowboy Hall of Fame in Oklahoma City. Already a commercial artist, Stavrowsky was struck by their subject matter, and he decided to paint similar images from a contemporary standpoint.

I am forever experimenting and trying new approaches and techniques.

—OLEG STAVROWSKY

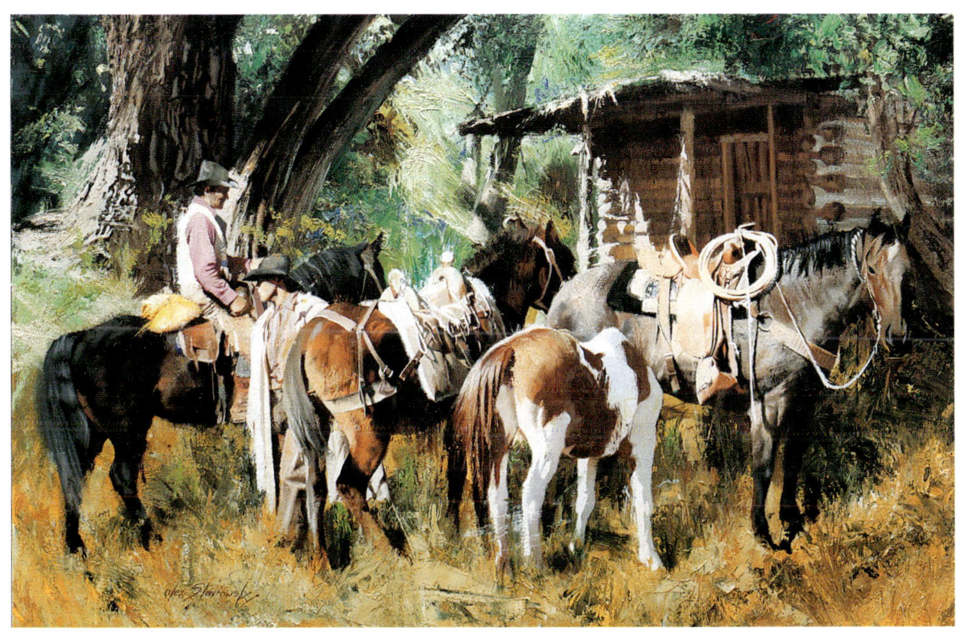

Oleg Stavrowsky,
CHIGGER COUNTRY,
oil on linen,
36 by 56 inches, 1994.
Private collection.

To accomplish this, though, Stavrowsky needed to learn about cowboys and horses, not easy for someone born in the Harlem area of New York. Now he knows horses, yet does not ride them, nor for that matter, go near them. "They step on me," he says, "and they don't like me. But they are beautiful, and I love the way they look." Stavrowsky served in World War II, then worked as a technical illustrator for McDonnell Douglas. Afterwards, he lived in a succession of Midwestern cities while employed as a freelance illustrator. Stavrowsky eventually settled in Santa Fe in 1991. An iconoclast about his career, Stavrowsky reflects, "I have never won any prizes or ribbons or awards, and it is seldom I attend an art show. I do not belong to any art clubs or groups of any kind. I am strictly a lone wolf and keep pretty much to myself. I am completely self-taught and intensely interested in my work even at my age. I am forever experimenting and trying new approaches and techniques."

Many of Stavrowsky's paintings are commissioned by clients. He starts an image from the photographs he takes of working cowboys, sometimes posed on fences or beside a horse. He creates a pencil sketch from a photograph's suggestions, to ensure he and a client agree on the basic composition. Then he proceeds to paint the image on a canvas. Stavrowsky's subjects are rendered in a loose, expressive fashion, the paint executed in a thick impasto with brush or palette knife. With paintings like *The Harnessers* or *Chigger Country,* Stavrowsky prefers to show figures from the back or side, focusing on graphic rather than narrative expression.

Attracted to the overlooked, fragmented aspects of Western art, **NELSON BOREN** (b. 1952) has developed a distinctive trademark style. Boren's watercolors present an intimate, close-up view of the life and trappings of the modern American cowboy. His large-scale compositions give insight into an unfamiliar lifestyle and create a singular mood. "I enjoy capturing the weathered look of old leather and rusty spurs," he says. "I see history in these elements of cowboy life." Among

Boren's exhibitions are shows at the Buffalo Bill Historical Center, the Desert Caballeros Western Museum, and the Scottsdale Center for the Arts. His work is located in such corporate collections as the Dallas Cowboys, the Minnesota Vikings, and Coca-Cola.

Boren and his family live on an eighteen-acre ranch outside Sandpoint, Idaho. Trained as an architect, he operated his own architectural firm for many years in Mesa, Arizona, then in 1990 moved to Idaho and became a full-time artist. Boren applies lessons learned as an architect to his watercolors, which he calls "fragments."

Boren's watercolors feature intricate, close-up details of cowboy boots, spurs, chap-covered legs, or gloved hands holding a rope. Unlike many watercolorists, Boren does not stretch his paper, and he paints directly on it, the wrinkles and puddles adding a more authentic look and texture. Boren spends considerable time at rodeo events, where he hangs around the "pits" in search of prospective ideas for his images. In addition, he uses live models and the cowboy material he has collected. He considers his paintings figurative, although they never include faces, and sometimes not a torso, either. Personality is established through the visual impact of colorful shirts, gloves, chaps, and jeans, like *Wrangler Shirt.* And in the case of *Arizona Boots,* it is spurs and neon cowboy boots. "I try with these subjects to capture emotions about them," Boren explains, "prompting viewers to imagine the rest."

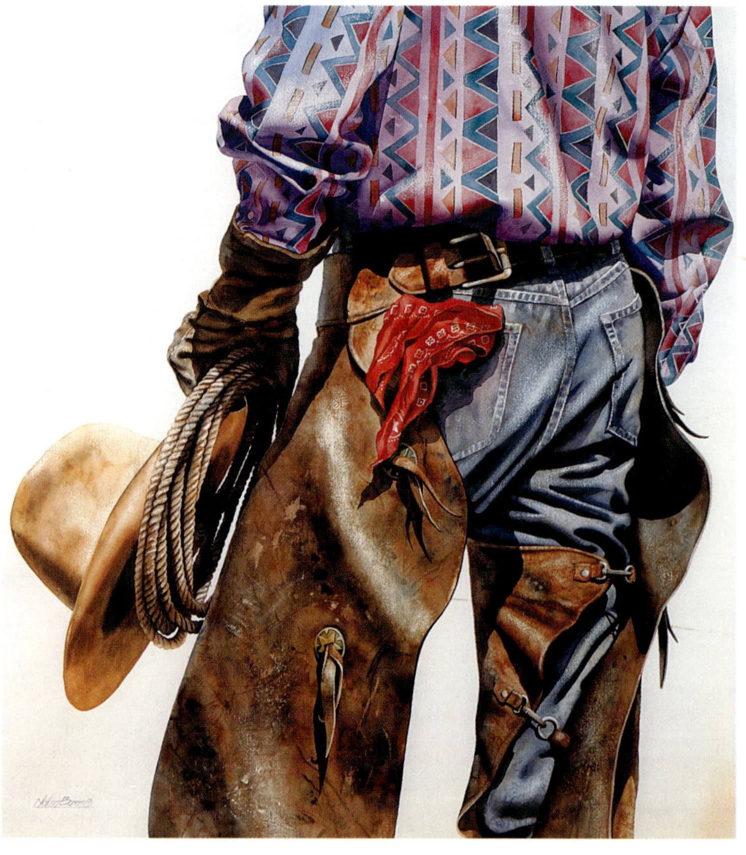

Nelson Boren,
WRANGLER SHIRT,
watercolor,
54 by 50 inches, 1993.
Photograph courtesy of Suzanne Brown Gallery.

The paintings of **DON COEN** (b. 1935) are filled with the varied imagery of rural ranch life—Hereford cattle, horses, cowboys, dogs, pickup trucks, and farm machinery. His massive canvases, devoid of clichés, their images deliberately commonplace, are macro-views that dissolve the

I try with these subjects to capture emotions about them,
prompting viewers to imagine the rest.

—NELSON BOREN

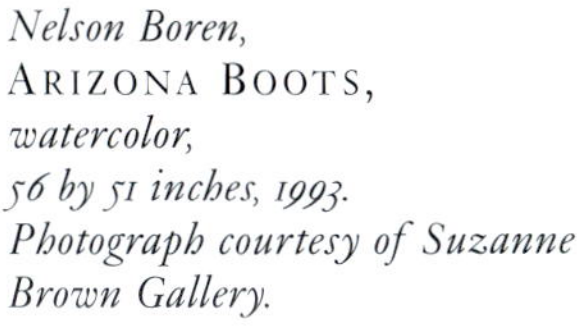

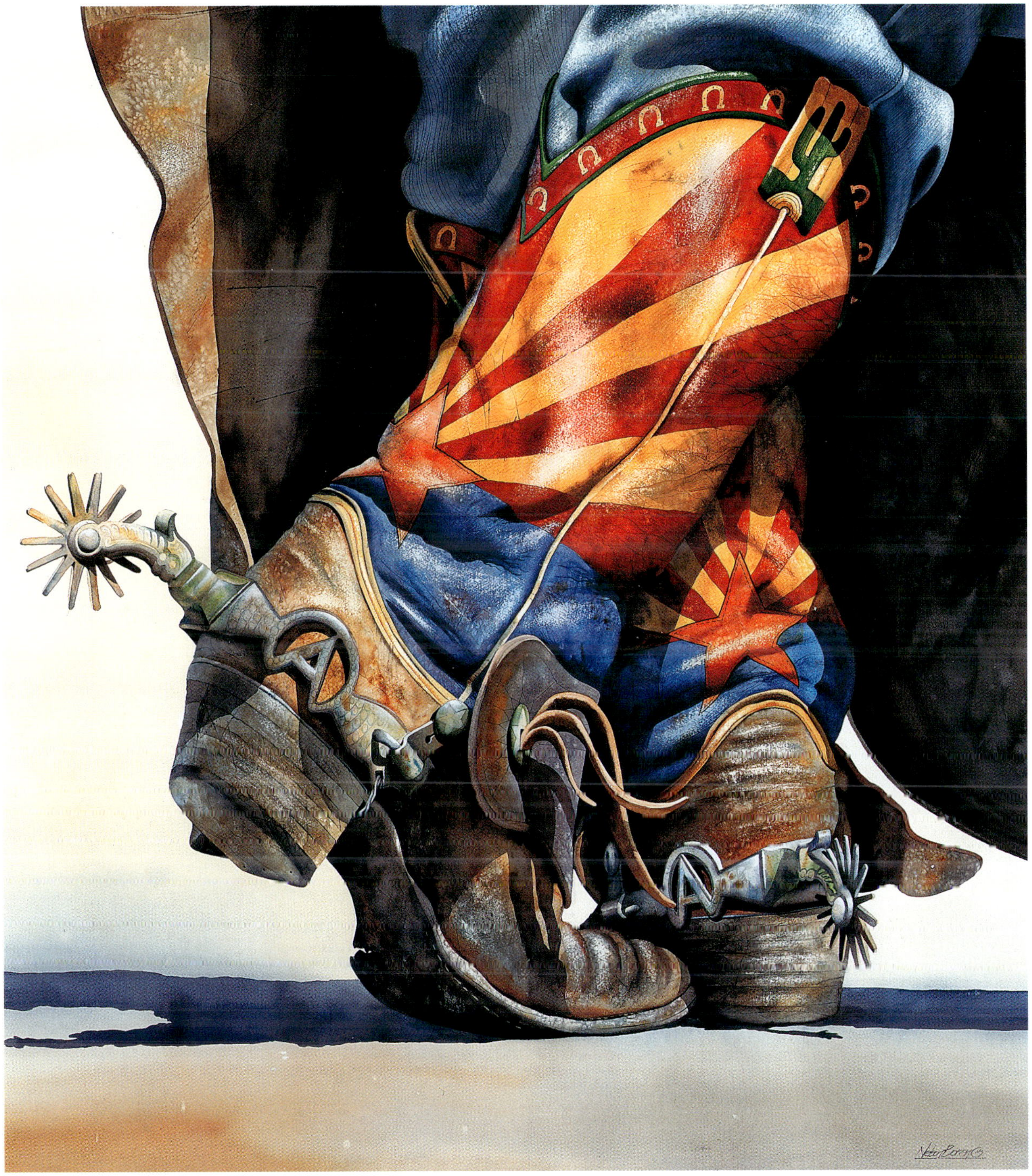

Nelson Boren,
ARIZONA BOOTS,
watercolor,
56 by 51 inches, 1993.
Photograph courtesy of Suzanne Brown Gallery.

boundaries between realism and abstraction. In fact, his airbrushed, nonobjective paintings venture beyond the large-scale, into epic proportions.

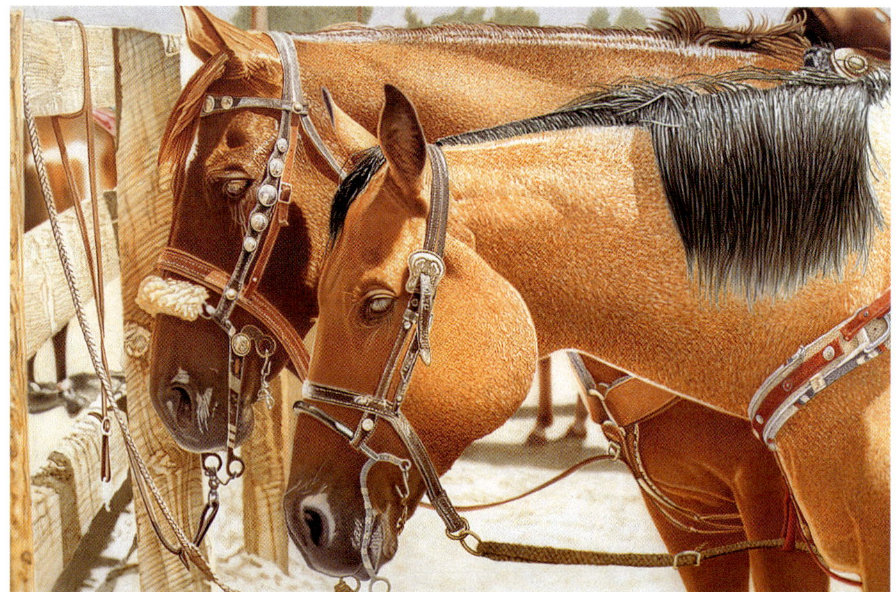

Don Coen,
PATTERNS OF THE WEST,
airbrush and acrylic on canvas, 6½ by 10 feet, 1996. Private collection.

Coen was born and raised in Lamar, Colorado, and now lives in Boulder. After graduation from the University of Denver, Coen worked for an aircraft manufacturer, then attended graduate school at the University of Northern Colorado. In the early 1960s, he turned to full-time painting. Since 1968, he has participated in over fifty one-man and group exhibitions, and is represented in both public and private collections. Recently, the Denver Art Museum purchased one of his paintings for their permanent collection.

Rural Western America, ranches and farms, with their truth and simplicity, but without nostalgia, are the subjects for Coen's art. He uses an airbrush to create the soft-focus backgrounds, telephoto close-ups, and enlargement effects in his paintings. "You get layers and layers of color, and subtle changes in color that are wonderful," he says. The paintings seem like movies to Coen, in that when you see them up close, the images dissolve, but further away, they snap into focus. "Actually, when I'm doing an airbrush and acrylic painting like *Patterns of the West,* I think of it as a nonobjective painting, and not a realistic one," Coen says.

Like Don Coen, **JOHN FARNSWORTH** (b. 1941) paints large-scale canvases, usually of cattle and horses. The son of a Santa Fe Railway engineer, he grew up in small towns along the tracks in northern Arizona, places like Williams, Flagstaff, Ash Fork, Winslow, and Happy Jack. After graduation from Flagstaff High School, Farnsworth taught himself to paint. He worked as a preparator at the Museum of Northern Arizona in the middle 1960s, and in his free time he often teamed up with another artist to explore, camp, and paint at remote places scattered throughout the Navajo Reservation.

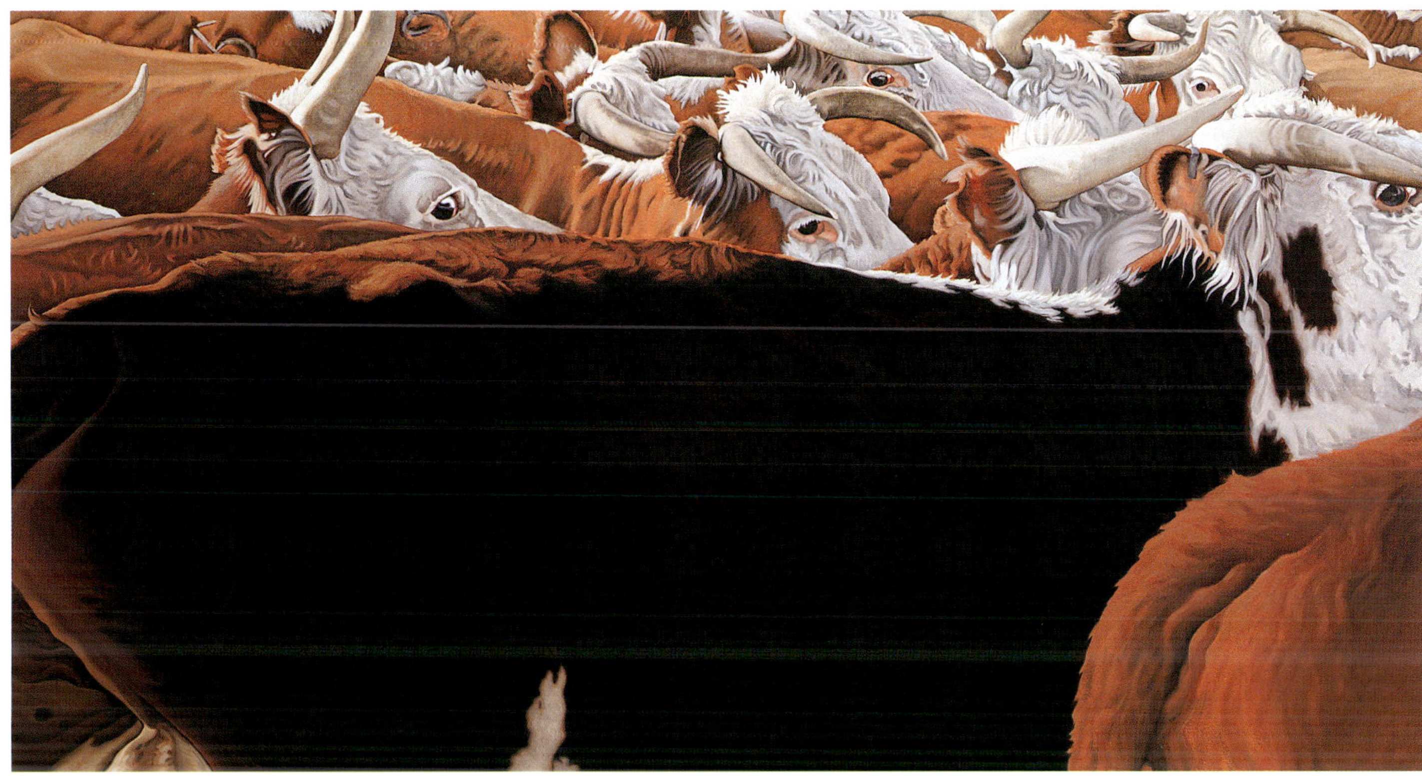

John Farnsworth, WHITEFACE, *oil on canvas, 48 by 96 inches, 1982. Private collection.*

Farnsworth, who now lives in Taos, New Mexico, has been a full time painter since 1968. His best-known work is the gigantic mural of a Wells Fargo stagecoach that adorns one wall at Phoenix's Sky Harbor International Airport. Some of the museum and corporate collections that have collected his work include the Millicent Rogers Museum, Northern Arizona University, and IBM.

Farnsworth's painting approach involves cropping, which enhances a viewer's involvement, eliminates unnecessary areas, and controls the relationships between image sections and the canvas edge. He believes this gives a greater illusion of depth. He alternates between large, developed

Light, design, texture, the Southwestern heritage, life, death, and mystery are elements embedded in my art.

—JOHN FARNSWORTH

acrylic paintings of horses and cattle, such as *Whiteface* (p. 147), and more spontaneous watercolors, often of Hopi Kachina faces. "For me, light, design, texture, the Southwestern heritage, life, death, and mystery are elements embedded in my art," he says. He finds his cattle and horse subjects at auctions and rodeos, and he is intrigued with their subtle colors, textures, shapes, and arrangement of forms. Farnsworth works from a combination of photographs, sketches, and his imagination to conceive each canvas.

ROBERT SHUFELT (b. 1935) loved horses before he ever thought of drawing cowboy art, and desperately wanted to be a cowboy before he could afford a horse. Now a resident of Hillsboro, New Mexico, Shufelt, known as "Shoofly," grew up in Illinois. He attended the University of Illinois, then experienced brief careers as a professional football player and a race car driver. Afterwards, he worked as a commercial illustrator in Chicago for twenty years.

In 1976, Shufelt moved to Wickenburg, Arizona, and started to draw Western subjects. Two years later he decided to embrace a career as an artist. Shufelt struggled for recognition, and not until 1979 would he achieve his first successful exhibition. Some of his recent exhibits include the Old West Museum in Cheyenne, Wyoming; the Desert Caballeros Museum in Wickenburg; and the Pro-Rodeo Hall of Fame.

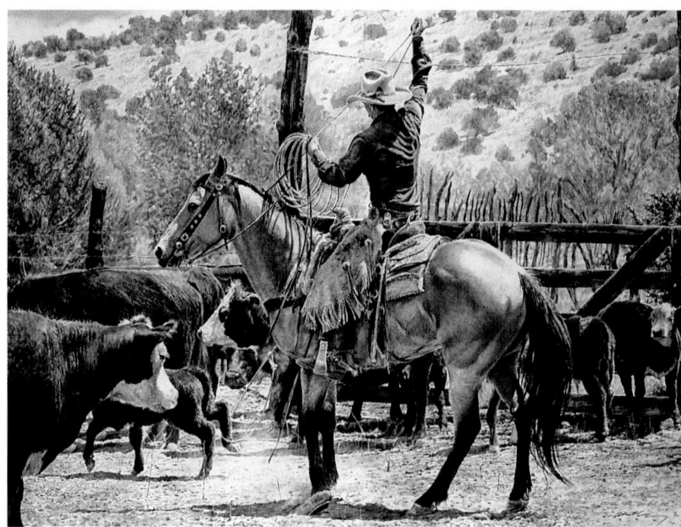

Robert Shufelt,
RATHER HAVE TWO, BUT ONE 'IL DO,
pencil,
22 by 30 inches, 1996.
Private collection.

Shufelt's drawings illustrate stories of the cowboy West with quiet subtlety, their intimacy found in the directness of pencil. He uses photographs as a tool, to capture reactions to quick situations and special moments. A drawing begins by layering graphite on graphite, building as one does in a painting. Fascinated by light and texture, Shufelt feels that good drawings, as *Rather Have Two, But One 'Il Do* or *Down Time,* bring life to the space that surrounds them, and color becomes irrelevant. The subjects are always cowboys and their horses. "A horse gives a man nobility," he remarks. "As for these cowboys, they work in forgotten country on forgotten ranches hoping nobody will remember and bring forth bulldozers. Keepers of the American spirit. I feel a deep sense of responsibility and joy in drawing them and drawing for them."

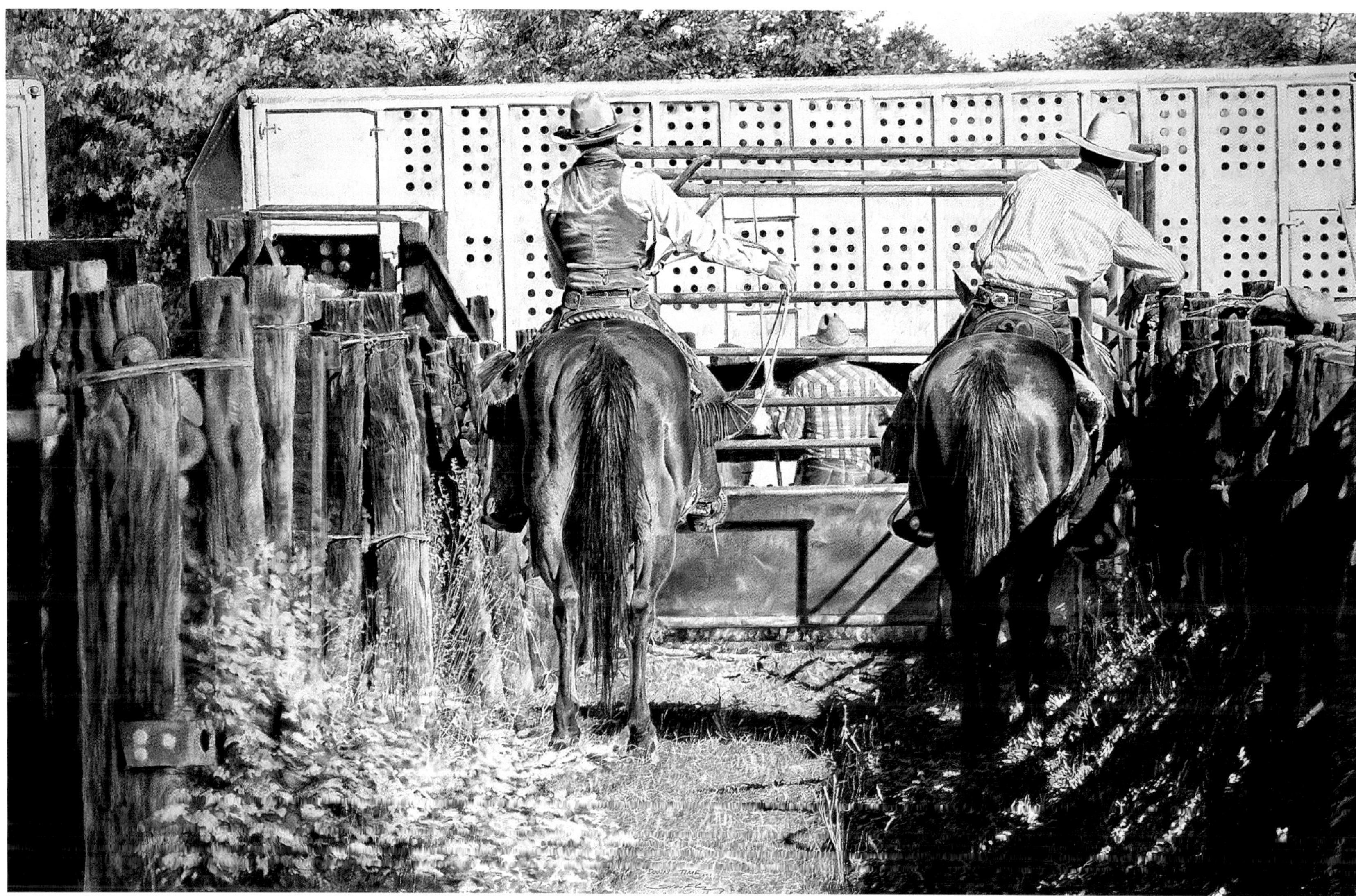

Robert Shufelt, DOWN TIME, *pencil, 29 by 40 inches, 1996. Photograph courtesy of Legacy Galleries.*

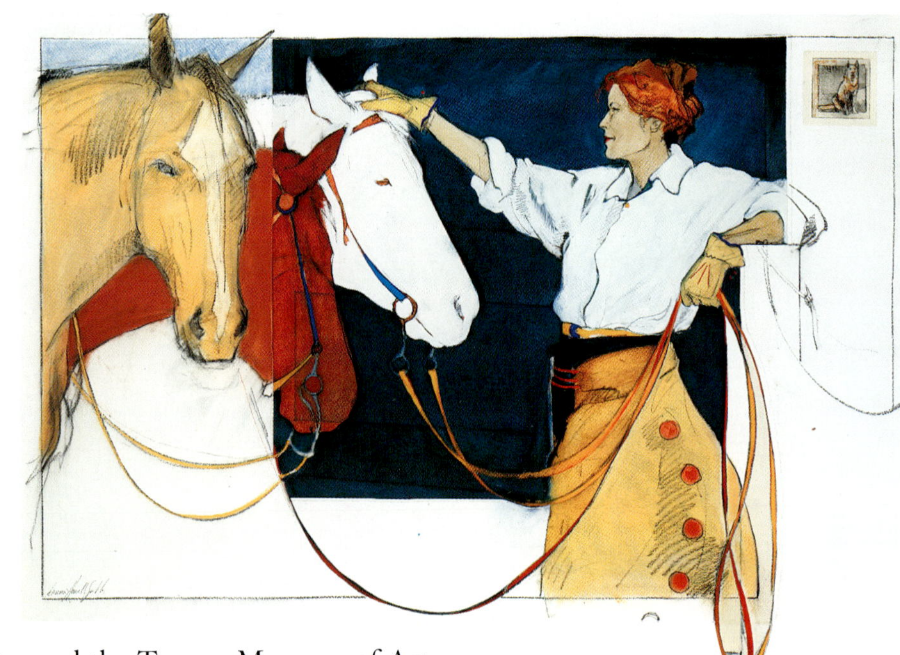

Donna Howell-Sickles, CANVAS REINS, *oil/multimedia on canvas, 40 by 60 inches, 1996. Private collection.*

Raised on a family ranch near the Red River in Texas, **DONNA HOWELL-SICKLES** (b. 1949) developed an early interest in the mythology of cowboy life. After she received a B.F.A. from Texas Tech University in Lubbock, Howell-Sickles taught for two years as a visiting artist in schools for the Washington State Arts Commission, then returned to Frisco, Texas, where she now resides, in the late 1970s.

Howell-Sickles has been the featured artist of the 1996 American Women Artists Show at the National Museum of Wildlife Art in Jackson, Wyoming, in addition to being the focus of more than a dozen one-woman gallery shows. Her work is in private, corporate, and museum collections such as the Buffalo Bill Historical Center and the Tucson Museum of Art.

Howell-Sickles's art revolves around the imagery of cowgirls, started when a friend gave her an old postcard of a cowgirl with smiling red lips, arrayed in Western attire. Fascinated, Howell-Sickles knew this was an invented image, an intangible character created by novels and movies of the early 1900s. Cowgirls evolved as the major theme in her work by 1979, particularly when she studied the women who participated in Wild West shows and early rodeos.

By the early 1980s, Howell-Sickles's art included additional detail to elaborate the differences and personalities she found in these women, with their faces more defined. Joy and contentment, that sometimes overlooked part of daily life, anchored by increased movement in her figures, define her work, such as *Canvas Reins,* enhanced with the symbolic touch between the woman and her horses, or *Earth, Air, Fire, and Water,* a presentation of four stylishly dressed cowgirls and two playful bears. "The cowgirl is my icon for women in general," Howell-Sickles says. "She gives us someone of warmth and humor with whom we can share a good laugh."

The art of Howell-Sickles reflects part of the American West's mythology. The quest for self, meaning, happiness, and camaraderie reside in her images. In her paintings, cowgirls, supported by wild and domestic animal companions, serve as spiritual icons, a visual legacy of women as intense, creative individuals who are inspired by life.

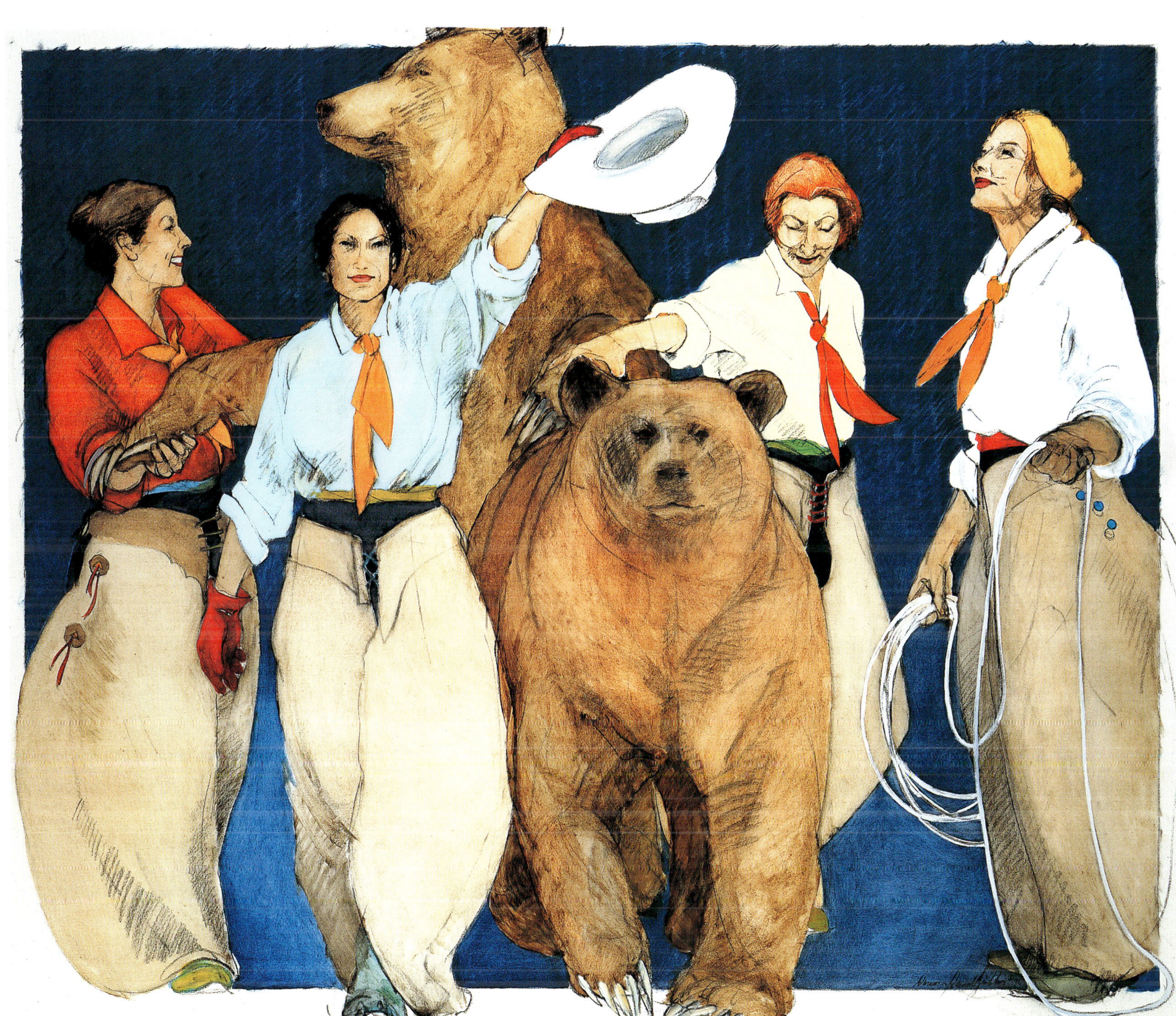

Donna Howell-Sickles, EARTH, AIR, FIRE, AND WATER, *oil on canvas, 60 by 72 inches, 1996. Private collection.*

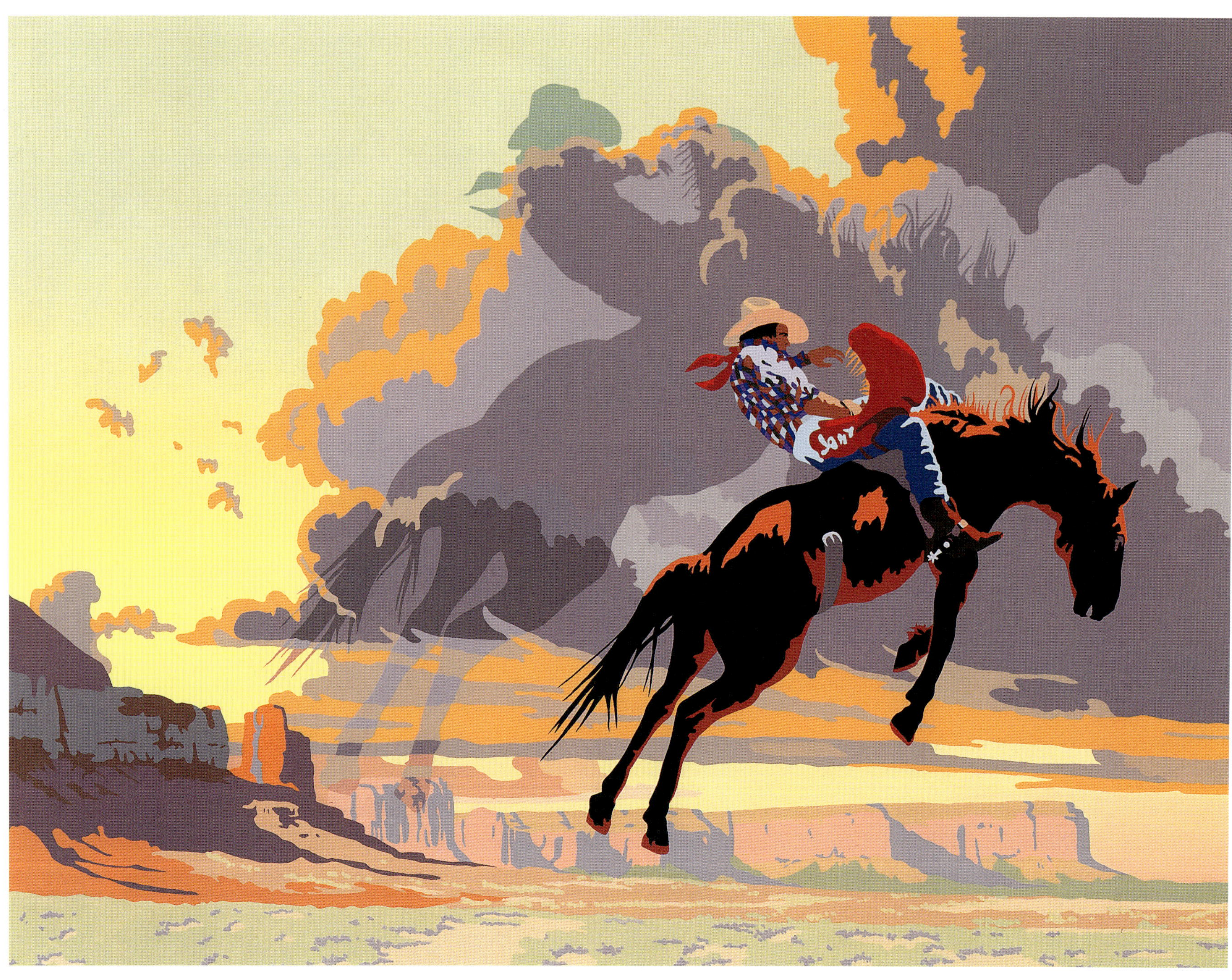

Bill Schenck, LEAPING INTO THE TWILIGHT OF HIS CAREER, *oil on canvas, 30 by 40 inches, 1995. Private collection.*

A visual satirist, **BILL SCHENCK** (b. 1947) paints images of the modern American West, his subjects cowboys, cowgirls, pickups, and Cadallics, old traditions and new values, done in the flat, simplified manner and vibrant colors of pop art. After receiving a B.F.A. from the Kansas City Art Institute in 1969, he moved to New York and embraced photo-realism. Schenck recalls that the original school of photo-realism demanded a remote, cool approach to an image. However, he discovered his romantic interest in the American West interfered with its modern tenets.

That romantic interest propelled him into a Western lifestyle, which included work as a rodeo performer for nearly four years, which led to painting images of rodeo and ranch life. By 1975, he started to paint cowboys and Cadillacs, along with paintings of cereal boxes, his parodies of contemporary American culture. Women appeared in Schenck's paintings by 1982, pop Western cowgirls, imagery that remains in his work. Since 1972, Schenck has had over 120 solo and group exhibitions. His work is in the collections of the Yellowstone Art Center, the Smithsonian Institution, the Wyoming State Museum, and Brigham Young University, among others, besides nearly twenty corporate collections.

Schenck practices a form of abstraction to debunk and demystify his subjects, tempered by use of flattened and stylized images drawn from photographs, a "paint-by-numbers" approach. This, along with exaggerated colors, gives his work a distinctive tone. Detail is removed, portions of several photographs are combined, solid color masses are emphasized, and black shadows are overstated for three-dimensional effects, as in *Leaping into the Twilight of His Career,* his perception of the final ride of a rodeo performer. Schenck explains, "My style of painting becomes a marriage of my earliest romantic remembrances of the West and my artistic roots in the 'pop' painting of the early 1960s. Out of this, I paint takeoffs from old black-and-white movie stills, slides from rodeo events, cowboys on the range, landscapes, comic book–style Western images, even Donald Duck as a cowboy, and gun-slinging cowgirls."

Cowboys, cowgirls, and ranch life still remain vital in certain regions of the West, icons of self-made individuals and enclaves of self-reliance. From the measured perspective of realist painting to the liberality of contemporary pop art techniques, images of the cowboy spirit still thrive as subjects for painters and sculptors. The open range and the free rider have long passed by, but contemporary artists throughout the West continue to find inspiration for a uniquely American subject matter.

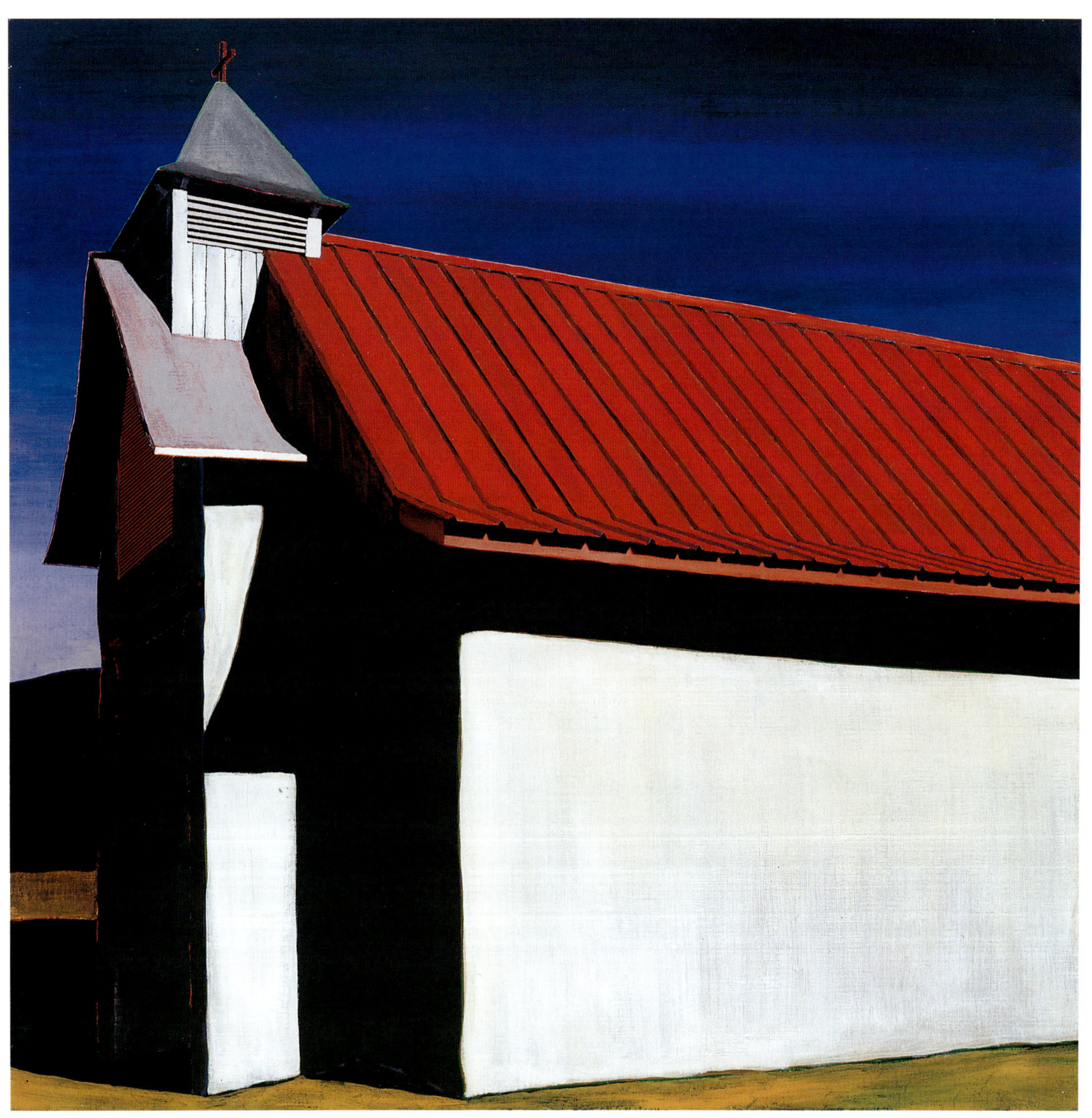

OTHER WESTS

Evidence of Something Else

THERE ARE ARTISTS AT WORK IN THE AMERICAN WEST WHO DO NOT FIT EASILY INTO ANY particular category. Their subjects resonate through such topics as past and present Hispanic traditions, family and community, Native American mythology and spiritualism, and agrarian-based life and environmental concerns. They respect the Old West, with its myriad cultural icons, yet know there is not only a Present West, but Other Wests, and New Wests poised over the horizon. Their expressive art, sometimes balanced on the tension between realism and abstraction, reflects the ambiguities of change, tragedy, alienation, and death. Yet others respond with reverence, hope, spiritualism, irony, and the sacred, as they search for ways to communicate what the West means to them. Some take old, shadowy myths and legends, rework them, then create new symbolic resolutions, reinvented traditions, through their paintings and sculpture.

Harold Joe Waldrum,
NEW RED ROOF AT PILAR,
acrylic on linen,
40 by 40 inches, 1993.
Collection of Mr. and Mrs. Richard L. Anderson; photograph by Bill McLemore Photography, courtesy of Joy Tash Gallery.

Many of these artists are disturbed by the modern version of what Frederic Remington called in his time "men in derby hats, the smoking chimneys, the cord-binder, the thirty-day note," only now it is in the form of population explosion, the sprawl of rural and urban development, racism, and environmental degradation. Most of them, especially the Native American and Hispanic artists, attempt to place in their metamorphic and symbolic art the inventive threads that bind the past to the present.

One of those threads, the solid timelessness of northern New Mexico's Hispanic churches, has inspired the paintings, etchings, and linocuts of **HAROLD JOE WALDRUM** (b. 1934). Born in Texas, Waldrum completed a music degree at Western State College in Colorado, then pursued graduate work in studio painting at Fort Hays State College in Kansas. He taught for fourteen years in the Kansas public school system, and for one year at Fort Hays State College.

In 1971 he moved to New Mexico, and in 1980 he started to paint the region's old Hispanic churches, repositories of personal faith, devotion, and daily life. These churches and *moradas* not only have personal significance for Waldrum, with their saints, angels, and dead ancestors; they also serve as the vehicle for the creative act of painting. Interested in aesthetic problems, along

When I make art, I concern myself with the amounts of reflection I perceive.

—HAROLD JOE WALDRUM

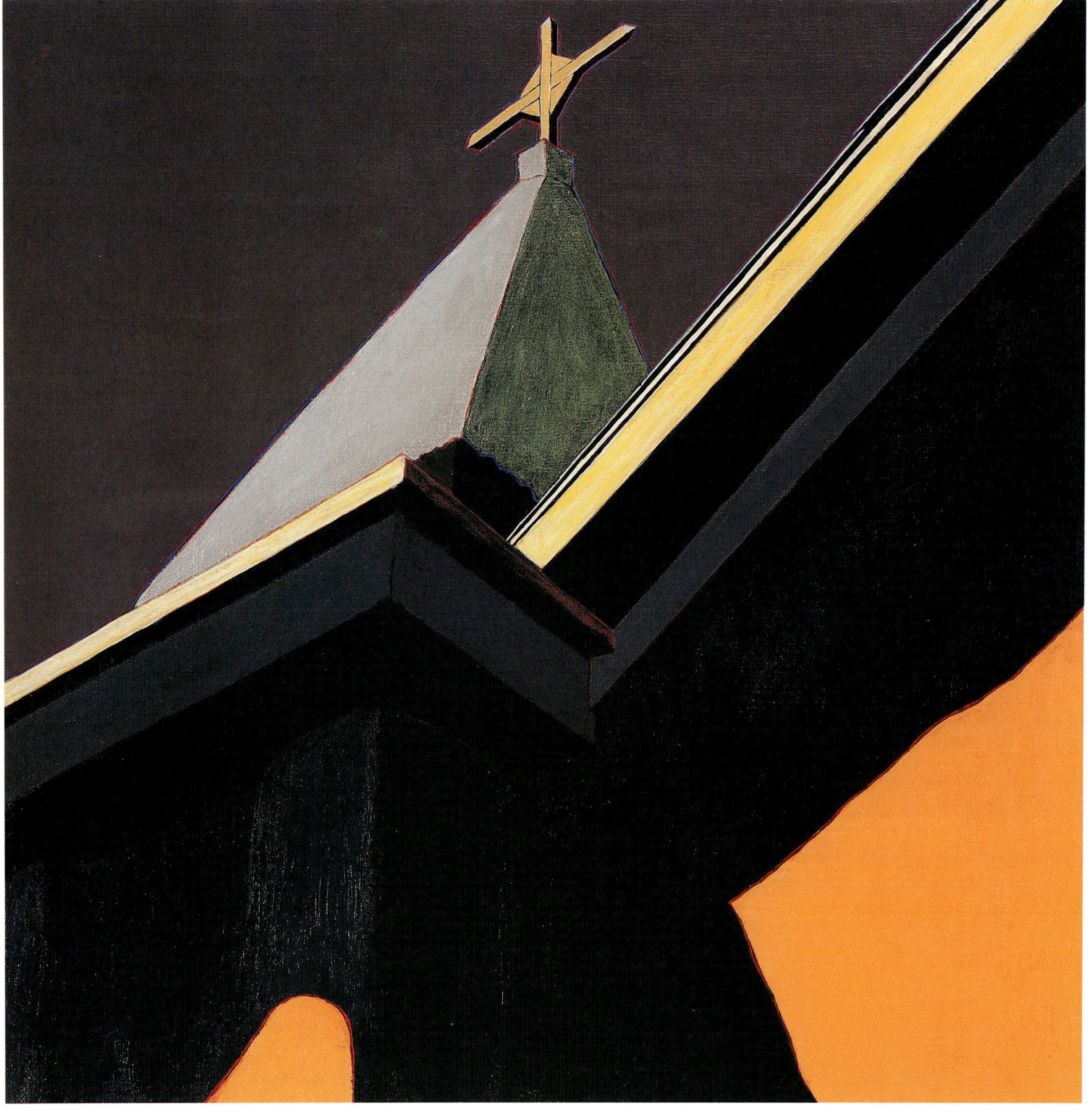

Harold Joe Waldrum,
BELFRY AT CORRALES,
acrylic on canvas,
40 by 40 inches, 1995.
Photograph by Mary Elkins,
courtesy of Joy Tash Gallery.

with their solutions, Waldrum finds inspiration in the formal creation of the space, color, and light that dance around these structures.

In order to solve the fundamental problem of New Mexico's variable light, Waldrum uses the camera as a tool, although with some limitations, to help him conceptualize the images he desires. He analyzed the region's almost celestial light, then developed a painting style that expresses *un divina luz,* "that divine light," on the religious architecture, their shapes anchored by single slabs of color, arranged in broad planes. "When I make art, I concern myself with the amounts of reflection I perceive," he says. For Waldrum, his paintings of austere churches, like *New Red Roof at Pilar* (p. 154) or *Belfry at Corrales,* each with its own character, reflect a timeless personal testament.

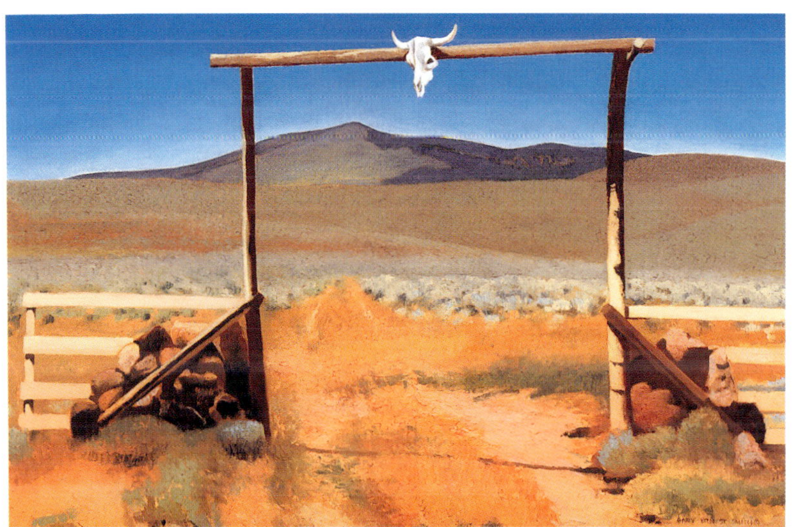

Gary Ernest Smith,
EASTERN OREGON GATEWAY,
oil on canvas,
48 by 84 inches, 1990.
Private collection;
photograph by Bill McLemore
Photography, courtesy of Overland
Gallery of Fine Art.

Like Waldrum's solitary churches, the human landscapes painted by Utah artist **GARY ERNEST SMITH** (b. 1942) often speak of acute loneliness and the dignity garnered from hard work and self-reliance, symbols that transcend arrangement of paint on the canvases. His art merges human figures with architectural shapes and natural surroundings, drawn from rural environments, from people shaped, hammered, and chiseled by the land. The paintings theatrically evoke the regionalist agrarian tradition, so much a part of the West's heritage.

Born and raised in a small, isolated farm community near Baker, Oregon, Smith lived in an environment that stressed hard work. He took his first art instruction through the Famous Artists Course, a correspondence school, then after discharge from the military obtained an M.F.A. from Brigham Young University. By then, enough commission and gallery contacts had accumulated that he decided to try his hand as a full-time painter.

Years of art study and his rural background eventually coalesced into a distinctive style: images of faceless men and women—pumpkin harvesters, potato farmers, ranch hands—solitary, mysterious figures. These people are icons reflective of the American West, Smith feels, rooted in

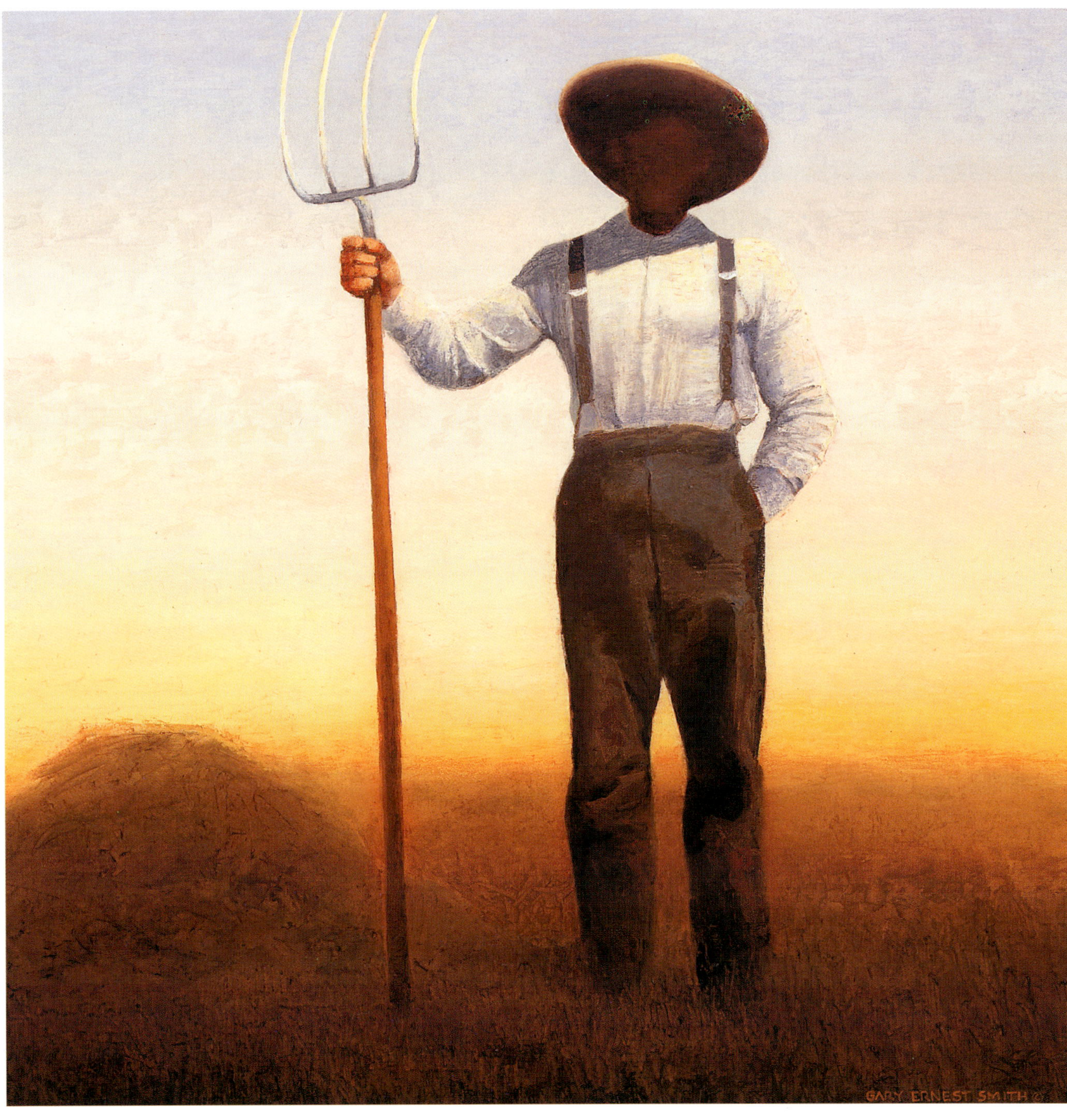

Gary Ernest Smith,
SOLITARY MAN OF THE FIELD,
oil on canvas,
48 by 48 inches, 1990.
Private collection; photograph by
Bill McLemore Photography, courtesy of
Overland Gallery of Fine Art.

the earth. Their faces are shadowed in the paintings, the perfect metaphor and universal symbol for everyman and everywoman.

Smith has exhibited his art widely in solo and group shows, including the Springville Art Museum (Springville, Utah) and the Sangre de Cristo Art Center. A one-man show, *Journey in Search of Lost Images,* originated at the Springville Art Museum in 1990, then traveled for two years to eighteen venues throughout the United States.

An exacting synthesis of realism and abstract designs, some of Smith's paintings are hard-edged and slightly surreal, based on the hidden layers of his early experiences in Oregon. In 1989, driven by a desire to reclaim the region of his youth, Smith traveled to the sagebrush and rimrock country of Baker County, Oregon. There, inspired by vast vistas, lonely roads, and independent people, Smith produced a series of paintings that he called Journey in Search of Lost Images, the work that ultimately served as the foundation of the museum show. One of them is *Eastern Oregon Gateway* (p. 157). As Smith explains, "Using animal skulls as figureheads is commonplace to Westerners. I chose to paint them in an almost surreal setting that suggests a haunting, majestic symbolism."

Most of Smith's paintings focus on an agrarian way of life that appears as timeless as the Western landscape, yet is slowly fading away. "I constantly look for images in my surroundings that distill the essence of the rural experience," he says. His paintings are endowed with diffused light effects, stark imagery, and an atypical point of view. These works, like *Solitary Man of the Field,* speak with formal clarity about the stillness and calm of everyday tasks, of people at peace with themselves and the land.

I constantly look for images in my surroundings
that distill the essence of the rural experience.

—GARY ERNEST SMITH

For **PAGE ALLEN** (b. 1951), the Western landscape lends itself not only as a subject for painting, with abundant light and space, but also as a metaphor. To Allen, there is a distinction between familiarity and awe, or for that matter, between realism and abstraction in her work.

After she graduated from Hampshire College in 1974, Allen received an M.A. from Northern Illinois University in 1980, then studied with Richard Diebenkorn and Garner Tullis. Among her solo and group exhibitions are shows at the Yellowstone Art Center and the Eiteljorg Museum.

Allen envisions herself as the spiritual descendant of those early modern artists clustered around Alfred Stieglitz; Georgia O'Keeffe, Arthur Dove, and Marsden Hartley. Like them, she paints a visible world, and like them, she seeks something invisible, something spiritual in her art. In her oils, watercolors, and monotypes, Allen does not imitate the look of nature, but rather attempts to discover a spiritual path through the use of myth, metaphor, symbol, and stories, visually expressed through her paintings.

Recently, Allen has produced images she calls "illuminations," similar to the illuminated manuscripts in the Middle Ages. "I aspire through these paintings to locate the sacred in the commonplace, to describe the small miracles of our visible world, and to open portals on the larger existence that they imply." Allen often uses the metaphor of roads, which she believes represent the ongoing, perhaps endless human journey. In these paintings, like *Blue Highway,* the Western landscape is bisected by a pristine road, which disappears over the horizon, the overall image painted with intense color. For Allen, who strives to intensify sensory experiences, roads through empty landscapes offer the possibility of epic journeys, along with choices to leave or stay, or to experience and inhabit.

I aspire through these paintings to locate the sacred in the commonplace,
to describe the small miracles of our visible world,
and to open portals on the larger existence that they imply.

—PAGE ALLEN

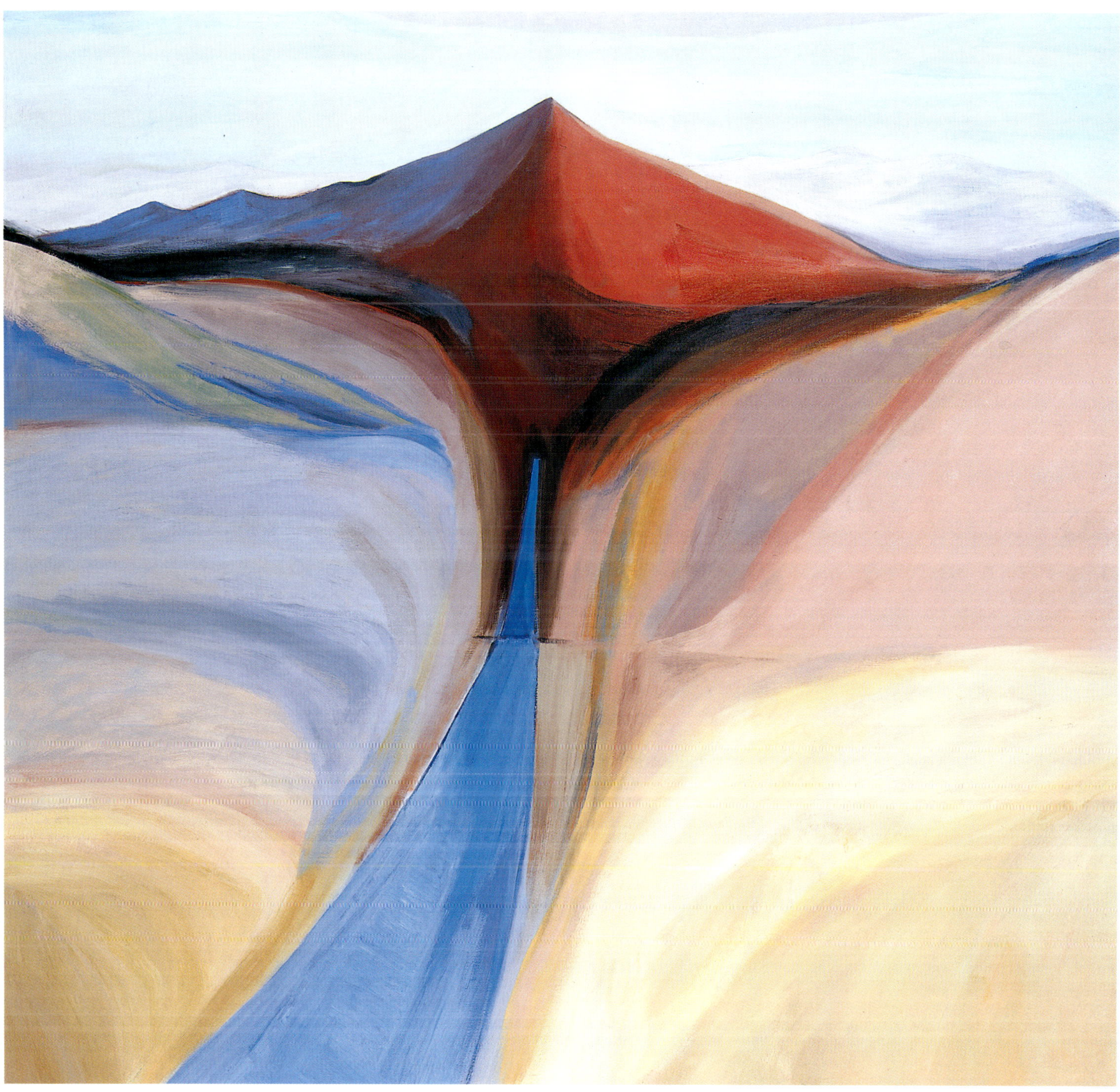

Page Allen, BLUE HIGHWAY, *oil on linen, 44 by 48 inches, 1996. Private collection; photograph courtesy of Owings-Dewey Fine Art.*

With unique vision, **Paul Pletka** (b. 1946) paints images of Plains Indian nomadic cultures and Pentitente rituals of New Mexico, where the illusion seems so real it can haunt the imagination. His narrative paintings are composed of assembled facts anchored by an extremely personal interpretation of those cultures. Ritualized suffering, pain, and death seem ever-present themes in his art. Pletka's work combines his interest in surrealism with an ability to extract fantasy from reality. In fact, he calls himself a "pictorial novelist."

Born in San Diego, California, Pletka moved to Grand Junction, Colorado, with his family in 1957. In high school, he painted Native American themes and landscapes, then in college, took studio courses in art. Eventually he worked as a collections manager and exhibits preparator for the Museum of Art and Science in Grand Junction, where he had his first exhibit in 1967. Later he moved to Tesuque, New Mexico, in 1977. Pletka has exhibited his work at such museums as the Colorado Springs Fine Arts Center, the Museum of Fine Art (Santa Fe), the Scottsdale Center For the Arts, and the Albuquerque Museum.

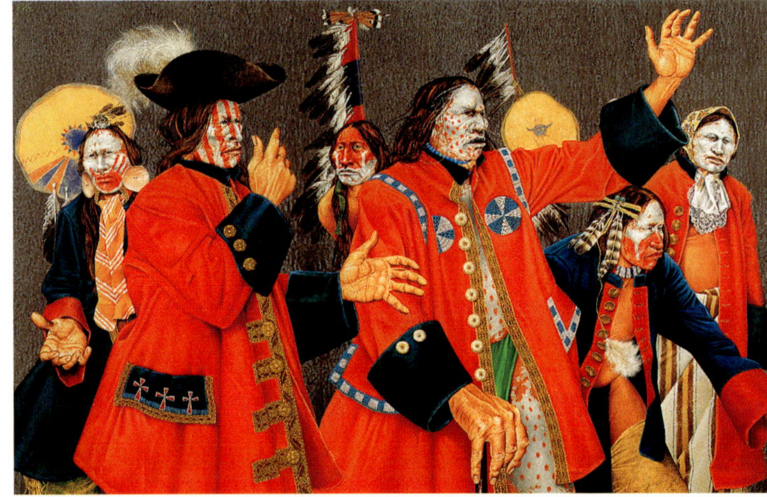

Paul Pletka,
LOS INDIOS DEL LLANO ESTACADO,
acrylic on linen,
52 by 80 inches, 1993.
Collection of Mr. and Mrs. Gerald Dorros.

Pletka's paintings are usually executed on a large scale. Comfortable with this format, he works his canvases in a slow, deliberate manner. Large, monolithic figures, surreal, monstrous, with exaggerated hands, swollen torsos, and diminished heads, as in *Los Indios del Llano Estacado,* are portrayed as if viewed through a convex lens. In particular, Pletka found Plains Indians and the Pentitente culture of New Mexico inspiration for his haunting visions. Fascinated with their artifacts, he collects and researches them, then uses the objects as the foundation for a personal narrative.

Pletka's art explores various themes—magic, superstition, ceremonialism, totemism, animism, or superstition. His paintings respond to something he has personally encountered. He viewed a Pentitente procession several years ago and was moved by the deliberate, measured, pious, reverent impression of the event. The result, executed with complex symbolism, is *The Arrest (Pentitente Procession),* an image evocative of death, power, and transformation. Pletka recalls, "I had never seen or read about the idea of Christ being led by a rope—a rope around his neck as if He were under arrest. The minute I saw it, I knew that's what I wanted to do with the painting."

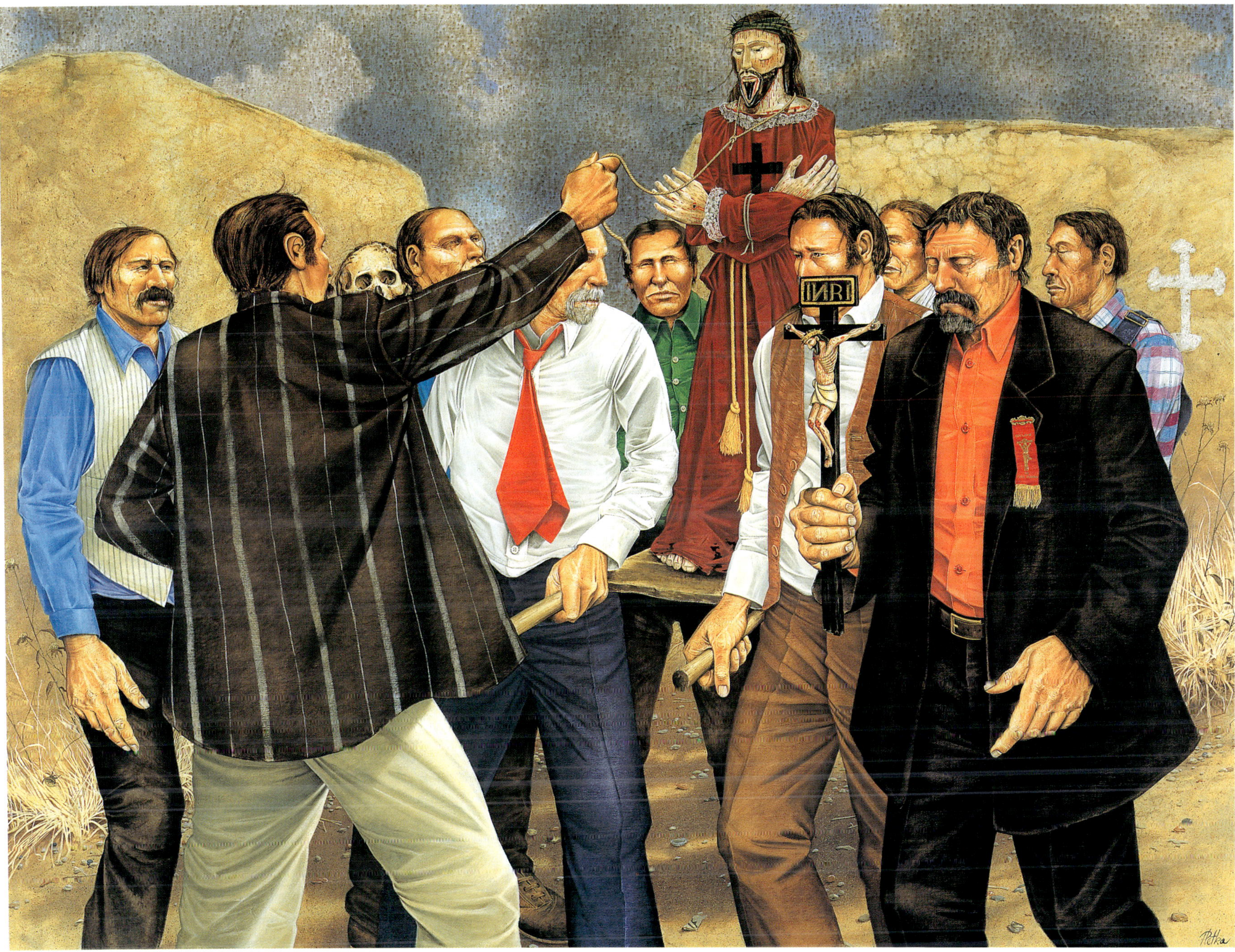

Paul Pletka, THE ARREST (PENITENTE PROCESSION), *acrylic on linen, 66 by 86 inches, 1995. Collection of Dennis and Janis Lyon; photograph courtesy of the artist.*

*I believe in the tradition, I am the tradition, but tradition is not copying.
What I do to continue my heritage is to renew it.*

—LUIS TAPIA

Throughout the Southwest, there are Hispanic artists whose work—sculpture, painting, textiles—is infused by the long history of tradition, art, community, and faith, yet charged with concern for contemporary artistic and social concerns. Their art is often linked to traditional motifs, but they innovate within that tradition. Through their efforts, a renaissance of Hispanic art has gained momentum.

Within this vibrant community of artists, **Luis Tapia** (b. 1950) finds religious and spiritual inspiration in tradition, but ventures beyond to comment on Hispanic secular life. His carved and painted wood sculptures depart from older, more traditional forms, while maintaining firm connection to earlier themes. Tapia has played a leading role in contemporary Hispanic art in the Southwest as he searches for nourishment through blending tradition with modern Hispanic culture.

A native of Santa Fe, New Mexico, Tapia went from elementary school through one year at New Mexico State University without the benefit of an art education. The 1960s and 1970s Civil Rights movement, though, alerted him to the existence of traditional Hispanic art and a vital Hispanic culture. Encouraged by his then wife, he studied the Spanish colonial art collections at the Museum of International Folk Art in Santa Fe, and was inspired to create carved and polychrome-painted *santos*. Now his subjects include not only *santos*, but altar screens, *caretas de la muerta* (death carts), and, in homage to present Hispanic life, low-rider automobiles and dashboard altars.

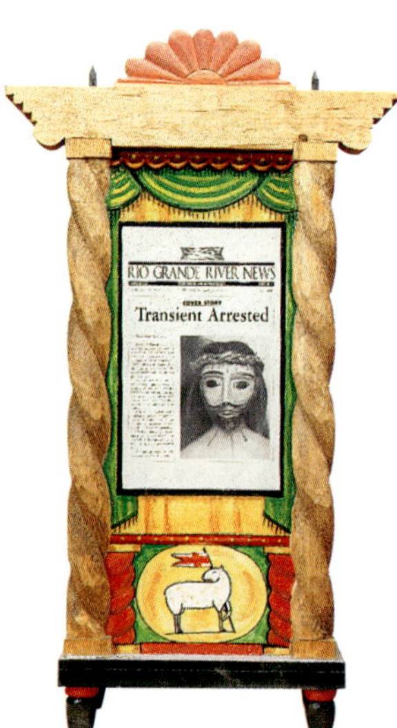

Luis Tapia,
CHRIST THE TRANSIENT,
carved and painted wood,
29 by 16 by 7 inches, 1996.
Photograph courtesy of Owings-Dewey Fine Art.

Prompted by their passion to redefine and expand traditional and contemporary Hispanic art, Tapia and six other Santa Fe artists established *La Cofradia de Artes y Artesanos Hispanico* in 1978. By the time La Cofradia (The Brotherhood) disbanded in 1982, they had mounted four major exhibitions and increased the visibility of Hispanic art.

Tapia's work is in the collections of the Smithsonian Institution, the Museum of American Folk Art (New York), the Museum of New Mexico, and the Albuquerque Museum, among others. In addition, his art has been included in major exhibitions, such as the landmark *Hispanic Art in*

Luis Tapia,
CHIMA ALTAR—BERTRAM'S CRUISE,
carved-and-painted wood,
life-size, 1992.
Collection of Museum of Fine Arts, Museum of New Mexico, museum purchase with funds donated by Lynn Stevr; photograph courtesy of Owings-Dewey Fine Art.

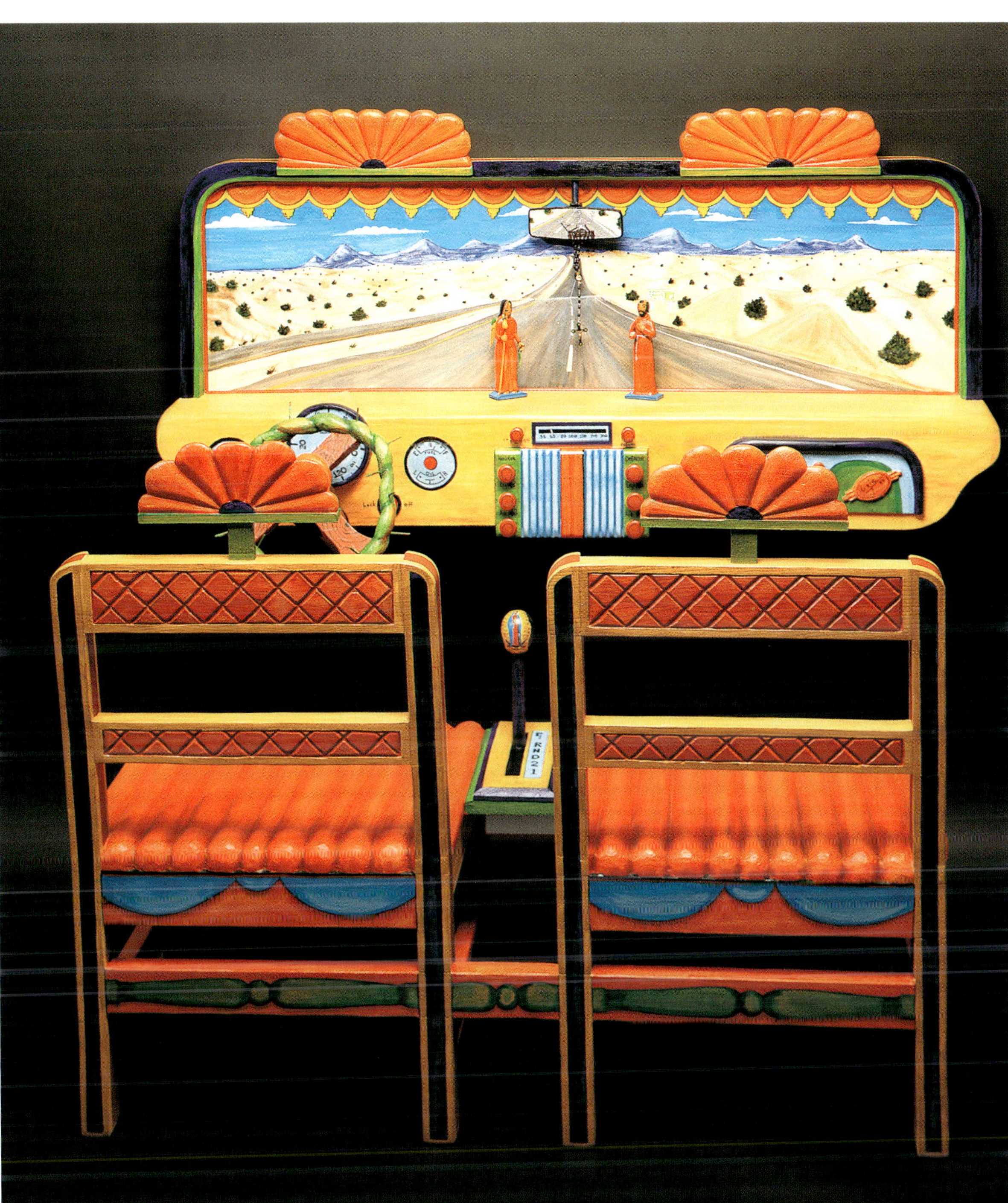

the United States organized by the Museum of Fine Arts in Houston. In 1994, Tapia received the Santa Fe Rotary Foundation's Distinguished Artist Award.

Among Tapia's interests is the restoration of old New Mexico furniture. Beneath the yellowed varnish and grime of accumulated years, he noticed paint colors lay bright and vibrant. He took this tradition and adapted it to his art. "Color is an important aspect of my work," he says. "I am just reviving an old tradition, but I use acrylic. I believe in the tradition, I am the tradition," he continues, "but tradition is not copying. What I do to continue my heritage is to renew it."

For example, in *Christ the Transient* (p. 164), Tapia has transformed Jesus into a modern version of the homeless man, exchanging an old image for a new one, and in *Chima Altar—Bertram's Cruise* (p. 165), he transformed an automobile's dashboard into a religious altar. "I remember as a child my mother would place plastic figures of Jesus on the dashboard," Tapia reflects. "This work is based on altars. It also implies automobiles are an important part of our culture. They are used as hot rods, for everyday occurrences, and as an altar in a way."

Like Luis Tapia, the paintings of Denver artist **ANTHONY ORTEGA** (b. 1958) celebrate aspects of Hispanic culture, especially family and community. Through the use of pure, unabashed color and strong shapes, Ortega celebrates the concept of community in combinations that intertwine Spanish Colonial, Indian, folk art, and mural traditions with Hispanic life. Born in Santa Fe, Ortega moved to Denver with his mother, but returned to the small village of Pecos, New Mexico, each summer to spend time with his grandmother, uncle, and cousins. From those experiences, his paintings eventually assumed the visual reality and sensory impact of family, neighborhood, religion, school, and work, set in rural and urban environments.

Anthony Ortega,
LAS FAMILIAS CAMPESINAS,
pastel on paper,
22 by 30 inches, 1996.
Private collection.

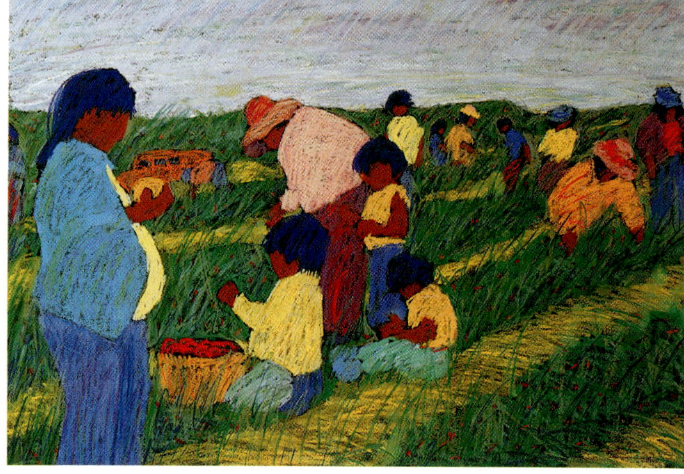

Ortega graduated from the University of Colorado, studied at two schools in Mexico, then returned to obtain an M.F.A. from the university in 1995. Since 1982 he has been a part of solo and group exhibitions including the Eiteljorg Museum, the Colorado Springs Fine Arts Center, and the Huntington Beach Art Center, in addition to international tours in Germany, France, and Spain. His art has been acquired by the Denver Art Museum, the Orange County Museum of Art, and the Mexican Museum in San Francisco.

Paint is what my painting is all about.

—JOHN FINCHER

The figures in Ortega's oils, pastels, and monotypes—and there are always figures—seem part of the tempestuous color he uses. Often he works on a large scale, tending to favor pastel. His images echo the vigor of present-day Chicano-Mexican life in the Southwest, figures stopped for a moment of time to chat, migrant workers next to trucks in a field, people clustered around a bakery, or parishioners on the steps of a church. One of his pastels, *Las Familias Campesinas,* is an image of family groups who share work together in the agricultural fields of southern Colorado's San Luis Valley. While Ortega acknowledges the influence of light by painters like Edward Hopper, this is now secondary. "Shape, color, form, and texture have overtaken it," says Ortega.

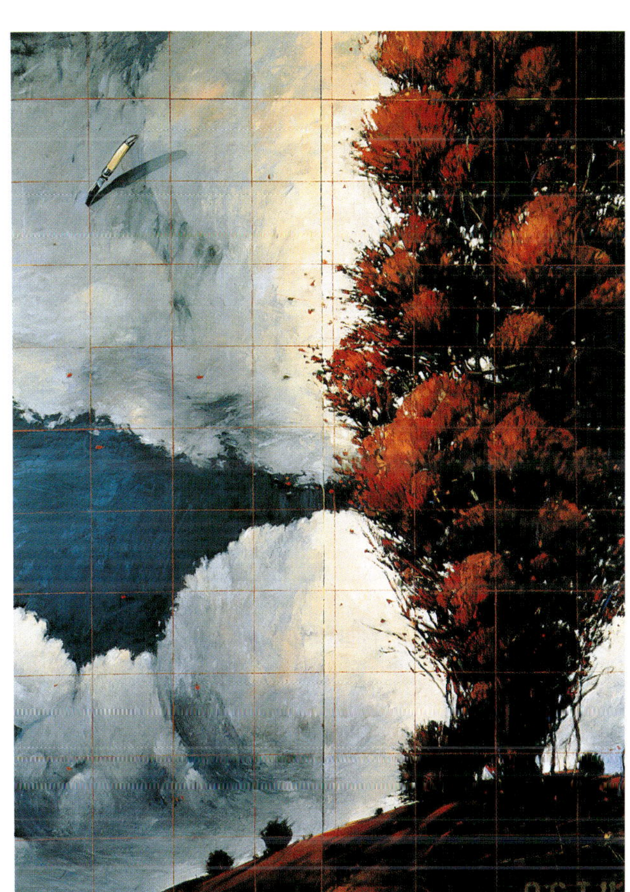

John Fincher, OCTOBER II, *oil on linen, 82 by 52 inches, 1992. Private collection.*

Other artists throughout the West, such as **JOHN FINCHER** (b. 1941), explore the role of irony and humor in their art. Irony relies on difference, on the exposure to the mixing of boundaries, and hinges on humor. Fincher paints subjects similar to pop art—arresting icons, bright color, cropped borders, and objects included obtrusively and incongruously.

A native of Texas, Fincher now lives in Santa Fe. He graduated from Texas Tech University in 1964, then obtained an M.F.A. from the University of Oklahoma. Besides having numerous solo and group exhibitions, Fincher has work in corporate collections such as the Bank of America, the El Dorado Hotel in Santa Fe, Texas Instruments, and the Marshall Field Company. In addition, over a dozen museums have obtained his paintings for their permanent collections.

Fincher's painting vocabulary includes Western artifacts such as chaps, boots, belt buckles, and spurs, and in recent years, landscapes. Ironic contrasts are used in these works, and occasionally personal souvenirs and calligraphic messages. There is often a grid placed on a landscape painting, as in *October II,* in which the images of tree and clouds are partitioned. The grid serves to stop the movement of clouds, and bring order to the chaos of nature. An ironic addition, almost trompe l'oeil, is the open penknife painted as if embedded in the image. To Fincher, this is a visual pun that reinforces the sense of irony. Overall, his technique includes brilliant color and objects scattered on

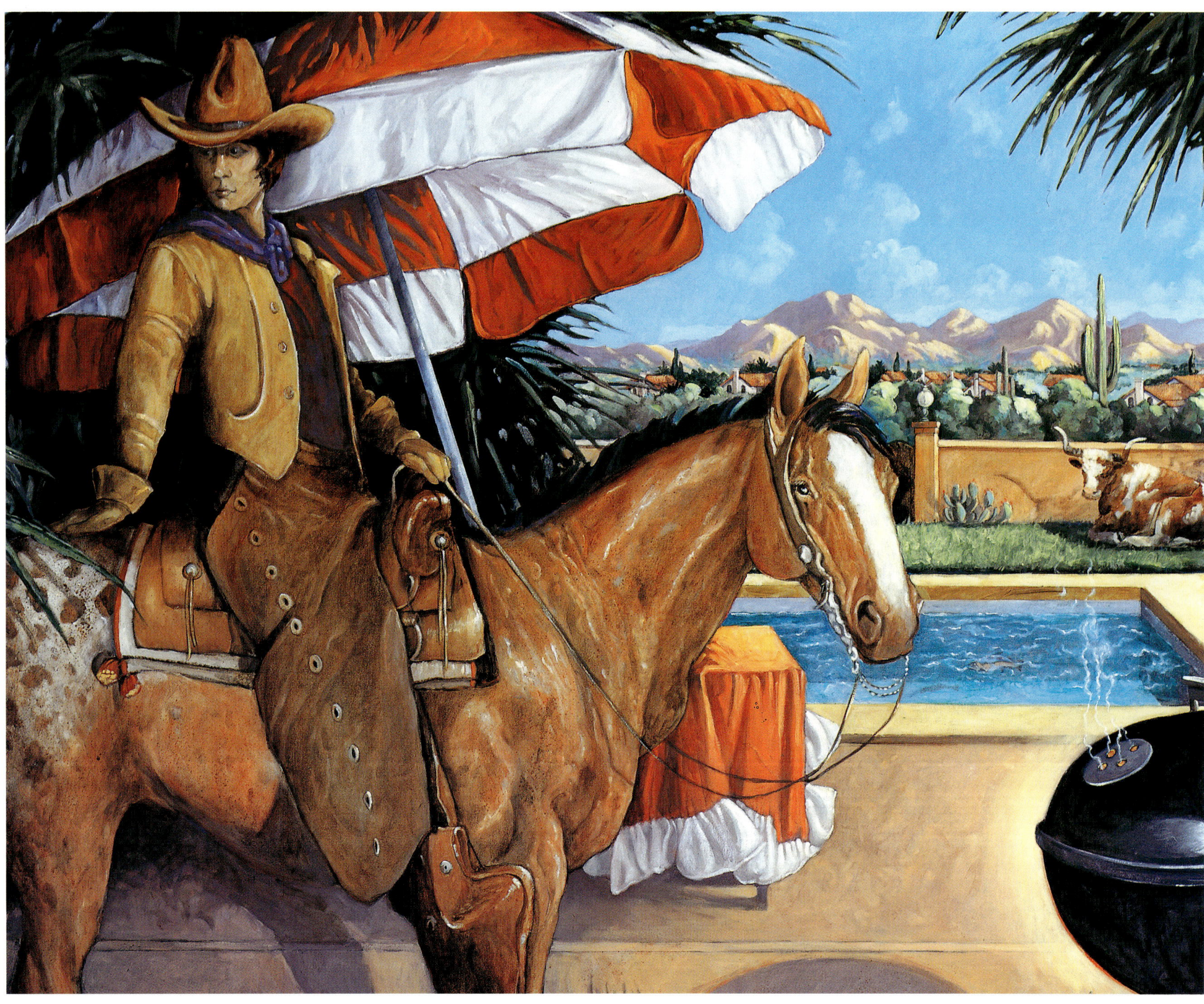

Anne Coe, SUBURBAN RANCHETTE: UTOPIAN BLISS AT THE END OF THE MILLENNIUM, *acrylic on canvas, 40 by 48 inches, 1996. Photograph by Bill McLemore Photography, courtesy of Joy Tash Gallery.*

I have always used humor as a vehicle for my messages.

—ANNE COE

the surface. The landscape is secondary, and there is no political agenda. "Paint is what my painting is all about," Fincher says.

ANNE COE (b. 1949) is known for an art that combines narratives of exaggerated landscapes and stylized animals—Godzilla-sized Gila monsters, coyotes drag-racing pink Cadillacs, or fez-wearing monkeys. Coe lifts concepts from Western art and introduces humor, manipulates her idiosyncratic images to fabricate parody, and sometimes confronts viewers with blatant irony.

Coe, a fourth-generation Arizonan, grew up in Wellton, Arizona, near the Mexican border. She received an undergraduate degree from Arizona State University in 1970, then an M.F.A. in 1980. She has had a long list of exhibitions, including the Mesa Southwest Museum, the Eiteljorg Museum, the Tempe Fine Arts Center, the Scottsdale Center for the Arts, and the Museum of National Heritage in Lexington, Massachusetts. Her work is found in many museum and corporate collections.

An environmentalist, Coe resides on the outskirts of Apache Junction, at the base of Arizona's Superstition Mountains. She participates in numerous environmental organizations, including the Superstition Area Land Trust, in an effort to forestall the development and destruction of her beloved Sonoran Desert. Environmental messages are embedded in her work, political statements that articulate the pressures of urbanization and a concern for wildlife.

Coe's fertile, imaginative art explores the interface between the wild desert and urban life, through the mocking humor of outrageous situations, such as *Suburban Ranchette: Utopian Bliss at the End of the Millennium.* The civilized content of suburban life is disrupted by her inclusion of a cowgirl astride a horse and a longhorn steer next to the swimming pool. "I have always used humor as a vehicle for my messages," Coe says. Part of her Chronicles of the Millennium series, the painting is a response to our times at the end of the century. Her vision for this painting arises from the "American Dream" north of Scottsdale, where everyone rushes to purchase their part of the desert. "Yes, people can live in the desert, but the cost is an acre an hour taken by development. There are times we need to evaluate where we are and where we are going," Coe says. The paintings are Coe's visual Rorschach test, anchored by her views on humor and pathos of contemporary Southwestern life.

Considered a primary exponent of contemporary sculpture in the Native American art movement, **BOB HAOZOUS** (b. 1943) takes a provocative approach to sculpture. His work, like Coe's, is marked by exaggeration and powerful observation. Born in Los Angeles, the son of the acclaimed Apache sculptor Alan Houser, Haozous is a Warm Springs Chiracahua Apache who retained the traditional family spelling of his name. Haozous grew up in northern Utah, where his father taught art. After service in the U.S. Navy, he attended the California College of Arts and Crafts in Oakland, California, graduating in 1971.

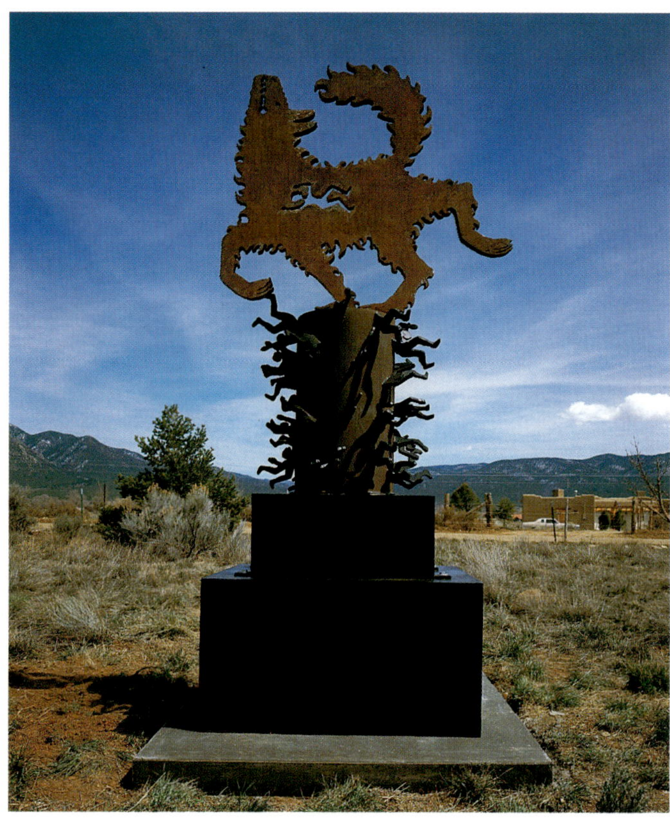

Bob Haozous,
WOLF,
steel,
96 inches high, 1987.
Private collection.

Since the early 1970s, Haozous has participated in over one hundred solo and group exhibitions in the United States and in Japan, Mexico, Norway, Germany, and Switzerland. His steel sculptures are in the collections of the Hood Museum at Dartmouth College, the City of Tulsa, the Joslyn Art Museum, the Heard Museum, and many others.

There are messages in Haozous's work, expressed in steel. Sculpture, to him, offers clues, yet few precise conclusions. Haozous's own conclusions present contradictions about environmental destruction and the inhumanity of man. "Whites walk on the earth; Indian people are supported by the earth," he says. "I'm filled with a passion to present this through contradiction, thus rescuing my tribe from a position of maintenance to one of development, and ultimately to excitement about life itself." Steel and the environment to which it contributes reflect Haozous's messages about the paradoxes in contemporary American life.

Haozous's energy and talent are channeled into an educational art that speaks to the average person, as *Wolf* does. While this image is reminiscent of the coyote mania that has permeated Southwestern folk art, Haozous intends deeper meaning. The wolf still survives, despite efforts to

Whites walk on the earth; Indian people are supported by the earth. I'm filled with a passion to present this through contradiction.

—BOB HAOZOUS

eradicate its presence. Like the steel with which it is formed, this image, with hard-edged, sardonic portrayal, states "I am still here." "I think common images say something best," Haozous says. "If I get too esoteric, people will miss the point."

For many Native American artists in the American West, their art is viewed as a continued extension of tradition, their themes and concepts vital as symbols of present tribal consciousness. To some degree, their work embodies messages about the experience of Native American life in the modern West. A number of these artists experiment with new mediums, new painting or sculpting techniques, and new subject matter. Sometimes Native American artists combine the dynamics of contemporary art, such as forms of abstract expressionism, with the traditions of their own cultures, in an effort to understand different realities.

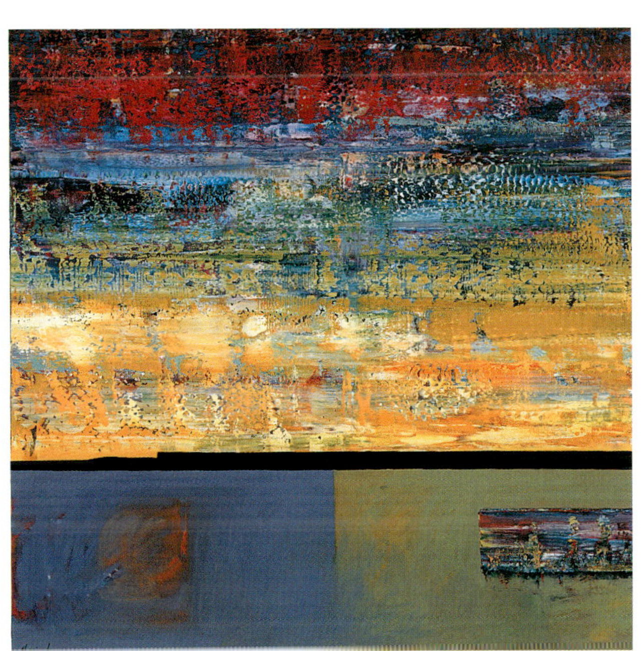

Dan Namingha, ANTELOPE MESA, *acrylic on canvas, 48 by 48 inches, 1994. Photograph courtesy of Niman Fine Art.*

One of them, Hopi-Tewa artist **DAN NAMINGHA** (b. 1950), the great-grandson of Hopi potter Nampeyo, is an artist dedicated to the use of symbols and stories extracted from his culture, filtered through the techniques of abstract expressionism. Born in the village of Polacca, at the foot of First Mesa on Arizona's Hopi Reservation, Namingha completed an art scholarship at the University of Illinois, studied at the Institute of American Indian Arts in Santa Fe, then pursued further studies at the American Academy of Art in Chicago. He now lives in La Tierra, just north of Santa Fe.

His paintings have been exhibited at major museums, both nationally and internationally. Namingha has been a guest artist for NASA at launches of the space shuttle *Discovery*, a judge at an art exhibition in Zimbabwe, and a guest on television shows for CBS and PBS. He won an art award in 1994 from the Harvard Foundation, in conjunction with a solo exhibition at the Fogg Museum in Cambridge, Massachusetts. The following year he received the 1995 Santa Fe Rotary Foundation Award. In 1996, the Museum of Fine Arts in Santa Fe organized a major retrospective of his work.

Namingha's richly textured art, rooted in Hopi spirituality, is founded on a half-personal, half-symbolic imagery of Kachinas, stars, clouds, lightning, the four directions, and spiral forms indicative of evolution, migration, and the umbilical cord of Mother Earth. Many of his recent

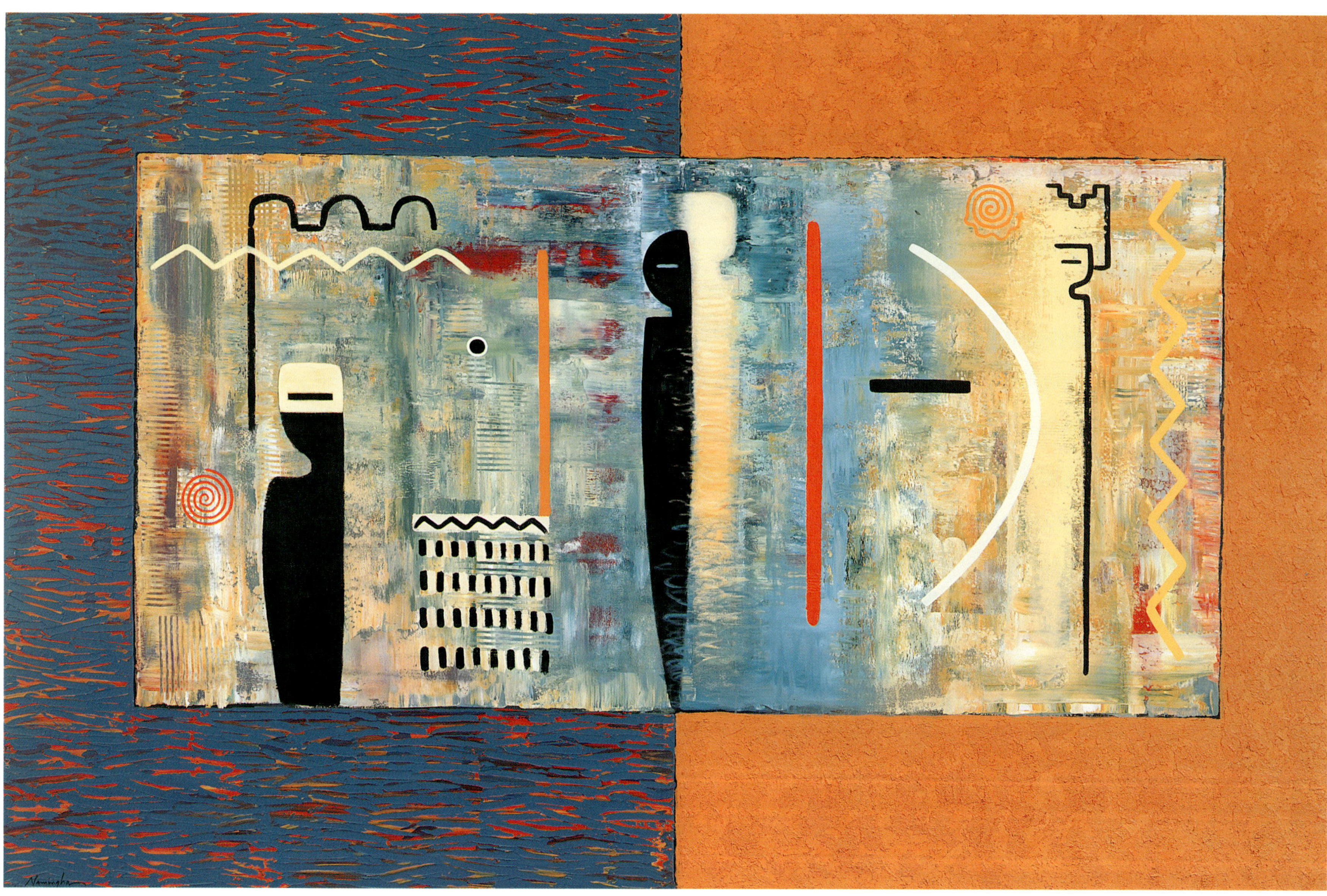

Dan Namingha, DREAM STATE SERIES, *mixed media on canvas, 78 by 120 inches, 1994. Photograph courtesy of Niman Fine Art.*

paintings are large-scale, heavily layered compositions, partitioned into geometric divisions. In an article for *El Palacio,* Namingha said, "I like the idea of contrast. I use flat blocks of color around the border, and within that space there is a band of texture, and within that space there is a band of texture with the symbols I use." On top of this, Namingha applies his symbols—fragments or abstractions of Hopi Kachina mask symbolism and ancient petroglyphs. "The symbols are ancient," he says, "but still in use at the present." These symbols are like ancient pottery shards to Namingha, fragments from other worlds. Namingha often includes in his paintings the stark silhouette of distant mesas and the sky above dark with the possibility of rain, as in *Antelope Mesa* (p. 171). For Namingha, the land and the sky are intricately linked together in this painting. He has also consistently used the motif of slits—windows or doors—pathways through which viewers might enter a transcendental world, as he has done in *Dream State Series.*

Not until he reached his early twenties did **Harry Fonseca** (b. 1946) learn to embrace his Nisenan Maidu background. Through the influence of tribal elder Frank Day, a respected Maidu painter, Fonseca discovered the magic embedded in his people's ancient myths. From realization of this tradition, he embarked on an exploration of how symbols from the past could enlighten present conditions. Since the early 1970s, Fonseca has had numerous group and one-man exhibitions at institutions including the Southwest Museum, the Museum of Northern Arizona, the National Cowboy Hall of Fame, the Millicent Rogers Museum, and most recently, a major exhibit at the Wheelwright Museum of the American Indian.

Largely self-taught, Fonseca explores different media: oil, acrylic, pen and ink, clay, wood, and lithography. Intrigued by pattern and design, he strives for a textural vibrancy. Some of Fonseca's early work portrayed Maidu sacred dances and the Maidu story of creation. He became well known for his Coyote Series in the 1970s, in which he transformed the traditional Indian image of coyote, the trickster, into a wily survivor quite at home in modern American culture.

The Stone Poems give me a chance to confront myself in a new world. It is a world where the black and whites are slowly turning into grays—with all their shades of uncertainty, fear, growth, and wonder.

—HARRY FONSECA

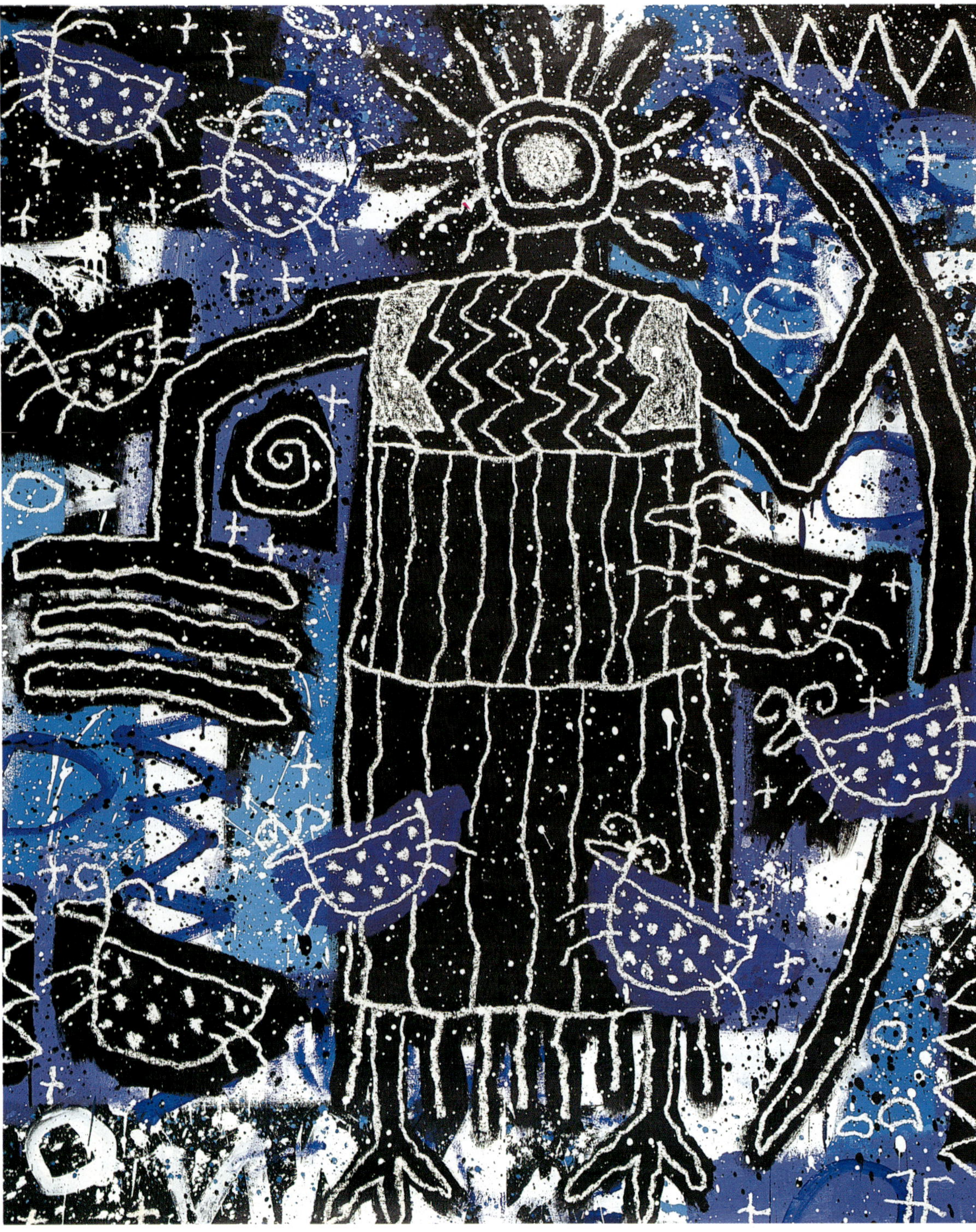

Harry Fonseca,
NOCTURNE #11,
mixed media on canvas,
72 by 58 inches, 1990.
Collection of Wheelwright
Museum of the American Indian;
photograph by Lynn Lown.

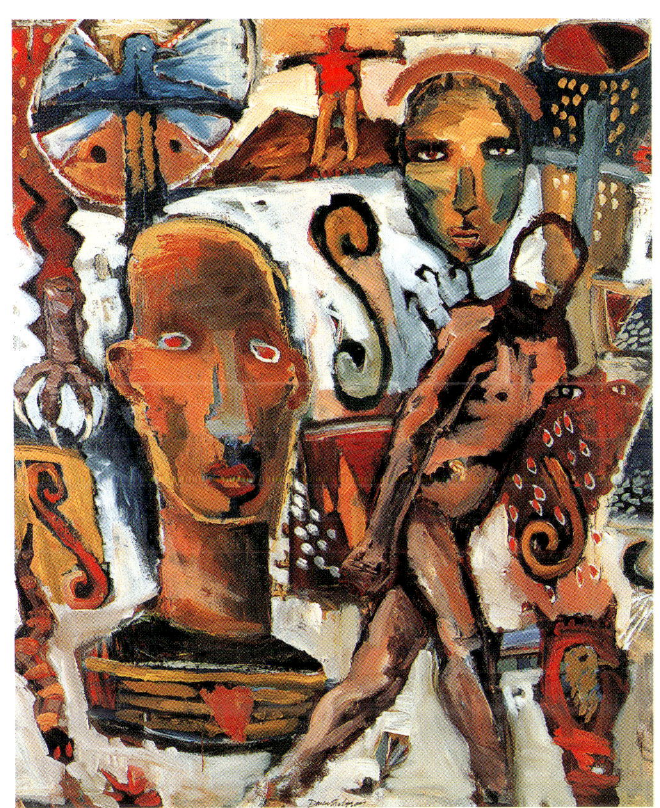

Darren Vigil Gray,
THE OPENING CHORD,
acrylic on canvas,
58 by 48 inches, 1995.
Photograph courtesy of Peyton-Wright

more mysterious things that I do. I prefer the idea of me as the mediator, the mediator between the earthly world of paint and the unearthly realm of artistic creation."

Sometimes half-human, half-bird figures appear in Gray's paintings, with birds and animal parts strapped to their heads, as in *After Praying Four Times* or *The Opening Chord.* The figures either look past or confront the viewer with impassive detachment, their eyes blank or distracted. But Gray does not consider them lacking emotion; rather, as he says, "I think of them as looking inward." Gray paints his canvases with explosive force, his color rendered with intense, almost savage execution.

Much like Darren Vigil Gray, **Emmi Whitehorse** (b. 1956) finds motivation for her art in the mysterious and the enigmatic. Born in Crownpoint, New Mexico, on the Navajo Reservation, Whitehorse lived in a government boarding school as a youngster, and while there she drew horses, people, everything and anything she encountered. In one instance, she drew so much she was prohibited to have a pencil or pen in one of the classrooms. At age sixteen, she attended the University of New Mexico, then eventually obtained an M.A. in printmaking from there in 1982.

She has had numerous exhibitions at institutions such as the Wheelwright Museum, the Millicent Rogers Museum, the Lowe Gallery, the National Museum for Women in the Arts, and the Tucson Museum of Art. Whitehorse's paintings can be found in the collections of the Heard Museum, the Phoenix Art Museum, the Saint Louis Art Museum, and the Joslyn Art Museum.

Whitehorse's work is an orchestration of abstract approaches, formal assemblages of organic, amoeba-like forms. She calls these paintings "scribbles," made-up images, yet one perceives leaf shapes, animal footprints, and spirals, similar to ancient petroglyphs, inside them. Whitehorse considers the paintings dreams, and she plumbs them to construct with paint on canvas or paper what has transpired in her mind. The work reflects her deep interest in nature and the land, and through that interest she creates small worlds with her imagery.

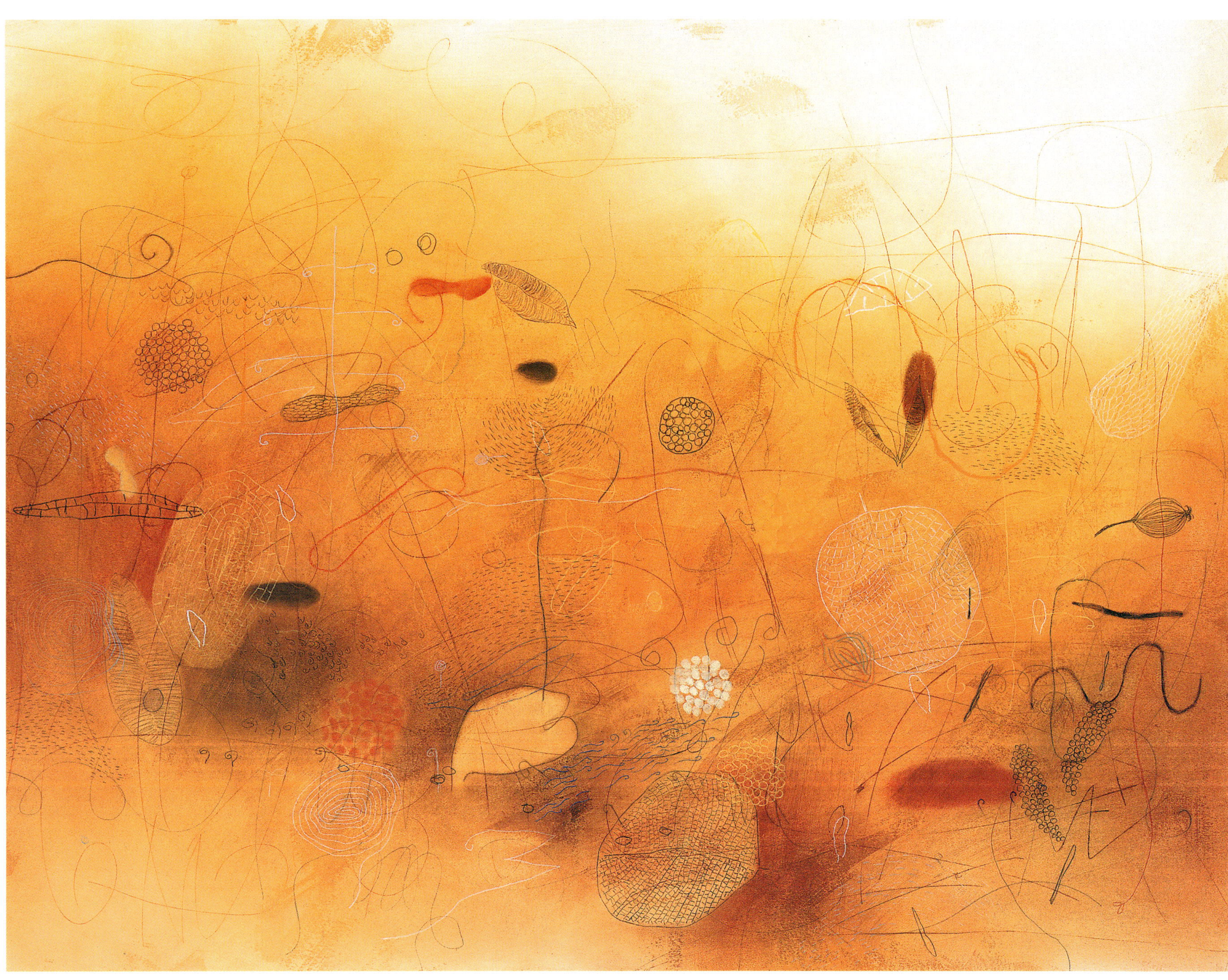

Emmi Whitehorse, SOLAR POND, *mixed media, 39½ by 51 inches, 1996. Photograph courtesy of Cline LewAllen Contemporary.*

A painting takes on its own persona.

—EMMI WHITEHORSE

Recently Whitehorse has ventured beyond some of the Native American mythology that infused her earlier work, into a more dreamlike, expressive status. "A painting takes on its own persona," she says. "The choice of colors is random, and the titles come after the work is completed." Still, recognizable symbols bob and float; a snake, seed pods, the fragments of a leaf, found, for example, in her painting *Solar Pond,* lie embedded in her work. Perhaps there is a supernatural world in Whitehorse's mind, the symbols on her paintings echoes of signs from long-lost spirits.

The art of **JAUNE QUICK-TO-SEE SMITH** (b. 1940), a member of the Flathead tribe, born on the Flathead Reservation in Montana, presents the juxtaposition of contemporary modern life and ancient Native American culture. Her style, which mines American popular culture, combines words, collaged motifs, and large, striking pictographs of animals and people in an effort to forge beneficial links and share ideas and skills between mainstream American culture and the Native American community. She views herself as an interpreter, a time traveler who ventures back and forth in order to translate ideas about the two worlds. Smith considers her paintings "narrative landscapes," with pointed commentary and sometimes sardonic humor.

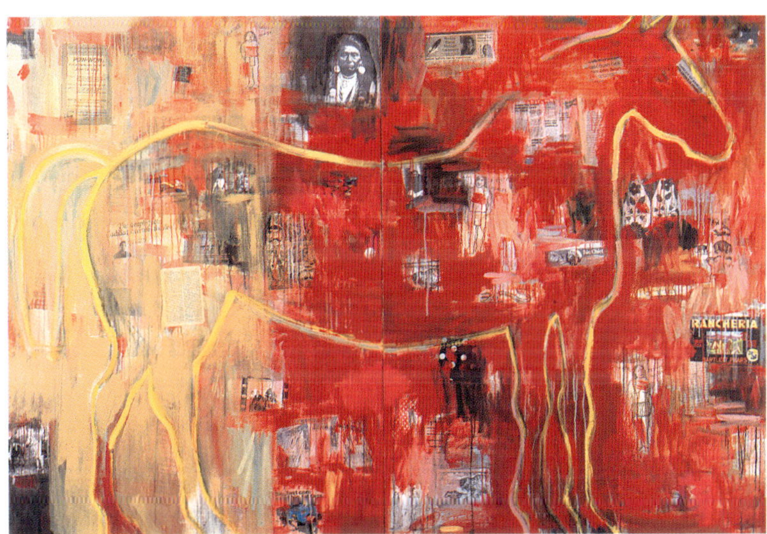

Jaune Quick-to-See Smith, INDIAN HORSE (diptych), *oil/collage/mixed media on canvas, 66 by 96 inches, 1992. Collection of Museum of Modern Art, Ecuador, Biennial International de Pintura, Cuenca, Ecuador, purchase award; photograph courtesy of Steinbaum Krauss Gallery.*

A painter and printmaker, Smith has exhibited widely, both nationally and internationally. She completed a public installation in collaboration with another artist at San Francisco's Moscone Center that honors the tribes of that area. She has also completed, in conjunction with a Japanese artist, a football field–sized floor for the new Denver airport, illustrating the history of Colorado in pictograph.

Smith's work is in many public collections, including the Museum of Mankind (Vienna), the Denver Art Museum, the National Museum of American Art (Washington, D.C.), and the Museum of Modern Art (New York). In 1992 she received an honorary doctorate from the Minneapolis College of Art and Design, and in 1995 the Wallace Stegner Award from the Center of the American West at the University of Colorado.

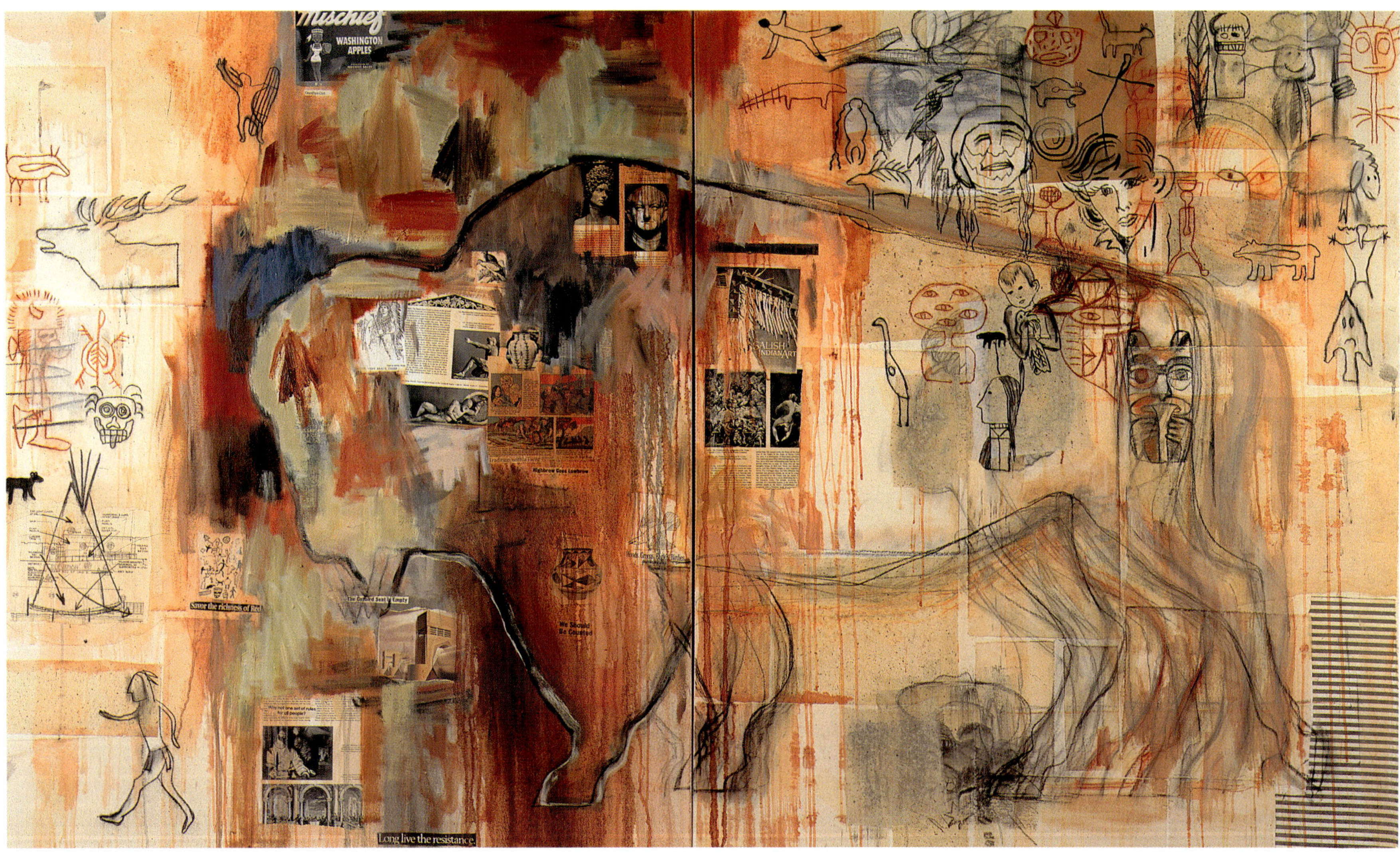

Jaune Quick-to-See Smith, INDIAN DRAWING LESSON (diptych), *oil/collage/mixed media on canvas, 60 by 100 inches, 1993. Collection of Nancy and Peter Gennet; photograph by David Vine, courtesy of Steinbaum Krauss Gallery.*

Large, identifiable Native American icons romanticized by movies, novels, and the popular media are often used in Smith's paintings. However, when the viewer moves closer, there emerges a reading of a different story about Native American life on and off the reservation. Animal images, outlined and pictographic in nature, play important roles in her work. Other material, clipped-out newspaper articles, images from magazines and books, sometimes sections from the *Yellow Pages,* are included. Not only can you view her paintings, you can read them. In *Indian Horse* (p. 179), a large, visually iconic horse figure is combined with the subtle reminders of the dislocation and ecological, economic, cultural devastation that dominates much of reservation life today. Another one of her creations, *Indian Drawing Lesson*, addresses the slaughter of horses in the headline "Burger or Being?, the Choice is Yours," and alludes to the mistreatment of Native Americans.

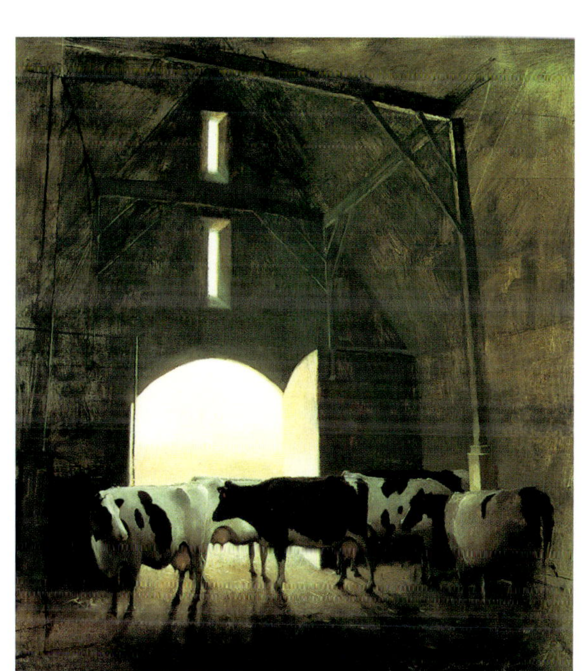

Michael Workman, IN THE BARN #2, *oil on panel, 40 by 36 inches, 1994. Private collection; photograph courtesy of Meyer Gallery.*

There are artists in the American West such as **MICHAEL WORKMAN** (b. 1960) who are, at first glance, landscape painters; yet their imagery reflects elements beyond traditional landscape painting. On the surface, Workman's art reflects the farm and ranch life of rural, pastoral Utah, yet it transcends specific place to explore spiritual concerns. Workman is a resident of the small town of Spring City, where he has a studio on the upper floor of an old store. There he can view the bucolic landscape and its sheep and dairy cattle, part of the town's mosaic of everyday life.

Workman, who received a master's degree in studio art from Brigham Young University in 1992, considers his paintings universal in nature, and does not necessarily believe they portray places in Utah. Marked by a modesty of subject matter, they are spiritual poems done in paint. In fact, Workman wants them to convey what he feels is a transcendental spiritualism. Workman's paintings offer a quiet sentiment influenced by the painters of the Renaissance and the baroque period, and in particular the tonalist painters and their ability to make subjective interpretations of nature with muted colors, diffused lighting, and gentle contours.

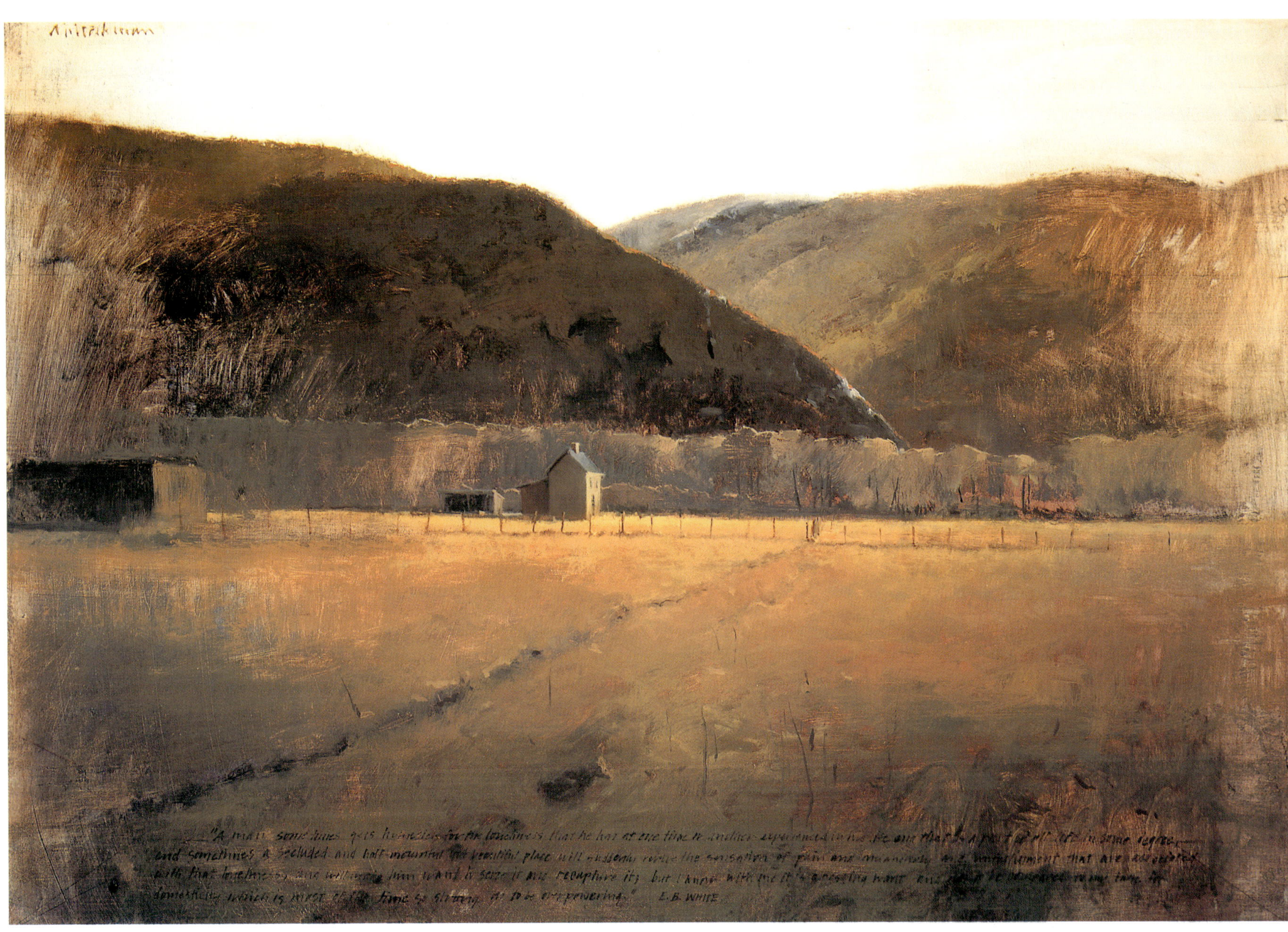

Michael Workman, THE OLD HERRICK PLACE, *oil on masonite, 14 by 20 inches, 1994. Private collection; photograph courtesy of Meyer Gallery.*

Some of the best paintings began as one thing
and ended as something else.

—MICHAEL WORKMAN

Workman does little planning for his paintings; he simply starts to paint, on canvas stretched over a wood panel. Sometimes when a work does not meet with his approval, he removes the paint using sandpaper and steel wool. Part of the residue remains, and Workman leaves these scraped areas visible, glazing portions with translucent layers of pigment. "Some of the best paintings began as one thing and ended as something else," he says. Each of his canvases is proportioned mathematically, the division of space calculated carefully. They are relationships with a purpose, although part of the painting is left unorganized so viewers can participate in the creation. Ultimately Workman attempts to combine this organized classical approach with loose, interpretive brushwork and romantic color, as he has done with *The Old Herrick Place.* Sometimes on a painting he includes phrases or quotes from writers; in this case the words are from E. B. White, essayist and children's book author.

An example of the spiritual foundation in Workman's art is *In the Barn #2* (p. 181), a portrayal of dairy cows in a dark, moody barn, their forms backlit by an open door. "For centuries, artists have used the idea of a passageway, or of light and dark contrasts, as symbols of the opposites we all experience as we go through life," Workman says.

In a similar fashion, **Lynn Taber-Borcherdt** (b. 1943) responds to the Southwest's deserts, leading her to focus inward in search of a balance between the landscape and her own thoughts about existence. After graduation with an M.F.A. from the Art Institute of Chicago in 1965, Taber-Borcherdt produced paintings she frankly calls, "dark, dark, dark." When she moved to Tucson in 1970 with her sculptor husband, she encountered the solitude and light-filled expanse of the Sonoran Desert. As her art evolved from this experience, Taber-Borcherdt's subject matter shifted toward a combination of actual and imagined sites in her paintings.

Among her individual and group exhibitions are ones at the Tucson Museum of Art, the Bakersfield Museum of Art, the Colorado Fine Arts Center, the Smith College Museum of Art, and the Phoenix Art Museum. Fascinated with the effects of luminosity and iridescence inspired by a trip to England, she started painting psychological interpretations of fairy tales and Native American creation myths. After she encountered neolithic sacred sites in Great Britain and Scotland in

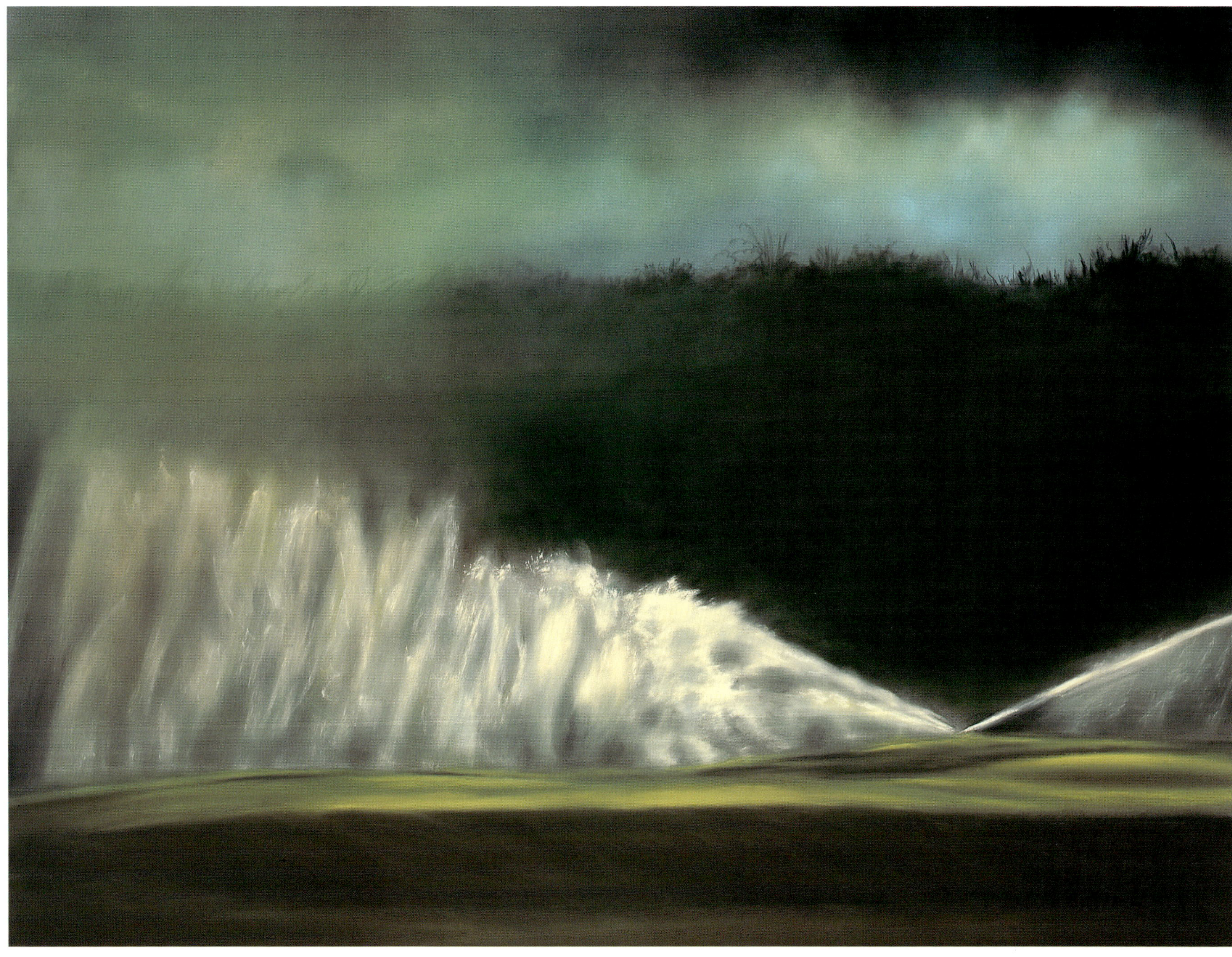

Lynn Taber-Borcherdt, HUMAN NATURE AT WORK IN THE COOL OF THE EVENING AT VENTANA CANYON, *pastel on sanded paper, 20½ by 25½ inches, 1996. Collection of the artist.*

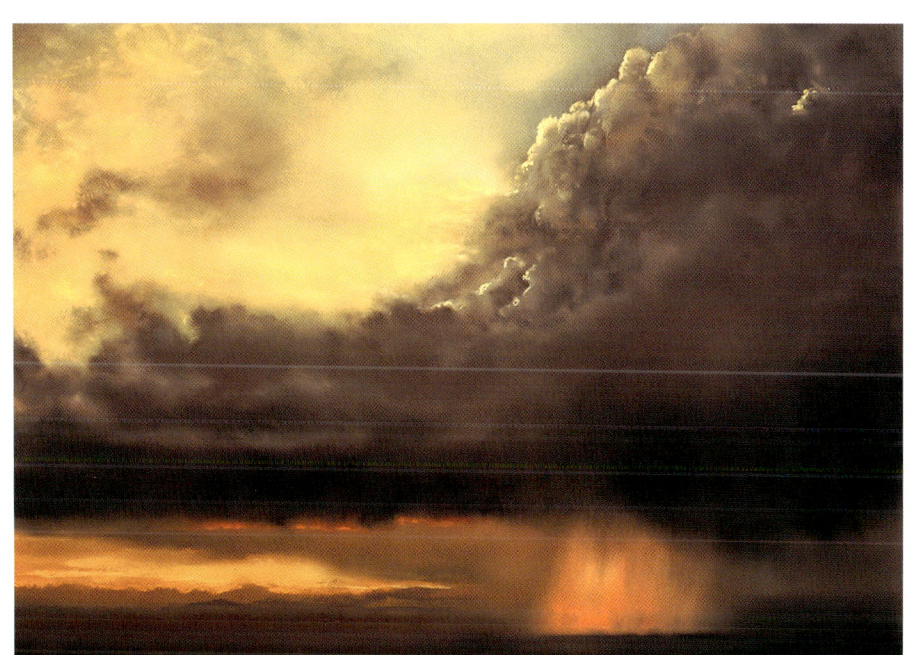

Lynn Taber-Borcherdt, JANUARY STORM, TUCSON, *pastel on sanded paper, 14½ by 19½ inches, 1996. Collection of the artist; photograph by Robin Stancliff.*

1990, her landscapes included ancient stone monuments. By 1993, Taber-Borcherdt started to use pastel exclusively as her medium, and to focus on sky and weather patterns, with their promise of rain to the astringent grandeur of the landscape.

Drawn to spiritual places and spiritual events, like the desert storms that periodically sweep over Tucson, Taber-Borcherdt need only look out the studio window at her home high above he city in the Santa Catalina Mountains for subject matter. Through her mastery of the pastel medium, she creates enigmatic, almost formless atmospheres, visions of magical worlds, endowed with redeeming rain, like *January Storm, Tucson.* The paintings are created through thousands of tiny pastel chalk strokes, executed with her fingertips. Each image takes several days to complete. Occasionally, giant irrigation water sprinklers appear as subjects in her work, as in *Human Nature at Work in the Cool of the Evening at Ventana Canyon.* These machines are Taber-Borcherdt's pictorial metaphor for the artificial replacement of natural processes, and the relentless depletion of underground water tables. "Water, the lifegiver, is showered upon the lands as humanity seeks to replace or augment natural rainfall," she says. "In the process, the visual power of the heavens is brought groundward, into the landscape, and man has, through artificial precipitation, usurped the role of Nature."

The art of **WOODY GWYN** (b. 1944) is infused with the Southwest's expansive silence and allure of light, along with the asphalt and concrete symbol of contemporary American life, the highway. Born in San Antonio, Gwyn grew up on the stripped-down landscapes that surround Midland, Texas. Artist Peter Hurd, the famous Southwestern regionalist, encouraged Gwyn to attend art school. Gwyn responded and studied for two years at the Pennsylvania Academy of Fine Arts.

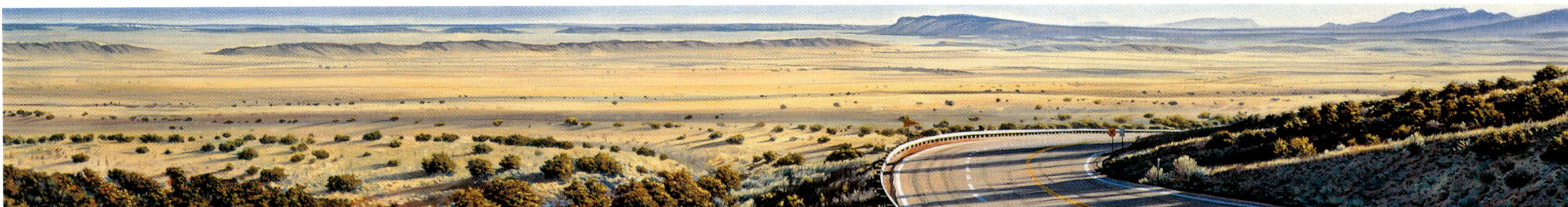

Woody Gwyn, 285 SOUTH, *oil on linen, 9 by 66 inches, 1990. Private collection.*

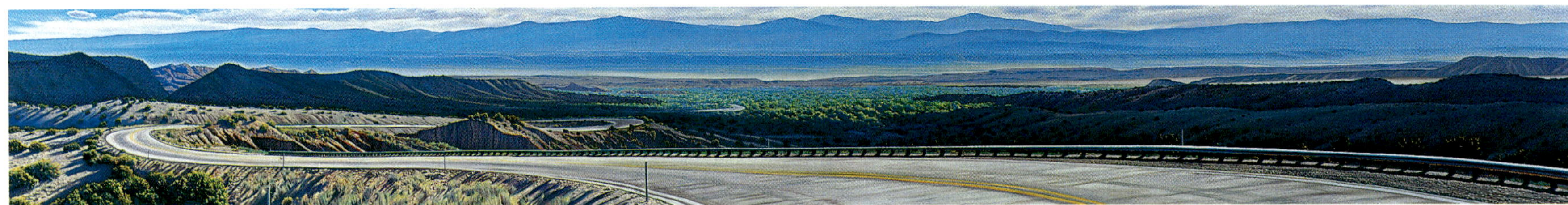

Woody Gwyn, CHIMAYO, *oil on linen, 24 by 180 inches, 1991–92. Private collection.*

Afterwards, Gwyn returned to Midland for ten years, then in 1974 moved to Santa Fe, where he now works out of a large converted warehouse studio. From the time he first exhibited in 1965 to the present, Gwyn has had numerous solo and group exhibitions, and his work hangs in many corporate, public, and museum collections throughout the United States.

Gwyn is noted for large-scale paintings that typically include a modern interstate or regional highway, work that embraces the relationship between the man-made and the pristine. His paintings are as much about dispersion as they are about the sense of community in the West. Small oil sketches remind Gwyn what it was that interested him about a particular scene; then he takes their messages into larger paintings. With pared-down realism, as neither strict naturalist, nor a hyper-realist, Gwyn paints not only what he sees, but provocatively questions traditional landscape painting. "The crucial thing for a realist painter is to care about the world around him that he is trying to express," he says.

For example, two of his road paintings, *285 South* and *Chimayo,* rendered almost in the style of Chinese scroll paintings, reflect Gwyn's awareness of landscape changes in the modern West. The first painting follows the highway south of Galisteo, New Mexico, the asphalt ribbon and the landscape energized by Gwyn's feel for the dry, clear atmosphere and piercing light of New Mexico. The other canvas depicts the upward, sinuous curves of the road to Chimayo. On the western horizon lie the Jemez Mountains. With these paintings, Gwyn has found the geometric ribbon of roads, overpasses, and viaducts, part of the ageless landscape. The highway is an elegant symbol of human achievement, homage to the phenomenon of flow. But with Gwyn's vision, no vehicles or pedestrians intrude in these pictures. "In some paintings I have included cars and trucks, but ended up taking them out because they stop the eye. I want the eye to flow, to weave in and out of the paintings," Gwyn says. As constructed, cultural landscapes, Gwyn's roads remain as empty and lonesome as the physical landscape.

Chuck Forsman, FEATHER RIVER, *oil on masonite, 57 by 84 inches, 1992. Photograph courtesy of Tibor de Nagy Gallery.*

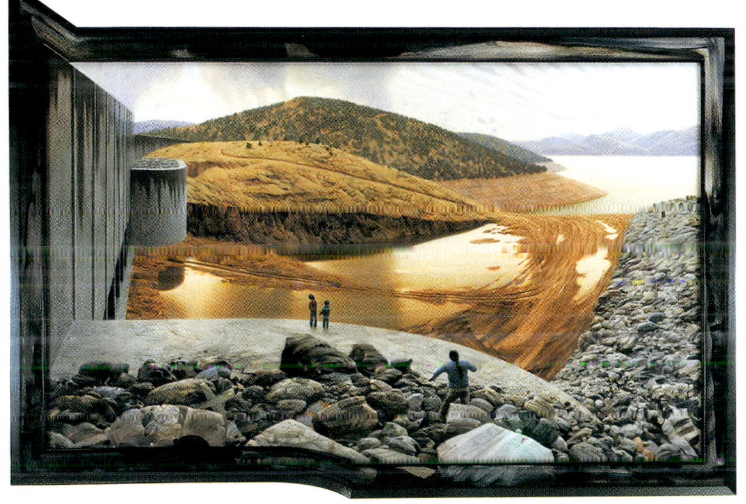

For most of his life, **CHUCK FORSMAN** (b. 1944) has been in the American West near streams and rivers. Baptized in the Deschutes River of central Oregon at the age of eight, he recalls the place seemed sheltered and cool. Later, a reservoir covered the location. When his family moved to Northern California, Forsman would often visit a place called Nelson's Bar on the Feather River. That, too, disappeared under a man-made impoundment.

Forsman received his undergraduate degree from the University of California, Davis, in 1967, and after service in Vietnam, where he received a Bronze Star, he returned to complete an M.F.A. Since 1971, he has served as a professor of art at the University of Colorado. He is the recipient of a National Endowment for the Arts grant, a purchase award from the American Academy of Arts and Letters, and a Colorado Council on the Arts Award.

To look honestly at the world around us is a sobering activity. Escapism may be possible, but escape is not.

—CHUCK FORSMAN

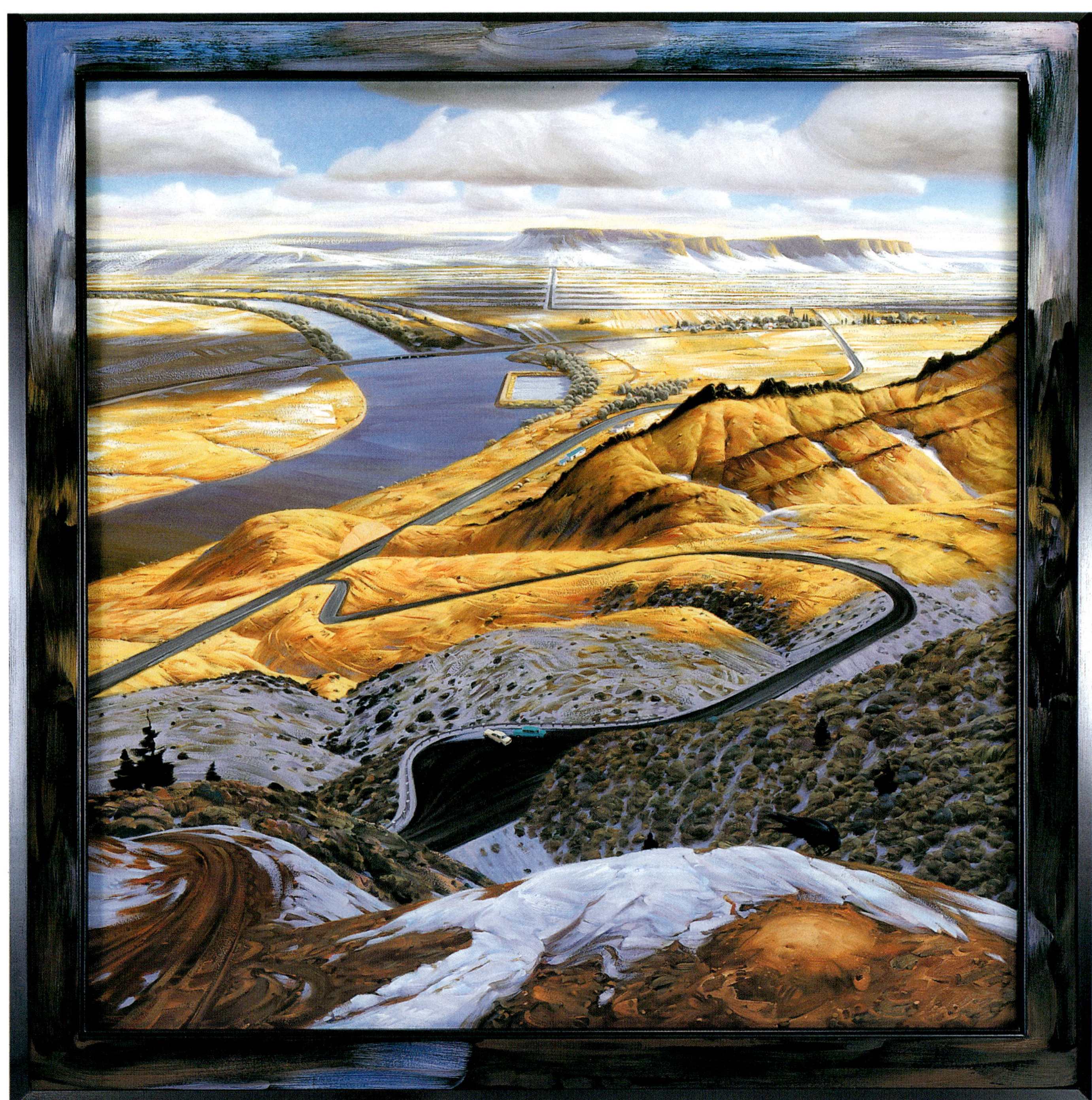

Chuck Forsman, CROW COUNTRY, *oil on canvas, 56 by 56 inches, 1993. Collection of Yellowstone Art Center.*

His work is in such places as the Metropolitan Museum of Art, the Denver Art Museum, the Phoenix Art Museum, Chase Manhattan Bank, the Anshultz Corporation, and Hallmark Cards. He has had many solo and group exhibitions, his most recent one *Arrested Rivers,* a national traveling exhibit organized by the University of Colorado.

In the early 1980s, Forsman started to concentrate on landscape painting, not pure landscapes, but a series of images that include dams and reservoirs as intrusive elements. "Arrested Rivers," he calls them. Forsman wants these paintings about the excessive control of water to convey what he feels is a crime, one we all share. In our rush to transform the West, magical, beautiful, and special places are destroyed, and like clogged arteries, they hasten our mortality. We have, in effect, created a new landscape, a hydraulic landscape, such as the one depicted in his painting *Feather River.* In this image of Northern California's Orville Dam, Forsman has left a subtle message, the cross in the middle foreground, a lament for the river's desecration. His paintings explore intersections of the West's lean, sparse, dehydrated terrain with human imprint, as in *Crow Country* (p. 188), a view of Yellowtail Dam on Montana's Crow Reservation. Not only is the earth disrupted by construction, our ability to look, to see vast distances, is likewise constricted and fragmented. "I have come to believe that the long tradition of celebration and optimism in landscape painting is on shaky ground," he says. "To look honestly at the world around us is a sobering activity. Escapism may be possible, but escape is not."

From the paintings of Clyde Aspevig, which celebrate the bountiful space and the effect of water on the timeless landscape, with no trace of human presence, to the roads of Woody Gwyn and the dams and reservoirs of Chuck Forsman, who offer meditation on the irrefutable proof of time's change, contemporary artists still chronicle the geographic and mythic core of the American West upon the collective imagination.

Artists continue to redefine, refine, and personalize their experiences with the West's immense, poetic landscape, and with the region's cultures, past and present, whose cast of characters have played and continue to play a vital role. The paintings and sculpture produced by the artists in this book, and their fellow practitioners, shape the concept of the West as a special place, a place that still informs the present. Most of this contemporary art is representational, with some nod toward abstract expressionism and other styles, since many artists strive to convey specific, detailed information about the West's landscapes and peoples. There is a remarkable array of documentary, illustrative, narrative, mythic, and formal aesthetic responses to the West that often combine to transcend space and time. This art ranges from the feel of fact to that of myth. No one subject prevails, except for the concept of the West itself. The myths and sagas of the Old West, of the lone, self-reliant cowboy and noble Native American, still remain compelling, and continue to shape contemporary attitudes, for both artists and non-artists. To show that the West of the cowboy and rancher remains vital, consider that the works sold by the twenty-six members at the 1996 Cowboy Artists of America show and sale grossed $1.7 million.

Still, many artists do not consider themselves "Western artists," especially Native American and Hispanic ones. Maybe they, and others, feel closer to "artists of the American West." Now more urban than rural, the New West seethes with a mosaic of highways, dams, bland suburban tracts, instant malls, sterile industrial parks, and military facilities, a plastic and neon topography. Within this rapidly fluctuating, commercialized, new human landscape, subject to change without notice, artists struggle to distill iconic meaning from the legacy and implied promise of the West, with new twists if possible. They focus on the beauty of the West and its inhabitants, yet dread the implications of the truth. Perhaps, though, they still heed Ralph Waldo Emerson's thought, "The health of the eye seems to demand a horizon. We are never tired so long as we can see far enough." Above all, they respond to that clarion call, "The West, the West, always the West!"

ARTIST BIOGRAPHIES

The information here has been compiled from materials supplied by the artists and their gallery representatives, in addition to published sources. This information reflects only recent achievements and activities. Exhibitions listed include only museum and professional organizations, and not gallery events. If an artist is not represented by any galleries, his or her representative is listed as "Self." Every attempt has been made to provide accurate and up-to-date information, but due to the fluid nature of the gallery business, some information may have changed.

Meredith Brooks Abbott

Born: 1938, Los Angeles, CA
Resides: Carpinteria, CA
Education: Art Center College of Design, Pasadena, CA
Recent Exhibitions: California Art Club, 1996, Pasadena, CA; Carnegie Art Museum, 1996, Oxnard, CA; Oak Group, 1996, Santa Barbara, CA
Collections: Cottage Hospital, Santa Barbara, CA; Leisure Technology, Lakewood, NJ; Santa Cruz Island Foundation, Santa Barbara, CA; State Capitol Building, Concord, NH
Representatives: The Craftsman Guild and California Heritage Gallery, 300 DeHaro St., San Francisco, CA 94103, (415) 431-5425; Maureen Murphy Fine Art Gallery, 1187 Coast Valley Rd., Santa Barbara, CA 93108, (805) 969-9215

William Acheff

Born: 1947, Anchorage, AK
Resides: Taos, NM
Education: Self-taught
Recent Exhibitions: National Cowboy Hall of Fame *(Prix de West Invitational)*, 1996, Oklahoma City, OK; Artists of America, 1995, Denver, CO
Award: Prix de West Purchase Prize, 1989, National Cowboy Hall of Fame, Oklahoma City, OK
Collection: National Cowboy Hall of Fame, Oklahoma City, OK
Representatives: J.N. Bartfield Galleries, 30 W. 57th St., 3rd Floor, New York, NY 10019, (212) 254-8890; Nedra Matteucci's Fenn Galleries, 1075 Paseo de Peralta, Santa Fe, NM 87501, (505) 982-4631; Settlers West Galleries, 6420 N. Campbell Ave., Tucson, AZ 85718, (520) 299-2607

Peter Adams

Born: 1950, Los Angeles, CA
Resides: Pasadena, CA
Education: Lukits Academy of Fine Art, Los Angeles, CA
Recent Exhibitions: Natural History Museum of Los Angeles County, 1996, Los Angeles, CA; Autry Museum of Western Heritage, 1995, Los Angeles, CA
Collections: ARCO Tower, Los Angeles, CA; Jonathan Club, Los Angeles, CA; Pacific Asia Museum, Pasadena, CA; Trust Company of the West, Los Angeles, CA
Representatives: The Craftsman Guild and California Heritage Gallery, 300 DeHaro St., San Francisco, CA 94103, (415) 431-5425; Galerie Gabrie, 597 E. Green St., Pasadena, CA 91101, (818) 577-1223; Joan Irvine Smith Fine Arts, 1550 South Coast Hwy., Laguna Beach, CA 92651, (714) 494-0854; Morseburg Galleries, 9089 Santa Monica Blvd., Los Angeles, CA 90069, (310) 273-5207

Page Allen

Born: 1951, St. Charles, IL
Resides: Santa Fe, NM
Education: Northern Illinois University, DeKalb, IL
Recent Exhibitions: DeWeese Gallery of Contemporary Arts, 1994, Bozeman, MT; Nora Eccles Harrison Museum of Art, 1994, Logan, UT; Arvada Center for the Arts and Humanities, 1992, Arvada, CO
Collections: Arvada Center of the Arts and Humanities, Arvada, CO; Eiteljorg Museum of American Indian and Western Art, Indianapolis, IN; Missoula Museum of the Arts, Missoula, MT; Museum of Fine Arts, Santa Fe, NM; Pepsi Cola/Frito-Lay Corporation, Dallas, TX
Representatives: Meredith Long and Company, 2323 San Felipe, Houston, TX 77019, (713) 523-6671; Owings-Dewey Fine Art, 76 E. San Francisco St., Santa Fe, NM, (505) 982-6244

Roy Andersen

Born: 1930, Temple, NH
Resides: Cave Creek, AZ
Education: Art Center College of Design, Pasadena, CA
Recent Exhibitions: National Cowboy Hall of Fame *(Prix de West Invitational)*, 1996, Oklahoma City, OKInternational Museum of the Horse, 1992, Lexington, KY
Award: Western Heritage Award, 1994, Favell Museum, Klamath Falls, OR
Collection: National Park Service, Pecos National Monument, Pecos, NM
Representatives: Claggett/Rey Gallery, 100 E. Meadow Drive, Vail, CO 81657, (970) 476-9350; Legacy Galleries, 7178 Main St., Scottsdale, AZ 85251, (602) 945-1113; Settlers West Galleries, 6420 N. Campbell Ave., Tucson, AZ 85718, (520) 299-2607

Tony Angell

Born: 1940, Los Angeles, CA
Resides: Seattle, WA
Education: University of Washington, Seattle, WA
Recent Exhibitions: National Academy of Design, 1996, New York, NY; National Cowboy Hall of Fame *(Prix de West Invitational)*, 1996, Oklahoma City, OK
Collections: Freye Art Museum, Seattle, WA; Gilcrease Museum, Tulsa, OK; U.S. West, Seattle, WA
Representatives: Foster/White Gallery, 126 Central Way, Kirkland, WA 98033, (206) 822 2305, and 311 1/2 Occidental Ave. S., Seattle, WA 98104, (206) 622-2833; Merrill Gallery of Fine Art, 1401 17th St., Denver, CO 80202, (303) 292-1401

Clyde Aspevig

Born: 1951, Havre, MT
Resides: Loveland, CO
Education: Eastern Montana College, Billings, MT
Recent Exhibitions: Gilcrease Museum, 1997, Tulsa, OK; National Cowboy Hall of Fame

(Prix de West Invitational), 1996, Oklahoma City, OK
Award: Robert M. Lougheed Memorial Award, 1993, National Cowboy Hall of Fame, Oklahoma City, OK
Collections: First Bank of Billings, MT; Montana Historical Society, Helena, MT; Museum of the Rockies, Bozeman, MT; Rockwell Museum, Corning, NY
Representatives: Kootenai Gallery, 573 Electric Ave., Big Fork, MT 59911, (406) 837-4848; Simpson-Gallagher Gallery, 1115 13th St., Cody, WY 82414, (307) 587-4022; Thomas Nygard Gallery, 127 Main St., Bozeman, MT 59715, (406) 586-3636; Trailside Americana Fine Art Galleries, 7330 Main St., Scottsdale, AZ 85251, (602) 945-7751, and 105 N. Center, Jackson, WY 83001, (307) 733-3186

Gerald Balciar
Born: 1942, Medford, WI
Resides: Parker, CO
Education: Self-taught
Recent Exhibitions: Gilcrease Museum, 1996, Tulsa, OK; National Cowboy Hall of Fame *(Prix de West Invitational),* 1996, Oklahoma City, OK
Awards: Bedi-Makky Foundry Prize, 1994, National Sculpture Society; Juror's Award, Northwest Rendezvous Group, 1993, Park City, UT
Collections: Denver Zoo, Denver, CO; Leigh Yawkey Woodson Art Museum, Wausau, WI; National Cowboy Hall of Fame, Oklahoma City, OK; University of North Texas, Denton, TX
Representatives: Altermann and Morris Galleries, 2727 Routh St., Dallas, TX 75201, (214) 871-3035, and 10000 Memorial, Ste. 230, Houston, TX 77024, (713) 688-1668; Canyon Spirit Gallery, 2340 Big Thompson Canyon, Estes Park, CO 80517, (970) 586-3888; Hawthorn Galleries, 1335 W. Hwy. 6, Branson, MO 65615, (417) 335-2170, and 375 Browd Ave. S., Naples, FL 34102, (941) 263-7994; Knox Gallery, 123 Beaver Creek Plaza, Avon, CO 81620, (970) 949-5564, and 1632 Market St., Denver, CO 80203, (303) 820-3925; Rice and Falkenburg Gallery, 325 Worth Ave., Palm Beach, FL 33480, (407) 833-9005; Trailside Americana Fine Art Galleries, 7330 Main St., Scottsdale, AZ 85251, (602) 945-7751, and 6th and Lincoln, Carmel, CA 93921, (408) 624-5071, and 105 N. Center, Jackson, WY 83001, (307) 733-3186

Joe Beeler
Born: 1931, Joplin, MO
Resides: Sedona, AZ
Education: Art Center College of Design, Pasadena, CA
Recent Exhibition: Phoenix Art Museum (Cowboy Artists of America), 1996, Phoenix, AZ
Awards: Living Legend Award, 1996, Canada Cowboy Art Council, Calgary, Canada; Arizona History Maker, 1995, Arizona Historical Association
Collection: Cowboy Artists of America Museum, Kerrville, TX
Representatives: Big Horn Galleries, 1167 Sheridan Ave., Cody, WY 82414, (800) 505-2639; Claggett/Rey Galleries, 100 E. Meadow Dr., Vail, CO 81657, (970) 476-9350; Hawthorn Galleries, 1335 W. Hwy. 76, Branson, MO 65615, (417) 335-2170; Trailside Americana Fine Art Galleries, 7330 Main St., Scottsdale, AZ 85251, (602) 945-7751, and 105 N. Center, Jackson, WY 83001, (307) 733-3186; Wickenburg Gallery, 1449 67 N. Tegner, Wickenburg, AZ 85338, (520) 684-7047

Nelson Boren
Born: 1952, Tempe, AZ
Resides: Sandpoint, ID
Collections: Dallas Cowboys, Dallas, TX; Minnesota Vikings, Minneapolis, MN
Representatives: Marcus Gallery, 213 Galisteo, Santa Fe, NM 87501, (505) 982-9363; Martin-Harris Gallery, 60 E. Broadway, Jackson, WY 83001, (800) 366-7814; Pitzer's of Carmel, 6th and Dolores, Carmel, CA 93921, (408) 625-2288; Suzanne Brown Gallery, 7160 Main St., Scottsdale, AZ 85251, (602) 945-8475

Harley Brown
Born: 1939, Edmonton, Alberta, Canada
Resides: Tucson, AZ
Education: Camberwill School, London, England
Recent Exhibition: National Cowboy Hall of Fame *(Prix de West Invitational),* 1996, Oklahoma City, OK
Awards: Silver Medal—Drawing, 1993, Gold Medal—Drawing, 1992, Robert M. Lougheed Memorial Award, 1990, National Cowboy Hall of Fame, Oklahoma City, OK
Representatives: Coeur d'Alene Galleries, Coeur d'Alene Resort, Ste. A, Coeur d'Alene, ID 83814, (208) 667-7732; Gateway Gallery, 1950 Juan Tabo NE, Albuquerque, NM 87112, (505) 292-2849; Jones Gallery, 7643 Girard Ave., La Jolla, CA 92037, (619) 459-1370; Settlers West Galleries, 6420 N. Campbell Ave., Tucson, AZ 85718, (520) 299-2607; Stagecoach Gallery, 1st Ave. N., Great Falls, MT 59403, (406) 761-8845; Vanier and Roberts Gallery, 7106 Main St., Scottsdale, AZ 85251, (800) 890-9559; Whiteside-Altermann and Morris Galleries, 38 New Orleans Rd., Hilton Head Island, SC 29938, (803) 842-4453; Wilcox Gallery, 1975 N. Hwy. 89, Jackson, WY 83001, (307) 733-6450

Kenneth R. Bunn
Born: 1938, Denver, CO
Resides: Denver, CO
Education: Self-taught
Recent Exhibitions: C. M. Russell Museum, 1996, Great Falls, MT; National Museum of Wildlife Art, 1996, Jackson, WY; Artists of America, 1993–1995, Denver, CO; National Cowboy Hall of Fame *(Prix de West Invitational),* 1994–1996, Oklahoma City, OK; Gilcrease Museum, 1992, Tulsa, OK; Leigh Yawkey Woodson Art Museum, 1993, Wausau, WI
Awards: National Academician, 1994, National Academy of Design, New York, NY; Distinguished Wildlife Artist, 1993, Leigh Yawkey Woodson Art Museum, Wausau, WI; Fellow, National Sculpture Society, 1992, New York, NY
Collections: Eiteljorg Museum of American Indian and Western Art, Indianapolis, IN; Gilcrease Museum, Tulsa, OK; National Museum of Wildlife Art, Jackson, WY; Royal Ontario Museum, Toronto, Ontario, Canada
Representative: Gerald Peters Gallery, 439 Camino del Monte Sol, Santa Fe, NM 87501, (505) 988-8961

Paul Calle
Born: 1928, Manhattan, NY
Resides: Stamford, CT
Education: Pratt Institute of Art, Brooklyn, NY
Recent Exhibitions: Hudson River Museum, 1995, Yonkers, NY; National Cowboy Hall of Fame *(Prix de West Invitational),* 1996, Oklahoma City, OK; Gilcrease Museum, 1991, Tulsa, OK
Awards: Nora Jean Hulsey Buyer's Choice

Award, 1995, Silver Medal—Drawing, 1992, National Cowboy Hall of Fame, Oklahoma City, OK
Representative: Self

George Carlson

Born: 1940, Elmhurst, IL
Resides: St. Maries, ID
Education: Art Institute of Chicago, Chicago, IL
Recent Exhibitions: National Cowboy Hall of Fame *(Prix de West Invitational)*, 1995–1996, Oklahoma City, OK; Fort Worth Zoo Museum, 1995, Fort Worth, TX; Gilcrease Museum, 1994, Tulsa, OK; Autry Museum of Western Heritage, 1993, Los Angeles, CA
Award: Idaho Governor's Award for Excellence in the Arts, 1996
Collections: C. M. Russell Museum, Great Falls, MT; Colorado Springs Fine Arts Center, Colorado Springs, CO; Denver Art Museum, Denver, CO; Eiteljorg Museum of American Indian and Western Art, Indianapolis, ID; National Cowboy Hall of Fame, Oklahoma City, OK
Representatives: Big Horn Galleries, 1657 Post Rd., Fairfield, CT 06430, (203) 255-4613; Bishop Gallery, 7164 Main St., Scottsdale, AZ 85251, (602) 949-9062; Nedra Matteucci's Fenn Galleries, 1075 Paseo de Peralta, Santa Fe, NM 87501, (505) 982-4631; Parchman Stremmel Galleries, 203 N. Presa, San Antonio, TX 78205, (210) 222-2465; Valley Bronze of Oregon, 186 N. Hemlock, Cannon Beach, OR 97110, (800) 559-2118

Ken Carlson

Born: 1937, Morton, MN
Resides: Kerrville, TX
Education: Minneapolis School of Art, Minneapolis, MN
Recent Exhibitions: Leigh Yawkey Woodson Art Museum, 1996, Wausau, WI; National Cowboy Hall of Fame *(Prix de West Invitational)*, 1996, Oklahoma City, OK; Gilcrease Museum, 1994, Tulsa, OK; James Ford Bell Museum of Natural History, 1994, Minneapolis, MN; National Museum of Wildlife Art, 1994, Jackson, WY
Awards: Distinguished Wildlife Artist, 1996, Leigh Yawkey Woodson Art Museum, Wausau, WI; Texas Turkey Stamp, 1996; Texas Waterfowl Stamp, 1994
Collections: Gallery of Sporting Art, Genesee County Museum, Mumford, NY; National Museum of Wildlife Art, Jackson, WY
Representatives: Collector's Covy, 15 Highland Park Village, Dallas, TX 75205, (214) 521-7880; Gallery at Midlane, 2500 Midlane, Ste. 7, Houston, TX 77027, (800) 659-9449; River Run Gallery, 291 1st Ave., Ketchum, ID 83340, (208) 726-8878; Russell A. Fink Gallery, 9843 Gunston Rd., Lorton, VA 22199, (703) 550-9699; Settlers West Galleries, 6420 N. Campbell Ave., Tucson, AZ 85718, (520) 299-2607; Trailside Americana Fine Art Galleries, 105 N. Center, Jackson, WY 83001, (307) 733-3186; Whistle Pik Gallery, 425 Main St., Fredericksburg, TX 78624, (210) 990-8649

Russell Chatham

Born: 1939, San Francisco, CA
Resides: Livingston, MT
Education: Self-taught
Recent Exhibition: C. M. Russell Museum, 1996, Great Falls, MT
Collection: Museum of the Rockies, Bozeman, MT
Representatives: Anne Reed Gallery, 620 Sun Valley Rd., Ketchum, ID 83540, (208) 726-3036; Barney Wycoff Art, 312 E. Hymn Ave., Aspen, CO 81611, (970) 925-8274; Chatham Fine Art, 120 N. Main St., Livingston, MT 59047, (406) 222-1566; Martin-Harris Gallery, 60 E. Broadway, Jackson, WY 83001, (307) 733-0350; Munson Gallery, 225 Canyon Rd., Santa Fe, NM 87501, (505) 983-1657; and Sutton West Gallery, 121 W. Broadway, Missoula, MT 59802, (406) 721-5460

Donna Clair

Born: 1939, Chicago, IL
Resides: Taos, NM
Education: Art Institute of Chicago, Chicago, IL
Collections: Sunwest Bank, Albuquerque, NM; Tee-pak Corporation, Chicago, IL; United Bank, El Paso, TX
Representative: Self

Anne Coe

Born: 1949, Wellton, AZ
Resides: Apache Junction, AZ
Education: Arizona State University, Tempe, AZ
Recent Exhibition: Scottsdale Center for the Arts, Scottsdale, AZ
Collections: Buffalo Bill Historical Center, Cody, WY; Center de Arte Moderne, Guadalajara, Mexico; Eiteljorg Museum of American Indian and Western Art, Indianapolis, IN; Mesa Southwest Museum, Mesa, AZ; Valley National Bank, Phoenix, AZ
Representatives: Aspen Mountain Gallery, 303 E. Hopkins, Aspen, CO 81611, (970) 925-5083; Denver Buffalo Company, 1109 Lincoln St., Denver, CO 80203, (303) 832-0885; Joy Tash Gallery, 4142 N. Marshall Way, Scottsdale, AZ 85251, (602) 945-0195; Martin-Harris Gallery, 60 E. Broadway, Jackson, WY 83001, (800) 366-7814

Don Coen

Born: 1935, Lamar, CO
Resides: Boulder, CO
Education: University of Northern Colorado, Greeley, Colorado
Recent Exhibition: Denver Art Museum, Denver CO
Collections: Central Bank and Trust, Denver, CO; Colorado Council of the Arts, Denver, CO; Denver Art Museum, Denver, CO; IBM Corporation, Boulder, CO; Oklahoma Art Center, Oklahoma City, OK
Representatives: Susan Duval Gallery, 525 E. Cooper Ave., Aspen, CO 81611, (970) 925-9044; Suzanne Brown Gallery, 7160 Main St., Scottsdale, AZ 85251, (602) 945-8475

Don Crowley

Born: 1926, Redlands, CA
Resides: Tucson, AZ
Education: Art Center College of Design, Pasadena, CA
Recent Exhibitions: National Cowboy Hall of Fame *(Prix de West Invitational)*, 1996, Oklahoma City, OK; Phoenix Art Museum (Cowboy Artists of America), 1996, Phoenix, AZ
Award: CA Award, Cowboy Artists of America, 1996, Phoenix Art Museum, Phoenix, AZ
Collection: Cowboy Artists of America Museum, Kerrville, TX
Representatives: Big Horn Galleries, 1167

Sheridan Ave., Cody, WY 82414, (800) 505-2639; Gateway Gallery, 1950 Juan Tabo NE, Albuquerque, NM 87112, (505) 292-2849; Husberg Fine Arts, 7137 Main St., Scottsdale, AZ 85251, (602) 947-7489; Legacy Galleries, 150 Center St., Jackson, WY 83001, (307) 733-2353; Settlers West Galleries, 6420 N. Campbell Ave., Tucson, AZ 85718, (520) 299-2607

Tom Darro

Born: 1946, Chicago, IL
Resides: Scottsdale, AZ
Education: Self-taught
Representatives: Lewis Art Gallery, 8025 W. Dodge Rd., Omaha, NE 68114, (402) 391-7723; Overland Gallery of Fine Art, 7155 Main St., Scottsdale, AZ 85251, (602) 947-1934; Settlers West Galleries, 6420 N. Campbell Ave., Tucson, AZ 85718, (520) 299-2607

Robert Daughters

Born: 1929
Resides: Tucson, AZ
Education: Kansas City Art Institute, Kansas City, MO
Recent Exhibition: Gilcrease Museum, 1990, Tulsa, OK
Collection: The Shansby Group, San Francisco, CA
Representatives: Altermann and Morris Galleries, 10000 Memorial, Ste. 230, Houston, TX 77024, (713) 688-1668; El Taller Gallery, 8015 Shoal Creek Rd., Ste. 109, Austin, TX 78757, (512) 302-0100; Elinor Oldham's Fine Art Gallery, 3623 Wyoming NE, Albuquerque, NM 87111, (505) 299-2829; Frame Works and Gallery, 309 Main St., Grand Junction, CO 81501, (970) 243-7074; Gustafson Galleries, 9606 N. May Ave., Oklahoma City, OK 73120, (405) 751-8466; MacLaren/Markowitz Gallery, 1011 Pearl St., Boulder, CO 80302, (303) 449-6807; Meyer Gallery, 225 Canyon Rd., Santa Fe, NM 87501, (505) 983-1434, and 7173 Main St., Scottsdale, AZ 85251, (602) 947-6372; Walnut Street Gallery, 217 Linden St., Fort Collins, CO 80524, (970) 221-2383

Joellyn Duesberry

Born: 1944, Richmond, VA
Resides: Littleton, CO
Education: Institute of Fine Arts, New York University, New York, NY
Recent Exhibitions: Denver Art Museum, 1993, Denver, CO; Eiteljorg Museum of American Indian and Western Art, 1990, Indianapolis, IN
Award: Rocky Mountain National Park Artist-in-Residence Award
Collections: AT&T, New York, NY; Cargill, Minneapolis, MN; First Bank of Boston, Boston, MA; Mobil Oil Corporation, Houston, TX; The State Department Art Bank, Washington, DC
Representatives: Hand Graphics Gallery and Atelier, 418 Montezuma St., Santa Fe, NM 87501, (505) 988-1241; James Graham and Sons, 1014 Madison Ave., New York, NY 10021, (212) 535-5767; Robischon Gallery, 1740 Wazee St., Denver, CO 80202, (303) 298-7788

John Farnsworth

Born: 1941, Williams, AZ
Resides: Rancho de Taos, NM
Education: Self-taught
Collections: Arizona State University, Tempe, AZ; Flagstaff Medical Center, Flagstaff, AZ; Millicent Rogers Museum, Taos, NM; Museum of Northern Arizona, Flagstaff, AZ; Sky Harbor International Airport, Phoenix, AZ
Representatives: Charlene Cody Gallery, 130 W. Palace Ave., Santa Fe, NM 87501, (505) 820-0010; Suzanne Brown Gallery, 7160 Main St., Scottsdale, AZ 85251, (602) 945-8475

John Fincher

Born: 1941, Hamilton, TX
Resides: Santa Fe, NM
Education: University of Oklahoma, Norman, OK
Recent Exhibitions: Site Santa Fe, 1996, Santa Fe, NM; St. John's College, 1996, Santa Fe, NM
Collections: Albuquerque Museum, Albuquerque, NM; ARCO, Los Angeles, CA; Cole-Taylor Financial Group, Chicago, IL; Dallas Museum of Fine Arts, Dallas, TX; El Dorado Hotel, Santa Fe, NM; University of Oklahoma Museum of Art, Norman, OK; Wichita Art Museum, Wichita, KS
Representative: Cline LewAllen Contemporary, 129 W. Palace Ave., Santa Fe, NM 87501, (505) 988-8997

Harry Fonseca

Born: 1946, Sacramento, CA
Resides: Santa Fe, NM
Education: California State University, Sacramento
Recent Exhibitions: Wheelwright Museum of the American Indian, 1996–1997, Santa Fe, NM; East Hawaii Cultural Center Gallery, 1993, Hilo, HI; Crocker Art Museum, 1992, Sacramento, CA; Shizouka City Gallery, 1992, Shizouka, Japan
Representatives: Cline LewAllen Contemporary, 129 W. Palace Ave., Santa Fe, NM 87501, (505) 988-8997; Solomon Dubnick Gallery, 2131 Northrop Ave., Sacramento, CA, 95825, (916) 920-4547

Chuck Forsman

Born: 1944, Nampa, ID
Resides: Boulder, CO
Education: University of California, Davis, CA
Recent Exhibitions: Philbrook Museum of Art, 1997, Tulsa, OK; William King Regional Art Center, 1997, Abingdon, VA; Denver Art Museum, 1996, Denver, CO; University of Colorado, 1994, Boulder, CO; National Academy of Sciences, 1991, Washington, DC
Awards: West Publishing Company, 1996, Egin, MI; Colorado Council on the Arts Recognition Award, 1995, Denver, CO
Collections: Chase Manhattan Bank, New York, NY; Denver Art Museum, Denver, CO; Kemper Financial Services, Chicago, IL; Metropolitan Museum of Art, New York, NY; Phoenix Art Museum, Phoenix, AZ; United Bank of Denver, Denver, CO
Representative: Robischon Gallery, 1740 Wazee St., Denver, CO 80202, (303) 298-7788; Tibor de Nagy Gallery, 724 5th Ave., New York, NY 10019, (212) 262-5050.

Joan Foth

Born: 1930, Elmira, NY
Resides: Chimayo, NM
Education: Barnard College, New York, NY
Collections: Hallmark Cards, Kansas City, MO; Topeka Public Library, Topeka, KS; Wichita Art Museum, Wichita, KS
Representatives: Munson Gallery, 225 Canyon Rd., Santa Fe, NM 87501, (505) 983-1657; Spotted Horse Gallery, 525 E. Cooper St., Aspen, CO 81611, (970) 920-6755

Alyce Frank

Born: 1932, New Iberia, LA
Resides: Arroyo Hondo, NM
Education: University of Chicago, Chicago, IL

Recent Exhibitions: Museum of New Mexico, 1991, Santa Fe, NM; Taos Art Celebration, 1991, Taos, NM
Representatives: Fenix Gallery, 228-B Paseo del Pueblo Norte, Taos, NM 87571, (505) 758-9120; Zaplin-Lampert Gallery, 3944 N. Marshall Way, Scottsdale, AZ 85251, (602) 970-6100, and 651 Canyon Rd., Santa Fe, NM 87501, (505) 982-6100

Edward J. Fraughton
Born: 1939, Park City, UT
Resides: South Jordan, UT
Education: University of Utah, Salt Lake City, UT
Recent Exhibition: National Cowboy Hall of Fame *(Prix de West Invitational),* 1996, Oklahoma City, OK
Award: Gold Medal—Sculpture, 1993, National Cowboy Hall of Fame, Oklahoma City, OK
Collections: City of San Diego, CA; Randolph-Macon College, Front Royal, VA; State Capitol Building, Cheyenne, WY
Representatives: Bronze Coast Galleries, 2234 N. Hemlock, Cannon Beach, OR 97110, (503) 436-1055; Drevitson Galleries, 27016 Church Hill Rd., Woodstock, VT 05091, (802) 457-1250; Huntsman Gallery, 521 E. Hyman, Aspen, CO 81611, (303) 920-1910; Miller Gallery, 2715 Erie Ave., Cincinnati, OH 45208, (513) 871-4420; Mountain Trails Gallery, 200 Old Santa Fe Trail, Santa Fe, NM 87501, (505) 988-3444; Taminah Gallery, 608 Main St., Park City, UT 84060, (801) 655-3265, Trails West, P.O Box 2360, Sun Valley, ID 83353, (208) 726-9261; Western Wildlife, 4 Embarcadero Center, San Francisco, CA 94111, (415) 398-4845; Wilcox Gallery, 1975 N. Hwy. 89, Jackson, WY 83001, (307) 733-6450

Luke Frazier
Born: 1970, Provo, UT
Resides: Logan, UT
Education: Utah State University, Logan, UT
Recent Exhibitions: National Museum of Wildlife Art, 1996, Jackson, WY; Art for the Parks, 1991–1996, Jackson, WY
Awards: National Wildlife Award, 1993 and 1996, Art for the Parks, Jackson, WY
Collections: CES Foundation, Jackson, WY; National Museum of Wildlife Art, Jackson, WY; Society of Illustrators, New York, NY
Representatives: Coeur d'Alene Galleries, Coeur d'Alene Resort, Coeur d'Alene, ID 83814, (208) 667-7732; DeMott Gallery, 12 S. Frontage Rd., Vail, CO 81657, (970) 476-8948; Legacy Galleries, 7178 Main St., Scottsdale, AZ 85251, (602) 945-1113; Meyer Gallery, 305 Main St., Park City, UT 84060, (801) 649-8160; Pitzer's of Carmel, 6th and Dolores, Carmel, CA 93921, (408) 625-2288

John D. Free
Born: 1929, Pawhuska, OK
Resides: Pawhuska, OK
Education: Self-taught
Recent Exhibition: National Cowboy Hall of Fame *(Prix de West Invitational),* 1996, Oklahoma City, OK
Collections: American Royal Association, Kansas, City, MO; Cherokee Historical Museum, Tahlequah, OK; National Cowboy Hall of Fame, Oklahoma City, OK
Representatives: Trails West Gallery, 1476 S. Coast Hwy., Laguna Beach, CA 92651, (714) 494-7888; Wichita Gallery of Fine Art, 100 N. Broadway, Wichita, KS 67202, (316) 267-0243

Charles Fritz
Born: 1955, Mason City, IA
Resides: Billings, MT
Education: Iowa State University, Ames, IA
Recent Exhibitions: Artists of America, 1996, Denver, CO; National Cowboy Hall of Fame *(Prix de West Invitational),* 1996, Oklahoma City, OK; Salmagundi Club, New York, NY
Award: Lee M. Loeb Award, Salmagundi Club, New York, NY
Collections: Denver Art Museum, Denver, CO; Leaning Tree Museum of Western Art, Boulder, CO; Texaco Corporation, New York, NY
Representatives: Grizzly Gallery, 111 S. Canyon West, Yellowstone, MT 59758, (406) 646-1030; Settlers West Galleries, 6420 N. Campbell Ave., Tucson, AZ 85718, (520) 299-2607; Turner Art Gallery, 301 University Blvd., Denver, CO 80206, (303) 355-1828

Walt Gonske
Born: 1942, Newark, NJ
Resides: Taos, NM
Education: Arts Students League, New York, NY
Recent Exhibition: National Cowboy Hall of Fame *(Prix de West Invitational),* 1991–1996, Oklahoma City, OK
Collections: Eiteljorg Museum of American Indian and Western Art, Indianapolis, IN; Gilcrease Museum, Tulsa, OK
Representatives: Hamdy Fine Arts Gallery, 234 W. Main, Fredericksburg, TX 78624, (800) 655-6088; Melton Park Gallery, 4300 N. Sewell, Oklahoma City, OK 73118, (405) 525-3603; Nedra Matteucci's Fenn Galleries, 1075 Paseo de Peralta, Santa Fe, NM 87501, (505) 982-4631; Robson Gallery, 535 4th Ave., San Diego, CA 92101, (619) 234-7356

Glenna Goodacre
Born: 1939, Lubbock, TX
Resides: Santa Fe, NM
Education: Art Students League, New York, NY
Recent Exhibitions: National Cowboy Hall of Fame *(Prix de West Invitational),* 1996, Oklahoma City, OK; Texas Tech University, 1995, Lubbock, TX
Awards: National Academician, 1994, National Academy of Design, New York, NY; Knickerbocker Artists Gold Medal, Distinguished Achievement in American Art, 1993, New York, NY
Collections: Colorado Springs Fine Arts Center, Colorado Springs, CO; National Park Service, Washington, DC; New Mexico State Capitol, Santa Fe, NM; Plains National Bank, Lubbock, TX
Representatives: Altermann and Morris Galleries, 2727 Routh St., Dallas, TX 75201, (214) 871-3035, and 10000 Memorial, Ste. 230, Houston, TX 77024, (713) 688-1668; Knox Gallery, 1632 Market St., Denver, CO 80203, (303) 820-2324, and 100 E. Meadow Drive, Vail, CO 81657, (970) 949-5564, and 375 Broad Ave, S., Naples, FL 32333, (941) 263-7991; Nedra Matteucci's Fenn Galleries, 1075 Paseo de Peralta, Santa Fe, NM 87501, (505) 982-4631; Pam Driscoll Gallery, 416 E. Cooper St. Mall, Aspen, CO 81611, (970) 925-3881; Perry House Galleries, 1017 Duke St., Alexandria, VA 22314, (703) 836-5148; R. Paul Mooney Fine Art, 7116 Main St., Scottsdale, AZ 85251, (602) 946-9946

Veryl Goodnight
Born: 1947, Denver, CO
Resides: Santa Fe, NM
Education: Self-taught
Recent Exhibitions: Artists of America, 1993–1996, Denver, CO; Governor's Invitational, 1993–1996, Cheyenne, WY; Northwest Rendevous Group, 1996, Park City, UT
Collections: George Bush Presidential Library Center, Texas A&M University, College

Station, TX; Houston Astrodome, Houston, TX; Lely Resort, Naples, FL; National Cowboy Hall of Fame, Oklahoma City, OK
Representatives: Altermann and Morris Galleries, 225 Canyon Rd., Santa Fe, NM 87501, (505) 983-1590, and 10000 Memorial, Ste. 230 Houston, TX 77024, (713) 688-1668; Taminah Gallery, 608 Main St., Park City, UT 84060, (801) 649-4514; Trailside Americana Fine Art Galleries, 7330 Main St., Scottsdale, AZ 85251, (602) 945-7751, and 105 N. Center, Jackson, WY 83001, (307) 733-3186; Whiteside-Altermann and Morris Galleries, 38 New Orleans Rd., Hilton Head Island, SC 29938, (803) 842-4433

Darren Vigil Gray

Born: 1959, Dulce, NM
Resides: Santa Fe, NM
Education: Self-taught
Recent Exhibition: El Mundo del Arte de Nuevo Mexico, 1994, Salon Guadalajara, Palacio Municipale, Guadalajara, Mexico
Collections: Heard Museum, Phoenix, AZ; Museum of Mankind, Vienna, Austria; Museum of the American Indian, Heye Foundation, New York, NY; National Museum of American Art, Washington, DC
Representative: Peyton-Wright, 131 Nusbaum St., Santa Fe, NM 87501, (505) 989-9888

Richard Greeves

Born: 1935, St. Louis, MO
Resides: Fort Washakie, WY
Education: Self-taught
Recent Exhibitions: National Cowboy Hall of Fame *(Prix de West Invitational)*, 1995–1996, Oklahoma City, OK
Collections: Buffalo Bill Historical Center, Cody, WY; High Desert Museum, Bend, OR; National Cowboy Hall of Fame, Oklahoma City, OK; Wyoming State Museum, Cheyenne, WY
Representatives: American Legacy Gallery, 5911 Main St., Kansas City, MO 64113, (816) 444-7944; Michael Wigley Galleries, 1111 Paseo de Peralta, Santa Fe, NM 87501, (505) 984-8986; Vanier and Roberts, Ltd., 7106 Main St., Scottsdale, AZ 85251, (800) 890-9559

Martin Grelle

Born: 1954, Clifton, TX
Resides: Clifton, TX
Education: Self-taught
Recent Exhibitions: National Cowboy Hall of Fame *(Prix de West Invitational)*, 1996, Oklahoma City, OK; Phoenix Art Museum (Cowboy Artists of America), 1996, Phoenix, AZ
Representative: Overland Gallery of Fine Art, 7155 Main St., Scottsdale, AZ 85251, (602) 947-1934

Woody Gwyn

Born: 1944, San Antonio, TX
Resides: Santa Fe, NM
Education: Pennsylvania Academy of Fine Arts, Philadelphia, PA
Recent Exhibitions: Site Santa Fe, 1996, Santa Fe, NM; Riverside Art Museum, 1993, Riverside, CA; West Publishing Company, 1993, Egin, MI
Collections: Albuquerque Museum, Albuquerque, NM; Amarillo Art Center, Amarillo, TX; Forbes Magazine Collection, New York, NY; Phoenix Art Museum, Phoenix, AZ; Museum of Fine Arts, Santa Fe, NM; Tower Records Company, Sacramento, CA
Representatives: Allan Stone Gallery, 113 E. 90th St., New York, NY 10128, (212) 988-6870; Cline LewAllen Contemporary, 129 W. Palace Ave., Santa Fe, NM 87501, (505) 988-8997

Bob Haozous

Born: 1943, Los Angeles, CA
Resides: Santa Fe, NM
Education: California College of Arts and Crafts, Oakland, CA
Recent Exhibitions: Wheelwright Museum of the American Indian, 1995, Santa Fe, NM; College of Santa Fe, 1994, Santa Fe, NM; Scottsdale Center for the Arts, 1992, Scottsdale, AZ
Award: Artist-in-Residence, 1992, City of Frankfurt, Germany
Collections: City of Phoenix, AZ; Cleveland Museum of Art, Cleveland, OH; Heard Museum, Phoenix, AZ; Joslyn Art Museum, Omaha, NE; Penn Treaty Park, Philadelphia, PA; Philbrook Museum of Art, Tulsa, OK; Tower Records Company, Sacramento, CA
Representative: Self

Peter Holbrook

Born: 1940, New York, NY
Resides: Redway, CA
Education: Brooklyn Museum School of Art, Brooklyn, NY
Recent Exhibitions: Foothills Art Center, 1997, Golden, CO; Mesa Southwest Museum, 1996, Mesa, CA; Hunter Art Museum, 1994, Chattanooga, TN; Northern Arizona University, 1994, Flagstaff, AZ
Collections: Art Institute of Chicago, Chicago, IL; Bank of America, San Francisco, CA; Brooklyn Museum, Brooklyn, NY; FMC Corporation, Chicago, IL; Indiana State University, Indianapolis, IN; Springfield Art Museum, Springfield, MO
Representative: Charlene Cody Gallery, 130 W. Palace Ave., Santa Fe, NM 87501, (505) 820-0010

Lindsay Holt II

Born: 1958, El Paso, TX
Resides: Santa Fe, NM
Education: Art Center College of Design, Pasadena, CA
Recent Exhibition: Foothills Art Center, 1997, Golden, CO
Collection: Museum of Fine Arts, Santa Fe, NM
Representatives: Cline Fine Art, 526 Canyon Rd., Santa Fe, NM 87501, (505) 982-5328; Medicine Man Gallery, 7000 E. Tanque Verde Rd., Tucson, AZ 85715, (800) 422-9382

William Hook

Born: 1948, Kansas City, MO
Resides: Englewood, CO
Education: Art Center College of Design, Pasadena, CA
Recent Exhibitions: Colorado Governor's Invitational, 1994–1996, Denver, CO; Artists of America, 1992–1996, Denver, CO; Covering the West, The Best of *Southwest Art*, 1995
Award: New Mexico Symphony Orchestra Poster Artist, 1995
Collections: Denver Art Museum, Denver, CO; Denver Convention Center, Denver, CO; World Trade Center, Los Angeles, CA
Representatives: Carson Gallery, 1601 Araphoe St., Ste. 6, Denver, CO 80202, (303) 825-6608; Howard Portnoy Gallerie, 6th and Dolores, Carmel, CA, 93921, (408) 624-1155; MacLaren/Markowitz Gallery, 1011 Pearl St., Boulder, CO 80302, (303) 449-6807; Meyer Gallery, 225 Canyon Rd., Santa Fe, NM 87501, (505) 983-1434; R. Paul Mooney Fine Art, 7116 Main St., Scottsdale, AZ 85251, (602) 946-9946

Donna Howell-Sickles

Born: 1949, Gainsville, TX
Resides: Frisco, TX
Education: Texas Tech University, Lubbock, TX
Recent Exhibitions: C. M. Russell Museum, 1997, Great Falls, MT; Nicolaysen Art Museum, 1997, Casper, WY; Buffalo Bill Historical Center, 1996, Cody, WY; Tucson Museum of Art, 1995, Tucson, AZ
Collections: Buffalo Bill Historical Center, Cody, WY; National Museum of Wildlife Art, Jackson, WY; Tucson Museum of Art, Tucson, AZ
Representatives: Big Horn Galleries, 1167 Sheridan Ave., Cody, WY 82414, (800) 505-2639; Contemporary Southwest Galleries, 123 W. Palace Ave., Santa Fe, NM 87501, (505) 986-0440; Martin-Harris Gallery, 60 E. Broadway, Jackson, WY 83001, (800) 366-7814; Meyer Gallery, 7173 Main St., Scottsdale, AZ 85251, (602) 947-6372; Pitzer's of Carmel, 6th and Dolores, Carmel, CA 93921, (408) 625-2288; Sally Harvey Fine Art, 174 Midland Ave., Basalt, CO 81621, (970) 927-0927

Wilson Hurley

Born: 1924, Tulsa, OK
Resides: Albuquerque, NM
Education: United States Military Academy, West Point, NY; George Washington University School of Law, Washington, DC
Recent Exhibition: Eiteljorg Museum of American Indian and Western Art, 1991, Indianapolis, IN
Award: Eiteljorg Award, 1991, Eiteljorg Museum of American Indian and Western Art, Indianapolis, IN
Collections: Albuquerque Museum, Albuquerque, NM; Buffalo Bill Historical Center, Cody, WY; Gilcrease Museum, Tulsa, OK; National Cowboy Hall of Fame, Oklahoma City, OK
Representatives: Altermann and Morris Galleries, 2727 Routh St., Dallas, TX 75201, (214) 871-3035; Nedra Matteucci's Fenn Galleries, 1075 Paseo de Peralta, Santa Fe, NM 87501, (505) 982-4631

Doug Hyde

Born: 1946, Hermiston, OR
Resides: Santa Fe, NM
Education: Institute of American Indian Art, Santa Fe, NM
Recent Exhibitions: Artists of America, 1996, Denver, CO; National Cowboy Hall of Fame *(Prix de West Invitational)*, 1995–1996, Oklahoma City, OK
Award: Distinguished Artist of the Year, 1996, Santa Fe Rotary Foundation, Santa Fe, NM
Collections: Amon Carter Museum, Forth Worth, TX; City of Palm Springs, CA; Heard Museum, Phoenix, AZ; Lewis and Clark State College, Lewiston, ID; National Cowboy Hall of Fame, Oklahoma City, OK
Representative: Glen Green Galleries, 6000 E. Camelback Rd., Phoenician Resort, Scottsdale, AZ 85251, (602) 990-9110; and Nedra Matteucci's Fenn Galleries, 1075 Paseo de Peralta, Santa Fe, NM 87501, (505) 982-4631

Oreland C. Joe

Born: 1958, Shiprock, NM
Resides: Kirtland, NM
Education: Self-taught
Recent Exhibitions: National Cowboy Hall of Fame *(Prix de West Invitational)*, 1993 and 1996, Oklahoma City, OK; Phoenix Art Museum (Cowboy Artists of America), 1993–1996, Phoenix, AZ; Cowboy Artists of America Museum, 1995, Kerrville, TX
Award: Purchase Award, 1992, Governor's Invitational, Cheyenne, WY
Collections: City of Ponca, OK; Northern Navajo Medical Center, Shiprock, NM; San Juan College, Farmington, NM
Representatives: Mountain Legends Gallery, 610 E. Hwy. 2070, Rudioso Downs, NM 88346, (800) 450-7927; Mountain Trails Gallery, Tlaquepaque A201/A109, Sedona, AZ 86336, (520) 282-3225; Pierce Fine Art, 7145 Main St., Scottsdale, AZ 85251, (602) 945-8100; Wadle Gallery, 128 W. Palace Ave., Santa Fe, NM 87501, (505) 983-9219

Gregory Kondos

Born: 1923, Lynn, MA
Resides: Sacramento, CA
Education: California State University, Sacramento, CA
Recent Exhibitions: Hearst Art Gallery, St. Mary's College, 1994, Moraga, CA; American Academy of Arts and Sciences, 1993, New York, NY; Crocker Art Museum, 1993, Sacramento, CA; Fresno Metropolitan Museum, 1993, Fresno, CA
Awards: National Academician, 1995, National Academy of Design, New York, NY; Distinguished Service Award, 1994, California State University, Sacramento, CA
Collections: Corcoran Gallery of Art, Washington, DC; Crocker Art Museum, Sacramento, CA; Oakland Museum, Oakland, CA; Phoenix Art Museum, Phoenix, AZ
Representatives: John Berggruen Gallery, 228 Grant Ave., San Francisco, CA 94108, (415) 781-4629; Medicine Man Gallery, 7000 E. Tanque Verde Rd., Tucson, AZ 85715, (800) 422-9382

Bob Kuhn

Born: 1920, Buffalo, NY
Resides: Tucson, AZ, and Roxbury, CT
Education: Pratt Institute of Art, Brooklyn, NY
Recent Exhibitions: National Cowboy Hall of Fame *(Prix de West Invitational)*, 1996, Oklahoma City, OK; Society of Animal Artists, 1995, New York, NY; Gilcrease Museum, 1994, Tulsa, OK
Awards: Elliot Lisken Award, 1995, Society of Animal Artists, New York, NY; Prix de West Purchase Prize, 1991, National Cowboy Hall of Fame, Oklahoma City, OK; Distinguished Wildlife Artist, 1990, Leigh Yawkey Woodson Art Museum, Wausau, WI
Collections: Gilcrease Museum, Tulsa, OK; Leigh Yawkey Woodson Art Museum, Wausau, WI; National Cowboy Hall of Fame, Oklahoma City, OK; National Museum of Wildlife Art, Jackson, WY
Representatives: Gallery at Midlane, 2500 Midlane, Ste. 7, Houston, TX 77027, (800) 659-9449; Settlers West Galleries, 6420 N. Campbell Ave., Tucson, AZ 85718, (520) 299-2607

Frank LaPena

Born: 1937, San Francisco, CA
Resides: Sacramento, CA
Education: California State University, Sacramento, CA
Recent Exhibitions: University Art Gallery, Sonoma State University, 1993, Roahnert Park, CA; University of California Museum of Art, Science, and Culture at Blackhawk, 1993, Danville, CA; Falkirk Cultural Center, 1992, San Rafael, CA; German-American Institute, 1992, Stuttgart, Germany
Collections: Mills College, Oakland, CA;

Museum of Modern Art, New York, NY; University of Utah, Salt Lake City, UT
Representative: Pacific Western Traders, 305 Wool St., Folsom, CA 95620, (916) 985-3851

Tom Lovell

Born: 1909, New York, NY
Resides: Santa Fe, NM
Education: Syracuse University, Syracuse, NY
Recent Exhibition: National Cowboy Hall of Fame *(Prix de West Invitational),* 1996, Oklahoma City, OK
Awards: Robert M. Lougheed Memorial Award and Lifetime Achievement Award, 1992, National Cowboy Hall of Fame, Oklahoma City, OK
Representative: Altermann and Morris Galleries, 2727 Routh St., Dallas, TX 75201, (214) 871-3035

Frank C. McCarthy

Born: 1924, Scarsdale, NY
Resides: Sedona, AZ
Education: Pratt Institute of Art, Brooklyn, NY
Recent Exhibition: Phoenix Art Museum (Cowboy Artists of America), 1996, Phoenix, AZ
Collection: Cowboy Artists of America Museum, Kerrville, TX
Representatives: Altermann and Morris Galleries, 2727 Routh St., Dallas, TX 75201, (214) 871-3035; Big Horn Galleries, 1167 Sheridan Ave., Cody, WY 82414, (800) 505-2639; Pierce Fine Art, 7145 Main St., Scottsdale, AZ 85251, (602) 945-8100

George McLean

Born: 1939, Toronto, Ontario, Canada
Resides: Bogner, Ontario, Canada
Education: Self-taught
Recent Exhibitions: Leigh Yawkey Woodson Art Museum, 1992–1996, Wausau, WI; Suntory Museum, 1995, Osaka, Japan
Award: Master Wildlife Artist, 1992, Leigh Yawkey Woodson Art Museum, Wausau, WI
Collections: Genesee County Museum, Mumford, NY; Glenbow-Alberta Institute, Calgary, Alberta, Canada; Royal Ontario Museum, Toronto, Ontario, Canada
Representative: Self

Merrill Mahaffey

Born: 1937, Albuquerque, NM
Resides: Santa Fe, NM
Education: Arizona State University, Tempe, AZ
Recent Exhibitions: Foothills Art Center, 1997, Golden, CO; Artists of America, 1992, Denver, CO; Chandler Fine Arts Center, 1992, Chandler, AZ; Eiteljorg Museum of American Indian and Western Art, 1992, Indianapolis, IN
Collections: Arizona State University, Tempe, AZ; Metropolitan Museum of Art, New York, NY; Phoenix Art Museum, Phoenix, AZ; University of Utah, Salt Lake City, UT
Representatives: Charlene Cody Gallery, 130 W. Palace Ave., Santa Fe, NM 87501, (505) 820-0010; Golden West Gallery, 101 W. Colorado Ave., Telluride, CO 81435, (970) 728-3664; MacLaren/Markowitz Gallery, 1011 Pearl St., Boulder, CO 80302, (303) 449-6807; Suzanne Brown Gallery, 7160 Main St., Scottsdale, AZ 85251, (602) 945-8475

William Matthews

Born: 1949, New York, NY
Resides: Evergreen, CO
Education: Self-taught
Recent Exhibition: National Cowboy Hall of Fame *(Prix de West Invitational),* 1996, Oklahoma City, OK
Collections: Autry Museum of Western Heritage, Los Angeles, CA; Eiteljorg Museum of American Indian and Western Art, Indianapolis, IN; Gilman Paper Company, New York, NY; National Cowboy Hall of Fame, Oklahoma City, OK; The Ritz-Carlton, Aspen, CO; Warner Western Records, Nashville, TN
Representatives: Broschofsky Galleries, 6th and Leadville, Ketchum, ID 83340, (208) 726-4950; Channing Gallery, 53 Old Santa Fe Tr., Santa Fe, NM 87501, (505) 988-1078; Sally Harvey Fine Art, 174 Midland Ave., Basalt, CO 81621, (970) 927-0927; Simpson Gallagher Gallery, 1115 13th St., Cody, WY 82414, (307) 587-4022; Spanierman Gallery, 45 East 58th St., New York, NY 10022, (212) 832-0208; William Matthews Gallery, 1617 Wazee St., Denver, CO 80202, (303) 534-1300

Ed Mell

Born: 1942, Phoenix, AZ
Resides: Phoenix, AZ
Education: Art Center College of Design, Pasadena, CA
Recent Exhibitions: Scottsdale Center for the Arts, 1996–1997, Scottsdale, AZ; Grand Canyon Association, 1995, Grand Canyon National Park, Arizona
Collections: Arbys, Phoenix, AZ; Brown and Bain, Phoenix, AZ; Loew's Ventana Canyon Resort, Tucson, AZ; Phoenix Art Museum, Phoenix, AZ; Scottsdale Center for the Arts, Scottsdale, AZ; Syntax Corporation, Phoenix, AZ
Representatives: Owings-Dewey Fine Art, 76 E. San Francisco St., Santa Fe, NM 87501, (505) 982-6244; Suzanne Brown Gallery, 7160 Main St., Scottsdale, AZ 85251, (602) 945-8475

Herb Mignery

Born: 1937, Bartlett, NE
Resides: Loveland, CO
Education: Wayne State College, Wayne, NE
Recent Exhibitions: Center for Great Plains Studies, 1994, University of Nebraska, Lincoln, NE; National Cowboy Hall of Fame *(Prix de West Invitational),* 1996, Oklahoma City, OK; Phoenix Art Museum (Cowboy Artists of America), 1996, Phoenix, AZ
Collections: American Express Corporation, New York, NY; Center for Great Plains Studies, University of Nebraska, Lincoln, NE; U.S. West, Denver, CO
Representatives: Altermann and Morris Galleries, 10000 Memorial, Ste. 230, Houston, TX 77024, (713) 688-1668; Columbine Gallery, 2683 N. Taft, Loveland, CO 80538, (970) 667-2015; Fallbrook Fine Art, 128 N. Main St., Fallbrook, CA 92028, (619) 728-0700; Settlers West Galleries, 6420 N. Campbell Ave., Tucson, AZ 85718, (520) 299-2607

Lanford Monroe

Born: 1950, Bridgewater, CT
Resides: Taos, NM
Education: Ringling School of Art, Sarasota, FL
Recent Exhibitions: National Cowboy Hall of Fame *(Prix de West Invitational),* 1995–1996, Oklahoma City, OK; National Museum of Wildlife Art, 1996, Jackson, WY
Awards: Landscape Award, 1995, American Academy of Equine Art, Louisville, KY; Judge's Award of Merit, 1995, Art for the Parks, Jackson, WY
Collections: Huntsville Museum of Art, Huntsville, AL; Leigh Yawkey Woodson Art Museum, Wausau, WI; National Museum of Wildlife Art, Jackson, WY
Representatives: Barney Wycoff Gallery, 312 E. Hyman Ave., Aspen, CO 81611, (970) 925-8274; Pachmann Stremmel Galleries, 203 N.

Presa, San Antonio, TX 78205, (210) 222-2465; Trailside Americana Fine Art Galleries, 6th and Lincoln, Carmel, CA 93921, (408) 624-5071, and 105 N. Center, Jackson, WY 83001, (307) 733-3186

Jim Morgan

Born: 1947, Payson, UT
Resides: Mendon, UT
Education: Utah State University, Logan, UT
Recent Exhibitions: Artists of America, 1996, Denver, CO; Leigh Yawkey Woodson Art Museum, 1993 and 1996, Wausau, WI; National Cowboy Hall of Fame *(Prix de West Invitational)*, 1996, Oklahoma City, OK
Awards: Ben Stahl Artist's Choice Award, 1995, Northwest Rendezvous Group, Park City, UT; Robert M. Lougheed Memorial Award, 1994, National Cowboy Hall of Fame, Oklahoma City, OK
Collection: Crescent Cardboard Company, Chicago, IL
Representatives: Pitzer's of Carmel, 6th and Dolores, Carmel, CA 93921, (408) 625-2288; Trailside Americana Fine Art Galleries, 105 N. Center, Jackson, WY 83001, (307) 733-3186

Dan Namingha

Born: 1950, Polacca, AZ
Resides: La Tierra, NM
Education: Institute of American Indian Art, Santa Fe, NM
Recent Exhibitions: Museum of Fine Arts, 1996, Santa Fe, NM; Harvard University, 1995, Cambridge, MA
Award: Harvard Foundation, 1995, Harvard University, Cambridge, MA
Collections: Delhem Museum, Berlin, Germany; City of Phoenix, AZ; Hallmark Cards, Kansas City, MO; Mountain Bell, Denver, CO; National Aeronautical and Space Administration, Washington, DC
Representatives: J. Cacciola Galleries, 125 Wooster St., New York, NY 10012, (212) 966-9177; Joy Tash Gallery, 4142 N. Marshall Way, Scottsdale, AZ 85251, (602) 945-0195; Niman Fine Art, 125 Lincoln Ave., Santa Fe, NM 87501, (505) 988-5091

Gary Niblett

Born: 1943, Carlsbad, NM
Resides: Santa Fe, NM
Education: Art Center College of Design, Pasadena, CA
Recent Exhibition: Phoenix Art Museum (Cowboy Artists of America), 1996, Phoenix, AZ
Awards: Gold Medal—Water Soluble, Cowboy Artists of America, 1992, Phoenix Art Museum, Phoenix, AZ; Hubbard Award of Excellence, 1991, Hubbard Museum, Rudioso, NM
Collections: Eastern New Mexico University, Portales, NM; State Capitol Building, Santa Fe, NM; Sunwest Bank, Santa Fe, NM; Texas Christian University, Fort Worth, TX
Representatives: Altermann and Morris Galleries, 2727 Routh St., Dallas, TX 75201, (214) 871-3035; Big Horn Galleries, 1167 Sheridan Ave., Cody, WY 82414, (800) 505-2639; Claggett/Rey Gallery 100 E. Meadow Dr., Vail, CO 81657, (970) 476-9350; Nedra Matteucci's Fenn Galleries, 1075 Paseo de Peralta, Santa Fe, NM 87501, (505) 982-4631; R. Paul Mooney Fine Art, 7116 Main St., Scottsdale, AZ 85251, (602) 946-9946

P. A. Nisbet

Born: 1948, Washington, NC
Resides: Santa Fe, NM
Education: University of North Carolina, Chapel Hill, NC
Awards: National Science Foundation, Artists and Writers Program Grant for Travel to Antarctica, 1995–1996
Collection: National Aeronautic and Space Administration, Washington, DC
Representatives: Self; Bentley Gallery, 4161 N. Marshall Way, Scottsdale, AZ 85251, (602) 946-6060

Anthony Ortega

Born: 1958, Santa Fe, NM
Resides: Denver, CO
Education: University of Colorado, Boulder, CO
Recent Exhibitions: Art Museum of South Texas, 1996, Corpus Christi, TX; Colorado Springs Fine Arts Center, 1996, Colorado Springs, CO; Eiteljorg Museum of American Indian and Western Art, 1996, Indianapolis, IN; Huntington Beach Art Center, 1995, Huntington Beach , CA
Award: Distinguished Alumni, 1995, Heritage Center, University of Colorado, Boulder, CO
Collections: AT&T Corporation, Denver, CO; Beech Aircraft, San Antonio, TX; Colorado Convention Center, Denver, CO; University of Colorado, Boulder, CO
Representatives: Charlene Cody Gallery, 130 W. Palace Ave., Santa Fe, NM 87501, (505) 820-0010; Squash Blossom Gallery, 1428 Larimar St., Denver, CO 80202, (303) 572-7979

Bill Owen

Born: 1942, Gila Bend, AZ
Resides: Dewey, AZ
Education: Self-taught
Recent Exhibitions: Gilcrease Museum, 1996, Tulsa, OK; Phoenix Art Museum (Cowboy Artists of America), 1996, Phoenix, AZ
Award: Frederic Remington Award, 1994, National Cowboy Hall of Fame, Oklahoma City, OK
Collections: Cowboy Artists of America Museum, Kerrville, TX; Gilcrease Museum, Tulsa, OK; National Cowboy Hall of Fame, Oklahoma City, OK
Representative: Pierce Fine Art, 7145 Main St., Scottsdale, AZ 85251, (602) 945-8100

Tom Palmore

Born: 1945, Ada, OK
Resides: Wister, OK
Education: Pennsylvania Academy of the Fine Arts, Philadelphia, PA
Recent Exhibitions: Philadelphia Academy of the Fine Arts, 1994, Philadelphia, PA; South Bend Art Center, 1991, South Bend, IN
Collections: Brooklyn Museum, Brooklyn, NY; Buffalo Bill Historical Center, Cody, WY; Philadelphia Museum of Art, Philadelphia, PA; St. Louis Art Museum, St. Louis, MO, Whitney Museum of American Art, New York, NY
Representatives: Betts Gallery, 123 Grant Ave., Santa Fe, NM 87501, (505) 988-4499; J. Cacciola Galleries, 125 Wooster St., New York, NY 10012, (212) 966-9177

Paul Pletka

Born: 1946, San Diego, CA
Resides: Tesuque, NM
Education: Colorado State University, Fort Collins, CO
Recent Exhibitions: Colorado Springs Fine Arts Center, 1996, Colorado Springs, CO; Albrecht-Kemper Museum of Art, 1993, St. Joseph, MO; Fred Jones Jr. Museum of Art, 1993, University of Oklahoma, Norman, OK
Collections: Buffalo Bill Historical Center,

Cody, WY; Colorado Springs Fine Arts Center, Colorado Springs, CO; Eiteljorg Museum of American Indian and Western Art, Indianapolis, IN; Museum of Fine Arts, Santa Fe, NM
Representatives: Gallery 10, 34505 N. Scottsdale Rd., Scottsdale, AZ 85262, (602) 945-3385, and 225 Canyon Rd., Santa Fe, NM 87501, (505) 983-9707; Susan Duval Gallery, 525 E. Cooper Ave., Aspen, CO 81611, (970) 925-9044

Howard Post

Born: 1948, Tucson, AZ
Resides: Scottsdale, AZ
Education: University of Arizona, Tucson, AZ
Recent Exhibition: Desert Cabelleros Western Museum, 1992–1993, Wickenburg, AZ
Collections: Bank of the Southwest, Houston, TX; First National Bank, Kansas City, MO; Smithsonian Institution, Washington, DC; Victorio Land and Cattle Company, Phoenix, AZ
Representatives: Barney Wycoff Gallery, 312 E. Hyman Ave., Aspen, CO 81611, (970) 925-8274; Contemporary Southwest Galleries, 203 Canyon Rd., Santa Fe, NM 87501, (505) 988-7271; Golden West Gallery, 101 W. Colorado Ave., Telluride, CO 81435, (970) 728-3664; Suzanne Brown Gallery, 7160 Main St., Scottsdale, AZ 85251, (602) 945-8475

Jeri Nichols Quinn

Born: 1939, Alamogordo, NM
Resides: Point Reyes Station, CA
Education: Art Center College of Design, Pasadena, CA
Recent Exhibitions: Tucson Museum of Art, 1996, Tucson, AZ; Bolinas Museum, 1995, Point Reyes Station, CA; Art for the Parks, 1992, Jackson, WY,
Awards: Award for Excellence, Top 100 Paintings, 1992, Art for the Parks, Jackson, WY; Silver Award, 1992, *Art of California* Magazine
Collections: Hedgerow Farms, Winters, CA; Sacramento Mountains Historical Society, Cloudcroft, NM
Representatives: Christopher Queen Galleries, John Orrs Gardens, Ste. 4, Duncan Mills, CA 95430, (707) 865-1318; Merrill Gallery of Fine Art, 1401 17th St., Denver, CO 80202, (303) 292-1401; Rosequist Galleries, 1615 E. Ft. Lowell Rd., Tucson, AZ 85719, (520) 327-5729

Thomas Quinn

Born: 1938, Honolulu, HI
Resides: Point Reyes Station, CA
Education: Art Center College of Design, Pasadena, CA
Recent Exhibitions: Leigh Yawkey Woodson Art Museum, 1996, Wausau, WI; National Cowboy Hall of Fame *(Prix de West Invitational),* 1994–1996, Oklahoma City, OK
Award: Gold Medal—Watercolor, 1994, National Cowboy Hall of Fame, Oklahoma City, OK
Collections: Monterey Bay Aquarium, Monterey, CA; National Museum of Wildlife Art, Jackson, WY
Representatives: Christopher Queen Galleries, John Orrs Gardens, Ste. 4, Duncan Mills, CA 95430, (707) 865-1318; Hayden Hays Gallery, Broadmoor Hotel, 1 Lake Ave., Colorado Springs, CO 80901, (719) 577-5744; Russell A. Fink Gallery, 9843 Gunston Rd., Lorton, VA 22199, (703) 550-9699

James Reynolds

Born: 1926, Taft, CA
Resides: Scottsdale, AZ
Education: Kahn Institute of Art, Los Angeles, CA; School of Allied Arts, Glendale, AZ
Recent Exhibitions: National Cowboy Hall of Fame *(Prix de West Invitational),* 1992–1996, Oklahoma City, OK; Gilcrease Museum, 1993, Tulsa, OK
Awards: Gold Medal, Prix de West Purchase Prize, Best Oil Painting, and Buyers Choice Award, 1992, National Cowboy Hall of Fame, Oklahoma City, OK
Representatives: Gallery at Midlane, 2500 Midlane, Ste. 7, Houston, TX 77027, (800) 659-9449; Texas Art Gallery, 5570 W. Lovers Lane, Ste. 396, Dallas, TX 75209, (214) 350-8500; Trailside Americana Fine Art Galleries, 7330 Main St., Scottsdale, AZ 85251, (602) 945-7751, and 105 N. Center, Jackson, WY 83001, (307) 733-3186

Andrea Rich

Born: 1954, Racine, WI
Resides: Santa Cruz, CA
Education: University of Wisconsin, Whitewater, WI
Recent Exhibitions: Grants Pass Museum of Art, 1996, Grants Pass, OR; Fort Hays State University, 1996, Fort Hays, KS; Leigh Yawkey Woodson Art Museum, 1996, Wausau, WI; Triton Museum of Art, 1995, Santa Clara, CA
Award: Purchase Award, 1995, Minot State University, Minot, SD
Collections: Coos Bay Art Museum, Coos Bay, OR; International Wildlife Federation, Vienna, IL; Leigh Yawkey Woodson Art Museum, Wausau, WI; Minot State University, Minot, SD; 3M Company, St. Paul, MN
Representative: Self

Kenneth Riley

Born: 1919, Waverly, MO
Resides: Tucson, AZ
Education: Art Students League, Grand Central School of Art, New York, NY
Recent Exhibitions: Cowboy Artists of America Museum, 1996, Kerrville, TX; National Cowboy Hall of Fame *(Prix de West Invitational),* 1996, Oklahoma City, OK; Phoenix Art Museum (Cowboy Artists of America), 1996, Phoenix, AZ
Award: Prix de West Purchase Prize, 1995, National Cowboy Hall of Fame, Oklahoma City, OK
Collections: National Cowboy Hall of Fame, Oklahoma City, OK; United States Air Force Academy, Colorado Springs, CO; West Point Museum, West Point, NY
Representatives: Altermann and Morris Galleries, 10000 Memorial, Ste. 230, Houston, TX 77024, (713) 688-1668; Settlers West Galleries, 6420 N. Campbell Ave., Tucson, AZ 85718, (520) 299-2607

Morris Rippel

Born: 1930, Albuquerque, NM
Resides: Albuquerque, NM
Education: University of New Mexico, Albuquerque, NM
Recent Exhibitions: National Cowboy Hall of Fame *(Prix de West Invitational),* 1996, Oklahoma City, OK; Royal Watercolor Society, 1992, London, England
Collections: Albuquerque Museum, Albuquerque, NM; National Cowboy Hall of Fame, Oklahoma City, OK
Representative: Concetta D. Gallery, 20 1st Plaza NW, Ste. 29, Albuquerque, NM 87102, (505) 243-5066

Ted Rose

Born: 1940, Milwaukee, WI
Resides: Santa Fe, NM

Education: University of Illinois, Urbana, IL
Award: Distinguished Artist, 1997, *New Mexico Magazine*
Representatives: Zaplin-Lampert Gallery, 651 Canyon Rd., Santa Fe, NM 87501, (505) 982-6100, and 3944 N. Marshall Way, Scottsdale, AZ 85251, (602) 970-6100

Tom Ryan
Born: 1922, Springfield, IL
Resides: Midland, TX
Education: Art Students League, New York, NY
Recent Exhibition: Cowboy Artists of America Museum, 1996, Kerrville, TX
Award. Lifetime Achievement Award, 1996, National Cowboy Hall of Fame, Oklahoma City, OK
Collections: Cowboy Artists of America Museum, Kerrville, TX; National Cowboy Hall of Fame, Oklahoma City, OK; Phoenix Art Museum, Phoenix, AZ
Representative: Self

Sherry Salari Sander
Born: 1941, McCloud, CA
Resides: Kalispell, MT
Education: Shasta College, Redding, CA
Recent Exhibitions: National Cowboy Hall of Fame *(Prix de West Invitational)*, 1995–1996, Oklahoma City, OK; Gilcrease Museum, 1995, Tulsa, OK; Leigh Yawkey Woodson Art Museum, 1996, Wausau, WI; Old Algonguin Museum, 1995, Algonguin Park, Ontario, Canada; National Academy of Design, 1994, New York, NY
Award: Elliot Liskin Memorial Award, 1993, Society of Animal Artists, New York, NY
Collections: Buffalo Bill Historical Center, Cody, WY; Denver Zoo, Denver, CO; Gilcrease Museum, Tulsa, OK; Leigh Yawkey Woodson Art Museum, Wausau, WI; National Museum of Wildlife Art, Jackson, WY
Representatives: Altermann and Morris Galleries, 2727 Routh St., Dallas, TX 75201, (214) 871-3035, and 10000 Memorial, Ste. 230, Houston, TX 77024, (713) 688-1668, and 38 New Orleans Rd., Hilton Head, SC 29928, (803) 842-4433; Big Horn Galleries, 1167 Sheridan Ave., Cody, WY 82414, (800) 505-2639; Cogswell Gallery, 223 Gore Creek Rd., Vail, CO 81658, (970) 476-1769; Trailside Americana Fine Art Galleries, 7330 Main St., Scottsdale, AZ 85251, (602) 945-7751, and 105 N. Center, Jackson, WY 83001, (307) 733-3186; Wadle Gallery, 128 W. Palace, Santa Fe, NM 87504, (505) 983-9219

Bill Schenck
Born: 1947, Two Guns, AZ
Resides: Apache Junction, AZ
Education: Kansas City Art Institute, Kansas City, MO
Recent Exhibitions: American Museum, 1996, El Paso, TX; Desert Cabelleros Western Museum, 1994, Wickenburg, AZ; Metro Center for the Visual Arts, 1994, Denver, CO
Collections: Buffalo Bill Historical Center, Cody, WY; Eiteljorg Museum of American Indian and Western Art, Indianapolis, IN; McDonald's Corporation, Chicago, IL; Scottsdale Center for the Arts, Scottsdale, AZ; St. Luke's Hospital, Phoenix, AZ; Yellowstone Art Center, Billings, MT
Representatives: Aspen Mountain Gallery, 303 E. Hopkins, Aspen, CO 81611, (970) 925-5083; Martin-Harris Gallery, 60 E. Broadway, Jackson, WY 83001, (800) 366-7814

John Schoenherr
Born: 1935, New York, NY
Resides: Stockton, NJ
Education: Pratt Institute of Art, Brooklyn, NY
Recent Exhibitions: Leigh Yawkey Woodson Art Museum, 1992, Wausau, WI; Hubbard Museum, 1991, Rudioso, NM
Award: Purchase Award, 1994, Hiram Blanvelt Art Museum
Representative: Carson Gallery, 1601 Arapahoe St., Ste. 6, Denver, CO 80202, (303) 825-6608

Elmer Schooley
Born: 1916, Lawrence, KS
Resides: Roswell, NM
Education: Iowa State University, Iowa City, IA
Recent Exhibition: Tucson Museum of Art, 1991, Tucson, AZ
Collection: Museum of Fine Arts, Santa Fe, NM
Representative: Munson Gallery, 225 Canyon Rd., Santa Fe, NM 87501, (505) 983-1657

Robert Shufelt
Born: 1935, Champaign, IL
Resides: Hillsboro, NM
Education: University of Illinois, Urbana, IL
Representatives: Gateway Gallery, 1950 Juan Tabo NE, Ste. J, Albuquerque, NM 87112, (505) 292-2849; Legacy Galleries, 7178 Main St., Scottsdale, AZ 85251, (602) 945-1113; Settlers West Galleries, 6420 N. Campbell Ave., Tucson, AZ 85718, (520) 299-2607; Wickenburg Gallery, 67 N. Tegner, Wickenburg, AZ 85338, (520) 684-7047

Gary Ernest Smith
Born: Baker, OR
Resides: Highland, UT
Education: Brigham Young University, Provo, UT
Recent Exhibitions: Brigham Young University, 1997, Provo, UT; Springville Art Museum, 1993, Springville, UT; Springfield Museum of Art, 1992, Springfield, OH
Representative: Overland Gallery of Fine Art, 7155 Main St., Scottsdale, AZ 85251, (602) 917-1934

Jaune Quick-to-See Smith
Born: 1940, St. Ignatius, MT
Resides: Corrales, NM
Education: University of New Mexico, Albuquerque, NM
Recent Exhibitions: Joslyn Art Museum, 1996, Omaha, NE; National Museum of American Art, 1996, Washington, DC; Site Santa Fe, 1995, Santa Fe, NM; Wabash College Art Museum, 1995, Crawfordsville, IN
Awards: Wallace Stegner Award, 1995, Center of the American West, University of Colorado, Boulder, CO; Honorary Doctorate, 1992, Minneapolis College of Art and Design, Minneapolis, MN
Collections: Chrysler Museum, Norfolk, VA; Denver Art Museum, Denver, CO; Museum of Mankind, Vienna, Austria; Museum of Modern Art, New York, NY; High Museum of Art, Atlanta, GA; National Museum of Women in the Arts, Washington, DC
Representatives: Cline LewAllen Contemporary, 129 W. Palace Ave., Santa Fe, NM 87501, (505) 988-8997; Steinbaum Krauss Gallery, 132 Greene St., New York, NY 10012, (212) 431-4224

Tucker Smith
Born: 1940, St. Paul, MI
Resides: Pinedale, WY
Education: University of Wyoming,
Recent Exhibition: National Cowboy Hall of Fame *(Prix de West Invitational)*, 1996, Oklahoma City, OK

Award: Prix de West Purchase Prize, 1990, National Cowboy Hall of Fame, Oklahoma City, OK
Collection: National Cowboy Hall of Fame, Oklahoma City, OK
Representatives: Carson Gallery, 1601 Araphoe St., Ste. 6, Denver, CO 80202, (303) 825-6817; Pitzer's of Carmel, 6th and Dolores, Carmel, CA 93921, (408) 625-2288; Trailside Americana Fine Art Galleries, 105 N. Center, Jackson, WY 83001, (307) 733-3186

Gordon Snidow

Born: 1936, Paris, MO
Resides: Los Lunas, NM
Education: Art Center College of Design, Pasadena, CA
Recent Exhibitions: Cowboy Artists of America Museum, 1996, Kerrville, TX; National Cowboy Hall of Fame *(Prix de West Invitational)*, 1996, Oklahoma City, OK; Museum of the Horse, 1995, Hollywood Park, CA; Millicent Rogers Museum, 1992, Taos, NM
Award: Artist of the Year, 1996, Tucson Festival Society, Tucson, AZ
Collection: Cowboy Artists of America Museum, Kerrville, TX
Representative: Trailside Americana Fine Art Galleries, 7330 Main St., Scottsdale, AZ 85251, (602) 945-7751

Grant Speed

Born: 1930, San Angelo, TX
Resides: Lindon, UT
Education: Brigham Young University, Provo, UT
Recent Exhibitions: Cowboy Artists of America Museum, 1994, Kerrville, TX; National Cowboy Hall of Fame *(Prix de West Invitational)*, 1994, Oklahoma City, OK
Award: Prix de West Purchase Prize, 1994, National Cowboy Hall of Fame, Oklahoma City, OK
Collection: National Cowboy Hall of Fame, Oklahoma City, OK
Representatives: Hawthorn Galleries, 1335 W. Hwy. 76, Branson, MO 65615, (417) 335-2170; Meyer Gallery, 305 Main St., Park City, UT 84060, (801) 649-8160; Mongerson Wunderlich Galleries, 704 N. Wells St., Chicago, IL 60610, (312) 943-2354; Texas Art Gallery, 5570 Lovers Lane, Ste. 396, Dallas, TX 75209, (214) 350-8500; Tivoli Gallery, 255 S. State, Salt Lake City, UT 84111, (801) 521-6288; Vail Village Arts, 194 E. Gore Creek Drive, Vail, CO 81657, (970) 476-2070

Oleg Stavrowsky

Born: 1928, New York, NY
Resides: Santa Fe, NM
Education: Self-taught
Representative: Self

Ray Swanson

Born: 1937, Alcester, SD
Resides: Carefree, AZ
Education: Northrop Institute, Pasadena, CA
Recent Exhibitions: Cowboy Artists of America Museum, 1996, Kerrville, TX; National Cowboy Hall of Fame *(Prix de West Invitational)*, 1996, Oklahoma City, OK; Phoenix Art Museum (Cowboy Artists of America), 1996, Phoenix, AZ
Awards: Silver Medal—Water Soluble, 1992 and 1994, Phoenix Art Museum (Cowboy Artists of America), Phoenix, AZ
Representatives: Claggett/Rey Gallery, 100 E. Meadow Drive, Vail, CO 81657, (970) 476-9350; Pierce Fine Art, 7145 Main St., Scottsdale, AZ 85251, (602) 945-8100

Lynn Taber-Borcherdt

Born: 1943, Bakersfield, CA
Resides: Tucson, AZ
Education: Art Institute of Chicago, Chicago IL
Recent Exhibition: Bakersfield Museum of Art, 1993, Bakersfield, CA
Award: Regional Fellowship in Painting, 1990, Western States Federation
Representative: Davis Dominguez Gallery, 6812 North Oracle Rd., Tucson, AZ 85704, (520) 297-1427

Luis Tapia

Born: 1950, Santa Fe, NM
Resides: Santa Fe, NM
Education: Self-taught
Recent Exhibitions: Millicent Rogers Museum, 1996, Taos, NM; Museum of International Folk Art, 1995, Santa Fe, NM; Autry Museum of Western Heritage, 1994, Los Angeles, CA; Heard Museum, 1992, Phoenix, AZ
Award: New Mexico Governor's Award for Excellence in the Arts, 1996; Distinguished Artist, 1994, Santa Fe Rotary Foundation, Santa Fe, NM
Collections: Museum of American Folk Art, New York, NY; Museum of Fine Arts, Santa Fe, NM; National Museum of American Art, Washington, DC; National Museum of American History, Washington, DC; Roswell Museum, Roswell, NM
Representative: Owings-Dewey Fine Art, 76 E. San Francisco St., Santa Fe, NM 87501, (505) 982-6244

Howard Terpning

Born: 1927, Oak Park, IL
Resides: Tucson, AZ
Education: Chicago Academy of Fine Arts, American Academy of Art, Chicago, IL
Recent Exhibitions: National Cowboy Hall of Fame *(Prix de West Invitational)*, 1996, Oklahoma City, OK; Phoenix Art Museum (Cowboy Artists of America), 1996, Phoenix, AZ
Awards: CA Award, Phoenix Art Museum (Cowboy Artists of America), 1995, Phoenix, AZ; Frederic Remington Award, 1992, National Cowboy Hall of Fame, Oklahoma City, OK
Collections: Cowboy Artists of America Museum, Kerrville, TX; National Cowboy Hall of Fame, Oklahoma City, OK
Representative: Settlers West Galleries, 6420 N. Campbell Ave., Tucson, AZ 85718, (520) 299-2607

Kent Ullberg

Born: 1945, Gothenburg, Sweden
Resides: Corpus Christi, TX
Education: Konstfack School of Art, Stockholm, Sweden
Recent Exhibition: National Cowboy Hall of Fame *(Prix de West Invitational)*, 1996, Oklahoma City, OK
Awards: Ellen P. Speyer Prize, National Academy of Design, 1995, New York, NY; Frederic Remington Award, 1995, National Cowboy Hall of Fame, Oklahoma City, OK; Texas State Artist, 1991–1992, State of Texas; National Academician, 1990, National Academy of Design, New York, NY
Collections: City of Fort Lauderdale, FL; Denver Museum of Natural History, Denver, CO; Gilcrease Museum, Tulsa, OK; Leigh Yawkey Woodson Art Museum, Wausau, WI; Museum of Natural History, Gothenburg, Sweden; National Cowboy Hall of Fame,

Oklahoma City, OK
Representatives: Corpus Christi Art Connection, 3636 S. Alameda, Ste. C, Corpus Christi, TX 78411, (512) 854-1057; Knox Gallery, 1632 Market St., Denver, CO 80203, (303) 820-2324; Taminah Gallery, 608 Main St., Park City, UT 84060, (801) 655-3264; Trailside Americana Fine Art Galleries, 7330 Main St., Scottsdale, AZ 85251, (602) 945-7751, and 105 N. Center, Jackson, WY 83001, (307) 733-3186

Harold Joe Waldrum

Born: 1934, Savoy, TX
Resides: Truth or Consequences, NM
Education: Fort Hays State College, Fort Hays, KS
Collections: Albuquerque Museum, Albu querque, NM; Harwood Foundation, Taos, NM; Museum of Fine Arts, Santa Fe, NM; Palm Springs Desert Museum, Palm Springs, CA; Rockwell Museum, Corning, NY; Wells Fargo Bank, San Francisco, CA
Representatives: Joy Tash Gallery, 4142 N. Marshall Way, Scottsdale, AZ 85251, (602) 945-0195; Lumina Gallery, 239 Morada Ln., Taos, NM 87571, (505) 758-7282; Munson Gallery, 225 Canyon Rd., Santa Fe, NM 87501, (505) 983-1657

Curt Walters

Born: 1951, Farmington, NM
Resides: Sedona, AZ
Education: Self-taught
Recent Exhibition: Foothills Art Center, 1997, Golden, CO
Collections: Hotel Senyo, Tokyo, Japan; National Park Service, Grand Canyon National Park, AZ
Representatives: Altermann and Morris Galleries, 225 Canyon Rd., Santa Fe, NM 87501, (505) 983-1590; Jones Gallery, 7643 Girard Ave., La Jolla, CA 92037, (619) 459-1370, Saks Galleries, 3019 E. 2nd Ave., Denver, CO 80206, (303) 333-4144; Trailside Americana Fine Art Galleries, 7330 Main St., Scottsdale, AZ 85251, (602) 945-7751, and 6th and Lincoln, Carmel, CA 93921, (408) 624-5071; White Dove Gallery, 2104 Charlevoix NW, Albuquerque, NM 87104, (505) 243-6901

Garland A. Weeks

Born: 1942, Amarillo, TX
Resides: Mason, TX
Education: Self-taught
Recent Exhibitions: Governor's Invitational, 1993–1996, Cheyenne, WY; Professional Rodeo Cowboy Artists Association, 1993–1996, Las Vegas, NV; Wichita Center for the Arts, 1995, Wichita, KS; National Cowboy Hall of Fame *(Prix de West Invitational),* 1994, Oklahoma City, OK
Award: Official State Sculptor, 1995, State of Texas
Collections: Cutter Laboratories, Shawnee Mission, KS; Mercedes Boot Company, Mercedes, TX; National Cattleman's Association, Denver, CO; Texas Tech University, Lubbock, TX
Representatives: Hawthorn Galleries, 1335 W. Hwy. 76, Branson, MO 65615, (417) 334-2170; Simpson Gallagher Gallery, 1115 13th St., Cody, WY 82414, (307) 587-4022

Emmi Whitehorse

Born: 1956, Crownpoint, NM
Resides: Santa Fe, NM
Education: University of New Mexico, Albuquerque, NM
Recent Exhibitions: American Academy of Arts and Letters, 1994, New York, NY; Millicent Rogers Museum, 1993, Taos, NM; National Museum of Women in the Arts, 1991, Washington, DC; New Mexico State University, 1992, Las Cruces, NM
Collections: Mountain Bell, Denver, CO; Hallmark Cards, Kansas City, MO; Heard Museum, Phoenix, AZ; Joslyn Art Museum, Omaha, NE; Museum of Fine Arts, Santa Fe, NM, Phelps Dodge Corporation, Phoenix, AZ
Representatives: Bentley Gallery, 4161 N. Marshall Way, Scottsdale, AZ 85251, (602) 946-6060; Cline LewAllen Contemporary, 129 W. Palace Ave., Santa Fe, NM 87501, (505) 988-8997

Wayne Wolfe

Born: 1911, Kansas City, MO
Resides: Loveland, CO
Education: Self-taught
Recent Exhibition: National Cowboy Hall of Fame *(Prix de West Invitational),* 1996, Oklahoma City, OK
Collections: Gilcrease Museum, Tulsa, OK; National Cowboy Hall of Fame, Oklahoma City, OK; Rockwell Museum, Corning, NY
Representatives: Altermann and Morris, 225 Canyon Rd., Santa Fe, NM 87501, (505) 983-1590; Claggett/Rey Gallery, 100 E. Meadow Drive, Vail, CO 81657, (970) 476-9350

Michael Workman

Born: 1962, Salt Lake City, UT
Resides: Spring City, UT
Education: Brigham Young University, Provo, UT
Collection: Springville Museum of Art, Springville, UT
Representative: Meyer Gallery, 7173 Main St., Scottsdale, AZ 85251, (602) 947-6372, and 225 Canyon Road, Santa Fe, NM 87501, (505) 988-5170

Star Liana York

Born: 1952, Washington, DC
Resides: Abiquiu, NM
Education: University of Maryland, College Park, MY
Recent Exhibitions: Tucson Museum of Art, 1994; Albuquerque Museum, 1993, Albuquerque, NM
Collections: First National Bank, Fremont, IN; State Capitol Building, Santa Fe, NM
Representatives: Hawthorn Galleries, 1335 W. Hwy. 76, Branson, MO 65615, (417) 335-2170; Rice and Falkenberg Gallery, 325 Worth Ave., Palm Beach, FL 33480, (407) 833-9005; Shriver Gallery, 401 N. Pueblo, Taos, NM 87571, (505) 758-4994; Toh-Atin Gallery, 145 W. 9th St., Durango, CO 81301, (970) 247-8277; Zaplin-Lampert Gallery, 3944 N. Marshall Way, Scottsdale, AZ 85251, (602) 970-6100, and 651 Canyon Rd., Santa Fe, NM 87501, (505) 982-6100

Barbara Zaring

Born: 1947, Zanesville, OH
Resides: Taos, NM
Education: DePauw University, Greencastle, IN
Recent Exhibitions: Eiteljorg Museum of American Indian and Western Art, 1994, Indianapolis, IN; Museum of New Mexico, 1992–1993, Santa Fe, NM; Headly-Whitney Museum, 1992, Lexington, KY
Collections: Compaq, Houston, TX; United Bank of Colorado, Denver, CO
Representatives: Cogswell Gallery, 223 Gore Creek Drive, Vail, CO 81657, (970) 476-1769; New Gallery, 2639 Colquitt, Houston, TX 77098, (713) 520-7053; Total Arts Gallery, 122-A Kit Carson Rd., Taos, NM 87571, (505) 758-4667

BIBLIOGRAPHY

Adams, Peter. "Peter Adams: Eastern Exposure." *Southwest Art* (May 1996): 80–86.

Ainsworth, Ed. *The Cowboy in Art.* New York: The World Publishing Company, 1968.

American Icons: The Art of Neo-Regionalist Gary Ernest Smith. Scottsdale, AZ: Overland Gallery, 1994.

Angell, Tony. "Voices of Stone: The Sculpture of Tony Angell." *Southwest Art* (June 1993): 71–75.

Art and the Animal: The Society of Animal Artists 36th Annual Exhibition. New York: Society of Animal Artists, 1996.

Baldinger, Jo Ann. "If You Can Paint a Beer Bottle . . . You Can Paint a Horse." *Focus/Santa Fe* (July 1995): 32–35.

Bartell, James. "Donald Crowley: Capturing the Contemporary Indian." *Art of the West* (November/December 1991): 39–44.

Behrens, Shirley. "Martin Grelle: New Directions. *Art of the West* (March/April 1996): 60–65.

Birds in Art, 1996. Wausau, WI: Leigh Yawkey Woodson Art Museum, 1996.

Broder, Patricia Janis. *The American West: The Modern Vision.* Boston: New York Graphic Society, 1984.

Brown, Franz. "Clyde Aspevig." *Southwest Art* (February 1991): 71–77.

Brown, Harley. "Perilous Trips." *Southwest Art* (September 1994): 60–64.

———. *Desert Dreams: The Art and Life of Maynard Dixon.* Layton, UT: Gibbs Smith Publisher, 1993.

Cauble, Dianne. "A Communal Culture." *Focus/Santa Fe* (August/September 1994): 72–75.

Chatham, Russell. "The Seasons." *Big Sky Journal* (Summer 1995): 14–17.

Chiapas!: Cultural Warriors of New Mexico. Phoenix: The Heard Museum, 1992.

Clyde Aspevig. Bozeman: Thomas Nygard Gallery, 1994.

Cohen, Joel H. "Don Coen: Home on the Range." *Air Brush-Action* (July/August 1992): 10–19.

Compton, K.C. "Where Seasons Matter and Time Moves Slowly." *Focus/Santa Fe* (May 1993): 28–31.

Cottrell, Sheila. "James Reynolds." *Southwest Art* (May 1993): 67–72.

Cowboy Artists of America, Thirty-First Annual Exhibition. Phoenix: Cowboy Artists of America, 1996.

Davis, Tom. "Classic Carlson." *Sporting Classics* (January/February 1995): 33–39.

Dicker, Kiana. "Anne Coe." *Southwest Art* (June 1992): 80–85.

Dickinson, Carol. "Tony Ortega." *Southwest Art* (July 1989): 66–69.

Doherty, Stephen M. "William Matthews: The Power of Positive Painting." *Watercolor* (Spring 1995): 106–111, 127–128.

Doing it All: An Exhibition of Paintings by Gordon Snidow. Ruidioso Downs, New Mexico: The Museum of the Horse, 1995.

Fraughton, Edward J. "Edward J. Fraughton: A Life in Progress." *Southwest Art* (May 1993): 75–80.

Francis, Anna B. "Ted Rose: Locomotion." *Southwest Art* (June 1993): 55–58.

Euaclaire, Sally. "Dan Namingha: Glimpses." *Southwest Art* (August 1996): 74–79.

———. "George Carlson: Whispering Muse." *Southwest Art.*" (May 1994): 68–71.

Ellis, Nancy. "Nelson Boren: Below the Belt." *Southwest Art* (March 1994):62–66.

Gillespie, Nancy. "Luke Frazier: He's Young, Restless, and Talented." *Art of the West* (March/April 1995): 52–57.

———. "Lanford Monroe: A Rolling Stone." *Art of the West* (January/February 1995): 20–26.

———. "Walt Gonske: Painting Feeds My Soul." *Art of the West* (May/June 1996): 42–48.

Goodwin, Martha Burnett. "Alyce Frank." *Southwest Art* (November 1991): 70–76.

Gregory Kondos: A Retrospective. Sacramento: Crocker Art Museum, 1993.

Gregory Kondos: Yosemite and Other California Landscapes. Moraga: Hearst Art Gallery, 1994.

Hagerty, Donald J. *Desert Dreams: The Art and Life of Maynard Dixon.* Layton, Utah: Gibbs Smith, Publisher, 1993.

———. *Beyond the Visible Terrain: The Art of Ed Mell.* Flagstaff: Northland Publishing, 1996.

Hall, E.T. *Page Allen.* Santa Fe: Owings-Dewey Fine Art, 1994.

Hedgpeth, Don. *Cowboy Artist: The Joe Beeler Story.* Flagstaff, Arizona: Northland Press, 1979.

Hait, Pam. "Paul Calle: The Road Less Traveled." *Southwest Art* (December 1993): 44–48.

Hall, E.T. *Page Allen.* Santa Fe: Owings-Dewey Fine Art, 1994.

Harrison, Helen Mayer, et al. *Arrested Rivers.* Niwot, CO: University Press of Colorado, 1994.

Hedgpeth, Don. *Cowboy Artist: The Joe Beeler Story.* Flagstaff, AZ: Northland Press, 1979.

Hedgpeth, Don, and Walt Reed. *The Art of Tom Lovell: An Invitation to History.* New York: William Morrow and Company, 1993.

Kelton, Elmer. *The Art of Frank McCarthy.* New York: William Morrow and Company, 1992.

Klein, Hilary Dole. "Meredith Brooks Abbott." *Art of California* (January 1991): 23–27.

Klinka, Karen. "Wilson Hurley: Windows of the West." *Southwest Art* (November 1994): 48–53.

Kollasch, Sheila. "Howard Post: Poetry and Paint." *Southwest Art* (December 1992): 58–63.

Krakel, Dean. *Adventures in Western Art.* Kansas City: The Lowell Press, 1977.

Kusel, Denise. "Sculptor a Rising Star." *New Mexico Magazine* (May 1993): 66–71.

Lester, Patrick D. *The Biographical Directory of Native American Painters.* Tulsa: SRI Publications, 1995.

McGarry, Susan Hallsten. "Bill Owen: Living the Life." *Southwest Art* (May 1996): 58–65.

———. "Bob Kuhn: Colorful Critters." *Southwest Art* (May 1994): 86–93.

———. "Kenneth Riley: History Painting as Storytelling and Poetry." *Southwest Art* (July 1993): 50–57.

———. "Tucker Smith." *Southwest Art* (July 1989): 58–64.

———. *West of Camelot: The Historical Paintings of Kenneth Riley.* Indianapolis/Tucson: Eiteljorg Museum/Settlers West, 1993.

———. "William Acheff: Every Picture Tells a Story." *Southwest Art* (November 1992): 60–64.

McGovern, Kris. "The Treasures of Nature." *Focus/Santa Fe* (February/March 1995): 16–19.

McGrath, Leah. "My Own Backyard." *Focus/Santa Fe* (June/July 1996). 16–19.

McIntosh, Michael. "The Art of James Morgan." *Wildlife Art News* (November/December 1994): 85–89.

Miele, Frank. "Sherry Sander: Mystical Countries." *Southwest Art* (May 1995): 70–74.

Minckler, Thomas. "Charles Fritz." *Southwest Art* (May 1991): 101–104.

New Art of the West: The Artist's Response to Nature: Second Annual Invitational. Indianapolis: Eiteljorg Museum of American Indian and Western Art, 1991.
O'Conner, Patricia. "Nelson Boren: The Detail Man." *Art of the West* (September/October 1993): 58–63.
Olsen, Michael. "Jim Morgan." *Southwest Art* (August 1992): 74–79.
Osburn, Annie. "Elmer Schooley." *Southwest Art* (October 1991): 79–83, 231.
Paul Pletka: Eyes of the Mystic, Hands of the Dreamer. Colorado Springs, CO: Colorado Springs Fine Arts Center, 1996.
Peter Holbrook: Paintings. Garberville, CA: Platypus Press, 1996.
Piburn, Gregg. "Gerald Balciar: Soulful Animals." *Southwest Art* (May 1996): 71–78, 88.
Preston, Marcia. "John Free." *Southwest Art* (July 1991): 71–75.
Price, B. Byron. *Lougheed.* Bozeman, MT: Nygard and Elliot Publishing Company, 1991.
Prix de West Invitational 1996. Oklahoma City: National Cowboy Hall of Fame, 1996.
Pyne, Lynn. "Bill Schenck." *Southwest Art* (October 1990): 127–133.
———. "Gary Ernest Smith." *Southwest Art* (March 1991): 60–66, 131.
———. "Michael Workman: Transcendental Tonalism." *Southwest Art* (September 1996): 84–89.
———. "Tom Darro: Transcriptions of Life." *Southwest Art* (February 1994): 50–55, 84.
Simmons, Rita M. "Joellyn Duesberry: Freedom Integrated with Tradition." *Southwest Art* (November 1995): 72–76.
Snidow, Gordon. "Choices." *Southwest Art* (October 1994): 56–61.
——— "Gordon Snidow's American Woman Series." *Southwest Art* (October 1994): 56–61.
Runbech, Kathyrn. "The Oak Group: Caring for California." *Southwest Art* (June 1996): 68–73.
Russell Chatham: One Hundred Paintings. Livingston, MT: Clark City Press, 1990.
Sacks, Peter. *Woody Gwyn.* Lubbock: Texas Tech University Press, 1995.
Stavig, Vicki. "The Balciar Touch." *Art of the West* (January/February 1994): 42–47.
———. "Gary Niblett: A Good Age, A Good Time." *Art of the West* (January/February 1997): 24–30.
———. "Let it Flow." *Art of the West* (November/December 1996): 23–28.
———. "Veryl Goodnight: The Softer Side of the West." *Art of the West* (March/April 1995): 20–25.
Underwood, Ryan. "Namingha on Fire." *Santa Fean* (August 1996): 48–49.
Van Deventer, M.J. "Grant Speed." *Persimmon Hill* (Summer 1994): 21–25.
Versace, Candelora. "Dan Namingha: Coming Full Circle." *El Palacio* (Summer/Fall 1996): 36–43.
———. "Ted Rose: Off the Beaten Track." *New Mexico Magazine* (September 1996): 30–37.
Waldron, Joy. "Bob Haozous." *Southwest Art* (August 1992): 62–67.
Waldrum, H. Joe. *Ando en Cueros (I Walk Stark Naked).* Bosque, NM: Chinaberry Press, 1994.
Weeks, Garland. "Garland Weeks: How to Look at Sculpture." *Southwest Art* (August 1996): 88–93, 101.
Wieland, Terry. "Ken Bunn." *Wildlife Art News."* (March/April 1995): 46–51.
———. "Ken Carlson." *Wildlife Art News.* November/December 1994): 52–57.
———. "Thomas Quinn." *Wildlife Art News* (January/February 1995): 36–41.
Wildlife: The Artist's View. Wausau, WI: Leigh Yawkey Woodson Art Museum, 1996.
Wilkinson, Todd. "Coaxing Magic From Stone." *Wildlife Art* (November/December 1995): 37–40.
York, Star Liana. "Star Liana York: Unfamiliar Paths." *Southwest Art* (February 1995): 52–57.
Zanetell, Myrna. "Ken Carlson: Patience and Observation." *Southwest Art* (November 1994): 71–73.

INDEX

Artists featured in this book are listed in boldface type; page numbers in bold italic type refer to color plates.

ABOUT THE AUTHOR

DONALD J. HAGERTY recently retired from the University of California, Davis, after twenty-two years as a faculty member. Since 1981, he has also been a research associate in anthropology at the California Academy of Sciences in San Francisco. He now works as an independent scholar and consultant on the art and culture of the American West.

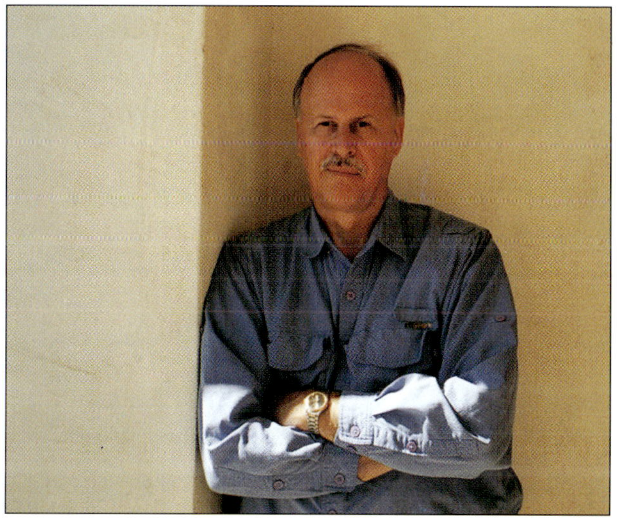

In 1981, Hagerty organized the first important exhibition on Maynard Dixon, *Images of the Native American,* held at the California Academy of Sciences. His biography of Dixon, *Desert Dreams: The Art and Life of Maynard Dixon,* was published in 1993 (Gibbs Smith Publisher). In conjunction with the book, Hagerty served as guest curator for a major retrospective exhibition of Dixon's work, also called *Desert Dreams,* which originated at the Museum of New Mexico in Santa Fe and traveled to six other museums.

In 1996, Hagerty published *Beyond the Visible Terrain: The Art of Ed Mell* (Northland Publishing), called "one of the best new art books of the year" by *Bookviews* and "highly recommended" by *The Bookwatch,* as well as *Canyon de Chelly: One Hundred Years of Painting and Photography* (Gibbs Smith Publisher); he has also written on art and artists for *Arizona Highways, Southwest Art, Pacific Historian, El Palacio, Russell's West, Art of California, American Art Review, Crosswinds,* and the Book Club of California. In addition, he has given numerous lectures for museums and other institutions.

Don Hagerty lives in Davis, California, with his wife and two children.